The Bible Speaks Today

Series editors: Alec Motyer (OT)
John Stott (NT)
Derek Tidball (Bible Themes)

The Message of Matthew

D0406332

Titles in this series

OLD TESTAMENT
(Series Editor J. A.
Motyer)

The Message of **Genesis
1—11**
David Atkinson

The Message of **Genesis
12—50**
Joyce G. Baldwin

The Message of
Deuteronomy
Raymond Brown

The Message of **Judges**
Michael Wilcock

The Message of **Ruth**
David Atkinson

The Message of
Chronicles
Michael Wilcock

The Message of
Nehemiah
Raymond Brown

The Message of **Job**
David Atkinson

The Message of **Proverbs**
David Atkinson

The Message of
Ecclesiastes
Derek Kidner

The Message of the **Song
of Songs**
Tom Gledhill

The Message of **Isaiah**
Barry Webb

The Message of **Jeremiah**
Derek Kidner

The Message of **Daniel**
Ronald S. Wallace

The Message of **Hosea**
Derek Kidner

The Message of **Amos**
J. A. Motyer

The Message of **Joel,
Micah & Habakkuk**
David Prior

NEW TESTAMENT
(Series Editor John
R. W. Stott)

The Message of
Matthew
Michael Green

The Message of the
**Sermon on the Mount
(Matthew 5—7)**
John R. W. Stott

The Message of **Mark**
Donald English

The Message of **Luke**
Michael Wilcock

The Message of **John**
Bruce Milne

The Message of **Acts**
John R. W. Stott

The Message of
1 Corinthians
David Prior

The Message of
2 Corinthians
Paul Barnett

The Message of
Galatians
John R. W. Stott

The Message of
Ephesians
John R. W. Stott

The Message of
Philippians
J. A. Motyer

The Message of
Colossians & Philemon
R. C. Lucas

The Message of **1 & 2
Thessalonians**
John R. W. Stott

The Message of
2 Timothy
John R. W. Stott

The Message of **Hebrews**
Raymond Brown

The Message of **James**
J. A. Motyer

The Message of **1 Peter**
Edmund P. Clowney

The Message of **2 Peter
& Jude**
Dick Lucas &
Christopher Green

The Message of **John's
Letters**
David Jackman

The Message of
Revelation
Michael Wilcock

BIBLE THEMES
(Series Editor Derek
Tidball)

The Message of the **Living
God**
Peter Lewis

The Message of the
Resurrection
Paul Beasley-Murray

The Message of Matthew

The kingdom of heaven

Michael Green

Senior Research Fellow,
Wycliffe Hall, Oxford University,
and Adviser in Evangelism
to the Archbishops of Canterbury and York

Inter-Varsity Press

InterVarsity Press
P.O. Box 1400, Downers Grove, IL 60515-1426
World Wide Web: www.ivpress.com
E-mail: mail@ivpress.com

Inter-Varsity Press
38 De Montfort Street, Leicester LE1 7GP, England

© 1988, 2000, by Michael Green
Study guide by David Stone © Inter-Varsity Press, 2000

All rights reserved. No part of this book may be reproduced, stored in a retrieval system or transmitted in any form or by any means, electronic, mechanical, photocopying, recording or otherwise, without the prior permission of InterVarsity Press.

InterVarsity Press® is the book-publishing division of InterVarsity Christian Fellowship/USA®, a student movement active on campus at hundreds of universities, colleges and schools of nursing in the United States of America, and a member movement of the International Fellowship of Evangelical Students. For information about local and regional activities, write Public Relations Dept., InterVarsity Christian Fellowship/USA, 6400 Schroeder Rd., P.O. Box 7895, Madison, WI 53707-7895.

Inter-Varsity Press is the book-publishing division of the Universities and Colleges Christian Fellowship (formerly the Inter-Varsity Fellowship), a student movement linking Christian Unions in universities and colleges throughout the United Kingdom and the Republic of Ireland, and a member movement of the International Fellowship of Evangelical Students. For information about local and national activities write to UCCF, 38 De Montfort Street, Leicester LE1 7GP, England.

All Scripture quotations, unless otherwise indicated, are taken from the Holy Bible, New International Version®. NIV®. Copyright © 1973, 1978, 1984 by International Bible Society. Used by permission of Hodder and Stoughton Ltd. All rights reserved. "NIV" is a registered trademark of International Bible Society. UK trademark number 1448790. Distributed in North America by permission of Zondervan Publishing House.

USA ISBN 0-8308-1243-1
UK ISBN 0-85111-536-5

Typeset in Great Britain by The Midlands Book Typesetting Company.

Printed in the United States of America ∞

British Library Cataloguing in Publication Data

A catalogue record for this book is available from the British Library.

Library of Congress Cataloging-in-Publication Data

Green, Michael, 1930
    The message of Matthew: the kingdom of heaven/Michael Green.
        p.cm.—(The Bible speaks today)
    Includes bibliographical references.
        ISBN 0-8308-12243-1 (paper: alk. paper)
        1. Bible. N.T. Matthew–Commentaries. I. Title. II. Series.
    BS2575.3 .G735 2001
    226.2'07—DC21

18	17	16	15	14	13	12	11	10	9	8	7	6	5	4	3	2
16	15	14	13	12	11	10	09	08	07	06	05	04	03			

For Jane Holloway
in gratitude for fourteen
years of shared ministry
at St Aldate's Church, Oxford,
at Regent College, Vancouver,
and in the Archbishops' Springboard Initiative

Contents

General preface   9
Author's preface   11
Chief abbreviations   13
Bibliography   15

Introduction   19
    Who wrote the Gospel?   19
    What do we know about the tax collector?   24
    What can we infer about the author? 25
    Who were the readers?   27
    What is the plan of the Gospel?   30
    Why was the Gospel so popular?   37
    When was it written?   38
    What were Matthew's main concerns?   39
    Matthew in recent study   50

PART 1: IN GALILEE
(Matthew 1 – 13)

A. BEGINNINGS (1 – 7)
  1. Jesus' pedigree and birth (1:1–25)   57
  2. Jesus' childhood (2:1–23)   65
  3. The beginning of Jesus' ministry (3:1 – 4:25)   75
  4. The first discourse: the manifesto of the kingdom
    (5:1 – 7:29)   88

B. DISCIPLESHIP (8 – 10)
  5. Who is this Jesus? (8:1 – 9:34)   113
  6. The second discourse: the mission of the kingdom
    (9:35 – 10:42)   128

C. RESPONSE (11 – 13)
7. Jesus' claim, and its ground (11:1–30)   137
8. Human response to Jesus: for and against (12:1–50)   144
9. The third discourse: the parables of the kingdom
   (13:1–58)   152

PART 2: TO JERUSALEM
(Matthew 14 – 28)

D. SHADOWS (14 – 18)
10. Shadows of the future (14:1 – 17:27)   165
11. The fourth discourse: relationships in the kingdom
    (18:1–35)   190

E. JUDGMENT (19 – 25)
12. Judgments on issues (19:1 – 20:34)   201
13. Judgment on Israel (21:1–27)   218
14. Parables and controversies on judgment (21:28 – 22:46)   226
15. The fifth discourse: 239
    (1) judgment on dead religion (23:1–39)   239
16. The fifth discourse: 249
    (2) the end of Jerusalem and of history (24:1 – 25:46)   249

F. FINALE (26 – 28)
17. A study in contrasts (26:1–16)   266
18. Jesus' last evening (26:17–56)   271
19. The trials of Jesus (26:57 – 27:31)   281
20. The cross and the tomb (27:32–66)   295
21. The end of the beginning (28:1–20)   311

Study guide   325

General preface

THE BIBLE SPEAKS TODAY describes three series of expositions, based on the books of the Old and New Testaments, and on Bible themes that run through the whole of Scripture. Each series is characterized by a threefold ideal:

- to expound the biblical text with accuracy
- to relate it to contemporary life, and
- to be readable.

These books are, therefore, not 'commentaries', for the commentary seeks rather to elucidate the text than to apply it, and tends to be a work rather of reference than of literature. Nor, on the other hand, do they contain the kind of 'sermons' which attempt to be contemporary and readable without taking Scripture seriously enough.

The contributors to *The Bible Speaks Today* series are all united in their convictions that God still speaks through what he has spoken, and that nothing is more necessary for the life, health and growth of Christians than that they should hear what the Spirit is saying to them through his ancient – yet ever modern – Word.

ALEC MOTYER
JOHN STOTT
DEREK TIDBALL
Series Editors

Author's preface

This Gospel according to Matthew is among the most influential books ever written. It is one of the four accounts we have of the good news of Jesus which derives from the apostolic circle. The ancient fathers quoted this Gospel more than any other, and with good reason. It is wonderfully complete, linking Jesus with his Jewish origins and Old Testament background, pointing forward to the growth of the Gentile Christian mission, and embodying in a memorably ordered fashion the teaching, actions, parables, miracles, death and resurrection of the central figure. It is the Gospel which not only proclaims the good news of Jesus but does so in such an organized way that it is ideal for any teacher.

I became thrilled with this Gospel some years ago when I was a Professor at Regent College, Vancouver. As I lectured on it, I became aware of the paucity of commentaries that one would want to pick up and actually read. They were often heavily preoccupied with scholarly details but missed the excitement of the material they were handling. So I determined to try to write a running commentary on the Gospel which would excite the readers, and carry them along, but would at the same time be academically responsible. One is never going to get unanimity among scholars in interpreting this Gospel, but I wanted to offer a framework that could be defended academically and would enable the thoughtful reader of the Gospel to gain a deeper understanding without becoming fogged by the minutiae of scholarship. That book, written without footnotes, was published some years ago by Hodder and Stoughton. It was entitled *Matthew for Today*. As a matter of fact I was invited by John Stott at that time to put it in *The Bible Speaks Today* series, and I should probably have done so! At all events, the publishers of *The Bible Speaks Today* came back to me when the designated authors of their exposition of Matthew had had to withdraw, and invited me to contribute the current volume. They asked me to do a thorough revision of my original book, so as to bring it up to date with

11

contemporary scholarship, while retaining the lively, readable style of *Matthew for Today*. This I have tried to do, and I hope this volume will be a spiritual blessing and not merely an academic aid to many students of this wonderful Gospel. I am deeply grateful to my friend the Rev. Dr David Stone for contributing an excellent study guide to the Gospel.

This exposition completes the New Testament series of *The Bible Speaks Today*, and it would be wrong to close this Preface without a glowing tribute to Dr John Stott, whose vision and initiative launched the series many years ago, and whose own superb expositions have enormously enhanced it.

MICHAEL GREEN

Chief abbreviations

mg.   margin
NIV   New International Version of the Bible (1973, 1978, 1984)
NRSV   New Revised Standard Version of the Bible (1989, 1995)
REB   Revised English Bible (1989)
RSV   Revised Standard Version of the Bible (NT 1946, 2nd
         edition 1971; OT 1952)

Bibliography

Commentaries and other works on Matthew

Frequently cited works are referred to by author's surname, or surname and date. References to commentaries are ad loc. unless otherwise stated.

Albright, W. F., and Mann, C. S. (eds.), *Matthew*, Anchor Bible (Doubleday, 1973)

Allen, W. C., *St Matthew*, International Critical Commentary (T. and T. Clark, 1912)

Augsburger, M. S., *Matthew* (Word, 1973)

Bacon, B. W., *Studies in Matthew* (Holt, Rinehart and Winston, 1930)

Barclay, W., *The Gospel of Matthew*, 2 vols., Daily Study Bible (St Andrew Press, 1975)

Beare, F. W., *The Gospel according to Matthew* (Blackwell, 1981)

Billingham, E. and I., *The Structure of Matthew's Gospel* (Brechinset Publications, 1982)

Blomberg, C. L., *Matthew*, New American Commentary (Broadman, 1992)

Bonnard, P., *L'Évangile selon Saint Matthieu* (Delachaux et Niestlé, 2nd edition 1970)

Bornkamm, G., Barth, G., and Held, H., *Tradition and Interpretation in Matthew* (SCM, 1963)

Butler, B. C., *The Originality of St Matthew* (Cambridge University Press, 1951)

Calvin, J., *Harmony of the Gospels* 1–3 (St Andrew Press, 1971)

Campbell Morgan, C., *The Gospel according to Matthew* (Oliphants, no date)

Carson, D. A., 'Matthew', in *The Expositor's Bible* 8 (Zondervan, 1984)

——, *The Sermon on the Mount* (Paternoster, 1986)

Chapman, J., *Matthew, Mark and Luke* (Longmans, 1937)

Crosby, M., *House of Disciples* (Orbis, 1988)

Davies, W. D., *The Setting of the Sermon on the Mount* (Cambridge University Press, 1963)

Davies, W. D., and Allison, D. C., *A Critical and Exegetical Commentary on the Gospel according to Saint Matthew*, 3 vols., International Critical Commentary (T. and T. Clark, 1988, 1991, 1997

Fenton, J. C., *St Matthew*, Pelican Gospel Commentary (SCM, 1963)

Filson, F. V., *The Gospel according to St Matthew* (A. and C. Black, 1971)

France, R. T., *Matthew: An Introduction and Commentary*, Tyndale New Testament Commentaries (IVP, 1985)

——, *Matthew: Evangelist and Teacher* (Paternoster, 1989)

Green, H. B., *The Gospel according to Matthew*, New Clarendon Bible (Oxford University Press, 1975)

Guelich, R. A., *The Sermon on the Mount: A Foundation for Understanding* (Word, 1982)

Gundry, R. H., *The Use of the Old Testament in St Matthew's Gospel* (Brill, 1967)

——, *Matthew: A Commentary on his Literary and Theological Art* (Eerdmans, 1982)

Hagner, D. A., *Matthew*, 2 vols., Word Biblical Commentary (Word, 1993, 1995)

Harris, J. R., *Testimonies*, 2 vols. (Cambridge University Press, 1916, 1920)

Hill, D., *The Gospel of Matthew*, New Century Bible (Marshall, Morgan and Scott, 1972)

Johnson, S. E., *The Gospel according to St Matthew*, Interpreter's Bible (Abingdon, 1951)

Keener, C. S., *Matthew*, IVP New Testament Commentary (IVP, 1997)

Kilpatrick, G. D., *The Origins of the Gospel according to St Matthew* (Oxford University Press, 1946)

Kingsbury, J. D., *Matthew: Structure, Christology, Kingdom* (SPCK, 1975)

——, *Matthew*, Proclamation Commentary (Fortress, rev. edition 1981)

——, *Matthew as Story* (Fortress, 1986)

McNeile, A. H. (ed.), *The Gospel According to St Matthew* (Macmillan, 1915)

Meier, J. P., *The Vision of Matthew: Christ, Church and Morality in the First Gospel* (Paulist, 1979)

Minear, P. S., *Matthew: The Teacher's Gospel* (Darton, Longman and Todd, 1984)

Morris, L., *The Gospel according to Matthew* (IVP, 1992)

Nepper-Christensen, P., *Das Matthäusevangelium – eine juden-christliches Evangelium?* (Aarhus, 1958)

Plummer, A., *An Exegetical Commentary on the Gospel according to St Matthew* (Stock, 1909)

Ridderbos, H. N., *Matthew* (Regency, 1987)

Rigaux, B., *The Testimony of St Matthew* (Franciscan Herald Press, 1968)

Schweizer, E., *The Good News according to Matthew* (SPCK, 1976)

Sim, D. C., *The Gospel of Matthew and Christian Judaism* (T. and T. Clark, 1988)

Stanton, G. N., *A Gospel for a New People: Studies in Matthew* (T. and T. Clark, 1992)

Stendahl, K., 'Matthew', in *Peake's Commentary* (rev. edition 1962, repr. Routledge, 1991)

——, *The School of St Matthew and its Use of the Old Testament* (Fortress, 2nd edition 1968)

Stott, J. R. W., *The Message of the Sermon on the Mount: Christian Counter-culture*, The Bible Speaks Today (IVP, 1978)

Thiede, C. P., *The Jesus Papyrus* (Phoenix, 1966)

Tilberg, S. van, *The Jewish Leaders in Matthew* (Brill, 1972)

Other works

Aland, K., *Did the Early Church Baptize Infants?* (SCM, 1961)

Aulén, G., *Christus Victor* (SPCK, 1931)

Bailey, K. E., *Through Peasant Eyes* (Eerdmans, 1980)

Banks, R., *Jesus and the Law in the Synoptic Tradition* (Cambridge University Press, 1975)

Beasley-Murray, G. R., *Baptism in the New Testament* (Eerdmans, 1962)

Blomberg, C. L., *Interpreting the Parables* (IVP, 1990)

Brown, R. E., *The Birth of the Messiah: A Commentary on the Infancy Narratives of Matthew and Luke* (Doubleday, 1971)

Burridge, R., *What are the Gospels? A Comparison with Graeco-Roman Biography* (Cambridge University Press, 1992)

Catchpole, D. R., *The Trials of Jesus* (Brill, 1971)

Dodd, C. H., *The Founder of Christianity* (Collins, 1971)

Dunn, J. D. G., *Jesus and the Spirit* (SCM, 1975)

Gerhardsson, B., *The Testing of God's Son* (Lund, 1966)

Gray, S. W., *The Least of my Brothers* (Scholars, 1989)

Green, M., *I Believe in the Holy Spirit* (Hodder and Stoughton, 1975)

——, *The Empty Cross of Jesus* (Hodder and Stoughton, 1984)

——, *I Believe in Satan's Downfall* (Hodder and Stoughton, 1988)

Haehner, H. W., *Herod Antipas* (Cambridge University Press, 1972)

Hengel, M., *Crucifixion in the Ancient World and the Folly of the Message of the Cross* (SPCK, 1977)

Jeremias, J., *Infant Baptism in the First Four Centuries* (SCM, 1960)

——, *The Lord's Prayer* (Fortress, 1964)

——, *New Testament Theology* (SCM, 1973)

Ladd, G. E., *Jesus and the Kingdom* (SPCK, 1966)

——, *The Presence of the Future: The Eschatology of Biblical Realism* (Eerdmans, 1974)

Machen, J. G., *The Virgin Birth of Christ* (James Clarke, 1930)

McKnight, S., *Light Among the Gentiles: Jewish Missionary Activity in the Second Temple Period* (Fortress, 1991)

Moule, C. F. D., *The Birth of the New Testament* (A. and C. Black, 1982)

Mounce, R. H., *Matthew*, Good News Commentary (Harper and Row, 1985)

Neusner, J., *Judaism in the Beginning of Christianity* (SPCK, 1984)

Plummer, A., *St Luke*, International Critical Commentary (T. and T. Clark, 4th edition, 1901)

Richards, J., *But Deliver us from Evil* (Darton, Longman and Todd, 1974)

Sanders, E. P., *Paul and Palestinian Judaism* (Fortress, 1977)

——, *Jesus and Judaism* (Fortress, 1985)

——, *Judaism: Practice and Belief, 63 BCE–66 CE* (SCM, 1992)

——, *The Historical Figure of Jesus* (Penguin, 1993)

Sherwin-White, A. N., *Roman Society and Roman Law in the New Testament* (Oxford University Press, 1963)

Stonehouse, N. B., *The Orgins of the Synoptic Gospels* (Tyndale, 1964)

Telford, W. R., *The Barren Temple and the Withered Tree*, JSNT Supplement 1 (JSOT Press, 1980)

Travis, S., *I Believe in the Second Coming of Jesus* (Hodder and Stoughton, 1982)

Verhey, A., *The Great Reversal* (Eerdmans, 1984)

Vermes, G., *Jesus the Jew* (Collins, 1973)

Walker, P., *The Weekend that Changed the World* (HarperCollins, 1999)

Wenham, D., *The Parables of Jesus* (Hodder and Stoughton, 1989)

Wenham, J., *Easter Enigma* (Paternoster, 1984)

Westerholm, S., *Israel's Law and the Church's Faith* (Eerdmans, 1988)

White, R. E. O., *Biblical Ethics* (Paternoster, 1979)

Woolmer, J., *Healing and Deliverance* (Monarch, 1999)

Wright, N. T., *Jesus and the Victory of God* (SPCK, 1996)

Yoder, J. H., *The Politics of Jesus* (Eerdmans, 1972)

Introduction

The Gospel according to Matthew is perhaps the most important single document in the New Testament, for in it we have the fullest and most systematic account of the birth, life, teaching, death and resurrection of the founder of Christianity, Jesus the Messiah. And yet it is a book that poses a number of questions which no commentators have been able to answer with certainty.[1] Let us examine some of them.

Who wrote the Gospel?

We do not know who wrote the Gospel. Like all the others, it is anonymous. The coming of Jesus sparked off an entirely new literary form, the 'Gospel'. It is not biography, though it contains it. It is not history, though it reflects it. A Gospel is the proclamation of good news: the good news of salvation which had long been looked for in Judaism, and which Christians were persuaded had burst upon the world in Jesus of Nazareth. The Gospels are utterly captivated by him, and none of them mentions the name of its author.

Second-century writers sought to remedy this situation. They do tell us who wrote them, and they may or may not have been right. In the case of Matthew, it is not at all easy to know whether they were right, because there is a major contradiction in the evidence. The external evidence points uniformly in one direction, the internal in another.

The external evidence is coherent and clear. Indeed, it is unanimous. It makes three main points. First, the Gospel according to Matthew is the earliest of the Gospels. Secondly, it was written in 'Hebrew'. This may mean Hebrew or Aramaic: at all events, it means

---

[1] An excellent background book, superbly written, about the emergence of this and the other Gospels, is C. F. D. Moule, *The Birth of the New Testament* (A. and C. Black, 1982).

that the early Christians were confident that it had not originally been penned in the Greek we have before us today. Most of the second-century writers were also persuaded that it was written for those who were converts from Judaism, which is a very likely assumption. The links between the Gospel and the Old Testament are many and obvious. The third conviction of the second-century church was that the Gospel was written by Matthew, one of the twelve apostles.

Such is the consensus of the external evidence, drawn from the second century. Irenaeus, a highly educated Christian bishop who wrote his *Against Heresies* in the last quarter of the second century, was born in the East, studied in Rome, and became Bishop of Lyons. He was the greatest theologian of the second century, and nobody rivalled the breadth of his experience of the worldwide church. He was clear about the origins of the Gospel according to Matthew. 'Matthew published a book of the gospel among the Hebrews, in their own dialect, while Peter and Paul were preaching the gospel in Rome and founding the church.'[2]

Origen, another massive intellect who flourished in Alexandria at the end of the second century and the beginning of the third, and who had access to the greatest Christian library in the world at that time, is no less clear. 'The first Gospel was written by Matthew, who was once a tax collector but who afterwards became an apostle of Jesus Christ, and it was prepared for the converts from Judaism and published in the Hebrew language.'[3]

Eusebius, the early fourth-century historian of the early church, says, 'Matthew had first preached to Hebrews, and when he was on the point of going to others [i.e. Gentiles?] he transmitted in writing in his native language the Gospel according to himself.'[4] And both he and Jerome (the greatest scholar in the ancient church, who published the Vulgate [Latin] translation of the Scriptures) tell us that Pantaenus, a leading and much-travelled Christian in the second century, found the Gospel of Matthew written in Hebrew letters (i.e. Aramaic) in India.[5] Jerome is particularly explicit: Matthew is the same person as Levi. He was a tax collector who became an apostle. He composed the Gospel in Hebrew letters and words for those who had come to faith out of Judaism. And he confesses: 'It is not clear who subsequently translated it into Greek. Moreover, the Hebrew text remains extant to this day.'

---

[2] *Against Heresies* 3.1.1.
[3] Cited in Eusebius, *Ecclesiastical History* 6.25. Origen says much the same in his *Commentary on John* 6:32, where he asserts that Matthew was the first to have published a Gospel, and that he did so for believers coming from Judaism.
[4] *Ecclesiastical History* 3.24.
[5] Jerome, *Of Illustrious Men* 36; Eusebius, *Ecclesiastical History* 5.10.

The origin of this tradition is very early indeed. It springs from Papias, who wrote his *Exposition of the Oracles of the Lord* about AD 130, if not rather earlier.[6] He was a disciple of John and companion of Polycarp, the influential bishop of Smyrna. Papias was very close to the earliest Christian tradition. Unfortunately his book has perished, but one tantalizing sentence remains about Matthew's Gospel: 'Matthew therefore composed the oracles (*logia*) in the Hebrew tongue, and each one translated them as he was able.'[7] To that statement we shall return. It may well be the original basis for the unanimous tradition of the early church that Matthew, the apostle and erstwhile tax collector, wrote the earliest Gospel in Hebrew for converts from Judaism.

However, the internal evidence is strongly against this. Indeed, the careful study of the text of the Gospels over the last 250 years has, until recently, yielded virtual unanimity on the three points cited above. First, Matthew does not seem to be the earliest Gospel. Secondly, it does not seem to have been written in Hebrew or Aramaic. Thirdly, it does not seem to have been written by an apostle, let alone Matthew.

Despite writers like J. Chapman, B. C. Butler and W. R. Farmer,[8] who maintained that Matthew is the earliest Gospel, hardly anybody else is persuaded. Irrespective of denomination, irrespective of theological position, those who have looked carefully into this matter are broadly convinced that the earliest documents about Jesus which have come down to us are the Gospel of Mark and the sayings of Jesus common to Luke and Matthew, usually known by the symbol Q. The order of events in Mark is clearly the basis for the order in Matthew and Luke, for Matthew and Luke never combine in order against Mark. Mark's order is primary. Moreover, if Matthew's Gospel had been written first, with its clear beginning, teaching, Lord's Prayer, and post-resurrection appearances, it would have been almost incredible for Mark to come and truncate the beginning and end, and leave out marvellous teaching like the Sermon on the Mount.

This is not the place to set out a detailed defence of the priority of Mark:[9] suffice it to say that few doubt it. If Mark's Gospel *was* the first to be written, however, that makes a big hole in the ancient testimony.

---

[6] Gundry (p. 620) puts the date before 110 AD.

[7] Recorded in Eusebius, *Ecclesiastical History* 3.39.

[8] J. Chapman, *Matthew, Mark and Luke* (Longmans, 1937); B. C. Butler, *The Originality of St Matthew* (Cambridge University Press, 1951); W. R. Farmer, *The Synoptic Problem* (Macmillan, 1964).

[9] The case is powerfully presented by G. M. Styler, 'The Priority of Mark', in Moule, *The Birth of the New Testament*, pp. 233ff.

An even bigger hole is created by the second consideration. The Gospel does not show any sign of having originally been written in Hebrew or Aramaic. It is a Greek Gospel, and is a fairly polished piece of writing. It irons out many of the stylistic infelicities found in Mark's 'market-place' Greek. Indeed, Mark bears many signs of the Aramaic substratum of the earliest preachers, Peter and others, which lay beneath his record. These signs are almost all removed by Matthew, along with the Aramaic words that are occasionally to be found in Mark. No, Matthew does not show any sign of having originally been translated from Hebrew. But all our ancient testimony relates not to our Greek Matthew but to a supposed lost Hebrew original. So what is that testimony worth?

The third consideration follows logically on from the previous two. How is it possible to imagine an apostle and eyewitness following the account of someone who, like Mark, was neither? It is very hard indeed to suppose that the Greek Gospel of Matthew as we have it, dependent as it is on Mark, could have been written by Matthew or Levi, the former tax collector who became an apostle of Jesus Christ.

The external and internal evidence are, therefore, in strong contradiction. Clearly there was some substantial link between the apostle Matthew and the Gospel that bears his name. If he did not write it, how can we account for his name being attached to it so universally and from such an early date? Three possible answers come to mind, and each of them has had its advocates.

First, the apostle Matthew may have written the sayings collection often called Q. Basic study of the Synoptic Gospels (Matthew, Mark and Luke), shows not only that Mark is their common source, but that both Matthew and Luke draw on another source, possibly oral but probably written, which was not known and used by Mark. This material consists entirely of sayings of Jesus. Somebody must have compiled these sayings very early indeed, perhaps in his lifetime. There is nothing surprising about this. The teaching of Jesus broke like a thunderclap on Judea. Nothing like it had ever been heard before. It would have been very surprising if nobody among the thousands who flocked to hear him ever thought of putting pen to paper to record some of that matchless teaching. Matthew, the tax collector, had the skills and the proximity to Jesus. Maybe he did the Christian church the marvellous service of collecting and writing down the sayings of his Master that are now brought to us in the teaching parts of Matthew and Luke. It would make good sense of Papias' cryptic claim that 'Matthew compiled the *logia* in the Hebrew tongue, and each one translated them as he was able.' On this interpretation, the *logia* would be not the Gospel as we have it, but the sayings of Jesus, taken down in Aramaic. People made their own translations of them until they got incorporated in one of the Greek Gospels later on. But, on this view, Matthew would not have written a Gospel himself.

However, there is another possibility, favoured by some. It is plain that Matthew's Gospel makes great play with the theme of fulfilment of the hints, predictions and prophecies of the Old Testament. In particular, it uses a formula such as 'All this took place to fulfil what the Lord had said through the prophet . . .' (1:22). There are ten or so such 'formula quotations' in this Gospel. Could it be that Matthew was the first to see this great theme of fulfilment? Could it be that he compiled the first list of 'testimonies' about Jesus? We know that such lists existed. A fascinating collection of messianic prophecies was discovered in Cave 4 at Qumran, where the Covenanters of the Dead Sea were earnestly awaiting divine intervention and deliverance. We know that Christians had such lists. One is extant from Cyprian, the third-century Bishop of Carthage. Rendel Harris, in his volumes entitled *Testimonies*,[10] argued that the early Christians, with their known interest in the Old Testament and their confidence that Jesus was the fulfilment of Old Testament prophecy, and with the example of contemporary Jewish writers before them, wrote down collections of Old Testament prophecies that could be used to back up their convictions about Jesus. Could Matthew have made the first such collection of testimonies? Is this what Papias is referring to by his *logia*? It is by no means impossible: *logia* can mean 'scriptures', not merely 'sayings', and does in fact mean that in Romans 3:2 and *1 Clement* 53. If so, it would not be difficult to see how Matthew's name became so firmly attached to the Gospel, even though he did not write it. He had compiled the testimony collection that formed such a prominent characteristic of it.

There is a third possibility. Matthew found a good deal of oral material about Jesus circulating among the disciples and early preachers of the gospel. He had heard a lot of it himself. He had preached a lot of it himself. And it is clear from the careful plan of the Gospel that he was a highly organized person. His great contribution was to assemble this teaching, and put it into some stereotyped form in which it could readily be handed on to others. This is what the great rabbis had done, and in Judaism the oral form from the rabbinic teacher was always preferred to the written product. There were two sources for authoritative tradition in Israel. One was the written *torah*, deriving from Moses. But the other was also ultimately derived from Moses, they believed. It was the stereotyped tradition of the elders of the nation, pointing back to their predecessors and ultimately to Moses himself. Is it not possible that

---

[10] J. R. Harris, *Testimonies*, 2 vols. (Cambridge University Press, 1916, 1920).

'Matthew', who shows some signs of being a sort of Christian rabbi, organized the material about Jesus into an easily remembered form that could be handed down for succeeding generations? No doubt he did so in Hebrew or Aramaic, and everyone translated it as he was able, just as Papias maintained, until a good deal of it was incorporated in the Gospel that subsequently came to bear his name. It is not hard to imagine some such 'shaping' activity going on in Jerusalem or Antioch in the early days while the oral tradition about Jesus was still fluid. Perhaps Matthew gave it the shape and organization that were retained in the Greek Gospel of Matthew, and did so before any of the canonical Gospels was written.

It may be in one of these ways (and I incline towards the first) that some reconciliation can be effected between the external and internal evidence about the authorship of this remarkable Gospel.

What do we know about the tax collector?

Most of what we know about Matthew the tax collector comes from Matthew 9:9–13, with its parallels in Mark 2:13–17 and Luke 5:27–32. We can make a number of very probable inferences.

First, Matthew got a new name. Mark 2:14 calls him Levi, son of Alphaeus. So does Luke 5:27. Clearly his name was originally Levi, son of Alphaeus, and after he began to follow Jesus, he received a new name, just as Simon had. 'Matthew' means 'gift of God'. Jesus saw what Levi was, and anticipated what he would become – God's gift. It is significant that only Matthew's account mentions the new name.

Secondly, Matthew belonged to a fascinating family. We learn from Mark and Luke that he was the son of Alphaeus. And so was James (Mark 3:18). They were therefore brothers. And at the end of the apostolic list (for all its variations) we find James ben Alphaeus, Thaddaeus, Simon the Zealot and Judas Iscariot as the last four mentioned. We know that Simon was a Zealot, that is to say a violent resistance fighter against the occupying Roman forces. Very likely Judas Iscariot was as well: one of the more probable derivations for his name is *sicarius*, the Latin for 'Zealot'. It is possible that James the son of Alphaeus shared the fierce, nationalistic patriotism of the Zealots. Most of the common people of Israel did in those days. But his brother, Matthew or Levi, was totally different. He farmed taxes for Herod Antipas. He co-operated with the occupying power that his brother seems to have been set on seeking to overthrow with bloody revolution. The quisling and the freedom fighter were brothers in the same family! This is not certain, but it is probable, and has often been noted by the commentators. It took Jesus of Nazareth to bring those two brothers together. Nobody else could.

Thirdly, Matthew was a tax collector, who left everything in his life for Jesus. The *publicani*, or tax collectors, were the people who raised the dues required by the Romans. They were much hated as social pariahs, and the Jews classed them with murderers. They were not even tolerated in the synagogues, and that is why, in the parable of the tax collector and the Pharisee in Luke 18:9–14, the tax collector stands 'afar off'. There were two main sorts of tax: the fixed taxes (ground tax, grain and wine taxes, fruit and oil tax, income tax and poll tax) and the more arbitrary taxes levied on customs, transport, exports and imports. The former had a fixed percentage, which was well known. It was in the latter category that there was limitless opportunity for the bribery and extortion that made the *publicani* so hated. Matthew had his tax office at Capernaum, on the main road from Damascus to Egypt, which passed through Samaria and Galilee. He was working under the direct employ of Herod Antipas, who, in turn, had to make massive block tax disbursements to Rome. It was a very lucrative place in which to work. This is the man who changed from his disreputable profession to become a wholehearted follower of Jesus.

Fourthly, Matthew threw a party for Jesus. That was both pathetic and glorious. Pathetic, because apparently he had no other friends apart from his fellow *publicani*, but delightful because his first instinct after discovering Jesus was to reach out to them and invite them to a meal to meet the Master (Matt. 9:10).

Finally, Matthew clearly brought his pen with him when he entrusted his life to Jesus. Most of the disciples of Jesus would have found that a fishing-net came more readily to hand than a pen. Not so Matthew. He was skilled at book work, and if we are to believe the united testimony of the early Christians he used this gift in the service of the gospel.

What can we infer about the author?

So much for Matthew, the man behind the Gospel. What of the actual author of the Gospel as we have it, however much he may have been dependent on Mark, on Hebrew material left by Matthew, on Q, or on a collection of Matthean testimonies? Four characteristics stand out.

First, he was a very humble man. He does not obtrude himself into the story at all. That is remarkable in a man who produced such a masterpiece. I recall that when Michelangelo heard people ascribing his *Pietà* to a rival, he slipped into the church at night and carved on to the statue the words *Michelangelo fecit*, 'Michelangelo made it'. It would have been understandable if the author of this Gospel had done something similar. But he did not. He must have been very modest. His gaze is directed towards his Master, not himself.

Secondly, he was a believer. He was clearly on the side of the disciples in his story, not the Pharisees. What he includes in his Gospel he includes because it will be useful for the community of which he is a part. He puts together material that will be valuable in confronting the successors of the Pharisees in his own day, and will serve to build up the believers in his own church. He was no academic author cloistered in his study, but a believer passionately involved in a local church.

Thirdly, he was a teacher. He was clearly among the leadership of his own church, and he must have been a very good teacher. Matthew 5:19 reflects a scribal background and a strong teaching emphasis. Similarly, 28:19 reflects his teaching role. These are only slight hints, to accompany the remarkable organization of the material in this Gospel, but for what they are worth they support the hypothesis that he was himself a gifted teacher concerned to produce educated Christians who knew what they believed and why, and would be able to defend the faith in controversy with hostile opponents and ignorant Gentiles. It is probable that he himself was engaged in obeying the Great Commission (28:18–20), in preparing new believers for baptism (which he alone of the evangelists mentions, 28:19), in debating with the Pharisees, and in building up the church members by what he said and what he wrote. No doubt he helped with the problems that arose in the early church, drawing on the resources which Jesus had left behind him. Matthew's Gospel handles several issues which do not get treated elsewhere in the Gospels. Clearly the author was a teacher.

Fourthly, he was a 'fulfilled' or 'messianic' Jew. There is a great deal of material in this Gospel to show that its author remained very much a Jew,[11] with whom Gentiles and tax collectors had everything in common. A Jew he remained, but a Jew whose relationship with Jesus had given him a world vision. No Gospel displays a greater commitment to world evangelization than Matthew's. It is one of the overriding characteristics of the book. The Magi, the Caananite woman, the centurion and others from Gentile backgrounds crowd into this Gospel set so firmly on Jewish soil. The author was probably a converted teacher of the law (scribe), perhaps leaving his mini-portrait in 13:52: 'Every teacher of the law who has been instructed about the kingdom of heaven is like the owner of a house who brings out of his storeroom new treasures as well as old.' Those words have struck most commentators as a brilliant description of just what the

---

[11] Attempts by P. Nepper-Christensen and others to make Matthew out to be a Gentile Gospel are very unconvincing. See his *Das Matthäusevangelium – eine judenchristliches Evangelium*? (Aarhus, 1958).

author of the Gospel was and did. He was once a teacher of the law, and now, as Jesus' follower, he uses his scribal background in the service of the gospel. His profession has been totally transformed. He is the interpreter not of a book, but of Jesus, who is the personal fulfilment of the law. This being so, the churches used Matthew's Gospel in debate with his former colleagues, and the material Jesus had left behind on the subject came in very handy. That is why it is preserved in this Gospel rather than in one of the others.

Who were the readers?

Three considerations seem to be significant in determining the readership for which the author wrote.

First, his readers were clearly, in the main, believing Jews, or Jews who were hovering on the verge of confessing Jesus as Messiah. This is very obvious from the large amount of Jewish material in this Gospel, and from all the links that are explicitly made with the Old Testament, from the first chapter onwards. Jews were manifestly in the centre of Matthew's vision. Gentiles were very much part of the original readership too. There was no apartheid in Matthew's church. They were probably not even called Christians yet. They claimed the name of the Messiah (10:40ff.; 19:29; 24:9). They were slaves, brothers, children, little ones of Jesus (5:22–24, 47; 7:3–5; 12:49; 18:1–14; 19:13–14; 23:8). They had most likely come to respond to Jesus through the messengers whom he had commanded to go through the cities of Israel and preach (10:5–23). They had accepted Jesus as Messiah and Lord. They had been baptized into his name. And now they wanted to know how best to live for him among compatriots who had branded them as enemies of the law, of the religion and of the people of Israel. They were struggling to find their own pattern of life, distinct both from the Pharisees with their synagogues, and from the Gentiles with their pagan lifestyle. Matthew's Gospel gives them a great deal of help in this area.

Imagine the situation. Here were little 'synagogues' (as the earliest Christian gatherings seem to have been called)[12] of messianic Jews who had come to the conviction that Jesus was the long-awaited Messiah promised in the Old Testament. They believed that the Law and the Prophets had been fulfilled in this carpenter of Nazareth. And that is why Matthew's Gospel lays such stress on the theme of fulfilment.[13] This was the crux of the debate between the infant church and the synagogue. The nub of it was whether Gentiles as well as Jews could enter into the full worship of God (see 4:15–16;

[12] The word translated 'meeting' in James 2:2 is *synagōgē*.
[13] France (1989), pp. 166–205.

8:11–13; 12:17–21). Christian insistence that they could do so produced strong reaction in the Jewish synagogue. The new sect was questioning behaviour patterns sanctioned for centuries as essential to Jewish life and religion. And here were these ignorant nobodies giving Jesus the status of Son of God, Son of Man, Messiah. They were claiming for him an authority greater than the law, greater than the temple. It was blasphemy! Moreover, if the Gospel was written after AD 70, they would also have attracted much odium because, although they were Jews, the Christians had not joined in the national struggle against Rome from AD 66 to 70. These were no patriots: they were cowards and deserters. Into their homes they accepted harlots, tax collectors and Gentiles. No wonder this Gospel so loudly echoes the bitter hostility that must have arisen between the Christian assembly and the synagogue down the road.

Secondly, it is probable that Matthew's Gospel was primarily addressed to teachers. In those days many people did not read, and so the role of Christian catechists and teachers was very important. They would need something like this Gospel so as to shape the material about Jesus into a memorable and manageable package in which it could be passed on. The church in the earliest period seems to have adopted the patterns of organization, training and worship that were prevalent in Judaism. That was very natural. The local church itself was, as we have seen, called a synagogue. Christian presbyters, or elders, took over from the lay elders who ran the synagogue. And Christian 'teachers of the law' were needed in order to do what their Old Testament counterparts had done. Their influence stemmed from knowledge of the Scriptures, acquaintance with the traditional interpretation of the Scriptures, and the ability to counsel people out of those Scriptures on how to live. These teachers were heirs to Moses' authority (23:2) and were honoured (23:6). They set the tone in prayer, fasting and almsgiving, the three central acts of Jewish piety (6:1–18). They exercised the power to bind or loose; that is to say to issue restricting or releasing enactments (16:19; 18:18; 23:23). Just as orthodox Jews would have asked, 'What do the scribes say?', so 'What do our Christian scribes say?' would have been the question in many an early Christian assembly. Jesus himself had anticipated the emergence of 'prophets and wise men and teachers' to correct the Pharisees (23:34). So I think we can imagine with some probability that Matthew's Gospel was a manual for such people. It was a tool for the Christian scribe. These scribes of Jesus were accredited by the Master himself. They were in line with the prophets of old. They were 'interns' of Jesus, the master rabbi, who had given them the keys to the mysteries of the kingdom (16:19). This Gospel was written for those coming over to Jesus the Messiah from Judaism, but it was written primarily with their teachers in mind. Christian scribes needed just such a tool for their ministry.

Thirdly, if we are to understand the readership of the Gospel properly, we must read the book at two levels.[14] On the one hand, it is the record of what Jesus said and did. On the other, it is written to correlate with Matthew's readers and their situation. The evangelist takes the material from the time of Jesus and intentionally applies it to the lives and times of his readers. And, significantly enough, in most of the chapters of this Gospel, there are three audiences in view. First, there are the disciples; second, the crowds; and third, the teachers of the law and Pharisees. Those three groups are apparent everywhere throughout this Gospel. Why? Surely because there is a correspondence between the audience in the days of Jesus and the readership for whom Matthew is writing. The 'disciples' correspond to the leadership in Matthew's church; they constitute, if you like, the 'prophets, wise men and scribes' of the second generation. The crowds are the ordinary church members, those who overhear what is said and are on the fringe of the action; and the teachers of the law and Pharisees correspond to the largely hostile leaders of the local synagogue. It is like a split-screen television picture: we need to watch both images at once. And all the time the writer is applying the teaching and example of Jesus, which he faithfully records, for the leaders of his own day to assimilate and pass on to the crowds of new Christians who are beginning to flood into the church. Also, he wants to help them all in the unpleasant confrontations they often had to endure with those Jews who were not messianic. When Matthew explains how Jesus trained the Twelve, and met the needs of the crowds, he was also, if you read between the lines, helping his colleagues to care for the 'little ones' in their congregations, and to nourish and train Christian leaders of the next generation.

Paul Minear, in his commentary *Matthew: The Teacher's Gospel*, adopts some such understanding of Matthew's purpose in writing. I am not persuaded by his detailed breakdown of the material, but, like Krister Stendahl before him, he is surely right in seeing that the Gospel as a whole was a manual to put into the hands of church leaders to help them in their work. Minear sees here a manual for church members (4:23 – 7:28), a manual for healers (9:35 – 11:1) a manual of kingdom secrets (ch. 13), a manual of discipline in the church (18:1 – 19:2) and a manual of signs pointing to the return of Christ (chs. 24 – 25). I doubt whether we have in the Gospel an amalgam of five manuals. What we do have, without doubt, is a most organized account of the life and teaching of Jesus, admirably adapted for the purposes of those who are called to teach the faith.

---

[14] Stanton, chs. 5–10.

What is the plan of the Gospel?

Although it is so manifestly well organized, it is by no means immediately apparent what the pattern of the Gospel is. However, practically everyone who has studied the book carefully would agree that it is built round five great blocks of teaching material given by Jesus, somewhat as follows:

chs. 1 – 4	*Introduction:* genealogy, infancy (chs. 1 – 2); baptism and beginnings of the ministry (chs. 3 – 4)
chs. 5 – 7	*Teaching 1: the Sermon on the Mount*
chs. 8 – 9	Jesus' miracles of healing (three groups of them)
ch. 10	*Teaching 2: the mission charge*
chs. 11 – 12	The rejection of John and Jesus by the Jews
ch. 13	*Teaching 3: the parables of the kingdom*
chs. 14 – 17	Miracles, controversies with Pharisees, Peter's confession, and the transfiguration
ch. 18	*Teaching 4: the church*
chs. 19 – 22	Jesus goes up to Jerusalem and teaches
chs. 23 – 25	*Teaching 5: judgment and the end of the world*
chs. 26 – 28	The last days, death and resurrection of Jesus

At first sight it may be surprising that Matthew has grouped material originally given on different occasions into a connected discourse which he presents in one of these major building-blocks of his Gospel. But that is a very western objection. Why should the evangelist *not* arrange material topically rather than chronologically? Most preachers do it every time they speak. That Matthew does make this grouping is rendered certain by the formula with which he brings each block of teaching to a conclusion, such as 'When Jesus had finished saying these things . . .' (7:28); 'After Jesus had finished instructing his twelve disciples . . .' (11:1), and similar phrases in 13:53; 19:1 and 26:1. It is no less obvious where he got the idea from; the five books of the Jewish Torah. Just as God had given the old covenant through Moses, so he gives the new covenant through the new Moses, Jesus, the one to whom Moses pointed forward. Matthew is underlining the continuity of the new law with the old, the new leader with the old. Here is one greater than Moses, giving to the people of God a new law, no longer externalized on tablets of stone, but written within their hearts. Nobody can turn the Sermon on the Mount into a legal code. Here are principles that can be applied by the Spirit of God to ever-changing situations. And Matthew has gathered from the teaching of Jesus a collection of such material, which he presents to us in the Sermon on the Mount. The same is true of the other blocks of teaching material. Few would dispute this.

But the divergence comes in different analyses of the contents of the Gospel apart from the five teaching blocks. There are many ways of breaking down that material. It is generally agreed that chapters 8 and 9, which contain nine acts of power by Jesus, complement his powerful teaching in the Sermon that precedes them. But the contents of the other chapters are not so easy to discern.

Perhaps the heart of the matter lies in chapter 13. It is the hinge on which the Gospel turns.[15] It is the break in the middle of the book, and the emphasis thereafter moves from the crowds to the Twelve. It may well reflect the theme of the Gospel, too. For here in chapter 13 we see the different responses to the planting of God's seed in the hearts of men and women: it is both reflective and challenging. And if chapter 13 is the hinge of the Gospel, we find two carefully balanced discourses on either side. Discourses 1 and 5 are similar in length and not dissimilar in subject matter. Both are about entry into the kingdom (now, and at the end-time). Discourses 2 and 4 are also similar in length and subject matter. They are concerned with the sending out of people, and the receiving of people, in the mission of the church and in the name of Jesus. Clearly, some care has been taken over the parallelism. The same evidence of care shows up in the narrative material as well. There are similarities between the accounts of the birth of Jesus and the resurrection. The birth of Jesus proclaims him as Immanuel, 'God with us'. The resurrection account enshrines his promise, 'Surely I am with you always, to the very end of the age' (28:20). Matthew's Gospel is very carefully designed indeed.

Nobody has perceived this better than Elizabeth and Ian Billingham, in a little book entitled *The Structure of Matthew's Gospel*, which is not as well known as it deserves to be. I find it rather persuasive. Their outline is to be found overleaf. They recognize the centrality of the five great blocks of teaching. They recognize the hinge nature of chapter 13. So far so good: there is nothing new here. But thereafter they develop a very detailed structure which, if it is correct, enables us to gain much insight into Matthew's purpose and pattern in writing.

The main division of the Gospel comes at 13:57. Part 1 is enacted in Galilee, Part 2 in Judea. This verse summarizes Part 1 and points forward to Part 2. Thus the rejection of Jesus in Galilee prepares us for a greater rejection in Jerusalem, as Israel turns her back on her rightful king. But although a prophet is rejected, often enough, in his own country, he is frequently accepted outside, and this prepares us for the fact that the cross and resurrection begin to forge a new

---

[15] *Pace* Blomberg, who sees 4:17 and 16:21 as the twin hinges of the book.

THE PATTERN OF MATTHEW'S GOSPEL

Part 1: In Galilee (1:1 – 13:58)

A. BEGINNINGS

1. Jesus' family tree
   1:1–17
2. Birth and childhood
   1:18 – 2:23
3. The beginning of Jesus' work
   3:1 – 4:25
4. TEACHING
   Basic teaching for disciples
   5:1 – 7:27

'When Jesus had finished saying these things, the crowds were amazed . . . because he taught them as one who had authority . . .'
7:28–29

B. DISCIPLESHIP

1. The disciples see Jesus' power to heal
   8:1–17
2. Jesus discourages some, but leads the disciples on. They see his power over nature, demonic forces and sin, and his disregard of convention (his call of Matthew)
   8:18 – 9:13
3. Those who see, and those who don't
   9:14–34
4. TEACHING
   Instructions to disciples, as they are sent out to do the work of Jesus
   9:35 – 10:42

'After Jesus had finished instructing his twelve disciples, he went on from there to teach and preach . . .'
11:1

C. ACCEPTING OR REJECTING JESUS

1. Grounds for accepting
   11:2–30
2. The Pharisees reject Jesus
   12:1–14
3. Acceptable to the Father
   a. Healings – leading to quotation from Isaiah
   b. Jesus accused of working in power of Beelzebub
   c. Jesus refuses to give sign
   d. 'Whoever does the will of my Father . . . is my brother . . .'
      12:15–50
4. TEACHING
   Parables about the kingdom
   13:1–52

'When Jesus had finished these parables, he moved on . . . to his home town . . . "Only in his home town . . . is a prophet without honour."'
13:53–54, 57

Part 2: To Jerusalem (14:1 – 28:20)

D. FORESHADOWING THE FUTURE

Introduction: the death of John the Baptist

1. The future for Israel
a. Feeding 5,000
b. Jesus and Peter (who will be leader of new Israel, the church) walk on water
c. Healings
d. True worship
   14:13 – 15:20

2. The future for the world
a. Healing a Gentile girl
b. Feeding 4,000
c. Interpreting signs of the times
d. Peter's declaration about Jesus
   15:21 – 16:20

3. The more immediate future – Jesus must go to Jerusalem and suffer
   16:21 – 17:27

4. TEACHING
   The kind of behaviour expected of those entering (on earth) the kingdom Jesus is about to set up
   18:1–35

'When Jesus had finished saying these things, he left Galilee and went into the region of Judea to the other side of the Jordan . . .'
   19:1

E. JUDGMENT – BY JESUS, OF JESUS, AND THE FINAL JUDGMENT

1. Reversal of human values
a. On divorce
b. On children brought to Jesus
c. On the rich young man
d. Parable of labourers in vineyard
'So the last will be first, and the first will be last.'
   19:3 – 20:16

2. 'Many are invited, but few are chosen.'
   20:17 – 22:14

3. The Pharisees attempt to trap Jesus into condemning himself
   22:15 – 23:39

4. TEACHING
   Predictions and parables about the time of the final judgment
   24:1 – 25:46

'When Jesus had finished saying *all* these things, he said to his disciples, ". . . the Passover is two days away – and the Son of Man will be . . . crucified." '
   26:1–2

F. THE END – AND THE BEGINNING

1. Events leading to the arrest of Jesus
   26:3–56

2. The trial of Jesus
   26:57 – 27:26

3. The crucifixion
   27:27–66

4. The resurrection
   28:1–20

'All authority in heaven and on earth has been given to me. Therefore go and *make disciples of all nations*, baptising them in the name of the Father and of the Son and of the Holy Spirit, and teaching them to obey everything I have commanded you. And surely I am with you always, to the very end of the age.'
   28:10–20

people of God among the Gentiles. There is thus a superb symmetry between the rejection that concludes Part 1 and the vindication that brings Part 2 to an end. Moreover, John the Baptist launches Part 2, and it is a particularly subtle link. He challenged Herod as Jesus challenged Jerusalem; and he came to a violent end, just as Jesus would. His death is proleptic.

Throughout the whole account there is a gradualness which ought not to be missed. Despite the formal end of Part 1 in the rejection of Jesus, there is no sudden and cataclysmic change. God's offer to Israel remains open during the chapters that follow, despite her seeming rejection of her Messiah. Yet all the time the new Israel is being formed, slowly and surely, and it is all centred round Peter and his colleagues. Like Peter, the church is to walk with Jesus by faith, despite the storms that assail them (14:33). A glimpse is given in chapter 15 of the coming world mission of the church. Chapter 16 shows Jesus determining to build his church on Peter's confession that he is Messiah and Son of God, and the transfiguration in chapter 17 confirms it. At last Jesus and his followers are ready to go up to Jerusalem for the denouement.

The Billinghams select three elements as worthy of comment from the five blocks of teaching material in the Gospel. First, Matthew is showing the continuity of the people of God throughout the ages. Secondly, Matthew shows how the people of God are Abraham's seed, and the promise of Genesis 15 is honoured. Abraham's descendants go and make disciples of all nations. The Great Commission fulfils God's promise that Abraham's descendants would outnumber the stars. Thirdly, the new Israel receives its new *torah*, law, which must be faithfully committed to succeeding generations.

Each half of the Gospel falls into three sections. B and E, the central sections in each half, are pivotal. Sections A and D, which respectively precede them, prepare the way for the two central themes of 'discipleship' and 'judgment'. Those that follow, C and F, carry these themes forward in such a way as to bring out the full implications of discipleship and judgment. The process comes inexorably to a head. Neutrality is impossible. Men and women have to decide how to respond.

We have, therefore, no simple story about Jesus in this Gospel. It is all very carefully planned to demonstrate authentic Christianity in action, showing the centrality of Jesus to every aspect of the Christian life and faith. Each item in the account has been carefully and precisely placed so as to make the greatest impact on the reader.

Let us examine these two halves a little more closely, beginning with section B, the linchpin of the first half of the Gospel. It is all about discipleship. The powerful presence of Jesus healing, exorcising and cleansing proclaims the kingdom of heaven. To follow him is a costly and serious business. So Jesus discourages those unwilling to pay the cost (8:18 – 22), and brings those who do into a closer relationship with himself (8:27 – 9:13). The disciples begin to see the face of the kingdom in the person of Jesus. They are ready for the trial run at mission which follows in chapter 10.

But before section B comes A, setting Jesus in the context of God's historic dealings with Israel by means of the genealogy and the infancy narratives. Matthew needs to show how Jesus' mission is linked with John's life, call to repentance, and arrest (3:1 – 4:17). He also needs to sketch a clear picture of what it means to be learners under Jesus as he enunciates the life of the kingdom of God. Hence the Sermon on the Mount that follows, and prepares the way for the subsequent central section on discipleship.

Section C emerges naturally from that same central section B. The challenge to discipleship is clarified. The kingdom of God is plainly seen to be embodied in Jesus, who is the kingdom in person. What will people do with the kingdom? What will they do with Jesus? This is the question that comes again and again in this section. First, the grounds for accepting Jesus are made clear through the material about John the Baptist (11:2–19). Jesus refers John in his doubts to the signs Isaiah (35:5–6; 61:1) said would mark the kingdom (11:2–6). Jesus then likens the Jews to unco-operative children playing street games. Refusal to see brings condemnation: but all can respond to his gracious invitation if they will (11:29). Jesus is the bridge between God and humankind; he is the locus of revelation. People should get yoked up with him!

Chapter 12 shows that on the whole the Pharisees are unwilling to accept his invitation. The atmosphere gets harsher. The claims of Jesus (to be Satan's victor, the ultimate judge, a greater than Solomon, Jonah and the temple) are more insistent. And the chapter that begins with the Pharisees' rejection of Jesus ends with the disciples' being welcomed into the most intimate relationship with him. The contrast is plain, and chapter 13, which follows, underlines it. The whole chapter is like a mirror flashed into the face of his hearers so that they can see themselves. Which way are they facing?

The second half of the book also has its crucial central section, E. And the content of that section is judgment. The theme rises to a crescendo in the last and most awesome of the parables, the great judgment.

The basis of judgment is whether people did or did not show mercy to those in need. The emphasis is on obedience to the implicit claims of the great Lover. It is the fitting conclusion of the Christian *torah*.

But this final judgment is preceded by a series of lesser challenges, represented by issues such as divorce (19:3) and marriage (19:10–12), the importance of God's children (19:14) and the matter of money (19:24). God's judgments are not made on the same basis as ours – hence the parable of the labourers in the vineyard (20:1–16). And so to the reversal of human values in the servant motif, rejected by Zebedee's sons, but embodied in Jesus (20:17–28). In that role Jesus enters Jerusalem humbly on a donkey, the Servant-Messiah (21:1–11). Immediately he is moved to act in judgment against the corrupt temple and the barren fig-tree (the emblem of Israel). The chief priests attempt to pass judgment on Jesus (21:23–27) but he shows that they are actually being judged by God (21:28–46). The judgment theme continues in chapter 22 in the parables of the marriage feast, taxes to Caesar, the great commandment, and the decision the Jerusalem leadership has made about messiahship (22:41–46). Chapter 23 contains Jesus' blistering judgments on the attitudes of the religious and on the city of Jerusalem (23:37ff.). This leads straight into the predictions of the end and the parables associated with it in chapters 24 and 25.

Section D precedes this central section E. And it is all about the future. The future of Israel comes under review, as does that of the Gentile world and the church that will penetrate it; so, indeed, does Jesus' own future. The teaching section that concludes it is all about the community of the future, the Christian church.

Section F is all about the end and the beginning. The events leading up to the cross are followed not by any new teaching section, but by the resurrection, the living Christ. The person has replaced the book. And this is a highly significant conclusion to the Gospel. This section spells out the implications of the judgment theme which preceded it in section E, the centrepiece of Part 2; just as section C had drawn out the implications of the discipleship theme in section B. Human judgment of Israel's Messiah is carried out through crucifixion, and that judgment will redound on those who cried out, 'Let his blood be on us and on our children!' (27:25). Yet despite humankind's judgment against God's Messiah, God's purpose is not thwarted. The resurrection is God's supreme vindication of Jesus and his claims, his teaching and his matchless life. 'He is not here; he has risen' (28:6). The crucified and risen Christ confronts people as the good news is proclaimed. And the question he poses is the heart of the whole Gospel. It is the question Pilate wrestled with: 'What shall I do, then, with Jesus who is called Christ?' (27:22).

It may be that we can argue about some of the detail. But I believe that the Billinghams have made out an excellent case for the centrality of chapter 13, the six sections of the Gospel and the skilful construction of those six panels embracing a central one in each half of the book. It is a pattern that enables us to see the design of the Gospel with some probability and no little clarity.

Why was the Gospel so popular?

Popular Matthew certainly was. In the second and third centuries it was constantly being quoted, whereas Mark was rarely consulted. Today, by way of contrast, it is Mark that enjoys favour, and Matthew is generally rather neglected. Why was it so much in vogue in the early church? Why was it placed first of the four when the Gospel canon emerged in the latter part of the second century?

There are a number of reasons. One of them is clearly that Matthew was the Gospel used by one of the great church centres. Certainty is not possible, but there is a lot to be said for the suggestion that the church at Antioch regularly used it, and thus gave it a lot of prestige. Ignatius, the early second-century Bishop of Antioch and martyr, was soaked in Matthew's Gospel, and there are strong traces of it also in the *Didache*, which seems to have originated in Antioch. The *Didache* was written around the end of the first century AD and comprised early teaching of the church. Interestingly enough, it was only in Antioch that the stater was worth four drachmas, and that is clearly the implication of Matthew 17:24–27. Antioch is a likely guess. In any case, some great city must have taken Matthew's Gospel to its heart if we are to account for its widespread use in antiquity.

A second reason is obviously that it was connected with the name of a great apostle. If Matthew the tax collector did not actually write it (and we have seen that he probably did not), he was widely believed to have done so, and clearly had something very significant to do with its origins, perhaps as the author of Q or of the *testimonia*. Having such an author obviously counted for a great deal.

Thirdly, the very Jewishness of this Gospel not only made it a valuable guide for those coming into Christianity from Judaism, but also provided a wonderful bridge into the Old Testament, showing the continuity and the difference between Christianity and Judaism.

Fourthly, the Gospel was magnificently arranged, as we have seen. It sprang from an orderly mind. It demonstrated a memorable plan. The evangelist arranged events and sayings into groups of three, five, seven or nine. Thus we have seven woes against the Pharisees (ch. 23), three typical examples of Jewish piety (6:1–18), seven parables (ch. 13), nine miracles in groups of three (chs. 8 – 9) and three series of fourteen generations in the genealogy (not forgetting that fourteen is the numerical value in Hebrew letters of the name David). Add to that the six panels of the Gospel and the five great blocks of teaching, and it is not surprising that this Gospel became so popular. It was easy to find your way around.

Fifthly, this Gospel is the most complete of the four. That is why it served as a manual for Christian teachers just as the *Manual of Discipline* did for the men of Qumran and the *Didache* did for the subapostolic church. Matthew's Gospel is complete, from the Old Testament background and genealogy to the Great Commission. It is an account of the origin, birth, ministry, teaching, mighty deeds, death, resurrection and continuing mission of great David's greater Son. In a word, this Gospel is an apology, defending the Christian faith against Jewish attacks. It is a manual to build up converts in Christian ethics and life. And it may well, as G. D. Kilpatrick[16] thought, have been used as an early lectionary, helping Christians to live a life of disciplined discipleship based on the words and deeds of Jesus set out in a systematic way that could be read week by week in the worship services.

Finally, Matthew's Gospel was succinct and clear. Matthew almost always shortens Mark's accounts, and his story is smoother, lacking Mark's harsh or vivid details. He also goes to some lengths to clarify what might have been misunderstood in the Markan account: the meaning of Jesus' baptism, for example, and the rumours about the grave-robbing. The faces of the disciples are often spared the blushes that are described in Mark, and there is more reverence about the person of Jesus himself. It all made for brevity and clarity.

When was it written?

We do not know for sure when Matthew was written. And the answer we give will depend very much on how we assess and value the ancient evidence that Matthew the apostle was the first to write a Gospel, and that it was the Hebrew prototype of our Greek Matthew that he composed. There is no compelling reason why, in the unlikely event that this is the correct attribution of authorship, the Gospel could not have been written in the forties. The Aramaist C. C. Torrey saw no reason why such a date need be rejected. If, however, the Gospel is a refined and polished edition of Mark with the addition of extra material, that makes a lot of difference to the date we give it. There are strong reasons to believe that Mark was written shortly before AD 70. If so, Matthew will have been written some years later, and a majority of scholars (for no very compelling reason, it must be confessed) assign it a date around AD 80. The most important internal hint may be found in 22:7: 'The king was enraged. He sent his army and destroyed those murderers and burned their city.' That certainly looks like an allusion to the destruction of Jerusalem by the Roman armies in AD 70. However, it may be a stock

---

[16] *The Origins of the Gospel According to St Matthew* (Oxford University Press, 1946).

description of a punitive expedition by a typical ancient king. The other bits of evidence can also be argued either way. For example, many scholars are impressed by the ecclesiastical organization (16:19; 18:17), the rise of false prophets (24:9) and the increased reverence paid to the disciples (8:26; 14:33; 16:9) and postulate a late date; but Krister Stendahl is not at all moved by this.[17] He sees a number of these factors already present in the Qumran community before Jesus was born! The truth is that we do not know the date of this Gospel. It was probably before AD 50 if the ancient fathers are right about its authorship. If they are wrong, somewhere in the 70s is more probable. Whatever the date of origin, it speedily established itself as the most important and most frequently quoted of the four Gospels.

What were Matthew's main concerns?

Among Matthew's many interests and emphases I suggest that these seven figured high.

1. Jesus, the centre of his vision

The author is entirely eclipsed by his subject, and Matthew has organized all his material to focus the reader's attention first on the person of Jesus the Messiah (1:1 – 4:16),[18] then on his public ministry (4:17 – 16:20) and thereafter on his death and resurrection. 'Jesus' is the main name used, and apart from 1:21 it is always a personal name. 'Jesus' is born in Bethlehem (2:1, 5–6), is raised in Nazareth (2:23) as a carpenter's son (13:55), and has brothers and sisters (13:55–56). As an adult he moves to Capernaum, which is called his own town (4:13; 9:1) where he apparently has a house (9:10, 28; 13:1; 17:25). Jesus is the climax of God's self-revelation; 11:27 shows him as both the author and the locus of God's self-disclosure.

The name apart, Jesus is often called 'Messiah' in Matthew's Gospel. The Hebrew word, and its Greek equivalent, *Christos*, simply mean 'the anointed one' (1:16, 18). Very soon it became almost a surname of Jesus, but in Matthew it often retains its basic meaning. Israel knew anointed prophets, priests and kings. After their demise the hope persisted that one day there would arise a figure who would recapitulate in his own person those three anointed strands of old. Those hopes were crystallized in the expectation of a Messiah, or sometimes (as at Qumran), two. The

[17] In his introduction to Matthew in *Peake's Commentary* (rev. edition 1962, repr. Routledge, 1991).
[18] For an introduction to the Christology of the Gospel, see Stanton, pp. 169–191; France (1989), pp. 279–317.

claim of Matthew is that the anointed one has come in Jesus of Nazareth (1:16, 18; 16:20–21). The title of 'prophet' was also accorded him, but it was soon seen to be inadequate (16:14; 21:11). He stands in David's royal line (1:1, 16–17, 20, 25). So 'Son of David' is used in this Gospel to shed light on who he is, especially when he heals those who are of no account in Israel (9:27–31; 12:22; 15:21–28; 20:29ff.). Often these despised folk see what the leaders of Israel are blind to, and Matthew makes full use of the ironic contrast. Jesus is David's anointed Son, and this description of him emphasizes God's faithfulness to his promises long ago, and so heightens the guilt of the chief priests in killing their Messiah.

A third way in which Jesus is described is as 'Lord'. The Greek word, *kyrios*, has a variety of nuances. It may mean no more than 'sir', as it does in modern Greek. That is the meaning in 27:63. It is often used of God, translating the Hebrew *ᵃdōnāy*. Occasionally in the Gospel it is applied to Jesus himself by those who have faith (e.g. 26:22; 16:22; 18:21). As J. D. Kingsbury showed,[19] this word 'Lord' has nuances of divinity about it when applied to Jesus by disciples. It was a confessional title in the earliest church.[20]

A fourth title of Jesus found often in this Gospel is 'Son of Man'. It is a public title, used among unbelievers and enquirers. The title is preferred by Jesus. It is always to be found on his lips and his alone. Jesus speaks about himself in this way when he is talking in general about his ministry (8:20; 9:6; 11:19; 12:8, 40), when he speaks about his cross (17:17, 22; 20:18–19; 26:2) and when he looks ahead to future vindication in glory (10:23; 16:27–28; 24:27, 30; 26:64–65). There was a marvellous ambivalence about it. It could be simply a periphrasis for 'I', as Geza Vermes never tires of stressing.[21] But it was also rooted in Daniel 7:14, as he is consistently unwilling to notice. And there it unambiguously stands for a towering figure, more divine than human, representing the 'saints, the people of the Most High',[22] to whom is given 'authority, glory and sovereign power'.[23] And it is this glorious figure who, as Jesus realized, was destined to stoop to assume the role of the suffering Servant whom Isaiah had long ago seen as the sin-bearer of the people. The highest in Judaism, the Son of Man, was to be identified with the lowest, the suffering Servant (Matt. 17:22). Thereafter God would hold out for him a glorious future seated 'at the right hand of the Mighty One and coming on the clouds of heaven' (26:64).

'Son of God' is the fifth and main title of Jesus in this Gospel. The Messiah is 'God's Son', not merely David's (27:40, 43, 54). In chapter 1 he is revealed as God's Son, conceived by the Holy Spirit,

---

[19] In his *Matthew: Structure, Christology, Kingdom* (SPCK, 1975), ch. 3.
[20] Phil. 2:11.   [21] See his *Jesus the Jew* (Collins, 1973).
[22] Dan. 7:27.   [23] Dan. 7:14.

not by Joseph (1:18). He is 'God with us' (1:23). In chapter 2 reference is repeatedly made to 'the child and his mother'; at his baptism his divine sonship is stressed (3:17). The temptation assumes it (4:3, 5–6). It is as divine Son that he heals, preaches and teaches, and this comes to a climax in Peter's confession of him as the Son of God (16:16). And so on through the passion to the resurrection. He has a unique relationship with the Father. He does on earth what his Father does in heaven. He has the right to call God Abba, 'dear Father'. Others can call God Father only in a derivative way. He speaks of God as 'my Father' or 'your Father', but never 'our Father', except in words he gives his disciples to say (6:9). His relationship to God is unique and incommunicable. Only he can reveal the Father (11:27ff.). He is totally endued with the Father's authority (28:18).

There can be no doubt that Jesus is the centre of Matthew's vision.

2. *The unity of revelation*

Matthew was sure that God had revealed himself in the Old Testament. Every Jew was sure of that. He was the God who had revealed himself to Abraham, Isaac and Jacob. He had done so by his words and by his actions. That was not an issue in Judaism. Everyone believed it. But if this is Matthew's conviction, how does he account for Jesus centuries later? How does he relate to God's revelation in the Old Testament? Matthew's answer is very clear. Jesus and the Old Testament correspond as fulfilment to promise. That is why Jesus is called by so many Old Testament titles. That is why he picks up so many Old Testament themes. That is why he quotes the Old Testament so freely and confidently, particularly with the 'formula quotations': 'All this took place to fulfil what the Lord had said through the prophet . . .' (1:22).[24] That is why Matthew stresses that Jesus came not to abolish the *torah* but to fulfil it (5:17). And when Jesus gives his great Sermon on the Mount, he does not scrap the Old Testament, but intensifies it. The commandment said, 'You shall not commit adultery.' To say, 'Don't look at a woman lustfully' does not negate the commandment; it intensifies it (5:27–28). That is what Jesus does time and again with the Old Testament. He applies it to the heart and makes it the more challenging.

It is the same with the formula quotations. When you look at them in their original Old Testament context, many of them seem to have almost nothing to do with the events to which Matthew applies them. They are, in a bizarre way, taken out of context. How can he do such a thing? Simply because he believes so strongly in the unity

[24] See also 2:15, 17, 23; 8:17; 12:17; 13:35; 21:4; 26:54, 56; 27:9, 35 mg.

of revelation. It is not that Matthew dreams up these allusions from the Old Testament. Had he done so, they would fit much better than they do. It is the action of Jesus that is primary. And the early Christians, such as Matthew, reflected, 'If Jesus really does bring us the final revelation of God, then it *must* be hinted at, however obscurely, in the Scriptures which come to us from God through Moses and the prophets.' So 'Out of Egypt I called my son' (2:15) must be seen, in its fullest sense, as a prediction of what in fact happened when the young Jesus came back from the sojourn he and his family had in Egypt and returned to Nazareth – though in the original passage of Hosea (11:1) no such thought was in the mind of the prophet. It may look like a misuse of the Old Testament, but actually it is not. It is a profound way of saying that the God who has revealed himself in the ancient Scriptures has now given a full and final disclosure of himself in Jesus. 'In the past God spoke to our forefathers through the prophets at many times and in various ways, but in these last days he has spoken to us by his Son.' Those opening words of the letter to the Hebrews could easily have been written by Matthew. He believed passionately in the unity of revelation. The time of fulfilment has come. But that fulfilment was foreshadowed in the Old Testament.[25]

3. *The life of discipleship*

Matthew's Gospel is strong on discipleship. He is clear that to decide for Jesus means repudiating old ways of behaviour. The law of the kingdom must mark the lives of the members of the kingdom. God's love brings us into the kingdom in the first place; that same love must have a practical outworking in our lives. We are the recipients of the love of God, who accepts us just as we are, unqualified tax collectors, sinners and the like. And that love transforms us. The practical outworking is delineated in the Sermon. That is how disciples are called to reflect the *agapē* which won them. The indicative of what members of the kingdom are in Christ is followed by the imperative of how they must behave. It is the outworking of what God works within them. Decision for Christ inevitably leads into discipleship of Christ. The Sermon assumes the indicative: it spells out the imperative. The gospel and ethics cannot be separated. And the ethic of the kingdom is spelled out in the Sermon on the Mount. It is meant to be lived out by the church in the midst of a secular society. We are not to expect everybody else to behave like that, but disciples are called to nothing less. That is the outworking of the love that has reached us in Jesus the Messiah. So discipleship is a major

[25] See Stanton, pp. 346–363.

concern of Matthew throughout his Gospel. And undoubtedly he intends the readers of his work to apply this truth to themselves. If Jesus is our rabbi, then discipleship is the name of the game.

4. *The kingdom of heaven*

The phrase 'the kingdom of heaven' (literally, 'the heavens') is a major concern in Matthew, and is peculiar to him. It shows how deeply rooted was his Judaism, for orthodox Jews used periphrases like 'heaven' so as to avoid using the sacred divine name. It means the same as 'the kingdom of God' in the other Gospels,[26] and is a specifically rabbinic trait. We shall look at seven aspects of the phrase.

The meaning of the kingdom
The phrase is used in four ways. First, it expresses the ultimate sovereignty of God over his world. Secondly, it stakes a claim: we, his creatures, should serve the King. Thirdly, it describes the realm in which his kingly rule is acknowledged. Thus you enter the kingdom, you are a child of the kingdom, you receive the kingdom, by responding to his kingly rule and surrendering to the King. And fourthly, it points to a future when God will be all in all, and his will shall be done on earth as in heaven. That is what the kingdom of God means in the Gospels. Thus Matthew speaks of the kingdom as already realized (in the person of the King, e.g. 4:17; 11:11) and yet also future (24 – 25; 16:28; 20:21). The kingdom of God has both a present manifestation and a future consummation. Men and women enter the kingdom by offering their allegiance to the King. And so the preaching of the kingdom means precisely the same as Jesus' appeal to people to repent (18:3), believe (18:6) and offer him their total allegiance (13:44–45).

The character of the kingdom
The character of the kingdom is very radical. It is the place where the Lord God is our Father (6:9). The fatherhood of God marks the kingdom into which we are invited. The forgiveness of sins is the very air we breathe (18:23ff.). We are brought into the new and eternal covenant (26:26). But we must not forget that the kingdom is an upside-down kingdom (11:25). It is the new order that means good news for the poor (11:5). It is the age to which the Scriptures pointed (11:2–6). It is the age of the Spirit (12:28). It is radically new and disturbing.

[26] A superb general introduction to the kingdom in Jesus' teaching may be found in G. E. Ladd, *Jesus and the Kingdom* (SPCK, 1966).

The coming of the kingdom

In one sense the kingdom is eternal and timeless, God's perpetual sovereignty over his world, his standing claim on people's allegiance. But in another sense it was brought in by Jesus. Matthew is clear on this matter. As we have seen, Daniel 7:13–14 are important verses in helping us to understand how Jesus and the kingdom are related. The kingdom spoken of there has three strands: authority, glory and sovereign power. And all three are major factors in the life of Jesus and emerge at major points in it. Take his birth, for example. There was the power of God's Spirit working with the virgin Mary to conceive Jesus. There was the glory of the angelic host worshipping at his birth. And there was the authoritative guidance that saved him from the slaughter of the small children in Bethlehem meted out by Herod. Or take the death of Jesus. It spoke of authority over Satan. It spoke of the power of God at that place of supreme weakness. And it was on the cross that his glory was revealed *par excellence*.

So it will be at the end of the world. It will be a demonstration of the authority of God breaking in to end human history. It will be the Son of Man returning in glory. And he will come to take his sovereign power. Here we have the same three great themes of the kingdom as were foreseen by Daniel long ago.

At the major events of Jesus' life all these three strands are present. At other times, one or other predominates. Thus at Pentecost his power is the main thing; at the ascension and at the transfiguration, his glory; at the destruction of Jerusalem, his authority as judge, a tiny cameo of the last day. This way of looking at the coming of the kingdom may help us to understand some of the difficult verses we find in the Gospel connected with it. Here are three. 'I tell you the truth, some who are standing here will not taste death before they see the Son of Man coming in his kingdom' (16:28). What does that mean? Well, it is clear what Matthew thought it meant. His narrative continues, 'After six days Jesus took with him Peter, James and John ... and ... was transfigured before them' (17:1–2). The evangelist clearly saw the coming of the Son of Man in his kingdom as at least prefigured in the transfiguration, which took place six days later. That was the coming in glory.

Or take 26:64: '... you will see the Son of Man seated at the right hand of the Mighty One and coming on the clouds of heaven'. The glory and the authority attributed to Jesus in that verse are manifestly part of his parousia, his return at the end of the age, no longer incognito but as rightful King. Or take 10:23: 'I tell you the truth, you will not finish going through the cities of Israel before the Son of Man comes.' This looks very much like the coming of the Lord in sovereign power in the judgment of AD 70. It means that they will not have completed the Jewish mission before judgment befalls Israel and the gospel is released widely into the Gentile world. Those are all difficult verses. The 'coming of the kingdom' is progressive and at different levels. But these three strands of authority, glory and sovereign power have a lot to do both with the events concerned and with the verses attached to them.

The demands of the kingdom

God's kingdom makes two main demands. First, you must enter into the kingdom (7:13, 21). This happens when you relate to the King. That is why Jesus called people to himself (11:28). For he is the embodiment of the kingdom (11:11). The Old Testament asserted God's kingly rule over his people Israel. But that idea was sadly marred in practice. On the one hand, the kings of Israel were generally a poor advertisement for God's kingship. They represented him very inadequately. And on the other hand, the people of Israel failed dismally to represent the servant response that is proper to the King. They were always breaking away to do their own thing, and obedience was hardly the supreme characteristic of God's people throughout their history. Both kingship and servanthood were very imperfectly embodied. But with Jesus all that changed. He expressed and embodied in his own person the kingly rule and claims of God Almighty. And he displayed in his perfect obedience all the marks of the Servant of the Lord. King and Servant met in his person. Jesus is thus both the founder and embodiment of the kingdom. He is the kingdom in himself. That is why he can call people to himself when he invites them into the kingdom of God (11:28). That is also why, in Acts, preaching about Jesus is, on occasion, referred to as preaching about the kingdom of God.[27] The message of the kingdom was entry by repentance and faith. And that is precisely the way in which to approach Jesus Christ. Thus Jesus tells people to repent (18:3), to believe (18:6) and to offer the allegiance proper to subjects (13:44–45) if they mean to enter the kingdom. The message of the kingdom was rightly and necessarily integrated with the person of the King.

Entry is one condition of the kingdom. The other is ethics. Once we enter in, we are reckoned to be sheep, not wolves; wheat, not weeds; sheep, not goats; good trees, not bad. New birth leads to new behaviour. New life leads to a new lifestyle. We must face the cost of the ethics of the kingdom. We cannot love God and materialism (6:24). In particular we must care for the poor and the powerless, who are called blessed by the King (5:3ff.).

[27] Acts 8:12; 19:8; 20:25; 28:23; 28:31.

The spread of the kingdom

In one sense it is nonsense to speak of the spread of the kingdom, because God is the ultimate and absolute ruler over all his creation. In another sense it is a good way of describing the growing response of rebel subjects, laying down their arms and surrendering to their rightful King. The circle of light expands as knees bow to acknowledge the King. This is reflected in the parables of the growth of the kingdom. The church carries the gospel to all the nations, and the kingdom grows as a result, until the parousia. Thus the mustard seed becomes, incredibly, a mighty tree and the birds of the air come and nest in it. This is a picture of empire in Daniel 4:10–17, 21 and Ezekiel 31:6. God's empire expands. It is the same with the leaven, which makes the dough rise until the whole is leavened. It is the same with the net that draws all sorts of fish in from the sea. The kingdom will spread until it reaches its climax in the return of Christ at the end of history.

The church and the kingdom

The church cannot be identified with the kingdom, which is a much broader and more wonderful thing: it would be sad indeed if God's rule on earth were confined to the church! No, it is not the same as the kingdom, but it is a major manifestation of that kingdom here on earth. It is a first instalment of the coming kingdom when God's will shall be perfectly done. It is intended by its message and way of life to be a colony of heaven. The church anticipates what the kingdom will be, but the church is not that kingdom. There is much mistaken talk these days about 'kingdom theology', taking what is ascribed to the kingdom and applying it uncritically to the church. Matthew's Gospel warns against any such facile identification. For the church is not the kingdom, although the association between the two is close. Thus Jesus can say in almost the same breath, 'I will build my church . . . I will give you the keys of the kingdom' (16:18–19). But the church is like the net, containing fish good and bad. The church is like the harvest field, weeds and wheat together. The church is at present a 'mixed economy', and at the end of time the day of judgment will sort it out. That day will see the final coming of the kingdom. The church is by no stretch of imagination the place where God rules, as yet. By no stretch of imagination is it holy, as yet. There are members of the church who do not understand and do not trust the King (13:19). There are false prophets in the church who lead people astray (7:15–23; 24:11). There are those in the church who collapse under the pressure of persecution (13:21; 24:9–10), or deny Jesus (10:33), or are seduced by wealth (13:12), and much else besides. No, the church cannot be identified with the kingdom, but it does represent that part of God's kingly rule which is no longer in open revolt against the rightful King but professes to have surrendered to him. And it is the job of the church to evangelize, so that the kingdom of God will spread as other rebel subjects come to accept the gracious armistice offered by the King.

The enemy of the kingdom

Jesus makes it plain that there is a determined enemy of God and his kingly rule: Satan. A strong counterpoint runs through the Gospel. Satan is totally opposed to the kingdom of God (6:13; 11:12; 12:24–29; 13:39). Satan, the tempter, the devil, the enemy, the evil one, Beelzebub, the ruler of this age – he is called by all those names – is the implacable foe of the kingdom of God. He assails Jesus constantly (4:1–11). He is the strong one, but Jesus is stronger than the strong (12:28–29). He even assails Jesus through Peter (16:21–23), through Jewish crowds (11:16–17), and Jewish leaders (16:1). He is the usurper prince of this world, and yet he is doomed to destruction, for Jesus goes up to Jerusalem to suffer many things from the elders, chief priests and teachers of the law, and on the third day he will be raised in triumph (16:21).

Satan assails the kingdom; he assails Jesus; and he assails the church. They will have to face persecution from without (13:39; 5:44; 7:21–23), and attack from within, especially through false prophets (7:15–23; 24:11, 24) who appear to be charismatic prophets but are in reality wolves (7:15), whose lives are loveless (7:10–20) and who lead others astray (24:11–12).

Such is the enemy. But his power is limited, his teeth drawn, and his destiny assured (25:41, 46).

5. The people of the Messiah

The noun 'church' is used twice in this Gospel and nowhere in any of the others. But the idea is much more prevalent than the mention of the word. Through the gracious summons of Jesus, the Messiah and Son of God, the disciples of Jesus become children of God and brothers and sisters in the company of the Messiah as they enter the sphere of God's kingly rule. In response to that gracious summons, the disciples begin to reflect in their lives the greater righteousness which eclipses that of the teachers of the law and the Pharisees, and they begin to show a deep determination to do the will of God and make it known. That is the theory, and Matthew's Gospel is an attempt to ground theory in practice.

If we are to retain Matthew's 'kingdom' language, then the members of the church are children of the kingdom (13:38). In Jesus they share the forgiveness of the kingdom (26:28). They hear and understand the word of the kingdom (13:19, 23) and so know the secrets of the kingdom (13:11). They seek the righteousness of the kingdom (6:33). They have been entrusted with the keys of the kingdom (16:19). They pray earnestly for the coming of the kingdom (6:10), and produce the fruits of the kingdom (13:8). At the consummation of the age they will enter into the kingdom (25:23) and inherit it (5:3).

Matthew directs the church strongly towards the end-time, because the empirical church is something of a mess, and Matthew knows that fact as well as we do. It is full of status-seeking (23:8–12), even hatred, among members (24:10), lack of love (24:12), luke-warmness (25:26), unwillingness to forgive (18:35). It is often marked by disciples' losing faith (18:6) and despising others in the community (18:10). Matthew encourages them to look towards the consummation, when the full glory of what God intends to do with his church will appear, on the day when the kingdom comes in power.

There is much more directed to the church in this Gospel. There are warnings: against hoarding wealth (19:23), against loss of faith and against presenting stumbling-blocks to others (18:6–7) – above all, against lack of readiness to meet Jesus (24:36–39; 25:11–13). There is also much encouragement: to trust the promises and live by them (5:3–10), to pray (6:9–13), to take up the cross and follow Jesus (10:24–25), to have no fear of enemies (10:28–31), to trust him like a child (18:3–4), to face the music (5:10–12) and to be ready for Jesus at his coming (24:27; 25:10).

6. *The end of the world*

The end of history is undoubtedly a major interest of the evangelist. The other evangelists all have it, but none to such an extent as Matthew. Jesus, the prince in rags, will come back as the crowned king of the universe. And the world is moving not towards chaos, though there will be plenty of that (24:3–31), but towards Christ and his return. Every movement worth its salt has an eschatology, an expectation of how it will all end. And Christians, Matthew believes, can hold their heads high. Their expectation is solidly grounded in the cross and resurrection. It is certain. That is the theme of chapter 24, distinguishing, as Mark does less clearly, between the fall of Jerusalem and the return of Christ later on. That is the theme of chapter 25 with its parables of the parousia. Christians live between the advents. They should fashion their lives and their ambitions accordingly. The parable of the nocturnal burglar (24:43–44) encourages expectancy among Christ's people; that about the disorderly servants (24:45–51) encourages holiness of life; the parable of the ten virgins speaks of the need for readiness (25:1–13); the parable of the talents stresses reliability (25:14–30), while the parable of the sheep and goats calls for practical love (25:31–46). Those are the characteristics that the expectation of Christ's return should bring about in his people. And in the light of his return they must evangelize.

Matthew and his readers do not rest their hopes on the future alone. They find the clue to the denouement in the middle of the story. The confidence that Christ will return is placed fairly and squarely in the coming and dying and rising of Jesus the Messiah. The ultimate has come into the world of the particular; the beyond has come into the midst. Absolute goodness is not an ideal that is beyond us. It has come to us in the person of Jesus. It has lived and died and risen. And in the last analysis it will prevail. That is why we can have confidence about the future; and that confidence was needed in the difficult days of the 70s and 80s of the first century, just as it is in our own age when people's hearts fail them for fear. Where is our world going? Are we running headlong into disaster? Or are we, like the French Resistance in the Second World War, actually on the side which, against all appearances, will win in the long run? The victory of Jesus in the midst of time points with certainty to his ultimate triumph at the end of time. And to that triumph Matthew looks with quiet but unshakeable assurance.

7. *The universality of the good news*

The gospel of the kingdom is meant for Jews and Gentiles alike. Matthew is a very Jewish Gospel, from 1:1 onwards. But although Jesus restricted himself almost entirely to ministry among Jews during his lifetime, there is nevertheless a constant outward thrust to this book. Judaism at its best did not sit comfortably, congratulating itself on its own election. It was meant to be a light to lighten the Gentiles. That was the call of the Servant of the Lord. And they looked for the day when the Gentiles would flow to Mount Zion. Jesus sets out to fulfil the call of the Servant, which nobody in Israel had ever previously undertaken. His mission was to the Jews first, but also to the Gentiles. And there is a surprising amount about the Gentile mission in this Gospel, which is at the same time so Jewish.

Gentile women such as Rahab are among Jesus' forebears (1:5). Gentile astronomers recognize and worship him when Israel's leaders do not (2:1–12). Jesus himself comes to his ministry from Galilee of the Gentiles (4:15). A Gentile centurion is commended for his faith above those in Israel (8:10), and we are told that many (i.e. Gentiles) will come from east and west and will sit down with the patriarchs while the sons of the kingdom will be ejected (8:11–12).

In fulfilment of Isaiah's prophecy Jesus will proclaim good news to the Gentiles and in his name the Gentiles will put their hope (12:17–21). A Caananite woman is commended for her faith in the Son of David, in striking contrast to the Jewish leaders (15:1–28). The capstone of the corner, rejected by the Jewish builders, will be the foundation of the Gentile mission (21:42–43), and in the parable of the vineyard in the same chapter it is said that 'he will rent the vineyard to other tenants, who will give him his share of the crop at harvest time . . . the kingdom of God will be taken away from you and given to a people who will produce its fruit' (21:41, 43).

Finally, there is the Great Commission to go and preach the good news to all the nations (28:18–20). It is not that Matthew has either a Jewish or a Gentile bias. He is well aware that the church must embrace social and political irreconcilables if it is to demonstrate to an unbelieving world that Jesus reconciles all people to God and to each other.

Matthew in recent study

Matthew's Gospel has, in recent years, replaced Luke-Acts as a major storm centre of New Testament studies. It is simply not possible to refer to more than a tiny fraction of the books and monographs that have emerged. So I shall be very selective.[28]

The person who wants a warm, devotional commentary designed for daily use can hardly do better than William Barclay's commentary. The best compact and very balanced commentary that faces up to the critical issues is that of R. T. France. Larger but still manageable commentaries have come from the hand of Craig L. Blomberg and Craig S. Keener; I did not find Keener as shrewd or helpful as Blomberg, though it has an impressively complete bibliography. Larger still are D. A. Carson's commentary in *The Expositor's Bible*, and R. H. Gundry's commentary, a solid if unexciting guide. And finally there is the massive New International Critical Commentary by W. D. Davies and Dale C. Allison, which I have not used. I have found the Word Commentary by Donald Hagner to be particularly wise, thorough and illuminating.

If those are only a few of the recent commentaries on Matthew's Gospel, other books which bear on the Gospel are legion. I can mention only a few here. R. T. France, *Matthew: Evangelist and Teacher*, is invaluable. It evaluates a great number of views on the Gospel, and then picks out major aspects of the Gospel – the literary character, the fulfilment theme, the place of Israel, Matthew's Gospel and the church and Matthew's portrait of Jesus. It is balanced,

---

[28] For details of all works cited here, see above, pp. 15–18.

comprehensive and full of insight. J. D. Kingsbury's *Matthew as Story* is the pioneer of the literary-critical approach to the Gospel, taking it as a story to be read in its own right and not as the product of editors working with small units of tradition. Robert Banks has done an exhaustive examination of *Jesus and the Law in the Synoptic Tradition*. Two important authors have given us fresh and much more positive light on Jesus and the Judaism of his day: Jacob Neusner's *Judaism in the Beginning of Christianity* is a short, irenic book, but E. P. Sanders is much more aggressive towards the traditional understanding of Judaism in his important books *Paul and Palestinian Judaism*; *Jesus and Judaism*; *Judaism: Practice and Belief* and *The Historical Figure of Jesus*. Michael Crosby's *House of Disciples* is an unusual and exhaustive 'reader-response' style of book examining issues of economics and justice in Matthew's church – and ours. He sees Jesus as putting into practice the kingdom ethic of reordering relationships and resources to meet the needs of people with justice.

N. T. Wright's big book, *Jesus and the Victory of God*, is very relevant, though it does not specialize in this Gospel. After a detailed assessment of major scholarly works on the historical Jesus he gives his own fascinating interpretation of how Jesus saw his mission (to remake Israel around himself), how he announced God's judgment on the Israel of his day, especially the temple and hierarchy, and how he saw the ministry of himself and his disciples as the fulfilment of Israel's destiny. Coming up to Jerusalem, he saw that he himself would die the death he had predicated of Israel. In obedience to that calling, he came to realize that he was going to do what, in Jewish thought, only God could do. This has the advantage of keeping all the teaching and actions of Jesus in an undeniably first-century framework.

I have found Graham Stanton's *A Gospel for a New People* one of the most seminal books on the subject in recent years. He too surveys much of the contemporary literature on Matthew, and suggests a variety of ways in which the Gospel can be read. Has the old form and redaction criticism anything to teach us still? Should Matthew, as J. D. Kingsbury believes, be read simply as a story without much attention being paid to sources and theological tendencies of the evangelist? Is it, after all, a biography somewhat like Greco-Roman 'Lives'? He is inclined to follow Richard Burridge (*What are the Gospels?*), in believing that it owes more to ancient 'Lives' than had previously been recognized. But he believes there is mileage in all three approaches. Seven chapters are then devoted to 'The parting of the ways' between church and synagogue. Stanton sees Matthew as a learned Jew who wrote for converted Jews who had accepted some Gentiles into their communities. These communities had recently experienced a painful parting from the local synagogue, hence both the anti-Jewish polemic and what he calls the 'legitimating answers' for the new people of God. In the final part of his book Stanton gives careful attention to the Sermon on the Mount, and to Matthew's use of the Old Testament. Above all, Matthew provided the 'new people' with a story that was new and satisfying, even though it had roots deep in Scripture. So here is a Gospel written about AD 80 as the church and synagogue part ways. I have believed for a long time that such was the case, but here is a major book making precisely this point, as well as offering other penetrating insights.

Can we draw together some agreed conclusions from this welter of academic study? Not many! But the following would command wide acceptance.

1. Matthew's Gospel probably dates to the 70s or 80s, after the fall of Jerusalem and perhaps after the Jewish Test Benedictions, though Gundry and more tentatively France go for a date in the 60s. If Dr Carsten Thiede[29] is right in believing that we have in the Oxford Magdalen papyrus part of a manuscript which should be dated in the mid- to late first century, then the case for an early date becomes unanswerable.

2. Much less confidence is placed these days in the hypothesis of Matthew's dependence on Mark and Q. Some do not believe in Q (a sayings source common to Matthew and Luke but largely absent from Mark). Some argue that Luke borrowed directly from Matthew. And some revert to the old view that Matthew was the first Gospel to be written! There are no agreed solutions. Scholars are inclined to opt for a rich collection of overlapping sources from which each of the evangelists quarried, sometimes using the same material and coming up with almost identical language. There is no certainty these days about the formation of the Gospel tradition and the priority of one Gospel over another. It would, however, be fair to say that most scholars still hold to the dependence of Matthew on Mark, and consequently reject Augustine's claim that Matthew was written first.

3. Many scholars see the Gospel as a vindication of Jesus and his message in a day when the church and the synagogue were moving in different directions in the last quarter of the first century.

4. Most scholars give some weight to the view (put forward originally by B. W. Bacon) that we should see in the five great discourses of the Gospel an allusion to the five books of Moses, and to Jesus as the new Moses. The organized teaching nature of the book has convinced most people of a catechetical purpose, whether

[29] C. P. Thiede, *The Jesus Papyrus* (Phoenix, 1966).

it was, as Paul Minear put it in the sub-title of his valuable commentary, 'the teacher's Gospel' or not.

5. Most scholars now recognize that the Jewish particularity and the Gentile universalism in this Gospel do not contradict each other; the gospel is 'first for the Jew, then for the Gentile'.[30]

6. Most scholars are persuaded that Matthew had a strong sense of promise and fulfilment, not only in the formula quotations but in the way he used the Old Testament in quotation, in allusion, in typology and in counterpoint with the teaching of Jesus.

7. Matthew's portrait of Jesus, as Son of God, Messiah, Son of David, Son of Man and supremely as God returning to Jerusalem as judge and redeemer, would win wide agreement.

8. Matthew is not an anti-Semitic Gospel, but it is directed against all forms of formalism and self-assertion before God, whether found in Jewish, Christian or other communities.

9. There is an increasing unwillingness among scholars to restrict Matthew to having one purpose only in his Gospel. He seems to have had several.

But now it is high time to allow Matthew to speak for himself.

[30] Rom. 1:16.

Part 1

In Galilee
(Matthew 1 – 13)

A. BEGINNINGS (1 – 7)

1:1–25
1. Jesus' pedigree and birth

The genealogy of Jesus (1:1–17)

What an amazing way to start a Gospel – with a great long list of names! But, to Jews, that was not surprising at all, as we shall see. It sets Jesus of Nazareth in the context of what God had been doing for his people from the earliest days. It ushers in the theme of fulfilment, which is so prominent in this Gospel. The climax of God's work for humankind throughout the centuries is – Jesus.

There is ample precedent for such genealogies in the Old Testament.[1] They were valuable for showing the purity of lineage that was so important to a Jew. Ezra 2:62 speaks of some of the returning exiles who 'searched for their family records, but they could not find them and so were excluded from the priesthood as unclean'. The great rabbi Hillel was gratified that he could trace his genealogy back to King David, and the Jewish historian Josephus, writing towards the end of the first century AD, begins his autobiography by relating his own pedigree. These documents were kept in the public records by the Sanhedrin. As a matter of fact, Herod the Great was so embarrassed that, as half Jew, half Edomite, his name was not in the official genealogies, that he ordered their destruction, so that nobody could claim a purer pedigree than his own! Far from seeing this as a bit of dull antiquarianism, therefore, the first readers of the Gospel would be fascinated that Jesus could trace his genealogy back to Abraham.

Matthew included Jesus' genealogy partly for the reasons of validation we have just considered, but mainly because he wanted to draw attention to the links Jesus had both with David and with Abraham. Jesus is the fulfilment of all history, and in particular of God's promise to Abraham that in his seed all the families of the earth would be blessed,[2] and of his promise to David that his throne and kingdom would be established for ever before the Lord.[3] And that, incidentally, is one of the texts found at Qumran in a list of

[1] E.g. Gen. 5 and 10.   [2] Gen. 12:1–3.   [3] 2 Sam. 7:16.

prophecies about the coming Messiah. So it was exceedingly significant.

The genealogy is carefully arranged in three groups of fourteen names each. So it is not intended to be comprehensive, but rather highly selective. It is designed, in fact, to make three names stand out: those of *Abraham* (2), *David* (6) and *Jesus* (16). The high point in the fulfilment of God's promise to Abraham in the Old Testament is undoubtedly King David. The climax of the genealogy is great David's greater Son. The whole thing is arranged with consummate artistry and care so that it could be easily memorized in an age when few could read and fewer still possessed books. The names are arranged as an acrostic on the name 'David' to make them easy to remember. In Hebrew, as we have seen, the numerical value of the name 'David' is fourteen, which is, accordingly, the number of generations Matthew has selected to mention. In Greek the verb *gennaō* (be *the father of*) does not necessarily indicate literal paternity: it can, and often does, mean 'be the ancestor of . . .' The Babylonian captivity was clearly important in this scheme of things (11–12, 17). Just as David represented the high-water mark of Israel's hopes and development and pointed forward to his descendant, Jesus, so the Babylonian captivity represented the nadir of Israel's fortunes, the frustration of her hopes, and the end of the royal line; and it too points forward to Jesus the Messiah and his people in whom those fortunes will be restored and those promises fulfilled.

A number of women figure in the genealogy. That might not seem strange in today's climate, but it was startling in a Jewish genealogy. In both Greek and Jewish culture a woman had no legal rights. She could not inherit property or give testimony in a court of law. She was completely under her husband's power. She was seen less as a person than as a thing. The Jewish man thanked God each day that he had not been created a slave, a Gentile or a woman. And yet here are four women in Jesus' genealogy.

And what women! *Tamar* (3) was an adulteress.[4] *Rahab* (5) was a prostitute from pagan Jericho.[5] *Uriah's wife*, Bathsheba (6), was the woman David had seduced and whose first child had died, but through whose subsequent son Solomon the royal line was traced.[6] *Ruth* (5) was not even a Jewess at all, but a Moabitess,[7] and Moabites and their descendants were not allowed near the assembly of the Lord.[8] These are the women introduced into the genealogy to prepare us for the climax of them all – *Mary* (16)! Matthew could not have found a more amazing selection of women wherever he had looked within the pages of his Bible. Why did he choose them?

It is clear from Mark 6:3; Galatians 4:4 and Revelation 12:1–5 that

---

[4] Gen. 38.   [5] Josh. 2:1–7.   [6] 2 Sam. 11 – 12.   [7] Ruth 1:4.   [8] Deut. 23:3.

people were well aware there was something strange about the birth of Jesus. It was different. The Jews put about the rumour that he was the illegitimate child of a Roman soldier and Mary. Nobody thought he was simply the child of Joseph and Mary.[9] So Matthew may well be alluding to such rumours when he points out that in Jesus' ancestry there are notorious women. Sinners they may be, but God works to rescue sinners and to use them in his service. Here at the outset of the Gospel, Matthew goes out of his way to show that the barriers between men and women are broken down: women share in the official genealogy of the Messiah alongside men. The barriers between Gentiles and Jews are broken down too: Ruth plays her part in the coming of one who was to be not only Messiah of Israel but Saviour of the whole world. And the juxtaposition of sinful women like Bathsheba and Tamar with Mary, the gentle mother of Jesus, shows that the barriers between good people and bad people have also come crashing down. As Paul put it, 'There is no difference, for all have sinned and fall short of the glory of God, and are justified freely by his grace' (Rom. 3:22–24). At the very beginning of the Gospel the all-embracing love of God is emphasized. Nothing can stand in its path. There is nobody who does not need it. Maybe the genealogy is not so dry after all!

The birth of Jesus (1:18–25)

Having prepared us through the genealogy for the appearance of the most important birth in all history, Matthew tells us in no uncertain terms who this baby is. He does so by unmistakable allusions to two Old Testament passages. The child is *Immanuel* and he is *Jesus*.

Immanuel (23) means 'God is with us'. It is not a prayer. It is a statement. It takes us back to Isaiah 7:14: 'The virgin will be with child and will give birth to a son and will call him Immanuel.' That child of prophecy, that child who was to be a 'sign', has come at last. And he is no less than God with us. The Hebrews had such an exalted conception of God that they did not even make any image of him – something which so amazed their Roman conquerors that they dubbed them 'atheists', people without gods. Against this background Matthew claims, not that God has given us a representation of himself, but that he has come in person to share our situation. What a claim, right at the outset of the Gospel! It is so ultimate, so exclusive. It does not fit with the pluralist idea that each of us is getting through to God in his or her own way. No, says Matthew. God has got through to us in *his* way. And Jesus is no mere teacher,

---

[9] The Greek of verse 16 is explicit: *ex hēs egennēthē* ('of whom [feminine] was born') emphasizes Jesus' descent from Mary, not from Joseph.

no guru, no Muhammad or Gandhi. He is 'God with us'. That is the essential claim on which Christianity is built. It is a claim that cannot be abandoned without abandoning the faith in its entirety.

The other great name accorded to the child of promise here is *Jesus* (21). That word, too, has a meaning: 'Yahweh saves.' 'God to the rescue', if you like. To be sure, it was a common name. It goes back to the frequent rescue of his people by God in the Old Testament days, perhaps most notably through a man who bore the same name, Joshua (its Hebrew form). But it is clearly very significant for Matthew. As with Immanuel, he explains what it means: *Jesus, because he will save his people from their sins.* This, too, was an Old Testament allusion. It comes from Psalm 130:8, where we are told that 'God will redeem Israel from all their sins.' Isn't that interesting? *God* promises that he will provide a rescue from sin; and, centuries later, *Jesus* comes to do it. This is one of many occasions where what is predicated of God in the Old Testament is applied quite naturally and unambiguously to Jesus in the New. Another classic example is Philippians 2:10–11, which asserts that Jesus has the right to that 'lordship' which God reserved for himself in Isaiah 45:23. This kind of usage needs to be borne in mind when some theologians assert that Jesus is never called 'God' in the New Testament writings.

So here, at the annunciation of Jesus' birth, we are brought face to face with the central theme of the Gospel. God, who has been at work on his people since the times of Abraham, has come among them in person. And he has come for the specific purpose of rescuing them from the mess they have got themselves into. Christianity is not good advice about morals. It is good news about God and what he has done for us.

And this good news is revealed in a variety of ways. First, God speaks through history: that is one of the points being made by the genealogy. Secondly, God speaks through dreams: five times in the first two chapters of Matthew God makes himself known in this way – and sometimes he still does. Thirdly, God speaks through angels (1:20; 2:13, 19), his spiritual messengers who appear in dreams or visions. Fourthly, God speaks through Scripture. *All this took place to fulfil what the Lord had said through the prophet*, says Matthew (22). Twelve times he uses this particular formula to speak of the Old Testament being fulfilled in the events of the New – an astonishingly high view of the accuracy and inspiration of the Old Testament, and a very clear perception of the unity of revelation down the centuries. But there is a fifth way in which God reveals himself, and that is through Immanuel, God with us. So the heavens are not brazen, and we do not live in a silent universe. God has spoken!

Indeed, we could go further. This passage is strongly, if

unself-consciously, trinitarian. God the Father reveals himself through his Son, Jesus Immanuel. But all this is brought about through the agency of the Holy Spirit. Mary was *found to be with child through the Holy Spirit* (18). What is conceived in her is from the Holy Spirit. Insistently Matthew underlines his point. In Judaism the Holy Spirit was supremely the one who revealed God's will to the prophets: he was equally at work in the creation of the world.[10] What is more, re-creation was seen to be the Spirit's work, as the marvellous story of the valley of the dry bones[11] makes so clear. And Isaiah had predicted long ago that when the coming great deliverer was born the Spirit of the Lord would 'rest' or 'remain' upon him.[12] So now the Spirit finds a perfect vehicle through whom to reveal God and re-create broken humanity. All three persons of the Trinity are brought before our gaze, and this is not a dogmatic construction but a very natural piece of writing. The doctrine of the Trinity is not something superimposed on Scripture, as Jehovah's Witnesses maintain; it emerges out of the natural allusions in the text itself.

Who is Jesus and why did he come? That is the question addressed so clearly in this paragraph. He is no less than God with us, and he came to rescue us. But that claim is so mind-boggling that inevitably problems arise. Four particular questions demand our attention.

First, is there not total confusion about the marriage situation of Joseph and Mary? There seems to be, at first sight. Joseph is said to be *pledged to be married* to Mary (18), then is said to be minded to *divorce* her (19), and then *took Mary home as his wife* (24). To our way of thinking this is most confusing, if not contradictory. But in Jewish marriage custom it is quite natural. Betrothal, the pledge to marry, was a solemn contract between the parties, and lasted for a year before the couple were married in the full sense. Thus it was far more binding than our engagement. Indeed, it could be terminated only by divorce. Way back in Deuteronomy 22:24 a betrothed girl is called a 'wife', though the preceding verse speaks of her as being 'pledged to be married'. And Matthew uses the terms *husband* and *wife* (19, 24) in this proleptic sense before they are fully married. Complete marriage, and the sexual union that goes with it, came at the end of the year of betrothal (25).

Secondly, what is the point of the genealogy if Joseph is not the father? Why does Matthew make such a point of the pedigree of Jesus if, as he himself maintains, he is not Joseph's son at all? Matthew is, as we have seen, interested not in strict biological descent but in legal standing. Legally Jesus was the son of Joseph, and inherited his pedigree. Biologically, Matthew maintains, he was not. He was born of the virgin Mary through the direct intervention

[10] Gen. 1:2; Ps. 104:30.   [11] Ezek. 37.   [12] Is. 11:2.

of the Holy Spirit. This may help us to understand the divergence in the genealogies of Jesus according to Matthew and Luke after they reach the Babylonian captivity. The line of kings had ended, and there were many collateral lines which could trace ancestry back to David. The rabbi Hillel, a contemporary of Jesus, could trace his ancestry back to David through one of these lines. It seems probable that Matthew is giving us Joseph's story and lineage, and that Luke is giving us Mary's. Matthew certainly gives us Joseph's story (angelic annunciation, perplexity and obedience), and this fits in well with his genealogy, which is clearly Joseph's. Luke, by contrast, tells us Mary's story (angelic annunciation, perplexity and obedience), which suggests that he may well be giving us her lineage as well. Thus Jesus would be legally 'the son of David' through Joseph, and biologically the descendant of David through Mary.

Is there any evidence for this? Yes, there is some. For one thing, Jesus' physical descent from David is given some prominence in the New Testament.[13] For another, Luke himself is clear that Jesus is the son of David as well as 'the Son of the Most High' (Luke 1:32). And the early patristic witness to his Davidic sonship is strong. Ignatius, writing shortly after AD 100, can say, 'For our God, Jesus the Christ, was conceived in the womb by Mary through God's good purposes, of the seed of David but also by the Holy Ghost',[14] and, 'He is truly of the race of David according to the flesh, but Son of God by the divine will and power.'[15] So we may be right in understanding Luke 3:23 as follows: 'Jesus ... was the son – it was thought, of Joseph – of Heli ...' (my translation). If we make this phrase about Joseph a parenthesis, as the Greek allows us to do, Jesus would be 'son', in the broad sense so common in the genealogies, of Heli: actually grandson, for there is evidence in the Jewish writings that Mary's father was Heli.[16] Because she was a woman, her name would not naturally be mentioned in a genealogy, which would account for the rather odd Greek construction. In a word, there is no reason why Mary should not have had Davidic blood in her veins as well as Joseph. If so, there is every point in having the genealogy as well as the assertion of a virgin birth.

Thirdly, can we believe in the virgin birth? Even if Matthew and Luke assert it, is this something we can credit today? David Jenkins, the controversial former Bishop of Durham, declared on television, 'I very much doubt if God would arrange a virgin birth.' But Christianity is concerned with what actually happened, and we are not at liberty to rewrite history in order to fit in with what we imagine to be likely.

---

[13] Mark 10:48; Acts 2:25–35; Rom. 1:3.   [14] *To the Ephesians* 18.
[15] *To the Smyrneans* 1:1.   [16] See *Chagig.* 77.4 in the Jerusalem Talmud.

Those who disbelieve the virgin birth make a number of points. First, there are two accounts of the genealogy of Jesus: may not both be rival literary constructions? There are pagan parallels to the story. The virgin birth is never part of the early preaching, and is confined in the New Testament to Matthew and Luke. What is more, it is intrinsically improbable, as well as being unnecessary to Christian belief in the deity of Christ.

Let us look at those points in turn. There are indeed two genealogies, and they do not precisely tally. Indeed, they arose in different parts of the church, and no convincing explanations have been given as to how they originated if they were legendary constructions. They are certainly not variants of the same tradition.

There are in fact no pagan parallels to the birth narrative. There are plenty of stories of Zeus impregnating mortal women for whom he lusted; but the purity, the restraint and the wonder of this story are unparalleled in pagan literature. Moreover, it is very Semitic in character, which is odd if it is supposed to be a Hellenistic creation. But it is even more odd to find such an account in the heart of Judaism, which was utterly repelled by any idea of God's being born among us. No, there are no parallels to this unique story. Not surprising, really: virgin births are uncommon!

To be sure, the virgin birth is not part of the early preaching of salvation such as we meet in Acts. Nor is it a normal part of evangelistic preaching today. But that does not mean it did not happen. There are, in fact, allusions to it in other parts of the New Testament.[17] Moreover, the virgin birth was regarded as fundamental by the earliest post-apostolic writers, particularly Ignatius,[18] while the Jewish and Roman opposition never suggested that Jesus was born to Joseph and Mary, but assumed that she had run off with a paramour.

As to its intrinsic improbability, that is true. But if you believe in the miracle of the incarnation and the resurrection, not to mention the other miracles, then there is no *a priori* reason why God should not select this different method for his Son to enter the world. Why should not the Spirit which brooded over creation not also brood creatively over the womb of Mary? The real objection to the virgin birth (or virginal conception, as it should properly be termed) does not spring from shortage of evidence at all: it springs from the assumption that God cannot or does not do miracles. And nobody who believes that God has entered our world in Jesus Christ should make that bland assumption.

However, it is only proper to say that there is nothing *necessary*

[17] Such as Mark 6:3; Gal. 4:4; Rev. 12:1–4; and the variant reading in John 1:13 ('who *was* born', instead of 'who *were* . . .', shows that the virgin birth was believed in very early, even though that reading is not likely to be original).
[18] See *To the Ephesians* 18 – 19; *To the Smyrneans* 1 – 2, etc.

about the virgin birth. The deity of Christ is not inextricably tied to it. God might well have entered his world in the normal manner, or chosen some unprecedented way of becoming one of us. He need not have come through a virginal conception. The documents, however, assert that he did. And if he did so enter our world, it is highly appropriate that one who is both God and human should be born through the fusion of the Holy Spirit and a human womb.[19]

Finally, did Matthew misread Isaiah 7:14? He seems to lay a lot of stress on the prophecy, *The virgin will be with child and will give birth to a son* (23), but does he realize that the Hebrew word translated 'virgin' (*'almâ*) can mean a young woman of marriageable age, and not necessarily a virgin? Matthew is often accused of misreading his Hebrew, but I fancy he knew the language rather better than his detractors. It is true that *'almâ* normally means 'virgin', but certainly can mean 'young woman'. Does Matthew make too much of it?

In point of fact, *'almâ* is used only seven times in the Old Testament, of girls or young women. In two cases[20] they are unmarried. Its use in connection with childbirth was so surprising to the writers of the Septuagint, the Greek translation of the Old Testament written some two hundred years before Christ, that they translated it by *parthenos*, a word which much more decisively means 'virgin'. They had sound instincts. For the prophecy received its immediate fulfilment in Hezekiah's own day and the destruction of the kings he feared,[21] but, as was characteristic in Hebrew prophecy, it had a deeper meaning.[22] The child would be a 'sign' – a word that suggests something more than the mere birth of a baby in the normal way. And by the time we reach Isaiah 9:6, this child is seen as 'Mighty God'. Matthew quite properly sees in this sign a further application, pointing forward to the fulfilment of 'Immanuel', God with us, in the person of Jesus.

It would be a pity if all these questions which arise in modern minds were to rob us of the main significance of this marvellous chapter. The Father loves us enough to send his Son, the one who shares both God's nature and ours. He comes to rescue his people from their sins, enemies far more deadly than Rome. If God loves like that, it is good news, *gospel*, indeed.

---

[19] There has been extensive discussion of the virgin birth of Jesus. See in particular J. Gresham Machen, *The Virgin Birth of Christ* (James Clarke, 1930), and R. E. Brown, *The Birth of the Messiah* (Doubleday, 1977), for more detailed discussion than is possible here.

[20] Gen. 24:43; Exod. 2:8.   [21] Is. 7:14–17.

[22] In Jewish exegesis of Scripture there were no fewer than five levels of meaning to be discerned!

2:1–23
2. Jesus' childhood

The wise men (2:1–12)

The birth of Jesus is passed over by Matthew with great economy. *Jesus was born in Bethlehem in Judea, during the time of King Herod* (1). No stable, no shepherds; just Bethlehem in Herod's day. Bethlehem had a long history in Israel. It was here that Jacob buried his beloved Rachel, when she died giving birth to Benjamin.[1] It was here that Benjamin's descendant, David, was born.[2] For ever afterwards it would be known as 'the city of David'. What is more appropriate than for David's great descendant to be born here, as Micah prophesied (6)?

But another king was in charge of Bethlehem and indeed all of Galilee and Judea at that time. Half Jew and half Idumean, Herod had been appointed king by the Roman Senate in 40 BC and gained control of the country by 37 BC. He died in 4 BC, and Jesus was clearly born before that date: the beginning of our era was miscalculated by a monk centuries later.[3]

Such was the climactic event of all history: Jesus, Immanuel, was born in the little town of Bethlehem, the ancient seat of the Davidic line. His coming always divides people, as we shall see time and again in this Gospel. Here, at the very start of his life, we see two camps forming: one full of praise and welcome; the other full of hatred and opposition. Herod and the Magi stand out in strong contrast, a contrast that will deepen as the story of Jesus' life unfolds towards the cross.

---

[1] Gen. 35:16–20. [2] 1 Sam. 16.
[3] Dionysius the Small, in the sixth century AD, who did not have accurate information about the death of Herod. But the switch from a Roman to a Christian calendar was based on his faulty calculations.

The Gentile theme

As we have seen (pp. 49–50), the theme of the Gentiles becomes a dominant motif in Matthew, and it begins here with the coming of the wise men.

A tremendous amount of legend has concentrated round these Magi: there is no reason to suppose that there were three of them, that they were kings, or that we know their names.[4] For centuries the Magi had been a tribe of priests in Persia, but the name had also come to be applied to magicians and astrologers, such as Simon Magus and Elymas.[5] Impressed by what they saw in the skies at night, some of these men journeyed west to Judea to find out what it meant. Is it not perfectly astonishing that men with so little to go on should venture so far, endure such hardships in travel, and face such uncertainties of finding the one the star betokened? What is more, they wanted to give him costly gifts and the worship of their hearts. They even recognized him as *king of the Jews* (2), a title that contrasts strikingly with Herod's position, and which does not recur in Matthew's Gospel until Jesus' crucifixion. Herod held jealously to his kingship by might of arms and by bitter repressive measures. Jesus showed his kingship by self-sacrifice for others. At Calvary he demonstrated that the weakness of God that is more powerful than mere mortals, and the Magi seemed to have had some inkling of it. I find their faith, their insight, their wholehearted search and adoring worship, utterly amazing. It is one of the many surprises in the Gospel. But then God is the God of surprises. Those who think they can predict his actions need to think again. How sad that in many churches, this element of surprise is almost entirely absent, and boring predictability governs all that happens!

Matthew, of course, has an eye for his own day as he records this story. By the time he wrote, Gentiles were flooding into the church, whereas most of his Jewish compatriots did not want to know. It was mysterious, paradoxical. But had not Isaiah[6] foretold something very similar? 'Arise, shine for your light has come, and the glory of the LORD rises upon you. See, darkness covers the earth, and thick darkness is over the peoples.' Well, that was happening all around Matthew among the Jews. 'But the LORD rises upon you, and his glory appears over you.' That, too, had happened to thousands: Matthew could give personal testimony to the fact. 'Nations will come to your light, and kings to the brightness of your dawn,' continues the prophet. That movement began with the visit of the Magi. It has continued like a swelling river to this day.

[4] Traditionally Gaspar, Melchior and Balthasar, first mentioned in the sixth century.
[5] Acts 8:9; 13:6.　　[6] Is. 60:1–3.

The fulfilment theme

The note of fulfilment is very prominent in this story. The king who was to sit on David's throne for ever would be born in Bethlehem. The shepherd who would care for Israel for ever would be born in Bethlehem. That is what Micah had predicted seven centuries beforehand[7] – an example of the way in which the New Testament fulfils the Old even to the smallest detail. It shows, too, that God's overarching plan of salvation spans the millennia. This is already the third example of promise and fulfilment that Matthew has brought before his readers. There will be many others. It is an essential quality in God as the Bible depicts him: he keeps his promises.

The contrast theme

The note of contrast is strongly emphasized in this short account. There is the contrast between Herod's kingship and that of Jesus: one inaugurated by Rome, an alien power, and based on aggression and cruelty; the other originating from love, shown in vulnerability and entering into its kingdom though the cross. Herod was thirty-three at his inauguration, and Jesus the same age when he died. What a contrast!

Matthew underlines particularly the contrasting responses to Jesus. We have seen how the Magi pursued what they knew to the utmost of their powers, and made an act of obeisance and dedication that takes our breath away. Those wise men sought him wholeheartedly: wise men and women still do. But over against them stood Herod and the Jewish clergy. Herod's response was hatred and fear: hatred of anything and anyone that threatened his self-centredness, and fear of a possible rival, however improbable. The lust for power blunted the better qualities in Herod's character. Power still has this corrupting tendency today. Hitler's Germany, Stalin's Russia, Saddam's Iraq and Milosevic's Serbia show the lengths to which self-seeking can go against what is known to be right.

Then there were the Jewish chief priests and scribes. Their attitude is almost as amazing as that of the Magi. They knew their Scriptures and had no problem in answering Herod when he wanted to know where the child would be born. Back came the answer, pointing Herod to Micah 5:2. He would be born in Bethlehem, of course. But did they go to greet him? Did they lift a sandal? Not at all. They knew it all, but they did nothing. That is a characteristic danger for clergy and scholars in any age. Their apathy hardened into outright opposition to Jesus as his ministry developed, and ended with

---

[7] Mic. 5:2.

frenzied lust for his blood – an awesome warning that knowledge is no substitute for obedience.

The polemical theme

There were doubtless people in Matthew's day who asserted that Jesus of Nazareth was born in Nazareth – and what people thought of Nazareth is made very plain in John 1:46. So Matthew puts the record straight. Jesus was not a Nazareth lad but born in Bethlehem, just as the prophet had foretold. Interestingly enough, Matthew does not know that Joseph was a native of Nazareth, although Luke knows it.[8] On returning from Egypt, Joseph 'went and lived in a town called Nazareth' (23). Despite the common subject matter covered by Luke and Matthew in the stories of Jesus' birth, they are totally independent of each other. That independence lends an added strength to their testimony.

The astronomical theme

In the ancient world most people believed in astrology. It is not surprising. The steady courses of the heavenly bodies represented the settled order of the universe. When some new astronomical happening took place, it was reasonable to suppose that God was breaking into his ordered world and making known some news.

A particular accident of history caused stars to be associated with kings and leaders. When Julius Caesar died in 44 BC, one of the most astonishing flukes in all history took place. A *nova* (thought to be a new star) appeared in the sky above his funeral pyre. Everyone assumed, of course, that he had gone to join the pantheon of the gods. Thereafter, stars for great men were emphatically in fashion!

Interestingly enough, there was a strong rumour around in the first century AD that world dominion would come out of Judea. Tacitus tells us that in the 60s of the first century 'there was a firm persuasion that at this very time the East was to grow powerful and rulers coming from Judea were to acquire universal empire'.[9] The same conviction is written up by the Jewish historian Josephus[10] and the Roman historian Suetonius.[11] Vespasian was the Roman general making war in Judea in the late 60s before becoming emperor, so he had good reason to be worried by rumours of this sort, before taking them over and using them in his own propaganda. There would therefore be nothing surprising if the Magi inferred impending political changes from the star they saw. That was a perfectly natural

---

[8] Luke 2:39.   [9] *Histories* 5.13.   [10] *Jewish War* 6.5.
[11] *Life of Vespasian* 4.5.

expectation in the pagan world. Moreover, a star formed part of Jewish messianic expectation. The famous prophecy of Balaam, 'I see him, but not now; I behold him, but not near. A star will come out of Jacob; a sceptre will rise out of Israel',[12] was very dear to Jewish hearts, and this again was one of the messianic proof texts found at Qumran. People mused on such verses, and drew much encouragement from them. So both Jewish and Gentile worlds were predisposed towards seeing in the stars an indication of what they might expect.

But what did the Magi see? There have been many suggestions. Some favour Halley's Comet, which was seen and recorded in 11 BC. But the most probable suggestion is that it was not one new star so much as the conjunction of Jupiter and Saturn in the area of the sky known as Pisces. This happened three times in the year 7 BC. It was seen on 29 May, 3 October and 4 December in that year. A cuneiform inscription from the observatory of Sippar in Babylonia gives us this fascinating information. The same conjunction took place in Kepler's day and highly impressed him. If this is in fact what arrested the attention of these star-gazing Magi, it is not difficult to see how they would have interpreted it. Pisces was reckoned by astronomers to mark the end of the sun's old course and the beginning of the new. Jupiter was the royal planet, and Saturn had long been the symbol of Israel. So this conjunction of planets, giving the impression of one very bright star, would have meant to the competent astronomer that a new age was beginning, in which the sovereignty of the world would shift to Judea. Jerusalem was the capital city of Judea, and it is natural that the Magi should have gone there first. They would have set out after the first conjunction of the planets, and the third would have occurred while they were in Bethlehem. It seemed to be almost overhead, and indicated to them that the end of their search was at hand.[13]

And so they came and found *the child with his mother Mary* (always in this order, 11, 13, 14, 20, 21) and gave him their offerings. How significant those were, in the light of the fulfilment theme which is so interwoven with this Gospel! Gold is the gift fit for a king – and the king in baby clothes was there. Frankincense was in constant use by the priests in the temple, and the ultimate priest, the one who was to make final reconciliation between God and humankind, lay before them. Myrrh was used to embalm the dead. The man born to be king was the man born to die. In those three gifts we see who he is, what he came to do, and what it cost him.

[12] Num. 24:17.
[13] For other suggestions about the star, see France (1985), Gundry, Blomberg, Keener and Hagner. New suggestions continue to emerge; the subject has a perennial fascination.

And, like the wise men, we bow in wonder before a God who could love us that much.

The escape to Egypt, and return (2:13–23)

Egypt had long been a refuge for Jews. The Jewish colony in Alexandria numbered more than a million at this time. So if Joseph sensed danger from Herod, as well he might (since Herod was distinctly inimical to anyone who might possibly displace him), then Egypt would be a natural place to go in order to be safe and to be among compatriots. Joseph also had a clear message from God that this was where he should go. So the family left for Egypt.

There are three points of particular interest in this narrative.

The link with Egypt

Many commentators do not believe the story of the escape to Egypt. They write it off as Old Testament symbolism. For instance, R. H. Gundry, in his commentary, interprets the chapter as a midrash (rabbinic-style comment) on Old Testament precedents at the time of the exodus and the Babylonian exile.[14] Thus the aggressive Pharaoh fails to destroy God's destined deliverer, Moses. Gundry believes we have to broaden our interpretation of 'happened' and 'fulfilled' when we read the formula quotations in this chapter, which he sees as embellishments of the tradition rather than fulfilments of the Old Testament. He sees Matthew as saved from fantasy because his embellishments rest on historical data, and foreshadow genuinely historical events such as the resurrection and the calamities to befall Judaism later on. But need we tread so radical a path? To be sure, there is plenty of symbolism in this chapter, plenty of emphasis on fulfilment of themes like the parallels between the childhood of Moses and that of Jesus, but that does not mean the account is unhistorical.[15]

The Talmud maintains that 'Yeshua was a magician and learned his skills in Egypt'. Though it comes from a hostile source, it is clear confirmation for the miracles of Jesus and for his stay in Egypt where the Jewish writers (wrongly) thought he was educated.

[14] Gundry expands this theory in his *The Use of the Old Testament in St Matthew's Gospel* (Brill, 1975).

[15] France (1985) helpfully notes that 2:13–23 consists of three brief narratives, each leading up to a 'formula quotation'. The focus is on the fulfilment of Scripture in relation to the childhood of Jesus. But he sees that alongside this there is a sub-plot, paralleling the childhood of Jesus and of Moses. Whereas the Moses typology does not figure large in the Gospel as a whole, it is clearly suggested in these infancy narratives.

Origen finds the same view in Celsus, an anti-Christian writer in the middle of the second century who held that Jesus was brought up as an illegitimate child in Egypt, that he discovered certain miraculous powers, and that on returning to his own country he used them to substantiate his claim to deity.[16] Yes, the escape to Egypt was historical, but it was also highly symbolic, and Matthew means us to understand this. It was a recapitulation, a fulfilment, of Israel's history. Israel became a nation after being called into Egypt, and the exodus from Egypt was the central point in the history of this nation that was becoming the people of God. Pharaoh tried to destroy the people in Egypt, but Moses brought them out of Egypt into the land of promise. Herod, a new Pharaoh, tried to kill the firstborn, Jesus, and in his rage and frustration he slaughtered other innocent firstborn in Bethlehem. He failed to kill the Saviour, just as Pharaoh had failed to kill Moses. Eventually, Moses brought the children of Israel out of the land of bondage and death, and Moses' successor was to bring the people out of a worse bondage and a worse death, the death of sin. Jesus is cast as the successor of Moses: he came to save his people from their sins. We shall see him in that role later on, for the five great blocks of his teaching in this Gospel take up and transcend the five great books of the Law revealed to Moses long ago. Here, Jesus is seen as the counterpart to Moses, not so much in revelation as in rescue. He is going to usher in the new exodus. That is why his time in Egypt is important in the symbolism of this Gospel.

The slaughter of the innocents

Sometimes people have wondered if Herod could have been so bestial as to destroy all the boys under the age of two in Bethlehem. Usually such people have been unaware of Roman history, for Herod could be a monster. To be sure, there is no independent record of this particular atrocity, but it is mild in comparison with some of Herod's other massacres. He slaughtered the last remnants of the Hasmonean dynasty of Jewish high-priestly kings who had ruled before him. He executed more than half the Sanhedrin. He killed 300 court officers out of hand. He executed his own Hasmonean wife, Mariamne, her mother Alexandra, and his sons Aristobulus, Alexander and Antipater. Finally, as he lay dying, he arranged for all the notable men of Jerusalem to be assembled in the hippodrome and killed as soon as his own death was announced. A man of ruthless cruelty and with a fanatical neurosis about any

[16] *Against Celsus* 1.38.

competition, it is quite in character that he should order the execution of the male children in Bethlehem. It was not a big place; there would probably have been only thirty or so of them, and their deaths would not have made a ripple on the history of the day.

Herod died in 4 BC, and his kingdom was split three ways. Herod Philip got Trachonitis in the north; Antipas got Galilee and the area beyond the Jordan known as Perea; and Archelaus took the lion's share, comprising Idumea, Judea and Samaria. He was loosely referred to as king (cf. 22, *reigning*), but this depended upon ratification by the Emperor Augustus. In due course, he went to Rome in AD 6 to get the title confirmed. Instead, he lost everything and was banished, and the Romans took up direct rule over his dominions. In many ways he carried on his father's policies during his short rule. It is not surprising that Joseph was chary of returning into his territory, but went instead to live in Nazareth, under the suzerainty of Antipas. The whole unsavoury story of Herod's activity in all this is an awesome reminder of how deeply opposition to Jesus can be rooted in the hearts of people who are not prepared to allow his gentle rule to control them. If we are determined to get our own way at all costs, we will go to any lengths to eliminate all trace of Jesus and his claims on our lives.

The quotations from Scripture

The use of Old Testament quotations in this narrative is very interesting and very characteristic of Matthew. He sees the authoritative revelation embodied in the Old Testament as being predictive of Jesus through prophecy, analogy, type and even verbal allusions. This would have been entirely understood by his Jewish readers. It was their own interpretative method.

In this short section we have no fewer than three 'fulfilment' citations from the Old Testament. The first, '*Out of Egypt I called my son*', comes from Hosea 11:1 and originally referred to God's calling the people of Israel out of Egypt under the leadership of Moses. Matthew sees in these words a deeper allusion, to the person and work of Jesus. The history of God's children is recapitulated in the history of God's Son. As Israel long ago was led down to Egypt, so was Jesus. As Israel came out, so did Jesus. He embodies and fulfils the history of the people of God in his own person.[17]

---

[17] Hosea's words are not a prediction, but an account of Israel's origin. And Matthew's quotation depends for its validity on Jesus' being seen as the true Israel. 'Israel's exodus from Egypt was taken already by the Old Testament prophets as a prefiguring of the ultimate Messianic salvation, and Matthew's quotation here thus reinforces his presentation of the childhood history of Jesus as the dawning of the Messianic age.' France (1985).

The second reference (18) comes in Jeremiah 31:15. Rachel's death in childbirth set her apart as the *mater dolorosa* (sorrowful mother) of the Old Testament. She was known among the rabbis as 'the mother of Israel for all time'. Yet her death in childbirth was the gateway to life for Benjamin. He, the child of her pain, was the ancestor of the Messiah. And again in Jeremiah's day Rachel's tomb near Bethlehem (*Ramah* [18] was Jeremiah's home) saw the lines of captives going past on their way to the Babylonian captivity. She entered, in a sense, into the pain and desolation of those departing exiles. And yet here again life came out of death, and the return from exile brought new life to Israel. Bereavement became the pathway to blessing. We are to see in God's disappointments the seeds of his ultimate purpose for our good.

The third reference, '*So was fulfilled what was said through the prophets: "He will be called a Nazarene"* ' (23), is the most remarkable of them all. Nowhere is it to be found in the Old Testament, nor is Nazareth even mentioned there.[18] We need to look a little deeper, if we are to hazard a guess at Matthew's purpose in including it. The fact that Matthew speaks vaguely of 'the prophets' in the plural may give us the key to this complex allusion. A man from Nazareth was despised in Jesus' day: it was an obscure town from which no good was thought to come, situated in 'Galilee of the Gentiles',[19] and there was plenty of indication among the prophets that the Messiah would be despised.[20] The word 'Nazarene' may also have sprung to Matthew's mind as a word-play on the Hebrew for 'Branch' (*nēṣer*) in Isaiah 11:1, a notable messianic text denoting a king from David's line. Another possibility is that Matthew might also have been thinking of Isaiah 49:6, part of one of the Servant Songs applied to Jesus in early Christian times. There the term 'those . . . have kept' could be interpreted, with a slight change of Hebrew pointing, as 'Nazarene', yielding the sense: 'It is too small a thing for you to be my servant to restore the tribes of Jacob and a Nazarene to restore Israel . . .' If this is so, then early in the Gospel we have the idea of Jesus, God's suffering Servant and child, preserved by him but rejected by the people. This is certainly a theme that will occupy us as the Gospel unfolds, but it is impossible to be sure which Old Testament allusions were uppermost in Matthew's mind. The very obscurity of the allusion shows that the infancy narratives are not fanciful, based on Old Testament prophecies. The history was primary, and the Old Testament, the acknowledged source of God's revelation, is ransacked by the evangelist in order to point it up.

[18] Matthew may know nothing of Joseph and Mary's original residence in Nazareth (Luke 2:4, 39), but he certainly does not contradict it. He states only what is relevant to his fulfilment quotation.

[19] Matt. 4:15; John 1:46.   [20] Ps. 22:6; Is. 53:3.

Looking back over this cycle of stories illustrating Jesus' childhood, a number of strands stand out.

First, Matthew makes it plain that God works through both surprise and continuity to bring about his purposes. The story of Jesus is utterly continuous with Abraham, with David and with the whole history of the chosen people. But it also bristles with surprises. Perhaps this is to encourage us to expect God to be working in our lives steadily and continuously, making sense of our past history; but also to be on the lookout for God's surprises in our lives, ready to grasp them and follow through their implications when they come.

Secondly, Matthew has a clear message for the readers of his day. By then the Gentile mission was in full flood, and the tensions with Judaism had reached snapping-point. The temptation to give up on the Jews would have been very great. But Matthew says, 'Don't give up on the Jewish people. God has not given them up. He has a special purpose for them. It stretches back to the dawn of time. It is from Jewish stock that Jesus was born. Do not forget it.'

Thirdly, Matthew has a word of encouragement about opposition. Opposition is inevitable, but it will never, in the providence of God, be allowed to quench God's mission. There was every possibility of quenching the Messiah: his mother Mary might have been stoned as an adulteress; he might have been killed by Herod; he might have been lost in Egypt. But no. God's hand was upon him. Opposition could not extinguish God's light. What an encouragement that would have been to Matthew's readers! The church, so frail, so exposed, would not be allowed to sink, however threatening the storms and waves that broke over it.

3:1 – 4:25
3. The beginning of Jesus' ministry

John the Baptist (3:1–12)

The scene is set for the beginning of Jesus' ministry.[1] First, we are introduced to his forerunner, John; then to his public inauguration ceremony, baptism; then to his temptation; and then to the first impact of his ministry, culminating in the Sermon on the Mount.

In all the Gospels the ministry of Jesus is prefaced by that of John. There is a very good reason, in addition to the obvious historical one: the central message of Jesus is repentance, and without repentance there is no way in which a person can respond to the good news and become a member of the kingdom of heaven. Repentance is the inescapable beginning.

We are brought up short by the stark immediacy of the opening words of the chapter. *In those days John the Baptist came, preaching in the Desert of Judea and saying, 'Repent, for the kingdom of heaven is near'* (1–2). He bursts upon the scene as the voice of prophecy. Prophets are a rare breed. They had been very rare in Israel for some 400 years. People did not know how to handle prophets. Nobody wanted them in their front room. And that is usually the way of the church. A prophetic voice is an embarrassment. It is rarely welcomed within the walls and plans of the Establishment. So John the Baptist operated in the desert of Judea, and became even tougher and more bizarre than he had been to start with.

A number of strands in this story are particularly illuminating.

The preacher

John is introduced in a fascinating way. No background information, no biography. Like Elijah of old,[2] he sweeps on to the stage

---

[1] The date (though of no interest to Matthew!) can be fixed with some confidence at AD 27, from Luke 3:1.
[2] 1 Kgs. 17:1.

with his call to repentance. Incidentally, this shows us that Matthew's Gospel is not written for those who know nothing of the events it contains. His readers know a bit about John, and that he fits into the story of Jesus at the outset. But we are bound to notice how he comes: *preaching* (1). 'Who are you, John?' we ask. *'A voice,'* he replies (3). Just that. He was actually a very great prophet, with a radical message of repentance to deliver. He lived a simple lifestyle which powerfully challenged the religious leaders of the day, who lived in considerable luxury. His message shook the state. His courage was phenomenal. And yet with striking humility he sees himself as nothing more or less than the voice through which God was addressing his nation. He takes no credit for his ministry. He is simply his Master's voice. What an example to preachers!

The quotation from Isaiah 40:3 to describe John is found in all the Synoptic Gospels and is highly significant. It forms part of God's comfort to his exiled people: her years of hard labour are over, her sins are forgiven. And it is against this backcloth that the voice calls in the desert, *'Prepare the way for the Lord'* (3). John is declaring the messianic salvation dreamed of long ago by the prophet. The fascinating thing is this: the desert community of scholar-ascetics at Qumran, in the wilderness of Judea, applied that very passage of Isaiah to themselves. They read it: 'A voice of one crying, "In the desert prepare a highway for our God." '[3] Salvation lay not in the desert community, however, but in the Messiah whom this rugged prophet from the desert (who may even have spent some time with the community at Qumran) proclaimed with such single-mindedness. He repunctuated the Isaiah quotation to give, *A voice of one calling in the desert, 'Prepare the way for the Lord.'* The Lord was Yahweh himself, of course, in the Old Testament prediction; but, as in 1:21, Jesus takes over the role there ascribed to God, and it is Jesus' way that John is preparing here. Preparing his way was the obsessive centre of John's vision. Would that it were ours!

In ancient Palestine, roads were simply tracks on the hard-baked earth, apart from the occasional highway built for prestige purposes by some king. For instance, Josephus tells us that Solomon built causeways of black basalt stone to Jerusalem in order to facilitate access for pilgrims 'and to manifest the grandeur of his riches and government'. These roads were built by the king's command and kept in order as the king required for journeys he was going to make. Then local inhabitants would be ordered to prepare the king's highway for him. That is how John saw his mission. His preaching was preparing the way for God's kingly rule, brought in by Jesus the King.

---

[3] 1QS 8:14; 9:19.

The desert

The desert is a second significant theme in this story. It was the scene of forty critical years in Israel's history. Moses, David and many of the nation's great leaders had spent time in the desert. Elijah had made its burning sands his home, periodically emerging to challenge King Ahab to repentance. And John, with heavy overtones of Elijah in his message, his dress and his location,[4] comes to fulfil what had been predicted of Elijah long ago: 'See, I will send you Elijah the prophet before that great and dreadful day of the LORD comes.'[5] It was Jewish belief that Elijah would return before the Messiah came, and that he would herald the coming king. Here, in the desert, John does just that.

The desert is the place where we meet God. Moses, David and the men of Qumran had found that. John found it. So did Jesus. It is still the place to meet God. Indeed, the apocalyptic description of the church's destiny in the time before Christ's return is given as 'the desert, where she would be taken care of'.[6] This is a lesson that many Christians today, engulfed in activism, could well heed.

The baptism

The baptism John administered was something shockingly new. Never had this been seen in Israel. The Jews knew about baptism, but it was something to be administered to outsiders, to Gentiles. Proselytes to Judaism underwent three elements in their initiation: the bath, circumcision and sacrifice. The baptismal bath was to wash away Gentile impurities. All members of the family went into the bath and washed themselves. They were then said to be born anew, to have had their sins cleansed, and other such phrases, which were picked up in the New Testament understanding of baptism.[7] In addition, the males in the family were circumcised, and the head of the family offered sacrifice. The bath was the most significant, not only for its symbolism, uniting the recipient with the Israelites in their passage through the Red Sea which constituted Israel a nation, but also because all members of the family received it.

Despite much learned discussion, it is plain that proselyte baptism existed in the time of John,[8] and it is likely that John's baptism owed something to it. There were, however, three striking differences.

First, John's baptism was given to Jews, and emphatically denoted that the recipients' Jewish heritage could not save them.

[4] See 2 Kgs. 1:8.   [5] Mal. 4:5.   [6] Rev. 12:14.
[7] The details are fully written up in J. Jeremias, *Infant Baptism in the First Four Centuries* (SCM, 1960).
[8] Cf. Matt. 23:15.

Secondly, it was not self-administered, as proselyte baptism was. If you were going to be fit for the kingdom, you could not make yourself so. You had to receive baptism at the hand of another.

Thirdly, John's baptism was eschatological. It looked for deliverance from *the coming wrath* (7), and it was administered in the running water of the river, not like the still bath of the proselyte or the repeated washings of the men at Qumran. Maybe John had in mind[9] the famous river that sprang from the threshold of the temple in Ezekiel's vision. In the burning aridity of the desert, wherever that river ran, life sprang into being: 'Swarms of living creatures will live where the river flows.'[10] So John insists that repentance means submitting to the judgment of God either in reality (*the coming wrath*) or else in symbol, by repentance and entering into the river. For the river was a picture of the judgment and mercy flowing from God's throne, and bringing forgiveness of sins and life in the Messiah's kingdom.

Religious observance and religious pedigree are not enough. The Pharisees and Sadducees had that and to spare. Orthodoxy is not enough. To be Abraham's seed is not enough. If there is no heartfelt repentance, there will be no spiritual life for you in the kingdom of the Messiah. That message is not out of place in the contemporary church, too prone to regard baptism and churchgoing as sufficient pledges of eternal security whether or not there is in the lives of the people any *fruit in keeping with repentance* (8).

The Spirit

The fourth fascinating theme here is the Spirit. The Spirit of God is clearly, though not exhaustively, explained in the Old Testament. It displays God's mighty power in the creation of the world.[11] It reveals God's will to the prophets.[12] It bestows particular skills or powers on certain people, maybe a Saul, a Gideon or a Sampson.[13] God's Spirit, *rûaḥ*, is not a natural possession of human beings. It is normally clearly differentiated from the *nepeš* or 'life' that sets a living person apart from a dead one. It is God's powerful invasion into the lives of humankind, and its coming is at his dictate alone.

The Old Testament prophets had longed for the day when this gift would be widely available among God's people, and their prophecies spoke of this.[14] What hopes these prophecies conjured up! Ezekiel, to go no further, looked for a personal and individual knowledge of God, a cleansing from sins, and a new moral power put within us as God's Spirit wrote his law on the heart. John may

---

[9] Like his namesake later on; cf. Rev. 22:1–2. [10] Ezek. 47:9. [11] Gen. 1:2.
[12] E.g. Ezek. 2:2. [13] 1 Sam. 10:1; Judg. 6:34; 14:6.
[14] Jer. 31:31ff.; Ezek. 36:25ff.; Joel 2:28ff.

well have had such promises in mind when he spoke of the coming Spirit. The men of Qumran had written a little about the Spirit, too. These were days of great ferment and expectation in Israel. But John the Baptist comes saying that the days when the Spirit is to be given are imminent. The forgiveness of sins and the bestowal of the Spirit, both functions of God Almighty, are to be exercised by this cousin of John's[15] whose sandals he was not worthy to 'untie' (Mark and Luke) or *carry* (Matthew).[16] It is noteworthy that John does not profess to be able either to give the Spirit or to proffer forgiveness of sins. The gift of the Spirit is emphatically said to come through Jesus; and John's baptism does not confer forgiveness of sins. As Mark and Luke make explicit, it is 'with a view to forgiveness of sins'.[17]

Both *rûaḥ* in Hebrew and *pneuma* in Greek are ambivalent. The words mean 'wind', 'spirit' or 'breath'. John may simply be developing his harvest imagery and saying that the day of judgment will come upon the impenitent like wind and fire: the wind that separates grain from chaff in winnowing, and the fire that burns up the chaff and stubble. But in view of the extensive Old Testament prophecies about the Spirit, and of the contemporary speculation about the Spirit at Qumran, there is no reason why John should not have had the premonition that God would offer not only forgiveness but his Spirit through the coming great one whose arrival he announced. And the Christian reader of Matthew would certainly reflect on the life-giving Spirit of God into which he had been baptized, and the cleansing fire of God's scrutiny to which he had been exposed through his repentance. On the Day of Pentecost, as Luke records, these twin characteristics of the Spirit – fire and wind – were prominent.[18] The Baptist's forecast had been fulfilled.

The baptism of Jesus (3:13–17)

The baptism of Jesus[19] is highly significant, and is recorded in all four Gospels. The moment he had been quietly waiting for, in the obscurity of his Nazareth home, had arrived. The whole country was buzzing with expectancy. The unthinkable was taking place. Jews in their hundreds were taking the unprecedented step of following John into the waters of the Jordan, confessing national and

[15] Luke 1:36.

[16] The two translations of the Aramaic word *skl*: Mark 1:7; Luke 3:16; Matt. 3:11.

[17] *Eis aphesin hamartiōn*: Mark 1:4; Luke 3:3, my translation. Matthew, in order to avoid any misunderstanding about the efficacy of John's baptism to forgive sins, reserves that phrase until the Last Supper, where it is explicitly related to Jesus' sacrificial death (26:28).

[18] Acts 2:2–3.

[19] See further my *I Believe in the Holy Spirit* (Hodder and Stoughton, 1975), chs. 3–4.

personal sins, and calling on God to cleanse them and make them fit for his kingdom. Not since the days of Ezra, and perhaps not even then, had there been such a national turning towards God. The time was ripe, and Jesus came forward to join others in the waters of baptism.

The story as Matthew records it is rich in significance. It points to Jesus' clear identification with all that John was teaching. He was prepared to go into the waters of judgment in that river and emerge impregnated with God's life. He was prepared to identify with the Servant motif, with the faithful remnant in Israel. It was an important moment for Jesus himself. But it would also have been important for the Christian reader in Matthew's day, who saw it as a pattern for Christian baptism. Matthew's readers would have been quick to pick out the key themes of repentance, forgiveness of sins and the fulfilment of all righteousness, noting too that baptism was a mark of sonship and a pledge of the gift of the Spirit. These five strands are woven into Christian baptism, and they stem from the baptism of Jesus. The placing of this incident as a frontispiece to the book, so to speak, shows what Jesus and we share in this area of Christian beginnings.

But there has always been a cluster of problems surrounding this act of Jesus. Here are three of them.

First, why was Jesus baptized? John was summoning people to repentance. What reason had Jesus to repent? The mid-second-century *Gospel according to the Hebrews* wrestles with this very point. In it, Jesus is represented as asking, 'Wherein have I sinned that I should go and be baptized by him?' Matthew feels the force of that question, and faces it head on with the exchange between Jesus and John. The answer Jesus gave was '... *to fulfil all righteousness*' (15). In the context here, *righteousness* refers to that quality of life that was demanded of candidates for baptism by John, who both displayed righteousness in his own life and uncompromisingly challenged others to do the same.[20] By submitting to baptism, Jesus acknowledged God's claim on him as on others for total consecration of life and holiness of character. It is part of his life of obedience, and John, though his 'inferior', should feel no embarrassment about taking part in it.

There were other reasons for Jesus' baptism. This was the moment in which John was publicly to announce the arrival of the Messiah and the start of his ministry. This was the symbolic anticipation of his full and profound baptism on the cross, which lay in the future, when he would taste for everyone the eschatological wrath of God and would proffer to anyone the unspeakable mercy of God. Just as

[20] Matt. 21:32.

on the cross he was to be fully and ontologically identified with the sins of humankind,[21] so it befitted him here, at the outset of his ministry, to set his hand to that awesome plough by undergoing its symbol and sacrament in the Jordan.

A further reason Jesus himself was baptized is not hard to guess. At the end of his ministry he urged baptism upon his followers.[22] He is here giving them the example they should follow.[23] It is difficult to understand the logic of those Christian groups today who claim they have no need of baptism or any sacraments. Their Master found them needful. And disciples are not higher than their Lord.

Secondly, did not Jesus already possess the Spirit and the sonship? Indeed he did. Matthew is at some pains to show that Jesus was conceived by the agency of the Spirit and was indeed Son of God. But the baptism was the public declaration of it. We must not forget that Jesus was human as well as divine. Must he not have felt many a hesitation about his nature and his mission? And here at this moment of self-humbling and obedience he receives (and others begin to perceive) a profound assurance that he is indeed Son of God, and has indeed been equipped by the Spirit of God to bring in the kingdom. The rabbis expected a great outpouring of the Spirit of God in the eschatological messianic age. Well, it had arrived. And Jerome sees the point: 'The mystery of the Trinity is revealed in the baptism.'

The dove is fascinating and perplexing. Is it an allusion to Genesis 1:2, depicting Jesus as God's in creation? Is it, perhaps, an allusion to that celebrated preacher of repentance in the Old Testament, Jonah (for in Hebrew Jonah means 'dove')? Or could it be an allusion to the salvation Jesus brings? When Noah survived in the ark the rigours of the flood, a dove he had sent out came and settled on him. And Jesus, who offers salvation in himself from the eschatological destruction of which John has been speaking, is marked out by the descent of the dove. We do not know for sure: nor does Matthew make it clear whether it was John or Jesus who saw the Spirit like a dove descending upon him. Much is wrapped in mystery. What is clear is that Jesus was empowered by the Spirit for his ministry as messianic Son who would preach repentance and the good news of the kingdom.

Thirdly, what did the voice from heaven mean? It meant that the age-long silence was ended. The heavens were no longer brazen and unyielding. The rabbis believed that 'when Haggai, Zechariah and Malachi, the last of the prophets, died, the Holy Spirit vanished from

[21] E.g. 2 Cor. 5:21; Gal. 3:13.   [22] Matt. 28:19.

[23] Matthew's expression 'Spirit of God' (v. 16) emphasizes the trinitarian aspect of Jesus' baptism, and its continuity with Christian baptism in the name of the Trinity (28:19).

Israel, but they were allowed to hear the *bat qôl*. The *bat qôl* meant the 'echo', or literally 'the daughter of the voice', an inferior substitute for the word of God, which had been withdrawn. It is sometimes said that this is an example of the *bat qôl*. I find the suggestion unpersuasive. This was no feeble substitute for the word of God. It was direct speech by the God who had long been silent. Now, as fulfilment is dawning, God attests his Son.

Amazing as the occurrence of this word from God was, its content was even more astounding. *'This is my Son, whom I love; with him I am well pleased'* (17). This seems to be a fusion of two Old Testament texts, Psalm 2:7 and Isaiah 42:1.[24] Psalm 2 addresses the king as 'son' of God. The kings had proved very disappointing sons, however, and there was a profound expectation and hope in Israel that one day God would bring into the world a messianic Son, a ruler worthy to inherit David's throne. There is now firm evidence from Qumran to show that 'Son of God' was a pre-Christian messianic title in Palestinian Judaism. The voice from heaven announced that the ultimate messianic ruler, the true Son, had come.

But that was only half the message. The other half, addressing Jesus as (literally) 'the Beloved, with whom I am well pleased', takes us back to the chosen servant of Yahweh, whose destiny is to suffer abuse and opposition, and eventually to die for the sins of the people.[25] The Isaiah passage continues, 'I will put my Spirit on him.'[26] That is what the voice from heaven meant! God Almighty was bringing in his long-promised deliverer to usher in the kingdom. He was both messianic Son and suffering Servant. And the descent of the Spirit not only marked him out for this ministry, but equipped him for the task.

The temptation of Jesus (4:1–11)

Why does God allow temptation? That is a question Christians often ask. Well, he allowed it for Jesus. And after a high spiritual experience, such as the baptism undoubtedly was for Jesus, temptation frequently comes, and properly comes. It sorts out the emotional 'high' from the reality of spiritual conquest and growth. We are not meant to live on spiritual highs. We are meant to live on the bread that comes from God alone, even if it is bread in the desert. God deliberately allows temptation. Its arrival does not mean that God's blessing has evaporated. It simply allows the ephemeral and the emotional to be separated from the lasting. Temptation builds spiritual muscle.

[24] Both texts were taken as messianic in the Qumran community, as it awaited God's salvation (4Q *Florilegium* 10–14).
[25] Is. 42:1 – 53:12.   [26] Is. 42:1.

But what did the temptation mean to Jesus? It would be a great mistake to suppose that the story of the temptations is included in the Gospel primarily to provide an example to Christian disciples, though they do provide that example. These temptations were messianic. They were uniquely appropriate to God's Son, who had just received a clear vision of his mission. How was he to carry it out? How was he to lead people back to God? Was he to adopt the path of the conquering king or of the suffering Servant?

The rabbis had all sorts of expectations about the messianic kingdom. One of them ran like this. 'When King Messiah comes, he will stand upon the roof of the holy place. Then he will announce to Israel, "Ye poor, the time of your redemption draws nigh." ' The rabbis were also sure that when Messiah came there would be a repetition of the gift of manna in the desert. That is why the Jews got so excited when Jesus fed the multitude in a desert place.[27] That is why they tried to make him king. They knew their Scriptures, and the writings of their rabbis. They knew that when manna in the wilderness came, that would be the sign of the kingdom breaking in. What temptations to bypass the cross, to short-circuit the path of obedience, and to adopt the role of the Son and the king without stooping to the role of the suffering Servant! That was the particular thrust of the third temptation: to gain universal dominion back from the usurper prince, but to do so by striking a bargain with him rather than by striking him through the heart with the wood of the cross. To be sure, the temptations to be selfish, to opt for the sensational and to compromise come the way of all Christians, but they are recorded here so that we may witness the testing of God's Son. Is his messiahship to be the slave of popular expectation? Or will he go to the cross to win the crown?[28]

What do the temptations mean for humanity? Adam had failed. Adam had tempted God: he had idolatrously gone for the tree in the midst of the garden when he had been told not to. Adam had disobeyed God, though he knew he was God's son. Adam had grabbed at sensual satisfaction because of the hunger of his body. And the last Adam won where the first Adam fell. Here is the recapitulation of history. Jesus succeeded where Adam had failed.

Moreover, Jesus succeeded where Israel had failed. The background to this story lies in Deuteronomy 8:1–5, from which Jesus quotes in his first reply to Satan. Moses recalls how God led the Israelites in the desert for forty years 'to humble you and to test you in order to know what was in your heart, whether or not you

[27] John 6:5–15.
[28] On the temptations of Jesus, and their counterpart in the Christian life, Blomberg is particularly helpful. See also the major work by Birger Gerhardsson, *The Testing of God's Son* (Lund, 1966).

would keep his commands'. And Israel failed comprehensively. They tempted God at Meribah and Massah. They were idolatrous with the golden calf. They grabbed at manna in the wilderness. Jesus, the fulfilment of Israel, succeeded where Israel, in its historical manifestation, had failed.

Notice how Jesus overcame these temptations. *'It is written ... it is written ... it is written ...'* The quotations come from Deuteronomy 8:3; 6:16, 13. They suggest that Jesus had been studying Deuteronomy in his own devotional reading. From within these two chapters he draws on material that he has learnt. And the Spirit, which came upon him so powerfully at his baptism, was able to take the Scriptures that he had learnt and use them in spiritual warfare. 'The sword of the Spirit ... is the word of God',[29] and if we do not know our way around the Scriptures and do not trust the Spirit in warfare against Satan we will not share in the victory of God's Son. But if we do, the Spirit will bring scriptures to our attention when temptation presses; and, like Jesus, we shall have the power to overcome. Christian readers of this Gospel in the 70s or 80s, conscious of being the followers of the last Adam, could learn much from this story. They must not go for a temporal kingdom, which Jesus refused; they must not grab fulfilment now, which Jesus declined; and they must not compromise with Satan, which Jesus rejected. They are to use the Spirit's sword in the ongoing battle against the forces of evil.

The start of the ministry (4:12–25)

Fresh from his baptism and temptation, Jesus launches his public ministry. Matthew stresses the fact that it continues that of John. John is arrested by Herod, and imprisoned in the terrible dungeons of Machaerus; Jesus immediately and boldly replaces him. John preached repentance, and that is precisely the subject of Jesus' preaching. Not for the first time, nor for the last, does Matthew stress the continuity of Jesus' work with all that had gone before. Very soon he will expand on the content of Jesus' teaching, but first of all he gives us some indication of his initial impact and the characteristics of the budding ministry.

Jesus' despised background

Jesus made a decisive break with Nazareth and came to live and work (probably based in Peter's house in Capernaum) in the area of the Sea of Galilee. This was a charming freshwater lake, fed by the

[29] Eph. 6:17.

84

Jordan, situated about 200 metres below sea level. It measured some 14 miles long by about 7 miles at the widest point. In those days there were nine or ten thriving townships clustered round its edge, and Capernaum lay at the northern tip. The province of Galilee was not large, only 50 miles by 25, but it was such a fertile area that it supported a dense population. Josephus, who was once its governor, tells us that there were no fewer than 204 villages in the province, none of them with under 15,000 inhabitants. So Jesus began his work in the most densely populated area he could have found anywhere in the Middle East. It was a population, moreover, that was volatile and open to change. Josephus again says that the Galileans were fond of innovation, by nature disposed to change, and always ready for sedition. They were tough and courageous, and thus formed a marvellous seedbed for the gospel. But they were much despised by the 'pukka' Jews down south in Jerusalem. *Galilee of the Gentiles*, these southerners called the area (15), which need not be a gibe (it was surrounded by heathen nations), but certainly was so used. For centuries, indeed for half a millennium before the second century BC, Galilee was in pagan hands, and it was an area where the Greek language, pagan customs and non-Jewish influences held sway. It was bound to be so: Galilee stood on one of the oldest and most important trade routes in the East, the Way of the Sea from Damascus down to Egypt. Nowhere could Jesus have had such a chance of gaining a large following as in Galilee. They may well have been living in the shadow of moral and spiritual death, as their more orthodox neighbours to the south asserted, but *on those living in the land of the shadow of death a light has dawned* (16). It is not uncharacteristic of God to go for the least likely place, where the orthodox would never expect to find him, among the greatest masses of unreached humanity.

A further hint of the Gentile mission

The Gentile mission would soon become the predominant thrust of the Christian church. Here we have only a hint of it, but an emphatic one. The very area that was once so ravaged by Assyria is flooded with light by the Saviour. The darker the night, the brighter the light shines. The quotation comes from Isaiah 9:1–2, where one of the most famous messianic prophecies in the Old Testament is to be found. 'In the past he humbled the land of Zebulun and the land of Naphtali [i.e. through the renewed and devastating assaults of Tiglath-Pileser in 734 and 732 BC], but in the future he will honour Galilee of the Gentiles.' And honour them he did: the people who walked in darkness saw the light of the world, and he made their area the centre of his ministry.

Jesus' immediate challenge to the Jews

The Gentile mission would lie in the future. In the meantime Jesus was preaching the good news of the kingdom[30] to his Jewish hearers, and that message demanded a response. The first to make that response were Andrew and Peter, two tough brothers in a fishing firm who were so captivated by Jesus that they left behind their belongings, their jobs and their families in order to become his disciples. Rough and ready they may have been, but they had the courage and decisiveness necessary to make these sacrifices and to follow Jesus, a step that proved too costly for the religious and the educated. There may have been something about fishermen, too, that made them particularly suitable for the 'fishing for people' that they would be doing in future. A good fisherman in those waters needs courage, for dangerous squalls erupt on that treacherous lake. He needs perseverance, patience and flexibility in the use of different methods (three types of fishing-net were used). He must keep himself unobtrusive so as not to frighten the fish away, and he must have a sense of timing. All these qualities were essential in the new kind of fishing to which this landsman introduced them.

A summary of the gospel of the kingdom

There were three sides to the gospel Jesus proclaimed.

First, he preached (17, 23). The word *kēryssein* was used to describe the work of the herald in a Greek city. It involved bold, clear, challenging proclamation. When the herald had something to proclaim, people had better listen. It was important. It came with the authority of the civic authorities. Effective preaching today has an arresting quality and a sense of authority that far transcend the personality of the preacher.

Secondly, Jesus gave himself to teaching (23), explaining the difficulties people found in his preaching, clearing up misunderstandings and changing attitudes. Teaching is directed primarily towards informing the mind; preaching towards reaching the will.

And thirdly, Jesus healed. He healed every kind of illness, demonic influence and paralysis. Kingdom ministry embraces preaching, teaching and healing. When the church exercises this ministry, she will often lack the power, immediacy and effectiveness of Jesus; he shared God's nature in a way the church does not. But wherever the church is truly carrying out the work of the kingdom, those three strands – challenging preaching, clear teaching and

---

[30] On the meaning of *the kingdom of heaven* see the Introduction, pp. 43–47.

healing (of physical disease, inner hurts and grip by dark forces) – will be seen.

These few verses have sketched the beginnings of the work of Jesus with deftness and speed. They have made clear the spread and the power of his ministry. Its impact, be it on two fishermen or on great crowds from all over the area, is plain. The direction is set for the next twelve chapters. Matthew makes this obvious. For in 4:17 he says, *from that time on Jesus began to preach . . . the kingdom,* and in 16:21, 'From that time on Jesus began to explain . . . that he must . . . suffer.' At once it is clear that this is a natural watershed in the book. We are entering a major section on the nature and proclamation of the kingdom. In Matthew 16 we shall begin another great section on the suffering and crucifixion of the King.

5:1 – 7:29
4. The first discourse:
the manifesto of the kingdom

The Sermon on the Mount is the supreme jewel in the crown of Jesus' teaching. I have found one of the most stimulating treatments of it to lie not in massive tomes such as W. D. Davies's erudite *The Setting of the Sermon on the Mount*, but in John Stott's exposition in this series: *The Message of the Sermon on the Mount*, to which I am much indebted.[1] I hope some readers will purchase it for themselves.

The placing of the Sermon

The placing of this first great discourse is important in the tidy plan that Matthew has devised for his Gospel. With it he brings to an end the first of six main panels in the book. The next four panels end in a similar major address by Jesus, and the final panel of the Gospel offers us, instead of the teaching of Jesus, the person of Jesus, risen from the dead. By then, we have reached the end which is also the beginning.

Not only is the placing of this material significant as well as tidy, but it presents a Christian manifesto of the kingdom. In all probability it was not all preached on one occasion, but was assembled by Matthew out of many talks by his Master, to show in a coherent whole what the essence of the teaching of Jesus was, and what it demanded of the men and women who were enlisting as his disciples. There is an inner logic in the placing of the material at this juncture. Jesus has just begun his ministry. It is taking off rapidly. What does it involve? What is it like to be a follower of Jesus?

To follow Jesus demands a totally different way of life, and is vital for the people of God. Right at the outset of his ministry Jesus lays it on the line. The new age has dawned. And the Sermon shows what

---

[1] Blomberg mentions thirty-six interpretations of the Sermon, and itemizes seven. I agree with him that the Sermon represents inaugurated eschatology, the 'now' and the 'not yet' that characterize the kingdom. Its teaching is a goal for disciples in every age, but will never be fully realized this side of heaven.

human life is like after repentance and commitment to the King.[2] In a word, life is very different. The injunction *'Do not be like them'* (6:8) encapsulates the tone of the whole Sermon. A sharp contrast is constantly being drawn between the standards of Jesus and those of all others. Here we meet a distinctive lifestyle, with radically different values and ambitions. Everything is at variance with life outside the kingdom.

The context of the Sermon

Jesus withdraws to teach. The crowds are not excluded, but he directs his teaching towards his disciples. He sits down like a rabbi to teach them; that was the accepted method. And he chooses a *mountainside* for the purpose. Probably that refers to one of the hills by the Sea of Galilee where the concave slopes and sounding-board of the sea make good acoustics for large numbers of people. Mountains are very interesting in this Gospel. We have the mountain of temptation (4:8), the mountain of the Sermon here, the mountain of transfiguration (17:1), and the mountain of farewell (28:16). These are all peaks in Matthew's emphasis. But the main point about the mountain here is the parallel to Mount Sinai. Moses went up Mount Sinai to get the law from God to give to the people of Israel. And now Moses' great successor ascends a mountain to receive from his Father and transmit to his disciples the law of the kingdom. We have a new law for a new people given on a new mountain by a new Moses. That is the context of the Sermon.

The content of the Sermon

The Christian life, as outlined in the Sermon on the Mount, is coherent and all-embracing. The citizens of the kingdom are called to put God first in their motives and their actions, in their business and their language, in their thought life and their priorities. All life comes under his royal control. There are seven main sections in the Sermon.

1. *Jesus addresses our character (5:3–12)*

The Beatitudes come like a bolt out of the blue for any who think of religion as a sad and miserable affair. Maybe 'religion' is. But the kingdom of God is quite different. In participating, we are the way God meant us to be, and so it is inevitably the happy life. And that is what *Blessed* means: made happy by God. It is as if Jesus is saying

---

[2] The Sermon is no mere code of ethics that can be detached from loyalty to Christ, as Marx and Gandhi wished to understand it. This is all about the lifestyle of the disciples of Jesus Christ.

that life in the kingdom with him is a life of profound joy, a joy that no person and no circumstance can take away. And this blessedness is not reserved for some nebulous future. It is for now! It is the mark of those who have really surrendered to the King and tasted his grace, although of course there is a future to rejoice in too.

Jesus singles out no fewer than eight aspects of the character and conduct of citizens of the kingdom. I doubt if they would constitute programmes on which party politicians would contest elections, but they sink deep roots of lasting joy.

The *poor in spirit* are happy – not the hard-boiled, who push others around. The phrase 'poor in spirit' has a long history in the Old Testament, particularly in the Psalms, and refers to those who have confidence only in God, ground down as they are by longstanding social and political distress. They have learned to put their trust in him alone, and to their unspeakable joy they find that the kingdom is God's free gift to them. Their joy springs from sheer, undreamed-of grace.

Those who mourn are happy, happier than guests at a party. For they have seen the depth of the world's suffering and of their own sin, and it has broken their heart. When that is true of us, we are wide open for the comfort that God longs to give. Had not Jesus come 'to bind up the broken-hearted' (Is. 61:1)?

The *meek* are happy, deeply happy in a way to which the big-headed can never aspire. The background to this verse is Psalm 37:11: 'The meek will inherit the land.' It is revolutionary stuff. It says that victory goes not to the wise or to the strong, but to those who are so small before God (which is what 'meek' means) that God can afford to exalt them without the danger of their getting proud.

It is *those who hunger and thirst* who are happy, not the bloated. Jesus is talking, of course, not of physical starvation, but of spiritual. There is a profound happiness in having a desperate *hunger*, a burning *thirst* for goodness (for this is the main meaning of 'righteousness' in this Gospel). Indeed, the intensity of that desire is underlined by a peculiarity in the Greek. 'Righteousness' is in the accusative instead of the genitive, which is normally used after words of desiring. These hungry ones desire the whole thing, complete righteousness, rather than a part of it. The phrase breathes whole-heartedness. If we have a passionate desire to be right with God and stay that way, he is going to meet that desire to the full, and we are going to be happy.

The *merciful* are happy in a way the legalist can never understand. They have tasted the sheer mercy of God who received them into the kingdom. They have come to share that quality of divine love. And they will be shown mercy throughout their lives and at the day of judgment.

The *pure in heart* have a joy to which lust is a complete stranger. 'Pure' means unalloyed, unadulterated. We see only what we are able to see. And if we train ourselves by an open heart of undivided loyalty to gaze on the Lord, we shall one day be able to appreciate the supreme vision of the unutterably beautiful one in all his glory. Double vision reduces our capacity to focus, and mars the joy of the vision of God.

There is a special joy for the *peacemakers*. Self-assertiveness and a divisive spirit know nothing of peacemaking. But those who reconcile the estranged are doing something just like God: he is always making peace. Sadly, this characteristic has been sadly missing from vast tracts of the church down the centuries. The children have been very unlike the Father, and have rendered him incredible to many.

Even the *persecuted* can be happy. They may appear to lose all: it is not so. They gain the kingdom of heaven. All down the centuries there have been a peace and a joy about those who for the sake of conscience have been willing to face opposition and death, and never more than in the last hundred years. Jesus is, however, speaking not of persecution as such but, as verse 11 makes plain, of persecution because of him. It is moving and significant that the suffering church in lands where it is oppressed does not want to be like the church in the West. It looks for our prayers, not that it may have an easy time, but that it may be faithful unto death, and know the joy of utter faithfulness to Jesus. There is no joy like that.

That is Jesus' prescription for the happy life. It is paradoxical, but immensely profound. He looks for qualities like those in the members of his kingdom.

2. Jesus speaks of our influence (5:13–16)

We are meant to be *salt* and *light* in society, and we shall be if the characteristics of the blessed life are seen in us.

There's a purity about salt: the Jewish sacrifices were offered with it. Salt is a preservative. But most of all, we look to salt for flavour. And that is what Christians are meant to be. If they are insipid they are useless to their Lord. There should be a flavour of Christlikeness, a sparkle of joy and unselfishness about them that is immensely attractive.

The light, too, is a most evocative image. A light is often a warning; think of a lighthouse. It is often an attraction; think of a lighted window looming out of the fog when you are lost. A light is often a guide; think of a torch or a flare path. Above all, a light is visible. You don't hide a lamp under an inverted bowl; you put it on a stand. There is no excuse for secret discipleship. '*A city on a hill cannot be hidden*' (5:14). And all this is possible only because Christ is the light of the world. Until he has illuminated us we can never shine with his reflected light. The imperative of shining is based on the indicative of being lit up by him. Then people will see our *good deeds and praise* not us but our heavenly *Father*, who is the source of the light they see reflected.

Both images have something important to say about Christian involvement in society. They militate against all forms of separation and withdrawal. We are meant to get involved and be a light and a preservative. We are not promised that we shall be able to Christianize the legislation and values of the world, but we are challenged to be an irritant, marching to a different drum and calling on society to heed God's standards.

3. Jesus speaks of our righteousness (5:17–48)

The main thing here is the attitude to God's law. The category of law is not abolished for the followers of Jesus. He came not to abolish the law but to fulfil it. Of course, some of the elements in the Old Testament law were abolished by being fulfilled. They had pointed forward to what had now eclipsed them in the fuller light brought by Jesus. But the moral law had not been abrogated. Indeed, Jesus goes on to intensify its demands. He is concerned to show his disciples in the kingdom that their righteousness must transcend the formal obedience which, at its worst, Pharisaism was capable of: the attitude that said, 'Right, I have fulfilled precisely what is required of me, but I didn't want to do it, and I shall not throw in one iota of extra commitment.' Jesus looks for the inner disposition as well as the outer action. The law is not the limit of obedience; it is to be seen rather as the springboard for a life of devotion to Jesus and his Father. It is the kerbstone along the road of love. And Jesus proceeds, in the verses that follow, to give a number of examples of the outworking of that wholeheartedness. Greatness in God's kingdom is measured by wholehearted obedience.

No-one can even enter the kingdom of the Righteous One without a righteousness greater than that of the Pharisees: that is to say, greater than that demonstrated by external rectitude.[3] To follow the letter of the law while ignoring its spirit, to keep laws externally so as to gain merit with God while at the same time breaking them inwardly, is unthinkable for children of the kingdom. There needs to be some correspondence between inner disposition and outward

---

[3] E. P. Sanders has given us a much more sympathetic appraisal of the Pharisees in his *Jesus and Judaism* (Fortress, 1985). Many were inspired by love towards God and the desire to please him. However, their emphasis on external performance paved the way for the formalism that Jesus denounces here and in ch. 23.

action. There needs to be some correlation between heart and deed. God is interested in loyalty, not legalism. The Jews aimed to satisfy the law of God. The members of the kingdom aim to respond in wholehearted gratitude to the love of God. And that attitude knows no limits. It never cries, 'Enough!'

Jesus has no quarrel with *the Law* and *the Prophets* (17). These were, along with 'the Writings', the three divisions of the Old Testament. He validates them completely as God's revelation which will never fail in the least degree (5:18). But he is totally against the externalism induced by the enormous legislative superstructure which the scribes and Pharisees had erected as 'a fence for the law'. Much of this legalism was contained in oral pronouncements, readily memorized in middle-eastern lands where writing was not very common. But even now we can see how vast and how repressive it was. In the third century AD some of it was codified in the Mishnah, which runs to some 800 pages (in English). Then commentaries emerged, to explain the Mishnah. These were known as talmuds. There are twelve printed volumes of the Jerusalem Talmud and sixty of the Babylonian Talmud! The pettifogging nature of the legislation was often heartbreaking. Broad principles of the law, such as keeping the Sabbath holy, were encrusted with a thousand rules and regulations which must have cowed the spirit of the normal Israelite. Glancing, for example at *Shabbath* 3–6 in the Mishnah we note that a new lamp can be moved from one place to another on the Sabbath, but not an old one; hot food may be kept warm by covering with clothes, feathers or dried flax, but not by covering with damp herbs or straw – which could engender fresh heat (and thus 'work') on the Sabbath day. An ass may go out on the Sabbath day wearing its saddle cloth if this was fixed on before the Sabbath, but may not wear a bell even if it is plugged (that would be work for the ass). Goats may go out with a protective cloth on their udders if it is to keep them dry, but not if it is intended to collect the milk ... and so forth. And all this was intended to preserve scribal righteousness. No wonder Jesus said that '*unless your righteousness surpasses that of the Pharisees and the teachers of the law, you will certainly not enter the kingdom of heaven*' (5:20).

In the verses that follow, 5:21–48, Jesus gives six examples of the 'greater righteousness' that he is talking about, referring to murder, adultery, divorce, oaths, revenge and love. In each case he rejects the scribal traditions, reaffirms the authority of the Old Testament principle, and draws out its implications. And he does it all with an astounding authority. The prophets of old had said, 'Thus says the LORD ...' when they spoke. The rabbis, aware that they were not inspired, never spoke on their own authority. They normally introduced a saying either by repeating it from some previous rabbi or by saying, 'There is a teaching that ...' But here is one who quietly but with immense authority juxtaposes his own view, fully supportive of the authority of the Old Testament, to centuries of its scribal interpreters: 'But I tell you ...' Who is this 'I', who speaks with such breathtaking assurance?

First, Jesus takes the subject of murder (5:21–26). The law had commanded, '*Do not murder*' (and the verb means 'murder', as in Exodus 20:13, not plain killing).[4] '*Anyone who murders will be subject to judgment*' is the scribal addition. Jesus goes far deeper. He traces murder to its dark lair in human hearts: hatred. The God who sees in secret is affronted not only by the fruit, murder, but by the root, hatred. Hatred may not be accountable in a court of law, but it is to have no place among members of the kingdom. Anger will have to face the judgment of God.

The scribes properly tried to safeguard citizens from gratuitous insult. To call someone *Raca*, an Aramaic swearword for 'blockhead' could lead to a hearing before the village council. No, says Jesus, that attitude of arrogantly dismissing one of God's creatures as an idiot will face the judgment of God. It is an attitude fit only for the rubbish dump. The word translated *hell* is 'Gehenna', imagery drawn from the local rubbish pit in the Valley of Hinnom outside Jerusalem. How important, then, to get right with your brother speedily, and not allow misunderstandings and resentments to fester (23–25)! It is no good supposing God will be pleased with your worship if your heart is full of bitterness against someone else. Among children of the kingdom, acceptable worship involves repairing relationships. And reconciliation with others flows from reconciliation with God. Verse 25 makes it plain that we are on the way to judgment. Those who spurn the mercy of the King will end up not in the kingdom but in *prison*. The good news is not to be trifled with. It is literally a matter of life and death.

Secondly, Jesus turns to the seventh commandment, against adultery (5:27–30). Here again it is not merely the act that is condemned, but the attitude from which it comes. Deliberately to foster lust, by erotic books, plays, films, magazines and websites, is to fly in the face of this commandment. For who is to know when the bridle of decency or convention will snap under the strain, and the racehorse of our passions break loose? 'Man looks upon the outward appearance, but the LORD looks at the heart.'[5] Some Christians have taken verses 29–30 literally. Origen, for example, castrated himself because of the imperious urge of lust. But that is

---

[4] This is recognized by the strong variant reading 'without cause' – which is not original but gives the correct meaning.
[5] 1 Sam. 16:17.

not what Jesus means. He is telling us that we must deal with sin as drastically and radically as necessary, and cut off avenues that we know to be unhelpful to cultivating that purity of heart which is part of the 'blessed' life (5:8).

Thirdly, Jesus turns to divorce (5:31–32). This was as hot an issue then as now. Divorce was rife throughout ancient society in the first century. It required no formality in Graeco-Roman circles: a written or oral notification sufficed. The first-century poet Martial speaks of women who have been ten times divorced. It was very common. But Jewish teaching on the strength of the marriage bond was exceedingly high, not only in the Old Testament but in rabbinic Judaism. Divorce can take place only when a man finds 'something indecent' in his wife and puts her away with a certificate of divorce.[6]

The precise meaning of 'something indecent' split the conservative school of Shammai from the liberal school of Hillel. The former restricted it to unchastity. The latter allowed it to include burning the toast at breakfast! Accordingly, there soon developed a great disparity between the ideals and the practice in Judaism concerning divorce. Given the fallenness of human nature, it is easy to see how the interpretation of Hillel won the day with the men. We shall comment further on this subject in 19:3, where it is raised again.

The plain meaning of Jesus' words is that divorce followed by remarriage is tantamount to adultery in the eyes of God. Jesus is even stricter than Shammai! As we see from 19:3, Jesus takes his hearers back to the purpose for which God instituted marriage. It was intended to be exclusive and lifelong. That is the ideal. To fail to keep this ideal is to spoil God's plan for man and woman. It does not mean that failure cannot be forgiven, or that a subsequent marriage cannot be happy and fruitful. It simply asserts that such a marriage is adulterous and can never bear testimony to the one-man-one-woman relationship, for good or ill, which marriage was intended by the Creator to be. And that was a shattering statement by the new Moses, going back behind the Mosaic concession in Deuteronomy 24:1 (designed, incidentally, not to facilitate divorce but to restrict it) to the original purpose of God. In the kingdom, as at the creation, marriage is meant to be exclusive and lifelong.

Chrysostom delightfully links this passage with the Beatitudes. 'For he that is meek, and a peacemaker, and poor in spirit, and merciful, how shall he cast out his wife? He that is used to reconcile others, how shall he be at variance with her who is his own?'

Fourthly, Jesus turns to oaths (5:33–37). Time and again in the Old Testament, God had insisted that oaths were to be honoured and

[6] Deut. 24:1.

95

kept.[7] The scribes devised a variety of escape clauses from binding oaths. Any oath which succeeded in avoiding the name of God was not absolutely binding: one could swear by one's head, by Jerusalem, by heaven, by earth, and so on. God was not thought of as a partner in such a transaction, so to break faith was not serious.

Jesus shows how frivolous and essentially sinful this attitude is. Our words should be trustworthy, as citizens of the kingdom. Oaths are required only because people are so often liars. Let them not be required among disciples. *'Simply let your "Yes" be "Yes", and your "No", "No"'* (37). Jesus is maintaining that our speech is to be trustworthy and true. Since he himself responded to the oath of testimony at his trial, it is apparent that we are not meant to take this saying so literally as to preclude an oath in a court of law. It ought not to be necessary because *we* might otherwise perjure ourselves, however, but only because so many others do. Even God frequently bound himself by an oath in the Scriptures,[8] not because he was untrustworthy but in condescension to our unbelief. That consideration alone should justify oaths on the lips of disciples.

Fifth comes retaliation (5:38–42). The famous *'Eye for eye, tooth for tooth'* in Exodus 21:24 was designed not to justify retaliation but to limit it. It was not permissive legislation but restrictive. And once again Jesus takes that restrictive tendency of Moses deeper, into the very attitudes of his followers. Private revenge is not to be part of their lives at all. The Christian community must not act according to the principle of retaliation in asserting legal rights. 'This attitude surpasses the spirit of legal codes', remarks David Hill, 'but does not supersede them.' Jesus is not talking about global pacifism or the abolition of police forces or the rights and wrongs of war. He is not talking about the responsibilities of states at all. Paul does that in Romans 13:1–7. No, he is prohibiting for members of the kingdom the attitude that says, 'The so-and-so has cheated me. Wait till I get even with him!' Natural – but wrong.

When the wronged party shows generosity to the one who has committed the wrong, it is immensely powerful. I was speaking about this once to a black Christian leader in South Africa. I asked him how he responded on the many occasions he had been humiliated and pushed around by whites. He replied along these lines: 'When I have been unjustly forced into some menial action[9] I complete it, and then turn and ask my "boss" if there is anything else that he would like me to do to help him. This totally takes the wind out of his sails: he can hardly believe any wronged party would respond like that.'

---

[7] E.g. Lev. 19:12; Num. 30:3; Deut. 23:22. [8] E.g. Gen. 22:16.
[9] That is the meaning of the word *forces* in v. 41 – literally 'pressgangs'.

That is precisely the point. Members of the kingdom should cause utter amazement by the way they respond to being grossly insulted (that is the meaning of being struck on the cheek, even today in the Middle East) or unjustly used. There should be such a generosity of spirit about us that we give and give and give (42) just as God has given to us. As so often in this Sermon, we are hearing only Part 2 of the deal: Part 1 is God's generosity in ever making us members of his kingdom; Part 2 is the way we reflect that generosity in our lifestyle.

The last example Jesus chooses of the 'greater righteousness' of members of the kingdom is the most challenging of all. It makes explicit what has been implicit throughout the whole chapter hitherto: love (5:43–48). The Great Lover has poured his love upon us unworthy rebels. He has purified us, has adopted us into his kingdom, and wants us to be his ambassadors in the human kingdoms. How is it to be done, and how is our allegiance to be shown? Supremely, by love. Love is the mark which, above all else, should distinguish those who know themselves to have been found by a loving God.

The Old Testament had been clear on this. 'Love your neighbour as yourself: I am the Lord.'[10] Because he is like that, we must be like that. And of course *neighbour* was to be taken in the broadest possible sense of 'other person', like the neighbour in the parable of the good Samaritan. But that was too tough for many of the scribes. It was unrealistic to understand 'neighbour' so broadly. So they added yet another of their escape clauses: *'and hate your enemy'*. That command appears nowhere in the Old Testament. It is a concession to human frailty invented by the scribes. And it was emphatically underlined by the Essenes of Qumran, who enthusiastically awaited the final battle in which their enemies would be crushed. But Jesus will have none of it. It is not limited love, but unlimited love, love to the just and the unjust, to evil and good alike, that is the mark of the Great Lover. And it must not be sporadic, but a settled mark of our characters, just as the regular following of day by night is a mark of the settled character of God himself. That is the meaning of *perfect, teleioi* (48). Be like God in undiscriminating and undifferentiating love towards all and sundry. That is the mark of the Master. That is the mark of the disciple.

The word 'love' is significant. The ancient world knew about *philia*, friendship; it knew about *erōs*, sexual love; it knew about *storgē*, the love that binds families together; but *agapē* was something very different. That is why the word is practically unknown before Christ – the commodity itself was in such short

[10] Lev. 19:18.

supply. For *agapē* means a love that gives itself for the good of the recipient. It means love that springs from the nature of the donor rather than from the real or fancied worthiness of the recipient. Of course we cannot like our enemies. But we can love them, in this sense of *agapē* love. We can desire and work for their highest good. We can regard them as those for whom Christ came and died and who are therefore intensely valuable to him. At least, we can begin to move in that direction if we ourselves have been magnetized by the love of the God who treats us like that. And it is nothing less than that for which Jesus looks in his disciples. Like Father, like son and daughter.

There's a sting in the tail of this marvellous passage. For it is hard to miss the scorn in the designations *tax collectors* and *pagans* (46–47). Commentators often suggest that Matthew has failed to love the outsider with God's all-embracing love, and reverts here to prejudiced descriptions inherited from his past. That is to assume Matthew made the sentences up. But if they came from the lips of Jesus, a very different scenario emerges. He hoists the hearers with their own petard. For almost all of them would despise the hated tax collectors and the Gentile pagans. And with gentle irony Jesus shows them that their loveless attitude is identical with that of the very people they despise. Love is a tender plant, and those who live in glass houses should not throw stones.[11]

4. *Jesus highlights our devotion (6:1–18)*

Next, Jesus takes the three main areas of traditional religious devotion: prayer, fasting and almsgiving. He warns his hearers against the ostentatious devotion sometimes to be found in the religion of his day, as of ours; and equally against the mechanical formalism to be found in some pagan circles. No, sincere obedience to God's word is the key to an authentic devotional life. Not playing to the gallery, but humbly living in the light of the Father's will. Such is the attitude he can reward.

That simplicity, that lack of ostentation, applies to our giving (6:1–4). It goes without saying that disciples will be generous givers. But they will not make their donations in a way that will draw attention to themselves. They will not do it publicly or to gain respect. It will be quiet. It will meet real need. It will be offered in love and gratitude to the heavenly Father who has given us all we have. The idea of 'reward' in Christianity needs great care. We do not become

---

[11] In this Sermon, and particularly in ch. 5, Matthew is distancing the young Christian community from the Judaism from which they had recently and painfully parted. He is showing their legitimacy as fulfillers of the Old Testament law. See Stanton, ch. 5.

Christians because of what we hope to gain, but in adoring response to the incredible generosity of God. Such is his generosity that he does, in fact, lavish good things upon the objects of his love both in this life and, we are assured, after it. But reward is nothing to do with our merit: it is everything to do with his character of irrepressible generosity. Actually, one can see a sub-Christian idea of reward in the variant reading contained in verse 4. Some late manuscripts add 'openly', as if secret giving would result in God's open reward! That is not what Jesus said. It is not the view of Scripture, as some of the 'prosperity churches' seem to teach, that giving to God is good business, and that givers will get their capital back with massive interest.

The same simple directness should mark our prayer (6:5–15). We shall be heard neither because we pray very visibly nor because we use a lot of words. The former is pretence: it is playing at prayer, like the hypocrites. There are many who think Christians are like that, and one can see why. Religious showmen, looking for the admiration of their colleagues, already have the only reward they will ever get (6:5). They have already received it in full. There is a terrible irony in those words.

Verbosity in prayer was also a common ancient failing. Pagans tended to think that God could be bludgeoned into acquiescence if they prayed long enough, and many Jews shared that conviction. Rabbi Levi said, 'Whoever is long in prayer is heard.' That attitude has not died in church circles. It is often tacitly assumed (though rarely stated) that the longer the prayer, and the more ardently it batters on the door of heaven, the more likely it is to get the desired answer. But Jesus explodes this myth: '*Do not be like them*' (6:8). Prayer is not informing God of something he does not already know. Nor is prayer seeking to get God to change his mind. It is the adoring submission of the creature to the Creator, of the disciple to the Master. He knows. He cares. He is your Abba, your dear Father. So when you pray, say, '*Our Father in heaven, hallowed be your name . . .*' (6:9).

The marvellous prayer that follows has depths we shall never plumb. It comes in a rather different form in Luke's Gospel.[12] There is certainly a different thrust to it. Luke's account is focused on people who needed to know how to pray: most of his readers were Gentiles. Matthew's account is primarily directed towards Jewish people who already pray, but need to know how to pray correctly, with the simplicity and directness that Jesus longs to see in his disciples. And the prayer shows them. It is not, of course, the *Lord's* Prayer. He did not use it himself: he told them to use it. He never

[12] Luke 11:1–4.

needed to pray, *'Forgive us our debts.'* No, it is really the Disciples' Prayer, and it is only as we enter into the life of discipleship that we can appreciate its meaning.[13]

It begins with the word of intimacy, *Father*. In the Aramaic Jesus spoke, that would be 'Abba', Jesus' own characteristic address to God. Nobody had ever addressed God like that. The word was used by little children of their daddy. And Jesus, who alone had that intimacy or relationship with God as his dear daddy, gives his true disciples the right to come in on the same level of intimacy, and call God Abba. Amazing! The whole gospel is contained in that one little word, Abba – as Paul well understood.[14] Individual disciples may approach God in that family confidence; but they do not come alone. They come as part of the multitude whom no-one could count.[15] And so he is *'Our* Father', not just 'My Father'.

Having brought us within the Father's presence, the prayer makes three petitions about God and his glory, followed by three about ourselves and our needs. The order is significant. We are not to be so taken up with ourselves that we rush into God's presence and give him a shopping list of our needs. His name is to be hallowed: that is to say, we long for his name, or character, to have top place in the world and in people's hearts. 'Lord, may we make you our Number One.' What a marvellous note of adoration with which to begin a time of prayer! The second request is for his kingdom (which means in the Gospels not a geographical realm but his kingly rule) to come – that is to say, for the extension of his control in the lives of those who are at present rebels against his love. It is a prayer for the spread of the gospel. The third petition is perhaps more directed towards life in the kingdom. If the disciples are anxious to see God's rule conquering the apathy and self-centredness of their friends who are not yet disciples, they should be no less concerned to see his will being done in their own lives, changing them and making them more like their Master. It is only when these three priorities have been addressed that disciples should turn to their own needs.

With impressive succinctness Jesus teaches us how to pray for ourselves. We are to pray for daily bread, for forgiveness, and for deliverance from evil. All human life is there in those three petitions. Our *bread* contains all our needs. The word for *daily* may indicate the continual supply for which we beg. But *epiousios* is a very rare word and may well have a profound paradoxical meaning: 'Give us today the bread of tomorrow.' Give us here and now, struggling as we are, an anticipation, a foretaste of that eternal bread, that supernatural nourishment which will be our lot in the future of the

---

[13] A magisterial exegesis of the prayer is given by J. Jeremias, *The Lord's Prayer* (Fortress, 1964).
[14] Rom. 8:15; Gal. 4:6.   [15] Rev. 7:9.

kingdom. That would include physical bread, and much more. And 'Forgive us . . .' How vital that is! Disciples never get to the point where they do not need daily, hourly forgiveness. That is one reason why *teleioi* in 5:48 cannot mean 'perfect' (NIV) but rather 'mature', 'fitted for what we were made for'. We shall never be perfect this side of heaven. But we can become what we were made for, to love God and enjoy him for ever – and to allow that love to overflow to needy 'neighbours' all around. That is gloriously possible, but we shall never get beyond having to pray with contrition and deep sincerity, 'Forgive us.'

The latter part of that verse (12) is important. Notice the tense: '*as we also have forgiven our debtors*'. This is spelt out in 6:14–15. It is not as though God petulantly says, 'I won't forgive you unless you forgive those who have wronged you.' The fact is, he *cannot* forgive us in those circumstances. For if we are to open our hands to receive his gracious pardon, we cannot keep our fists tightly clenched against those who have wronged us. So often our prayers are nullified because there is someone we think we cannot forgive. We can forgive them, and we must, if we hope ourselves to receive the daily renewing forgiveness of God. For he cannot and he will not pardon the impenitent, including those who nurse grievances against others. It is an impossibility while the condition of forgiveness – repentance – has not been met.

The third of the 'we' petitions is for God's guidance and strength against the enemy. The word translated *evil* is a genitive which could be either neuter or masculine. That is to say, it may refer to 'evil' (*to ponēron*) or to 'the Evil One' (*ho ponēros*). Maybe there is a nuance of both. Jesus had no illusions about the power of the Evil One, whom he had just defeated in the wilderness. All evil is inspired by him. And so Jesus, well aware of the dimensions of the spiritual battle which beset him and would always beset his disciples, bids them daily seek the Father's strength to be delivered from the seductions of the Evil One, leading them into temptation, and from the power of the Evil One, inducing them to sin.

God, our dear heavenly Father! His name hallowed, his kingdom extended, his will done. Our needs supplied, our sins forgiven, our temptations overcome. What a prayer! And all in fifty-seven (Greek) words – no vain repetitions here! The earliest church was soon accustomed to add words of adoring praise at the end of the prayer: 'For yours is the kingdom and the power and the glory for ever. Amen.' Not original, but very much in the spirit of the prayer itself. If his is the kingly rule in our lives, we can confidently claim his power, and we promise that we will not keep for ourselves the glory for anything that is achieved, but return it to where it belongs, to God himself.

Almsgiving, prayer, fasting. Fasting (6:16–18) is the third of the great devotional characteristics of Judaism at its best which Jesus takes over and underlines for members of the kingdom. Notice that he does not say, 'If you fast...' but *'When you fast...'* He takes it for granted that they will fast. In Judaism fasting was common, as a mark of sincerity and of repentance, and as a reinforcement to prayer. The greatest passage on fasting in the whole Bible comes in Isaiah 58:1–9a. The power of fasting is gradually being rediscovered by Protestant Christians; the Catholic Church had never lost it. Fasting strengthens self-discipline, it lessens the hold of material things upon us, it shows God that we mean business, it lessens the power of habit, and it enables us to seek God without distraction. Blessing follows fasting, time and again. Yes, there will be *reward* (18). But once again there is to be no ostentation. We are not to tell others that we are fasting; for once we start to take credit for ourselves, we rob God of his glory. Almsgiving is to be *only to your Father*: so is prayer. So is fasting. How could it be otherwise with those who against all hope had been allowed to call God their Abba?

5. Jesus examines our ambitions (6:19–34)

The worldliness that we are called to avoid can take a religious or a secular form. And so we differ from those who are not Christians both in our devotional life, which Jesus has dealt with in the first half of the chapter, and also in our ambitions. These are disclosed principally in two ways: 'What do we really value?' and 'What do we worry about?' It is to these twin areas of money and worry that Jesus now turns, as he seeks to show with embarrassing directness what it means to be a citizen of the kingdom.

Verses 19–24 are all about money. Jesus is unambiguous on this subject, which many preachers dare not face. *'You cannot serve both God and Money'* (24). *Money* is literally 'Mammon', who seems to have been the Carthaginian god of wealth. You cannot have divided loyalties in this matter. God has to come first, and money a poor second. Jesus is specific, too, about the sorts of things that grab our spending power. He warns against giving priority to items such as clothes, which will wear out and are so readily perishable. He warns against overvaluing precious metals, which rust can spoil. He warns against putting our treasure where it can be stolen. Wise people, the true children of the kingdom, put their treasure where they cannot lose it, where it will never wear out, and where it can never be eroded. Their treasure is in heaven. It is safe with the Father.

Verses 22–23 have a general application: the *eye* is the window to the soul. You can often tell how things are with people by the message relayed through their eyes. Jealousy, prejudice, resentment,

MATTHEW 5:1 – 7:29

greed, lust – these are like films that can creep over the eye and distort the vision. All this is true. But the particular application of this image is to money. And it is not without significance that the words *good* (literally 'single') and *bad* often have a financial nuance in the Greek language. 'Single' means generous, open-hearted, warm. 'Bad' means miserly, niggardly. So it would seem that Jesus is developing his theme about money. Not only is it important to have your treasure in the right place; it is also vital to approach life with a generous, warm appraisal of other people. There are few things so distorting as an ungenerous, mean and critical spirit.

Hence the conclusion: you cannot be devoted to God if you are devoted to money and the things money will buy (24). They are rival affections. Money, the ancients came to see, is like sea-water. The more you drink of it the thirstier you get. The love of money is indeed a root of all kinds of evil.[16] In May 1987 *Time* magazine came out with an issue all about the corruption in high places brought about by wrongly placed priorities. 'Whatever happened to Ethics?' was splashed across the cover. More than a hundred of the Reagan administration either had to resign through scandals, many of them financial, or were under deep suspicion. 'Not since the reckless 1920s have the financial columns carried such unrelenting tales of vivid scandals, creative new means for dirty-dealing, insider-trading, money-laundering, greenmailing.' And this was all pitilessly documented by *Time* magazine. Money possesses a terrible power to corrupt. Believers must make sure that they are not overcome by it. And yet they are.

There are few areas where the standards of the world have so invaded the church as in this area of money. Christian giving is frequently at an abysmal standard, and when it rises to 10% or so, there is often the implicit or explicit assumption that God will bless you in financial terms for what you give. It is very convenient to forget that the preacher of this Sermon was penniless and remained that way until devotion to God drove him to a cross of wood. He practised what he preached. He did not try to serve God and Money. William Barclay makes an interesting point. 'Mammon' has a Hebrew root which means 'entrust'. Mammon was the wealth people entrusted to bankers to keep safe for them. But as the years went on, Mammon came to mean not that which is entrusted but that in which people put their trust. God entrusted us with all we have. It is the supreme treason to prize the gift above the donor. This generation is accountable at this point. Things that have been entrusted to us by God to support us have become, in effect, our god. Disciples are marked out clearly by their attitude to money.

[16] 1 Tim. 6:10.

Closely allied to the theme of money is *worry* (6:25–34). On the whole, the more money people have, the more anxious care they expend on how to keep it, increase it, and stop others stealing it. Secular people are preoccupied with their lives and bodies (25), and in particular with three areas which Jesus takes as examples: food, drink and clothes. Disciples should stand out in sharp contrast. We should not be consumed by *merimna*, anxious care, over these things.

Worry is not a little weakness we all give way to from time to time. It is a sin that is strictly forbidden. R. H. Mounce says, 'Worry is practical atheism and an affront to God', and Jesus gives good reasons for the truth of this.

Worry is unnecessary, even for the hardworking. Nobody works harder for a living than a bird, but birds do not worry. Yet the heavenly Father looks after them. How much less should we worry!

Worry is useless. Anxious care cannot *add a single hour* to life (27; or, as *hēlikia* may be translated, 'a few centimetres to height'). The past cannot be changed: the future cannot be charted. So worry about them is useless and debilitating.

Worry is blind. It refuses to learn the lessons of God's providence taught us by the birds and flowers. Short-lived as they are, in their quiet dependence on their environment they display that 'peace' that should mark believers who know that behind their environment there is a loving heavenly Father.

Worry is essentially a failure to trust God. And for disciples to be *of little faith* (30) hurts God greatly. It means we do not trust him, and that is always grievous. It means that we do not put him first, but instead *all these things* (33) come first. Our ambition as disciples must be to put God and his kingly rule at the top of our list of priorities, and we shall find that God takes care of the necessities of life.

But what if he does not? What of the hardships of believers? Is Jesus being unfeeling and unrealistic here? No. He himself knew the pinch of near-starvation and was to taste in his flesh the bite of cruel nails. But these things did not rob him of his loving trust in his heavenly Father, whose overarching providence would not allow anything to befall him which was not, in the last analysis, for good. That analysis might not be apparent until eternity, but it could be relied on, and it still can. For it depends on the faithfulness of God to his creation. Christians, like their Master, are totally secure in their relationship with the Father – and in all other respects totally insecure. In a world marred by sin and suffering, hardship is inevitable for everybody, and particularly for those who seek to live for God. After all, we follow a crucified Messiah and cannot expect a bed of roses. We were never promised one. What we are promised is the endless, unremitting, detailed, loving care of the Father over every aspect of our lives. Even in deep need, even in the hour of death, the fruits of trusting him are evident in the way believers behave. There should be a quiet glow, a radiance, about us that comes from acknowledging God's rule in our lives, and from seeking to act righteously and so to stay in that right relationship with him. When those things are in place, a Christian life stands out as a beacon in the surrounding gloom.

There is, in the life of the fourteenth-century German mystic Johann Tauler, a remarkable story that shows something of the attitude Jesus was looking for in his disciples. One day Tauler met a beggar. 'God give you a good day, my friend,' he said.

The beggar answered, 'I thank God I never had a bad one.'

Then Tauler said, 'God give you a happy life, my friend.'

'I thank God', said the beggar, 'that I am never unhappy.'

In amazement Tauler asked, 'What do you mean?'

'Well,' said the beggar, 'when it is fine I thank God. When it rains I thank God. When I have plenty I thank God. When I am hungry I thank God. And, since God's will is my will, and whatever pleases him pleases me, why should I say I am unhappy when I am not?'

Tauler looked at the man in astonishment. 'Who are you?' he asked.

'I am a king,' said the beggar.

'Where, then, is your kingdom?' asked Tauler.

The beggar replied quietly, 'In my heart.'

'*Do not worry about tomorrow*' (34). In anxiety, as in money matters, disciples are to demonstrate that they are governed by ambitions different from those of others. Our ambition should be to put God first; to avoid the pious worldliness of religious showmanship described in the first part of Matthew 6; and to avoid also the secular preoccupation with wealth and the daily concerns of life outlined in the second part. Incidentally, lest we allow the force of what Jesus says to pass us by through long familiarity, it might do no harm sometimes to check up on our finances and see how extravagant we are in our spending on food, drink and clothes, to mention just those three examples Jesus took. Our findings might disturb us.

6. Jesus turns to our relationships (7:1–12)

These verses hint at a complex web of relationships within the kingdom. Jesus' concern is that our allegiance to the kingdom should be manifest in them all. Once we are right with the Father, our relationships with other people are inevitably affected too.

We are not, therefore, to *judge* our brothers and sisters (7:1–5) but to serve them. After all, they are accountable to God, not to us. We can never know the whole story about them; but God does. And all too often what we condemn in others are the weaknesses we dare not face up to in ourselves. So it ill befits us to point out the speck of sawdust in our brother's or sister's eye when we have a great plank sticking out of our own, but are too blind to see it. Who said Jesus had no sense of humour? No, instead of the critical spirit, disciples should be known for their humility, recognizing their own shortcomings. They should also be known for their helpful spirit, willing to alleviate the troubles of others by practical help rather than adding to them by carping criticism.

Jesus goes on to warn his disciples against wasting time on the hardened (6). Some people hear the message of God's kingdom and do not want to know. It is an irresponsible use of time and effort to continue to hammer on a door that is firmly closed. The disciples should push on a door and, if it is ajar, enter in. If it is firmly bolted, that is the indication to move on elsewhere. 'Do not throw your pearls to pigs,' he says. They would rather have truffles or acorns! Disciples of Jesus are not to be storm-troopers for the kingdom of God. They should be equipped with the most sensitive radar to see where the Spirit of God is already preparing the way, and only then move in.

Disciples need in all this to keep prayerful and close to God (7:7–11). That relationship is crucial. Ask, seek, knock! God will not refuse our prayers: ask, and it will be given you. God will not mock our prayers, giving us stones for bread or snakes for fish. He will not give us what will harm us, and for that reason he will often answer our prayers differently from what we ask. We do not know what is for our good. He does. He is a good Father, and longs to give good gifts to his children. In Luke's account Jesus wraps up all those good gifts in one wonderful parcel, the Holy Spirit.[17] All other gifts are contained within that parcel. And if you, evil as you are (what a throwaway piece of realism about human nature!) know how to give good gifts to your children, how much more will a perfect God look after his children?

These wonderful promises lift our heart to pray. They do, however, hint at conditions to answered prayer, and the ones listed here are not exhaustive. It is assumed that I, the pray-er, am a disciple. It is assumed that I pray seriously and persistently (notice the present imperative in Ask ... seek ... knock, indicating continuous prayer to show we mean business). It is assumed that God may answer in a way I did not want or expect: he is sovereign, and he knows what is best. It is assumed that I ask in filial faith and expectancy. It is not a case of getting anything I want. There is no

[17] Luke 11:13.

suggestion that if only I ask hard enough and believe passionately enough it will turn out as I ask. What we are promised is that it will turn out for our ultimate good.

The final set of relationships Jesus mentions is the most demanding and all-embracing. It describes the generous and self-sacrificial attitude of the disciple to everybody he or she meets. Verse 12 is one of the most famous things Jesus ever said, and it is without parallel in the teachings of the world. There is some sort of a parallel for most of the things Jesus said in some ethical teacher or other if you rummage deep enough and range widely enough, but not for this. There is even a negative edition of this 'Golden Rule' to be found in Confucius. When asked for a one-word rule of life, he replied, 'Is not reciprocity such a word? What you do not want done to yourself, do not do to others.' But that is not nearly as demanding and challenging as the positive form that Jesus gives his disciples as the keynote for relationships with others.[18] Confucius' maxim could become the basis for law, and frequently has become just that. You can legislate against people doing to others what they would not want done to themselves. That is one of the ways of making a fair society. But you can never legislate to bring about what Jesus is teaching. That generous attitude of going out of your way to encourage the depressed, to forgive those who have wronged you, and to help the disadvantaged requires positive action, often self-sacrificial action. You don't do that to fulfil some law. You do it only if the love of the kingdom burns in your heart. It is one thing to say, 'I must not harm my fellows.' It is quite another to say, 'I must go out of my way to help them.' The first could be fulfilled by inaction; the second only by self-sacrificial love – the very thing that God evidenced in bringing people into his kingdom in the first place.[19]

As so often in this Sermon, the message is clear. God wants to see his characteristics embodied in his servants. Like Father, like child. And nowhere is that more important, and more noticeable, than in our relationships.

7. Jesus examines our wholeheartedness (7:13–27)

The last section of this amazing sermon is perhaps the most amazing of all. It turns on the place of Jesus in the life of the disciple. The ultimate issue of the Sermon is the authority and identity of the preacher. This is widely discounted by those who think the Sermon

[18] The positive form of the Golden Rule is found in some late Jewish writings, such as the *Epistle of Aristion* 207 and *1 Enoch* 61:1.

[19] 'For Matthew, the Golden Rule and the "love commandments" express the very essence of Scripture. These sayings of Jesus . . . are a lens through which his followers now read the law and the prophets.' Stanton, p. 304.

on the Mount is a collection of ethical maxims such as might have been devised by any cultivated humanist. Not so. The Sermon on the Mount ends with the most emphatic assertion of the ultimacy of Jesus Christ. What he has said with such power and precision in the Sermon derives from who he is.

And who is he? He is the one who can confidently call God *my Father* (21). He is the one who can tell us what will stand in the day of judgment (22). He is the one who can declare the tree of an individual's life bad or good, who can say of the road of life 'Through road' or 'No access' (13–14). Indeed, as the Fourth Gospel makes so abundantly plain, he is the gate, the door of the sheepfold. He is the way that leads to the Father. He is the true vine, and only by incorporation in him can the branches be really good.[20]

But we do not need to go to the Fourth Gospel to find Jesus' explicit claims to be the Beyond. They are very plain here. People prophesy in his name (22), and that was something which in Israel was done only in God's name. People call him 'Lord' and are not rebuked for it. Someone can be rejected from the kingdom of heaven if he or she does not know Jesus and is not known by him (23). Jesus inherits that character of God Almighty referred to in the Old Testament: he is the Rock.[21] Any 'house' of someone's life built on him will stand. Any house built on anything else will crash in ruins. What claims! Was there ever such a paradox between the sanity and profundity of the teaching in this Sermon and the lunacy of the preacher's claims if he is not what he claimed to be? Jesus calls for humankind's unalloyed adherence. He is the eschatological Judge. And he claims the place reserved for God in their lives. That is how the Sermon ends.

This devastating challenge is brought home in three main ways.

First, the *gate* and the *road*. That image (7:13–14) poses the question, 'Have you gone through the gate? Are you on the road?' You cannot get on to the road until you have gone through the turnstiles. And they are not roomy. No room for baggage, for pride, for irresolution. Enter! Notice how here, as so often in the teaching of Jesus, we are challenged to decide. There is no comfortable middle ground embracing most of us, and leaving on either side the very good and the very bad. How comfortable it would have been were that the case! But Christianity is not about being very good, or very bad, or very comfortable. It is about being in God's kingdom or staying out. It is about allegiance to God, or rebellion. It is about being on the road that starts narrow but opens out into the life of heaven, or staying on the broad road of our self-centredness until it

[20] John 10:4; 14:6; 15:1–8.
[21] See Deut. 32:4; 2 Sam. 22:2, 32; 23:3; Pss. 18:2, 31; 28:1; 31:2–3; 42:9; 62:2, 7; 71:3; 78:35; 89:26; 92:15; 94:22; 95:1.

contracts to a dead halt in final destruction. An awesome choice. And we find that at the end of the Sermon we are not permitted merely to admire the teaching; we are challenged to bow to the preacher. Have you entered in? Are you on the road?

Secondly, the *tree* and its *fruit* (7:15–23). How can you know if you are dealing with a disciple of the kingdom or not? You can tell from the fruit of his or her life. The question is not only 'Have you entered in?' but 'Is there real change?'

A profession of faith that makes no difference to the way we behave is barren and will never save anybody. There must be fruit, consistent, attractive fruit on the tree of our lives. Fruit that will show there is a Gardener at work. Fruit that will satisfy the hunger of the passer-by. How evil are the fruits to be found in many professing Christians! – an arrogance that alienates; an externalism that does not touch the heart; a separation between religion and life; a faith that makes no demands, or that consists in legalism; a religion that takes refuge in charismatic jargon about prophecy, or miraculous healings, or the driving out of demons, but may not even really know Jesus, and does not really do the will of the heavenly Father (22–23). Matthew may well have had in mind wild, charismatic 'prophets' current in his day, as he recorded these words of his Master. I fear that so much that passes as Christianity will shrivel up in the day of judgment and be found to be bogus and worthless. People judge the tree by the fruit. The awesome truth Jesus teaches here is that so does God! If the fruit is not real, we may take leave to doubt the nature of the roots.

Thirdly, the wise and foolish builders (7:24–27). The final way Jesus presses his claim brings us to the end of the Sermon. In this age of permissiveness and pluralism (which we forget was much the same in Jesus' own day), his claims stand out sheer and stark. He does not agree that it does not matter what you believe in so long as you are sincere. He does not allow that we are all climbing up to God by the route of our choice. He does not fit in with our shallow pluralism. Instead he says there are only two ways we can build. Not many ways, just two. We can either build on him and his teaching, which we will find is as solid as rock; or else we can build on any other religion or philosophy in the world, and we will find that it is sand, and in the last day it will spell ruin.

This last image is meant to follow up the previous two. The question is not only 'Have you entered in?' and 'Is there real change?' but 'How do you build?' He wants the hearers to ask themselves whether or not they are building on the only foundation that will bear their weight.

In our postmodern, relativistic and plural culture, how do Christians justify this exclusivism, which seems to be so arrogant? It is not that we are defending Christianity and saying it is better than anything else. Often it is not. Often it is shoddy and does not stand comparison with the ethos of what is best in other faiths or in liberal humanism. No, it is not the religion of Christianity that disciples are concerned to vindicate. With Dietrich Bonhoeffer, we believe that Jesus Christ came to destroy religion. Religion, if conceived as a human attempt to become acceptable to God by whatever system of beliefs and practice, is a beggar's refuge. It will not keep out the wind and the hail. What Jesus offers is totally different. It begins not from our reaching up, but from God's reaching down. It is not a religion at all, but a revelation and a rescue. Jesus is the revelation of what God is like; never has there been such a true likeness. The King has come to bring in the kingdom. He is no less than God's rescue for men and women lost in self-centredness and sin.

I could never claim ultimacy for Christianity as a system. I do claim it for Jesus Christ. In him God has broken with blinding light into our darkness. In him God has provided for sinners a way back to himself. The question is, how shall we respond? 'But', you say, 'what about those who have never heard the gospel?' Let us leave those who have never heard to the God who came to rescue those who had never heard. They can safely be entrusted to his justice and his love. The Judge of all the earth will do right.[22] And the one who loved them enough to come for them and die for them will not wrong them. Of that we can be sure. The end of Matthew's Gospel tells us one thing we can do if we care about them. We can go and tell them the good news of Jesus and the kingdom (28:19). And the end of the Sermon here informs us of the other thing we can do if we really care. We can make sure that we personally are wholeheartedly committed to Christ. Until we are sure where we stand ourselves, we shall be no use at helping others.

So, we must build on the Rock. How? Jesus' reply to that question is the heart of Old Testament religion. We must hear and obey. Not just hear, but obey. The theological and religious world is full of hearing; it is overloaded with God-talk. What will thrill the heart of God and make the pagans realize that the gospel is true is practical, generous obedience – obedience that transforms our characters (5:11–12), affects our influence (5:13–16), shows itself in practical righteousness (5:17–48), touches our devotional life (6:1–18), radically alters our ambitions (6:19–34), transforms our relationships (7:1–12) and marks us out as totally wholehearted servants of the King (7:13–27). That is what Jesus is looking for. That is the mark of the disciples he calls. That is the kingdom manifesto detailed with immense authority at the outset of his public ministry.

[22] Gen. 18:26.

The purpose of the Sermon

Finally, we must enquire what is the purpose of the Sermon.[23] There has been an enormous amount of discussion on this matter. Is it unpractical idealism? Is it, as Leo Tolstoy thought, a blueprint for Utopia? Or is it, as Albert Schweitzer thought, an interim ethic until the (imminent) arrival of the final kingdom of God which Jesus wrongly expected in his own lifetime? Martin Dibelius stresses that it is all about attitudes in contrast to legalism. Gerhard Kittel and Alec Vidler, however, see it as intensifying the claims of the law and thus issuing a terrifying call to repentance. No. The life the Sermon indicates is meant to be lived out by citizens of the kingdom, but they cannot even begin to live it until they enter that kingdom. The moral imperative is rooted firmly in the indicative of relationship with God. The standards of the Sermon are neither readily attainable nor totally unattainable. To put them beyond anyone's reach is to ignore the purpose of Christ's Sermon. To put them within everyone's reach is to ignore the reality of human sin. They are attainable, but only by those who have experienced the new birth, which is the indispensable condition of seeing and entering God's kingdom. For the righteousness described in the Sermon is an inner righteousness. It is the very antithesis of the inner evil that mars our hearts. There is only one solution. The tree must be made good if the fruit is to be good. Only belief in the necessity and possibility of a new birth can keep us from reading the Sermon with foolish optimism or hopeless despair. It is all of a piece with the ethical teaching of the whole of the New Testament, which can be summed up in the phrase, 'Become what you are.' Disciples are called by their Master to become in practice what they already are in the election and calling of God. Christian ethics is inextricably tied to Christian beginnings. You cannot have the fruit of righteousness without the root of relationship with the Righteous One.

And so, as A. M. Hunter suggests, we have here an ethic which has five characteristics. It is a religious ethic, for the imperative is based on an indicative. What we do springs from what we are. It is a disciples' ethic, given to the new Israel – to the church and not to the world. It is how disciples should behave. It is a prophetic ethic, not a new law. It is revolution, not legislation. It is a comprehensive ethic, pointing to the working out, in all aspects of life, of that *agapē* love which has grasped us. And it remains an unattainable ethic,

---

[23] See Stanton, chs. 12–13; D. A. Carson, *The Sermon on the Mount* (Paternoster, 1986); W. D. Davies, *The Setting of the Serman on the Mount* (Cambridge University Press, 1963); and R. Guelich, *The Sermon on the Mount: A Foundation for Understanding* (Word, 1982) – but the literature is enormous.

which we must nevertheless strive to attain. 'A man's reach should exceed his grasp,/Or what's a heaven for?'[24] It remains before citizens of the kingdom as a standard. It is a spur for those who possess the Spirit of Jesus, who laid it down.[25]

---

[24] Robert Browning, *Andrea del Sarto*, lines 97–98.

[25] We must remember that Matt. 5 – 7 is the evangelist's way of explaining the person and significance of Jesus for the life of his community, struggling as it was with growing alienation from the synagogue down the street. They, not the Jews, had the true insight into the Old Testament *torah*, and they, not the Jew, were its true followers because of their allegiance and obedience to Jesus, who encapsulated and eclipsed the law and the prophets.

B. DISCIPLESHIP (8 – 10)

8:1 – 9:34
5. Who is this Jesus?

The first great section of the Gospel has been concluded. It has dealt with the beginnings of the good news, the birth and early years of Jesus, the inauguration of his ministry, and the manifesto of his kingdom. We are now about to begin the central panel in the first part of the book, embracing chapters 8 – 10.[1] It is all concerned with the nature of discipleship. It flows naturally out of a consideration of Christian beginnings, and it leads naturally into the major theme of the next panel in chapters 11 – 13 on accepting or rejecting Jesus. Chapters 8 and 9 introduce the birth of discipleship, and it all depends on who Jesus really is. Matthew sets out to tell us.

The Sermon has faced us with the solemnity of choice. Chapters 8 and 9 follow that up. They concentrate on challenging the reader with one single, critical question. Who is this Jesus? The one who has just been portrayed as so mighty in word is about to be displayed as no less mighty in deed. In these chapters the authority of the King and the challenge of discipleship, explicit and implicit, are writ large. In broad terms:

the disciples see Jesus' power to heal (8:1–17)
the cost and difficulty of discipleship are brought before us (8:18–27)
the power of Jesus over nature, sin and the demonic is stressed (8:28 – 9:8)
the call and transformation of Matthew clearly form a paradigm (9:9–17)
Jesus' disregard for convention is evident, changing the lives of tax

---

[1] The Sermon has superbly illustrated the teaching aspect of 4:23. Now Matthew turns to the healing aspect. His teaching impressed the crowds with his authority. Now his healings make an equally great impact. Chapter 9 verse 35 neatly ends the section begun in 4:23. Jesus is Son of God, mighty in word and deed. His authority is without parallel.

men, women in need, and the blind and dumb – all outsiders (9:18–33)

This section is all working up to the call, commissioning and sending out of the disciples in chapter 10. It drives us inexorably to the conclusion that Jesus is indeed Immanuel, God with us. Once that is understood, Jesus can send his disciples out on mission.

We need to look more closely at the way Matthew has constructed this part of his story. Chapters 8 and 9 largely consist of three sets of miracles, and each set contains three miracles.

The first trio: the healings of Jesus (8:1–17)

Chapter 8 opens with three miraculous healings of Jesus. The authority of God is manifest not only in his preaching but in his mighty deeds. In verses 1–4 he heals a Jewish man with leprosy, in verses 5–13 a Gentile centurion, and verses in 14–17 a disciple's relative. The signs of the breaking in of the kingdom are plain.

The variety in these three healings is important.

The Jewish leprosy sufferer (8:1–4)

If Matthew meant leprosy proper, rather than skin disease in a more general sense (see the NIV margin), it is highly significant, for leprosy sentenced sufferers to a living death. It cut them off from civilization and made them live alone. 'He remains unclean. He must live alone; he must live outside the camp.'[2] The disease gradually spread and sensation ceased; more and more parts of the anatomy became disfigured or fell off. The outcome was death. Never was there a disease that so separated victims from their fellows. Never has there been a condition that so illustrated the spiritual condition of humankind. For sin is a terrible disease that separates us from our fellows and from God; it spreads, and it is fatal. No wonder the man with leprosy had to cry, 'Unclean!' to warn bystanders to keep their distance.[3] Significantly, whereas other diseases are 'healed', this alone is said to be 'cleansed'. The trouble was, of course, that leprosy sufferers did not get healed! There was no known cure.

There is therefore a dramatic appropriateness in the fact that the first mighty act of Jesus, in Matthew's presentation, was the cleansing of a man with leprosy. It was something extraordinary and eloquent, even more so than the memorable television pictures of Princess Diana touching people with Aids at a time when many were afraid to do so. Here is someone who actually touched a man whom

[2] Lev. 13:46.   [3] Lev. 13:45.

others shunned. It was unthinkable: but so is the love of God to sinners. Here is someone who can do what Judaism never succeeded in doing: heal a person with leprosy. Could the fulfilment of Judaism have come? Interestingly enough, here in Matthew's account, the fulfilment of the law is the climax of the story. *'Go, show yourself to the priest* (wouldn't it have been marvellous to see his face when a healed leprosy sufferer walked in?) *and offer the gift that Moses commanded, as a testimony to them'* (4). A testimony to what? To the fact that one greater than Moses had come; to the fact that what Judaism could not do, in cleansing from leprosy and from the disease of sin that it represented, the fulfiller of Judaism was doing.[4] Here was no intrusion: it was the completion of all that Judaism pointed to. What a frontispiece for the book of miracles!

The Gentile centurion (8:5–13)

The apostolic gospel was 'first for the Jew, then for the Gentile'.[5] That is exactly what we find prefigured in the Gospels. To be sure, Jesus concentrated on Israel during his ministry, but there are a number of pointers to the Gentile mission that would later develop. This is one of them. Jesus reaches out to this Gentile army officer. His concern is universal. We never read of him entering a Gentile home, but we do find him saying *the word* (8), and that word of Jesus is mighty to heal. The word of the risen and ascended Jesus was mighty both to transform lives and to heal bodies, in the Gentile mission as well as among those Jews who were responding to their Messiah. A story like this would be an enormous encouragement to those Gentile believers (many of them, no doubt, in Matthew's own congregation) who had never seen Jesus, but who had trusted his word and felt his power in their lives. And the attitude of this pagan centurion was a great example of the proper approach to Jesus. For it spoke of simple, profound faith. That was what brought Abraham to experience the power of God. Abraham believed God and it was credited to him as righteousness.[6] But in Israel in Jesus' day there was not too much of that living trust in God's power to heal. Forty years later, as the gospel spread from a hardening Judaism to the Gentiles, there was less. That is why Jesus' words to this soldier were so treasured and remembered: *'I tell you the truth, I have not found anyone in Israel with such great faith'* (10). Abraham's descendants will indeed be as numerous as the stars in the sky, just as God had promised,[7] but their identity would be a surprise to the Jews. For many of them would be Gentiles, coming alongside those heroes of

[4] The testimony 'may be both negative (a witness *against* those who reject Jesus; so in Mk. 6:11) and positive (a call to belief; see 24:14 and probably 10:18)'. France (1985).
[5] Rom. 1:16.   [6] Gen. 15:6.   [7] Gen. 15:5.

long ago who really trusted God: Abraham, Isaac and Jacob. They would take their place at table with the patriarchs, while the heirs to the kingdom would be thrown out. This was staggering.[8] The Jews looked forward to the messianic banquet as their private preserve, yet here is Jesus saying that the banquet would see many Jews excluded and many of the despised pagans welcomed. The Jews had to learn the lesson, which their ancestors knew and Gentiles were beginning to discover, along with the centurion in the days of Jesus, that faith is the key to entry into the messianic banquet, and faith is the key to experiencing the power of Jesus.

Peter's mother-in-law (8:14–17)

Tired though he was with his ministry of healing and exorcism,[9] Jesus still put himself out by healing one from whom he could well have expected a refreshing meal. When he got to Peter's home, he found Peter's mother-in-law in the grip of a high fever, probably malaria. He touched her hand and the fever left her – an immediate and wonderful cure. The result? She got up and served them.

I am sure that Matthew means us to learn from this. The disciples in Matthew's day had their family lives and their measure of domestic sickness. This story must have encouraged them greatly to pray for healing among their nearest and dearest. Had not Jesus bothered to heal someone closely related to Peter, an early disciple? Then let them expect him to do the same in their day and in their homes. There is reason to believe, as we have seen, that Matthew's Gospel had a particular purpose: to equip Christian leaders. The purpose of this particular miracle story was surely to lift their faith that God would heal in their own homes and those of people near to them. Jesus laid his hand on the woman, and she was healed. And the disciples should do likewise.

In recent years I have repented of my earlier scepticism in this matter, and have often followed the example set out here. And I have often seen healings result. But many people are not healed. It is a mystery which we shall never plumb. We can never be dogmatic about when God will heal and when he will not. But what happened regularly and without a failure rate in the life of Jesus does happen

---

[8] This passage is highly relevant to Matthew's own day, when church and synagogue were going their separate ways. It would be an enormous encouragement to Gentile believers to be assured that they, not the unbelieving Jews, were heirs to Abraham's faith. The story is a great endorsement of their legitimacy. See Stanton, p. 131 and passim.

[9] Mark tells us that it all took place in the synagogue in Capernaum on a Sabbath day: Mark 1:21–31.

occasionally and with many failures when his disciples pray in faith and call on God to heal. It is a sign of the kingdom. We should be surprised if we never see it. The powers of the age to come have broken into our world; but the powers of this age are there too. We have to live with that ambivalence. We are in a 'betwixt and between' state in this mortal life: we shall see the pain and the failure, but we shall also see the power and the glory, at least sometimes, if we maintain that attitude of simple trust in the heavenly Father which Jesus so movingly displayed.

Matthew goes on to tell of other healings and exorcisms on that astonishing Sabbath day. Notice the differentiation between deliverance ministry (*he drove out the spirits with a word*) and healing (*and healed all the sick*; 16). We shall need to look further into this later. But the evangelist's conclusion of this trio of healings is remarkable. He sees it as the fulfilment of Isaiah 53:4. That was, of course, a messianic prophecy, but it applied in the first instance to the sinbearing which Jesus undertook for us upon the cross. There are many passages in the New Testament which show how important this chapter, Isaiah 53, was for the early Christians. It helped them to understand what Jesus achieved for them at Calvary. But here the Isaiah passage seems to be used with a secondary application. It is related not to the death of Jesus but to his healing ministry. And it seems to say that so costly was this healing that Jesus *took up our infirmities* on himself, *and carried our diseases* (17). He bore our sicknesses as well as our sins. There is no suggestion of Calvary here. There is no justification for the claim of some charismatics that Jesus bore our sicknesses as well as our sins upon the cross. But Matthew does see the healing ministry of Jesus as part of the pain and hardship which Isaiah foresaw for the Servant of the Lord in chapters 40 – 55 of his book. Of course, sickness is related (though not, according to Scripture, directly related) to sin, and so it is not possible entirely to dissociate the healing ministry from the vicarious suffering in this picture of the Servant.[10] But Matthew sees him here coming from the mountain of revelation (chs. 5 – 7) and entering into the valley of the shadow, where sickness and demonic forces held sway. And he was willing to carry the burden of the pain, ostracism and defilement of broken humankind, just as he would later bear its sin. Here is a fulfilment of the prophet's words deeper than he could ever have imagined.

---

[10] Gundry (p. 150) acutely comments: 'The healings anticipate the passion in that they begin to roll back the effects of the sins for which Jesus came to die.' See also J. Woolmer, *Healing and Deliverance* (Monarch, 1999), by far the best modern book on this subject.

Two short pieces on discipleship (8:18–22)

The next two passages pick up the challenge of what we have just read, and prepare the way for the next trio of miracles that will follow.

A call to costly commitment (8:18–20)

In response to the enthusiastic '*I will follow you wherever you go*' (19), Jesus points out the cost of commitment. To follow him will involve hardship, insecurity and homelessness. That was his lot. It would be the lot of his disciples too. It is remarkable that a teacher of the law should honour Jesus as highly as is reported here,[11] for Jesus had not been educated at the scribal schools. But admiration will not suffice. Discipleship demands sterner stuff: blood, toil, tears, sweat. Is he prepared for the cost?

Discipleship begins now (8:20–22)

Another would-be disciple wants to follow Jesus but hopes to put it off. To 'bury one's father' (21) meant to wait until one's father was dead and buried.[12] This man was presented with the urgency of decision. Those who love parent or child more than Jesus are not worthy of him. The challenge of the kingdom will not brook delay. '*Let the dead bury their own dead*' (22) in all probability means, 'Let those who have not found the life of the kingdom attend to matters like burial'; but perhaps we should accept a slight change in the underlying Aramaic which would give the meaning, 'Let the waverers bury their dead.' At all events it is a warning against missing the boat, and a challenge to respond and begin discipleship while opportunity knocks. It may well be that in so well-planned a Gospel as Matthew's there is an intended run-on to the next story, the stilling of the storm. The waverer, poised on the brink of discipleship, is given a promise of security in the midst of rough seas if only he will keep his eyes on Jesus.

The second trio: the power of Jesus (8:23 – 9:8)

This section is as carefully presented as the last. Matthew gives us three mighty acts of Jesus, demonstrating his power over nature (8:23–27), his power over the demonic (8:28–34) and his power over

---

[11] However, there may be significance in the fact that the scribe sees him only as a rabbi (*Teacher*), while the true – if reluctant – disciple sees him as *Lord* (v. 21).

[12] See K. E. Bailey, *Through Peasant Eyes* (Eerdmans, 1980), pp. 26–27.

sin (9:1–8), followed, as before, by two pieces on discipleship: first the call of Matthew, and secondly the discussion of new wine in old wineskins (9:9–17).

The power of Jesus over the forces of nature (8:23–27)

It is important to recall that the Hebrews were land-lubbers. They did not enjoy the sea. Accordingly, in the Gospels with a Hebrew background such as Matthew and Mark, Galilee, though no bigger than many a Scottish loch, is a 'sea', whereas to Luke with his wider horizons it is just a *limnē*, a lake. The sea represented to Jews the forces of chaos: in heaven there would be no more sea![13] From earliest days the terrifying sea had been the habitation of Rahab and Leviathan and other unspeakable monsters. It is out of the sea that the Lord builds the firmament of the earth. He is sovereign over all those threatening forces.[14] Thus Psalm 65:5–8 worships 'God our Saviour'. Why? Because by his strength he formed the mountains, and he 'stilled the roaring of the seas, the roaring of their waves'. Again, Psalm 89 celebrates the greatness of the Lord: 'you rule over the surging sea: when its waves mount up, you still them. You crushed Rahab . . .' (verses 9–10). And so when Jesus stills the storm that had suddenly whipped up from nowhere on that treacherous lake, the awe of the disciples was beyond words. *'What kind of man is this? Even the winds and the waves obey him!'* (27). And the question began to dawn in their minds: could this Jesus be exercising God Almighty's own prerogative to quiet the storm?

So the main point of this passage is to demonstrate the power of Jesus over nature. He exercises God's own power over the forces of chaos. That is why he sleeps quietly in the back of the boat: partly natural exhaustion, no doubt;[15] but Matthew also wants us to see the utter confidence which Jesus exudes. He is in control of the situation. And what a situation! Those freak storms on the lake can easily be fatal. But so could the frequent squalls which beset the ship of the church (that analogy is common in the apostolic fathers). Matthew's readers must trust the power of Jesus in the storms of their lives.[16]

---

[13] Rev. 21:1. [14] Job 9:13; 26:12; 38:8–11; Pss. 74:13–14; 93:3–4; 104:7–9.
[15] Cf. Mark 4:1, 38.

[16] In a famous book by G. Bornkamm, G. Barth and H. Held, *Tradition and Interpretation in Matthew* (SCM, 1948), Günther Bornkamm in effect launched the discipline of redaction criticism with this passage. He sees Matthew as not merely the hander-on of this Markan story, 'but also its oldest exegete, and in fact the first to interpret the journey of the disciples with Jesus in the storm and the stilling of the storm with reference to discipleship, and that means with reference to the little ship of the Church'. In other words, this story shows us one of Matthew's theological intentions.

Maybe that is why, alone of the Synoptists, Matthew records Jesus' rebuke to the disciples (*'You of little faith, why are you so afraid?'* 26) in this rather unnatural position before he has dealt with the storm. There is no doubt that the Lord has power to *save* (25). The crucial condition is faith. Jesus has God's own power to quell any force exercised against his disciples. He asks only one thing: implicit trust. The lesson would not be lost on Matthew's hearers.

One interesting detail here leads in to the next story. Remarkably, the word translated *storm* (24) is *seismos*, which generally means an earthquake; some mighty force had suddenly stirred up the placid lake into frenzy. And Jesus, in quelling the storm, is said to 'rebuke' it (26). Remarkable! The inference is that that storm was yet another attack of the powers of darkness to snuff Jesus out before his work was done. In and under the natural phenomenon of a sudden storm, Jesus discerned the work of the devil. We should be very careful before we make the same assumptions, but we cannot rule them out.

The power of Jesus over the demonic (8:28–34)

This story of the Gadarene[17] demoniacs shows Jesus' absolute authority over the forces of evil. It was universally believed, in both Jewish and pagan circles, that there are forces beyond what we can see and hear, and that some of them are good (angels) and some evil (demons). This is not a dualistic belief, at least not in Judaism, which acknowledges God as sovereign: Satan and his demonic forces were originally made to know and enjoy God, but have rebelled. They have great power, but not unlimited power. God is still in ultimate control. And here are two men, eaten up by these dark forces in their lives, driven berserk and living in the tombs (frequently associated with the occult, both then and now). The Jews knew well that when the day of judgment arrived God and his Messiah would utterly destroy all demons.[18] The demonic awareness in these two men sensed that Jesus was indeed that Messiah. Had the day of judgment come? That fear lies behind their question, forced up through the voices of the men: *'What do you want with us, Son of God? . . . Have you come here to torture us before the appointed time?'* (29). Jesus does not parley with the evil spirits. He simply utters one word of command, *'Go!'* (32), and they go – into the herd of pigs, which stampedes over the steep bank into the lake.

Much ink and compassion have been spilled upon the pigs by scholars who no doubt enjoy their bacon for breakfast and their

---

[17] There is uncertainty both about the name (Gadarenes? Gerasenes? Gergasenes?) and the location.
[18] *1 Enoch* 15 – 16; *Jubilees* 10:8–9; *Testament of Levi* 18:12.

pork for dinner. But the main point is not the pigs. It may be that Jesus foresaw their fate. It may be not. The main points are first that Jesus exercises God's almighty power over the demons, and secondly that human beings are of much more value than a herd of pigs.

Yes, God's ultimate authority over Satan is vested in this man. That is what the story underlines. But there are a number of fascinating details. Why does Matthew mention two demoniacs, whereas Mark and Luke know of only one? Perhaps because only one of them became a Christian and was known in the Christian community. But Matthew does this 'doubling' on other occasions (e.g. 9:27; 20:30), so we must look deeper. It seems that we are met by a Semitic cast of expression. The 'two' may not mean that there were literally two, but that this sort of thing happened more than once. Or it may allude to the Jewish maxim that 'A matter must be established by the testimony of two or three witnesses'.[19] That is a strong feature in John's Gospel,[20] where Jesus points out that he and his Father are both testifying, and that his words and his works both testify to who he is. Two witnesses establish the veracity of an event. It may seem a very strange form of expression to us, but it made good sense to the Semitic mind. Matthew, by this curious duplication of people in some of the stories, may simply be emphasizing the veracity of his account. It is, however, not possible to be certain what prompted Matthew's duplication.

One is also prompted to wonder why the people were keeping pigs anyhow. If the area was Jewish, pig farming was forbidden. If it was the more pagan area of Perea, as it seems to have been (*the region of the Gadarenes*, 28), then it represents Jesus' first visit outside Jewish soil, and he is immediately introduced as Lord over the demonic forces that kept pagan people in thraldom. The demoniacs' question 'Have you come *here* to torture us?' would acquire added force. It would point to the ongoing exorcism on Gentile soil which was such a mark of the progress of the church. And the opposition the incident precipitated (unrelieved, as in Mark, by even a mention of the healing of the two men) may give us a glimpse of how difficult the mission of the church was in that area of Transjordan in Matthew's day. Finally, the phenomenon of evil spirits moving from one carrier to another is attested both in antiquity and today: I have seen it myself during ministry. The destruction of the herd of pigs served as a graphic assurance to the men in question that they really were free at last and that the evil spirits would never return. Jesus is Lord over all the forces of Satan.

[19] Deut. 19:15; cf. 17:6.　　[20] E.g. John 8:12–18.

The power of Jesus over sin (9:1–8)

Having shown Jesus as the one who wields God's power over two massive areas, nature and the demonic, Matthew chooses to insert a third story at this point. He wants to show that Jesus is authorized to exercise divine authority in yet another area, the forgiveness of sins. As in the previous story, Matthew's account is much more abbreviated than Mark's: he has so much other material he wants to include within the limits of a single scroll.

Matthew accentuates elements in Jesus that point to his divine nature. He sees the vicarious faith of the paralysed man's friends. He knows the thoughts of his scribal critics. He shows God's power to heal. He evokes glory to God who had given such authority to human beings. But the heart of the matter on which Matthew concentrates is the forgiveness of sins. Jesus takes it upon himself to do what only God can do – forgive sins. It is a preposterous claim. It immediately induces the charge of blasphemy. And it looks to us as if such a claim was empirically unverifiable. Not, however, to the scribes. There was a deeply rooted conviction in Judaism that all suffering was a result of personal sin, and that nobody could be cured until he or she was forgiven. For instance, Rabbi Chija ben Abba said, 'No sick person is cured from sickness until all his sins have been forgiven him.' Rabbi Alexander agreed: 'The sick does not arise from his sickness until his sins are forgiven.' With that understanding, imagine the impact that the healing of this man would have had. Not only would it have shown that the word of Jesus was mighty to effect change, just as the word of God had been from the beginning of time.[21] It would have given the most powerful evidence to them that Jesus really was authorized to forgive sins. If not, how could he have cured the sick man? And that led to the corollary that he was performing on earth the very task that God reserved for himself in heaven.

The impact of the authority of Jesus is impossible to miss. Matthew has laid enormous stress on it. It is seen in his teaching (7:28–29). It is seen in his power over sicknesses as varied as leprosy, fever and paralysis (8:1–17). It is seen in his authority over nature (8:23–27) and over the demons (8:28–34). And now, climactically, he claims the authority to exercise the divine function of forgiving sins.[22] And he backs it up by a spectacular healing. The implication is obvious; the challenge inescapable.

[21] Gen. 1:3.
[22] The suggestion made by some scholars, that *the Son of Man* in 9:6 should be taken in its corporate sense to denote humankind at large, is ridiculous. It makes no sense of the context, and nowhere in Scripture is humankind in general given this authority, which belongs to God.

In these three stories, then, Jesus is laying claim to divine authority. The claim is explicit. It is superbly documented. It challenges the hearers to the roots of their being. Some, like the disciples, are awed (8:27). Some, like the people of Gadara, do not want anything to do with him (8:34). Some, like the scribes, are scandalized (9:3) – the first indication of the Jewish opposition that will eventually send him to his death. Some, like the crowd who had witnessed the healing of the paralytic, praise God (9:8). But none of these is an adequate response. Nothing less than complete and immediate obedience to such a call and allegiance to such a person will suffice. And this, therefore, is the precise moment for the call and response of Matthew to be recorded. There is a deep inner logic in it. 'If Jesus Christ be God and died for me, no sacrifice can be too great for me to make for him,' said England cricketer and missionary pioneer C. T. Studd many centuries later. Matthew had no such clear light as Studd, but the three preceding stories demonstrate that Jesus was no mere human. He was bringing in God's kingdom. Matthew was challenged to respond.

The calling of Matthew (9:9–13)

Matthew[23] exacted taxes for the Roman invaders. The system of taxation lent itself to corruption, and tax collectors were proverbially rich and fanatically hated. Not only did they fleece you; they worked for the hated oppressors the Romans, either directly or under a client kingdom such as Herod ran. Matthew will have heard the teaching of Jesus in the Capernaum area. He will have seen the miracles of Jesus. He will have been wondering about this amazing man everyone was talking about. And then suddenly Jesus stood in front of him, and said, *'Follow me'* (9). Matthew did just that. That is truly amazing – amazing that Jesus should bother about someone so universally despised and hated; amazing that Matthew should leave everything to follow this carpenter; amazing that Jesus had such authority that when he said to a businessman, 'Follow me', the man obeyed; and amazing the transformation in Matthew's life that resulted. And we owe to Matthew the first written records about Jesus, contained, along with other material, in this Gospel. He would have had facility with a pen, and Jesus took this quality and used it in his cause. He can do the same with any who, like Matthew, get up and follow him.

Such a conversion is worth a party. Matthew throws one, and we

---

[23] Matthew is called Levi in the parallel passages in Mark and Luke. Probably 'Matthew' ('gift of God') is the new name Jesus gave him, just as he called Simon Cephas. His Capernaum tax office would control goods entering or leaving Antipas's territory.

see Jesus totally at home among a bunch of crooks who were Matthew's friends and colleagues. Unlike some church people in many parts of the world, Jesus was totally relaxed in the presence of 'sinners' and outsiders of every kind. They loved to be with him. He was so attractive, such good company. When the Pharisees saw this they were scandalized.[24] But Jesus was quite unabashed. *'It is not the healthy who need a doctor, but the sick. But go and learn what this means: "I desire mercy, and not sacrifice." For I have come not to call the righteous, but sinners'* (12, quoting Hos. 6:6). He charged the Pharisees with being immaculate in their pattern of sacrifices, but devoid of mercy. They despised people like Matthew, and God will not tolerate it. The divine mercy welcomes sinners like Matthew when they repent and follow Jesus. But the Pharisees choose to exclude themselves from the party. Here we see among the Pharisees a tendency, which will reappear more strongly as the story unfolds, to judge Jesus rather than revel in the mercy he offers, and to pride themselves on their own fancied goodness instead of recognizing his. The Pharisees could not tolerate the generosity of God to the paralysed man, to Matthew or to his crooked friends. Those who think they are healthy do not need a doctor: ironic words. There are, of course, no 'healthy' under God's expert examination, but there are lots of people who think they are. Such people do not see their need of a doctor, although they harbour germs of the same fatal disease of sin which they condemn in its cruder forms in others. There is no room for the Pharisee spirit in the kingdom. The word means 'separated ones', proud that they stand out from the crowd and are good people. Such an attitude stinks in God's nostrils. The kingdom is a one-class society – for sinners only.

So, after the three demonstrations of Jesus' power, the evangelist has given us a call to commitment. He follows it with a claim to uniqueness.

A question about fasting (9:14–17)

The disciples of John come and ask, *'How is it that we and the Pharisees fast, but your disciples do not fast?'* (14).[25] There is something very typical and ironic about this enquiry. Here are the disciples of John and the Pharisees wondering why on earth they fast! Typical of religious people. They engage in all sorts of actions and ceremonies and have not the least idea why they do it. But Jesus

---

[24] The Pharisees saw 'righteousness' as fulfilling the regulations of the covenant. Jesus saw it as God's mission to needy people. 'A healer must get his hands dirty' France (1985).

[25] Fasting was obligatory only on the Day of Atonement, but in addition the Pharisees fasted twice a week, a practice Jesus did not share.

is clear that his coming marks a discontinuity with all that. The old skins cannot contain the new wine he is bringing. Old regulations about ceremonial defilement cannot stand before the joy of forgiveness, fellowship, excitement and new direction which the coming of the kingdom inaugurates. How can the guests of the bridegroom mourn while the bridegroom is with them? At a Jewish wedding, open house was maintained for a week. It was a time of great rejoicing and hospitality, dancing and fun, such as might rarely come into the lives of poor people. And it was all paid for by the bridegroom's family. It was free to all comers. What a description of the kingdom Jesus came to usher in! And there may be the hint that Jesus plays the bridegroom role that was ascribed to God in the Old Testament.[26] Jesus brings joy. But there is clear prediction of sorrow too, as he looks ahead to his death: *'then they will fast'* (15). Joy and sorrow are inextricably wound together in the lives of disciples as they were in the life of the Master.

One thing is clear as the claims of Jesus are brought before us: here is something new. It simply is not tolerable to make Jesus a patch in the garment of Judaism to cover a threadbare area. No, for as soon as that garment goes to the wash the new piece will shrink, and the tear will get worse. It is the same with new wine and new wineskins. Old wineskins are shrivelled hard, and cannot cope with effervescent new wine. New wineskins, new garments are needed.

So ends the second great cycle of miracles recorded in these two chapters. We have read of three demonstrations of Jesus' power, the power attributed to God himself; and two responses, for him and against him.

The third trio: the newness of Jesus (9:18–34)

The newness that has just been brought before our imagination in the garments and the wineskins is perhaps the dominant theme in this third trio of miracles. First we find the healing of two women 18–26). Then the healing of two blind men (27–31). Then the healing of a dumb man (32–34). All of these are *'ammê hā'ares*, 'people of the land'. They are the unprivileged, the outcasts. A woman with a menstrual flow was unclean. So was a dead girl. And the blind and dumb were outsiders. And by definition, an *'am hā'ares* could not be holy. The rabbis were clear about that. Jesus scorns public opinion. A rabbi would never bother with the *'ammê hā'ares*, but Jesus cares for the despised outsider. New sight for the blind, new speech for the dumb, new health for the sick, new life for the dead. That is what the newness of Jesus means! And that is what these

[26] Is. 62:5; Hos. 2:16; cf. Rev. 21:2.

three miracles are intended to teach. What marvellous preaching material they make! How apt to the continuing mission of the church in Matthew's day, struggling against the syncretism of the pagan world and the pain of separation from the parent Jewish community!

These three stories stress several points in common. Yes, the new has come, but it is accessible only to faith. That is the clear burden of all three of these miracles. In each one, faith is the hand that grasps the astonishing new thing presented in Jesus. Faith is what brings us into contact with Jesus. It was so with the woman in the crowd, and with the father of the little girl: both touched, and so experienced, his power. It was the same, too, with the demonized man who could not speak. It was when he was brought face to face with Jesus that he was set free. Faith is not an intellectual construct: it is a primary means of cognition, like touch.

Even if it is full of error and inadequacy, faith can avail, so long as it is located in Jesus. As a matter of fact, the evangelist draws attention to the imperfect faith of all three people in these stories. The synagogue ruler came to Jesus as a last resort, desperate to see if anything could be done about his child. The woman in the crowd had a superstitious faith: she thought that if she touched his clothes the miracle might occur. The blind men called Jesus 'Son of David', a title which, though true, was one he sought to avoid because of its nationalistic associations. Defective faith all round, but it availed, because it reached out and touched Jesus. Faith brings salvation, and it does so as soon as we stretch out and make contact with the Lord. That is the message. *'Your faith has healed you'* (22). *'Do you believe that I am able . . .?'* (28). That is the critical question to the two blind men. When they replied, *'Yes, Lord'*, they received what they had asked for. The ruler of the synagogue got more than he dreamed possible.

However, the power of Jesus is not displayed in the climate of unbelief. The crowd round the woman did not believe, and they received nothing. The professional mourners round the girl did not believe, and they were ejected (24–25). The Pharisees did not believe (34) and, like the crowd they despised, they too received nothing. It is possible to jostle Jesus in the crowd and still remain utterly unchanged. It is possible to see miracle after miracle and ascribe them to the devil's activity. It is not the case, as people sometimes say, that 'If only I'd been there I would have believed.' No, there were plenty of people there who did not believe although unimpeachable evidence was spread repeatedly before their eyes. The human heart is capable of profound resistance and deep self-deception. It is only when we trust that we find salvation. The faith may be a last resort, it may be superstitious, it may be theologically deficient, but if it is placed in Jesus, it binds the sinner and the Saviour together. And that is what he came to bring about.

So ends the narrative part of the central section in the first half of Matthew's Gospel. It has given us three trios of miracles, pointing inescapably to the one who wields God's power on earth. We can respond and become disciples, like Matthew. Or we can ascribe his power to the devil, like the Pharisees. The issues are clear.[27] And now Matthew brings this great section on discipleship to a wonderful climax in the charge he gives his disciples to share in the mission of their Master.

---

[27] G. E. Ladd has a delightful summary: 'The scribes taught and nothing happened. Jesus spoke and demons fled, storms were stilled, dead were raised, sins forgiven ... his authority in deeds and words was nothing less than the presence of the kingdom of God.' *The Presence of the Future* (Eerdmans, 1974), p. 166.

9:35 – 10:42
6. The second discourse: the mission of the kingdom

It is difficult to miss the skill in Matthew's writing and arrangement. Just as the first section of his Gospel had found its climax in the Sermon on the Mount, informing us what the kingdom of heaven is about, so now the second section finishes with the mission charge, informing us that disciples must spread the good news of the kingdom.

This section needs to be read at two levels. It primarily describes the historical mission of the Twelve in the time of Jesus. He did not merely preach, teach and heal by himself, or even by taking his disciples out with him. He also sent them out to further his mission. But there can be little doubt that this material was also cherished by Matthew and other Christian leaders because of what it had to say about the continuing mission of the church in Matthew's own day.

After all, the shepherds of Israel had long neglected the flock entrusted to them by God. Ezekiel 34 depicts the sheep as neglected, maimed and scattered. Nobody seemed to care. The chapter goes on to say that the LORD himself would seek out his sheep, to care for them and bring them back. He himself would shepherd the flock. And a great conviction of Matthew's Gospel is that the Shepherd of Israel *has come!* What God was planning has come to pass, through the action of Jesus. He has *compassion* (9:36), for he sees the crowds *harassed and helpless, like sheep without a shepherd.* He comes as shepherd,[1] but he also sends his disciples to join in his work and continue it. That is how the early readers of the Gospel must have perceived it. That is how we perceive it today when reading or preaching on this passage. What was primarily directed towards the Twelve with their restricted historical mission has much to say about the continuing mission of the church down the ages, called to continue the shepherd mission of its Master.

If we read the material at these two levels, we shall gain a better

---

[1] John 10:1–18.

insight into the purpose both of Jesus and of the evangelist concerning the mission. At the level of the historical mission of the Twelve a number of important points need to be noticed.

The first is that Matthew sees this mission of the Twelve as so important that he has added a variety of other sayings of Jesus about mission to the basis he found in Mark 6:7–13. For the most part these extra sayings emphasize the urgency of the mission and its costliness due to the rejection and persecution of the missionaries. What was becoming increasingly plain (earlier in the chapter) for the Master is about to befall his disciples: namely, ever-increasing opposition to the proclamation of the kingdom.

Secondly, it is noteworthy that Jesus passes on to them the authority he has wielded so powerfully in word and deed since chapter 5. Their ministry is carefully presented as parallel to his own. The words of 4:23, describing Jesus' mission as one of teaching, preaching and healing, are almost repeated of his disciples in 10:7–8. They are to go and preach, to heal every disease. The evangelist is making it plain that the disciples of Jesus share his calling, his authority and his mission. They are to do and to preach what Jesus did and preached.

Thirdly, theirs is a strictly limited mission. It is limited in time and restricted in location (10:5–6). It is a preparation within Judaism for the wider mission that would become theirs after the death and resurrection of Jesus. Undoubtedly, some of the sayings of Jesus collected here by Matthew refer to this wider ministry to come. Verses 17–18, for instance, anticipate the situation we find in Acts when Christians are dragged before both Jewish and Gentile tribunals. The sharp family divisions envisaged in verses 21–22 and 34–39 relate to the painful divisions in the Jewish community of Matthew's day as different members of a family take up opposite stances with regard to Jesus. Some of them even have to face death, as Jesus himself did (v. 38). The persecution language of verse 23 prefigures the situation in Acts, and, on any showing, the famous key verse 23 looks forward to a date beyond this particular mission. Is it is a reference to the coming of the Son of Man after the passion to commission his disciples for the wider, Gentile mission (28:18–20)? Or does it suggest the coming of the Son of Man in judgment at the fall of Jerusalem in AD 70 – they will not have completed the evangelization of Israel before then? Or does it look further ahead, envisaging, as Paul did,[2] the salvation of the Jewish people at the end of time? Nobody knows for sure.

What is certain is that this chapter foreshadows mission in the churches that Matthew serves and the hardships the Christians are

---

[2] Rom. 11:25–26.

enduring. Moreover, it has enduring principles for subsequent disciples like ourselves to take to heart.

Mission is crucial

Mission is vital in any Christian ministry. If we are right in thinking that the Gospel was written primarily for leaders in the Christian community, those leaders have already been reminded in chapters 5 – 7 that it is the task of the shepherd to teach the flock. And now in this chapter they have it borne in on them that evangelism and outreach are just as important a part of their work. That, too, was part of the role of the shepherd in Ezekiel 34 from which the Israelite shepherds had drawn back. Matthew's church would not grow – no church will grow – unless evangelism lay at the heart of its life.

And this needs to be modelled by the leaders. They may well find that others are more gifted at evangelism than they are (and therein lies one of the values of working as a team), but it is vital for the leadership to get involved with this indispensable activity. Jesus sent his disciples out. He did not leave them in offices and studies. The Christian church at large needs to learn from this incident that its leaders are called by the Master to go out, yes, into open-air evangelism, to show how seriously they take the Lord's commission to the lost. Men like Irenaeus and Origen, Justin and Athenagoras, among the early Christians, combined major leadership roles and academic brilliance with front-line work in the market-places of the ancient world. They knew mission was vital. And they obeyed.

Mission is shared

The apostles[3] were not sent out on their own. They went out as a group. That is an enormous encouragement. Gifts emerge in such an enterprise that one never dreamed of. Mutual support leads one into a new dimension of fellowship. It will not merely be the minister aiding his colleagues. They will aid him, and the bond between them all will grow. One of the main reasons for burnout in Christian ministry is that it is generally carried out solo. Jesus never envisaged such a thing. Leadership in the New Testament is almost always plural. In the West these days, not a great deal of mission goes on. But where it does, some celebrated name is often expected to come in and do the evangelism. But that is not the New Testament pattern. People evangelized together, and they were a disparate team. One could hardly have engineered a greater contrast than between a

---

[3] Only here in Matthew are they called 'apostles'. The word means 'sent ones'; it denotes action rather than status. The disciples become apostles when they go out on mission.

contemplative like John, a fisherman like James, a hot-blooded Peter and a cool, calculating Matthew. They were a mixed bunch (10:2–4), but mission bonded them. It still does. And the impact of such a team, and the joy it brings to the members as they report back to their sending church, are hard to exaggerate. Mission needs to be shared.

Mission is sustained

The text does not actually say that mission is sustained, but that would be to look too narrowly. The mission began with the coming of Jesus and his call to the first disciples, 'Come, follow me' (4:19). It moves out into infinity in chapter 28 with the Great Commission to go to all the world and preach the good news. And now in the middle of the Gospel it is emphasized anew. For mission is a continuing responsibility. And within the sustained, regular outreach of the church, there are times for particular effort. This evangelistic trip by the Twelve was one of them.

As one who is regularly engaged in missions, I find that it is vital to go with a team. Sometimes it may be a couple of hundred, sometimes half a dozen. It may last for a long weekend, or for two or more weeks. It is most effective when it does not rely on central meetings with a celebrated preacher, but when it is carried on in the schools, pubs, working men's clubs and homes where people naturally meet, and where members of the team can chat with them in a relaxed way. Such missions are of course best when they transcend denominations, and I find increasingly that churches of a very wide spectrum will join together for a specific outreach to the community like this. It can make a marvellous focus for the much slower ongoing work of the churches in the area. It is generally a time of reaping.

Mission is complex

It is not hard to understand mission, but it is hard to do it in a balanced way. Most churches lack balance. They are strong in some areas and weak in others. But this mission of the Twelve had remarkable balance. Matthew has already made it plain that the mission inaugurated by Jesus involves teaching the word, healing and caring for social needs, and exhibiting his power. These three. Not just one of them. And each of those strands is represented in the mission of the Twelve (10:5–8). We should be seeking to regain that balance in our churches. We should expect God to exert his power among us. We should make teaching a priority. We should expect healings from time to time. We should take the risk of venturing forth in overt evangelism. And we should claim the power of Jesus over all the dark forces of the demonic. These strands are all to be found in the fast-growing churches of South East Asia. They should become a priority in the West.

Mission is strategic

Why should Jesus forbid entry into the Samaritan or Gentile towns (10:5)? It is not that he was not concerned about them. He was. But now was not the appropriate time. Jesus had a specific aim for this particular mission. Many churches have only general aims. Therein lies the difference. In his brief earthly ministry, to call them to repentance was his primary goal; it needed total concentration. He knew that the time for the Gentiles would come later, as the gospel spread out from its Judaic centre (24:14; 28:19–20). There is a place for strategy in mission. We should go here and not there at a particular time. Clear aims are necessary in church life. It is good when a congregation sits down to ask, 'What are we going to seek to do for God in the coming year, or five years?' If we aim for nothing we are sure to hit it.

Mission is demanding

Mission is very costly. It includes the hazards that characterized Jewish hostility to Christian evangelists in Matthew's day, as well as the hostility that met the Twelve on their mission. Hence verses 17–18. They will be brought not only before Jews but before Gentiles, governors and kings. Jesus is clearly looking beyond the mission of the Twelve to what is going to happen in the wider outreach of his church. And it was actually happening in Matthew's day; brother did betray brother to death, and father did deliver up child in the 60s and 70s of the first century (21). '*When you are persecuted in one place, flee to another*' (23) – that happened in AD 70 when Jewish Christians left Jerusalem in response to prophecy and migrated to Pella. Indeed, says Jesus, '*you will not finish going through the cities of Israel before the Son of Man comes*' (10:23). And he came, in a sense, in judgment in AD 70 when the Romans destroyed Jerusalem. That terrible judgment was intensified in AD 135, for then the Romans crushed the Second Revolt and made Jerusalem into a pagan city, from which Jews were banished, and on the ruins of the temple they built a shrine to Venus.

So Jesus sends them on this strategic, limited, temporary object-ive. It cost them all they had, just as mission cost him all he had. Their lot is identified with his (24–25, 32–33). In contrast to the 'prosperity cult' which is dominating certain areas of the Christian church today, Jesus does not offer his followers an easy ride. '*A student is not above his teacher, nor a servant above his master*' (24). They must share in the mockery, the opposition and the hard times of the Jesus they follow. '*Anyone who does not take his cross and follow me is not worthy of me*' (38). There is an identity of calling, of role and of destiny between Jesus and his ambassadors.

Mission is 'Jesus-shaped'

All the time, mission centres round Jesus. When the disciples are told to go and preach that '*The kingdom of heaven is near*' (7), what it really means is that Jesus is at hand. The kingdom has arrived in the person of Jesus. '*Whoever acknowledges me before men, I will also acknowledge him before my Father in heaven*' (32). The kingdom is Jesus-shaped. '*Whoever finds his life will lose it, and whoever loses his life*' – for the kingdom's sake? No, no: '*for my sake . . .*' – that is the person who will *find it* (39). Jesus' authorization commissions these disciples. Jesus' example directs them. Jesus' name determines their acceptance or rejection. Mission is Jesus-shaped: if it does not embody something of Jesus' life and point people in repentance and faith to him, it will fail.

We see in this mission charge some useful criteria for determining authentic Christian workers. How about their attitude to money, comfort and prosperity (9)? How about their peace in the midst of undeserved suffering (17–19)? How about their endurance (22)? How about their likeness to Jesus (24)? How about their cutting edge (34)? Have they the courage to face opposition?

An alternative way of reflecting on the mission charge could be summarized in five words: see, care, pray, receive, go. Remember that Jesus was training the Twelve by his own example, summarized at the end of chapter 9.

See (9:36)

When Jesus saw the crowds, he had compassion upon them, because they were harassed and helpless, like sheep without a shepherd. Jesus saw the situation: people were tormented, exhausted and led astray. Jesus perceived their need, as Ezekiel had done before him.[4] This is the supreme motivation for mission, to see the need of those who are perishing outside the kingdom. Motivation comes when you see people harassed by pressures, exhausted by the pace of life, going nowhere, and being led astray by many false ideologies. It comes when we see the church weak, out to entertain, self-related,

[4] Ezek. 34.

untrained, unwilling to sacrifice, powerless to witness, short of conviction, and prayerless. That is where the church in South Korea and Singapore has so much to teach us. It has seen the needs of the people. It has seen the weakness of the church. And it has acted. The results are celebrated throughout the world.

Care (9:36)

When Jesus *saw the crowds, he had compassion on them.* *Esplanchnisthē* means 'he was moved in his guts'. He was stirred deep down inside. Alas, the church is very unlike Jesus. We do not care. We do not go out in mission. Maybe we are too empty. Maybe we are too respectable. Maybe we are too similar to those who do not profess to know Christ: it would be embarrassing to approach them. We are, in all probability, too ignorant of the good news to share it naturally. We are too terrified of what people might think. We are too insulated in our Christian ghetto. We are too apathetic: we do not share the compassion of Jesus. The Gospels repeatedly tell us that when Jesus saw, he had compassion.[5] Perhaps we do not even look, let alone care.

Pray (9:37–38)

The harvest is plentiful but the workers are few. So it is vital to pray that *the Lord of the harvest will send out workers into his harvest field.* It is his harvest, and that is a relief. It does not all depend on us. We are not lords of the harvest. We are called on to pray. Why do we not go? Why do we not care? Because we do not pray. The harvest is great. Opportunity knocks. The labourers are few, pitifully few. But there is a Lord of the harvest; and what an encouragement that is. We are not responsible for the growth of the kingdom. He is. And he seeks our co-operation, in prayer and in going. We must be willing to answer our own prayers and, like Isaiah, to say, 'Here am I. Send me!'[6] The disciples must have been very surprised. It is one thing (and relatively comfortable) to pray that the Lord of the harvest will do something about it. It is quite another thing (and rather forbidding) to hear him say to us, 'Go.' We must be prepared to share in answering our own prayers.

Receive (10:8)

The disciples had to receive two things. The first was training, and they had already been receiving training from Jesus. I believe this is

---

[5] Matt. 14:14; 15:32; 20:34; Mark 1:41; 8:2; 6:34; Luke 7:13.   [6] Is. 6:8.

neglected in the churches at large. When I became Rector of St Aldate's Church, Oxford, I recall asking a respected Christian friend, John Stott, what I should concentrate on. His reply was unequivocal: 'Train, train, train.' We sought to do just that, and the results in the congregation became plain for all to see. The Twelve received training by watching the example of Jesus, by receiving the training that he offered, and by a practical assignment: they were sent out. They must have learnt an inestimable amount by this excursion. It is a marvellous way to train members of any congregation. The best way to train people in mission is not to give eloquent addresses on the subject, but to get people out on the streets or into the houses and prisons (where currently a major move to Christ is taking place). That is precisely what Jesus did to his followers on this occasion.

Important though it is to receive training, the Twelve and their successors down the years also need to receive authority (10:1). *'It will not be you speaking, but the Spirit of your Father speaking through you'* (10:20). Until our lives have been filled with the Spirit of God, we shall not be likely to engage enthusiastically in evangelism and mission. It is altogether too costly. We need empowering if we are to achieve anything for God. The power of the Lord and the mission of the Lord belong together.[7] That is emphasized at the end of this Gospel. Christ has all power. He is with us always, but he tells us to go and make disciples (28:18–20). In the charismatic movement there has sometimes been an emphasis on the power of the risen Lord without a corresponding commitment to evangelism. When that happens, things soon get shallow and introverted. The Holy Spirit is given us for mission. In the mainline churches, the Holy Spirit is given verbal recognition but is often a stranger. That is why not much detectable mission emanates from such quarters. We need to receive.

Go (10:6–7)

Who is to go? All of them. Luke says they went out two by two, for mutual encouragement and support. They were not all evangelists by temperament, but they were all sent to do the work of an evangelist. Regarding ten of these Twelve, we do not know if they ever preached a sermon: we are simply not told. But they all went out on mission. They were all witnesses. I know of no more effective way for a church to grow than for it to become a church full not of preachers, but of witnesses. God has no dumb children.

To whom do they go? They go *to the lost sheep of Israel* (10:6). They have a clear, limited, objective. They are to go to the lost, to the

---

[7] Acts 1:8.

distressed and poor (6, 8). Often it is the poor and the needy and the street people who respond to the good news, while the affluent keep themselves in icy isolation.

Their going will sometimes embrace a whole town or village (11). It will sometimes mean public preaching (7). It will sometimes mean open-air work: 'As you go, preach' (7). Jesus was an open-air preacher. What about his followers? It will sometimes involve visits and house meetings (11, 13). It will sometimes involve personal conversations (16). He sends them out in that variety of roles.

How are they to go? They must go expecting God to work (8). They must go expecting to be poor but to have enough (9–10). They must go trusting the Spirit of God to speak through them (20). Often disciples will have to speak totally impromptu on mission: it will be given them what they should say. They must go prepared for opposition (17–18). It is bound to come. Disciples who are not being opposed from some quarter or other are in all probability not saying anything worth opposing. They must go in confidence, because God is in control (26). Disciples have no need to fear: our God reigns. They must go and call for open confession of Christ (32). He needs to be confessed before others. Jesus called people openly, and so must his followers. They must go and put their whole life on the line (38–39). Disciples follow Jesus on the way of the cross (38). That is how Jesus' followers, including us today, are to go.

Disciples are called to see, to care, to pray, to receive, and to go. Those five words more or less summarize the mission charge. And the mission of the Twelve leads on to the third section of Part 1 of the Gospel: chapters 11 – 12. They are all about accepting the kingdom in the person of the King. Will people become disciples? The challenge of discipleship runs right through these coming two chapters.

C. RESPONSE (11 – 13)

11:1–30
7. Jesus' claim, and its ground

Once again Matthew's structure is beautiful in its simplicity, though subtle in its detail. It is clear that the previous panel has been completed with the address to the Twelve. A formula like *After Jesus had finished instructing his twelve disciples* (1) appears after each of the five great addresses which are such a feature of this Gospel. The first half of the book is drawing to a close, and the issue of whether people are for him or against him will be brought to a climax in the next great section of his preaching, chapter 13 – the parables. Those parables constitute a clear mirror held up to the crowds so that men and women may see themselves. Are they going to accept him or not?

It seems to me that Matthew works up to chapter 13 by setting out to answer four questions. What grounds are there for accepting Jesus (11:1–24)? What essentially is Jesus' claim (11:25–30)? What makes people reject those claims (12:1–45)? And who is the real family of Jesus (12:46–50)? We shall look at the first two questions in this chapter, and at the second two in the next.

What grounds are there for accepting Jesus? (11:1–24)

That was John the Baptist's problem. He was in trouble. Courageous man that he was, he had publicly rebuked Herod Antipas, ruler of Galilee, for his marital affairs. Herod had visited his brother in Rome and seduced his wife. He had then divorced his own wife and lured his sister-in-law to leave her husband and marry him. John had denounced this behaviour, and paid the penalty – prison in the fortress of Machaerus in the burning mountains by the Dead Sea. It is not surprising that he had questions and doubts in such a place as that. On the one hand, Jesus did not appear to be bringing an axe to the root of the trees, and so seemed a very different sort of Messiah from what John had imagined – if, indeed, he was Messiah at all. On the other hand, everything tends to get out of proportion when you are suffering for a long time in a confined space, as John was. Doubts grow in such a soil. Wisely, he did not allow them to fester. He sent his disciples to refer the matter to Jesus himself.

Jesus bids John's disciples to go and tell John what they *hear and see*: *'The blind receive sight, the lame walk, those who have leprosy are healed, the deaf hear, the dead are raised, and the good news is preached to the poor. Blessed is the man who does not fall away on account of me'* (4–6). And then Jesus launches into an encomium of praise for John. He was not only a prophet, but the messenger that was billed to come and usher in the coming of the Lord (14).[1] And guess who has followed him! In Malachi the expected coming one was God Almighty. But it is Jesus who brings that divine presence into the midst – a remarkable throwaway claim in the midst of singing John's praises.

There is nobody *greater than John the Baptist*, Jesus maintains. He is great because of his proximity to Jesus. But *he who is least in the kingdom of heaven is greater than* John (11). John's doubts and hesitations show that, great man though he was, he was not yet quite in the kingdom, for he remained unclear about the person of the King. When you are in the kingdom, committed with single-minded devotion to the King, you are even closer to him than John was. That seems to be the logic of Jesus' words. The kingdom is the thing. Don't miss the kingdom! From the days of John's preaching until now, the kingdom had been *forcefully advancing*, and *forceful men* were laying hold of it (12).[2] We must not forget that it was a time of unparalleled religious fervour in Israel. John's preaching had proved to be the signal for this invasion of the kingdom, but he could not see it because he had been thrown into prison. Whether he could see it or not, John the Baptist was the watershed in the history of God's revelation. He was the messenger of the Lord, sent to prepare his way; he was the fulfilment of Old Testament expectation. The quality of this man of iron stands out in striking contrast to his hearers. Nothing is ever to their liking. They resemble petulant children. When people are determined to harden their hearts, any excuse will do. But wisdom is shown to be right by action.[3] People

[1] The language of Mal. 3:1 is fused with that of Exod. 23:20. Mark uses the same combination (1:1–2). It was probably an early Christian *testimonium*.

[2] The verb translated *forcefully advancing* is particularly hard to interpret. Is *biazetai* middle ('forcefully advancing') or passive ('being forcefully advanced into', 'stormed')? And are the *forceful men* (*biastai*) hostile or friendly? Does it mean that since John started preaching, men of violence, the Zealots, have been forcing their way into it? Has the NIV got it right? Or does it mean that since John's imprisonment, the kingdom of God suffers violence, and violent men take it by force (thus RSV, NRSV, REB)? This latter interpretation would perhaps fit best with the flow of Matthew's recognition that opposition is increasing.

[3] Jesus, like the wisdom of God (cf. Prov. 8; Wisdom 7 – 8), will be vindicated by

might criticize John for his strange lifestyle (18), but he had moved the nation as nobody had done for centuries. They might criticize Jesus for his happy mixing with ordinary people (19), yet he brought the joy of God's kingdom into this needy world, and opened a new access to God.

What answer did Jesus give John? It is exceedingly profound. Only God can attest God. No other witness has the authority to do so. A great deal is made of this point in the Fourth Gospel.[4] Very well: how could God possibly give attestation to Jesus? In two ways, surely: by the fulfilment of his word in the Scriptures, and by the display of his power in the miracles. And so Jesus points to precisely these two areas.

John is told, in effect, to look at the fulfilment of Scripture. Verse 5 alludes to two passages in the Old Testament which were widely held to be messianic: Isaiah 35:5–6 and 61:1. If *the blind receive sight, the lame walk ... the deaf hear* and *the poor* have *the good news* preached to them, is it not clear that God's Spirit is upon Jesus, and that he is the one for whom John looked? There is, as we have seen, a strong stress on the fulfilment of Scripture in this Gospel. Matthew thought of the Old Testament both as embodying God's revelation and as looking forward to a fulfilment beyond itself. If, as Matthew believed, Jesus is that fulfilment, then inevitably he must fulfil, and not contradict, the Old Testament predictions. We see the same thing in 12:18–21, where Jesus counters the unwillingness of the Jews to see any outreach in a Gentile area by musing on the universalist outlook of the Old Testament prophecy in Isaiah 42:1–4.

And secondly, John is told of the mighty works of Jesus. They indicate the powerful breaking in of the kingdom of God. Signs and wonders are, however, by nature ambivalent. The same signs that led the disciples to believe were displayed at Korazin and Bethsaida (21), but the people were unwilling to face the change of lifestyle which commitment to him would involve. The same signs were evident to the crowd, and they did not get beyond discussing the matter (12:23). The same signs were evident to the Pharisees, and they ascribed to the devil the undoubted power exhibited in them (12:24).

Signs of God's power in the miraculous are veiled signs. They can warrant belief, but never compel it. There is always the possibility of producing an alternative explanation. If we are wilfully blind, no miracle can convince us to the contrary. These Pharisees, who had seen sign after sign, had the effrontery to say to Jesus, 'Teacher, we

what he does. The Son of Man is here identified with Wisdom, and to find Wisdom is to find life (Prov. 8:32–36).

[4] E.g. John 8:12–18.

want to see a miraculous sign from you' (12:38). His reply was sharp. 'A wicked and adulterous generation asks for a miraculous sign!' Wicked in hardness of heart: adulterous in the Old Testament sense of being 'married' to God and yet flirting with every other object of alternative desire. Such was their attitude. And Jesus says, 'None will be given it except the sign of the prophet Jonah.' Jonah was the preacher of repentance who spent three days in the belly of the great fish, and then was brought back from that watery grave. He is the best sign that Jesus can offer them. The word of God in the ancient Scriptures and the works of God displayed in the miracles of Jesus do indeed point him out as the King who has come to bring in the kingdom. They validate the 'greater than Jonah' who comes with that age-old and so unpopular message of repentance. In the resurrection of Jonah from that living death inside the fish we see a presentiment of the resurrection of Jesus the Messiah from the tomb.

Here is the nearest to a decisive sign it is possible to get. The resurrection will be God the Father's definitive vindication of his Son. Unlike the other miracles, there is no way in which a perverted imagination can dismiss that one as Satanic. It is the supreme ground for accepting who Jesus is and what he has done. 'As to his human nature [he] was a descendant of David, and . . . through the Spirit of holiness he was declared with power to be the Son of God by his resurrection from the dead.'[5] And that decisive ground for confidence in Jesus is hinted at in this chapter of Matthew's Gospel.

What essentially is Jesus' claim? (11:25–30)

What was that claim of Jesus that John was perplexed about, and that Korazin and Bethsaida found too much to accept? This amazing passage tells us.

'I praise you, Father, Lord of heaven and earth, because you have hidden these things from the wise and learned, and revealed them to little children. Yes, Father, [26]for this was your good pleasure.

[27]*'All things have been committed to me by my Father. No-one knows the Son except the Father, and no-one knows the Father except the Son and those to whom the Son chooses to reveal him.*

[28]*'Come to me, you who are weary and burdened, and I will give you rest.'*

Jesus is quietly claiming to be the locus of all revelation.[6] Whatever revelation there may be, dispersed in human intellect and

[5] Rom. 1:3–4.
[6] *The Son* is used here absolutely, as in 24:36, the only other such use in this Gospel. It means 'the Son of God', uniquely related to the Father (cf. 3:17; 14:33; 16:16).

values, in virtuous action, in nature and in the history of humankind, the centre of all God's self-disclosure is Jesus of Nazareth. He fulfils all the hopes of the Old Testament, and is the heart of all revelation. In a dark world lit by candles and lamps, he comes as a searchlight.

If we look closely at this claim, we will see five distinct elements in it.

First, Jesus maintains that God the Father conceals and reveals according to his will. People cannot grasp a Christian understanding of God and Christian relationship with God by their own efforts. They cannot discern who Jesus is, what the kingdom is, unless God shows them. He conceals these things from those who are wise in their own conceits, and reveals them to those who come with child-like trust and teachableness. Whenever anyone comes to faith, there is a divine disclosure to that person.

Secondly, Jesus claims to be the plenipotentiary representative of the Father. He comes from the Father's side, equipped with the Father's power and trenchancy, and displaying the compassion of the Father's heart. He fully represents God, and he comes with God's own claim on human hearts.

Thirdly, only the Father fully understands Jesus. Not John, not the disciples, not *the wise* or *little children*. The mystery of his person is inscrutable this side of heaven. Theologians have spent centuries seeking to reconcile his divine and human natures. It is like trying to square the circle. With the limited discernment of the human mind and heart it cannot be done. It takes God to know God. Only the Father knows the Son. What a claim!

Fourthly, only Jesus fully understands the Father. Great people have discovered and taught many true and noble things about God. Nobody has known him with the intimacy of Jesus, who could call him Abba, dear daddy. When that holy man Mahatma Gandhi was dying, one of his relatives came to him and asked, 'Babaki, you have been looking for God all your life. Have you found him yet?'

'No,' was the reply. 'I'm still looking.'

The humility, the earnestness, the sheer goodness of a great teacher like Gandhi shine through a remark like that. But it stands in the most stark contrast with Jesus' claim in this passage. *'No-one knows the Father except the Son'* (27). He does not know something about God. He does not even know everything about God. He knows God absolutely. It is simply breathtaking.

And fifthly, because Jesus shares the Father's nature as well as ours, he and he alone can reveal the Father. He can show us, because he knows. He can introduce us because he belongs: he is the Son.

These five elements go to make up the most astounding claim that has ever been heard on human lips, that the way to know the Father is through Jesus. It reminds us irresistibly of other words of Jesus: 'I am the way and the truth and the life. No-one comes to the Father except through me', and 'Anyone who has seen me has seen the Father.'[7] If you want to know what God is like, look at Jesus. If you want to get through to God, come to Jesus. If you want to discover the epicentre of God's self-disclosure, you will find it in Jesus.

That is the claim. That is what makes Christianity at once so widely attractive and so widely hated. The sheer exclusivity of the claims drives people in one direction or the other. They do not allow us the comfort of occupying middle ground. Nor can we shrug off the need for decision by saying that these exclusive claims are found only in the Fourth Gospel, which some scholars regard as late and theologically tendentious. The passage before us is every bit as challenging, exclusive and absolute in its claim as anything in the Fourth Gospel, and it is situated in one of the oldest strata of the Gospel tradition, the Q material, sayings of Jesus found in both Matthew and Luke but absent from Mark. Scholars ascribe a high degree of reliability to this material. C. S. Lewis was right when he said that there is no way of reconciling Jesus' humility of lifestyle, quality of character and profundity of teaching with the rampant megalomania which must colour his theological claims about himself if he is not God.[8] We are invited to choose how we shall respond to so staggering a claim.

The revelation and the rescue belong together. So Jesus, after making this claim to be the revelation of God, issues the most wonderful, warm invitation to all who feel in need of rescue by God (28–29). Notice again the breathtaking claim, 'Come to me' (28). Not 'Go to God' – we could not find the way. The Bible suggests that there is a twist in our human nature which would make us unwilling to embrace the highest when we saw it. 'Come to me – I have come to seek you out.' What grace, that God should come to seek his rebel subjects with no word of condemnation on his lips, but an invitation, 'Come'! That one word shows us the very heart of God. That is his attitude to sinners.

The weary and the heavily burdened are particularly invited. That may have a significance beyond the obvious, for the Greeks were exhausted by the search for truth, which had been proceeding for centuries without resolution. They anticipated modern existentialists in concluding that authentic experience was incommunicable: 'It is very difficult to find God, and when you have found him it is impossible to tell anyone else about him.' As for the Jews, they must have found religion a great burden. It had become a matter of endless regulations and duties. Did not the teachers of the law and the Pharisees 'tie up heavy loads and put them on men's shoulders'

---

[7] John 14:6, 9.   [8] C. S. Lewis, *Mere Christianity* (Bles, 1952), Part II, ch. 3.

(23:4)? Jesus came to end the search by taking us in his loving arms. He came to lift burdens off our aching backs, not tie them on. He offers 'rest', not cessation from toil, but peace and fulfilment and a sense of being put right. We have only to come, to entrust ourselves to him, and we shall find that rest. Millions have done so, and have enjoyed that given rest.

There is a deeper rest, which cannot be given but can only be found: the rest of taking his yoke upon us and entering into partnership with him. He wants not only to welcome back the sinner, but to train the disciple. 'Come to me' is followed by 'Take my yoke upon you' (28–29). The yoke was the wooden collar that ran across the shoulders of a pair of oxen and enabled them jointly to pull enormous weights. Metaphorically, the yoke was used to describe the law which the Jewish youth undertook to bind to himself in the bar mitzvah ceremony. It spoke of loyal commitment. And here the carpenter of Nazareth, who had made many a yoke, says in effect, 'My yokes fit well. They do not rub your neck and shoulders. Come to me. Get yoked up to me. Make an act of loyal obedience, like a bar mitzvah, to me. And you will find a deep peace and satisfaction that you could never find elsewhere. I have come for you. Come to me.'

Often in Judaism the 'yoke' is applied to the law.[9] Jesus brings a wonderful fulfilment to that imagery. He invites the weary and harassed not to go to the law but to come to him. However, the allusion seems to go deeper, to the wisdom literature where wisdom is almost personified and almost identified with God. In Sirach 51:23–27, Wisdom invites people to 'Draw near to me', to take on the 'yoke' of instruction, with the promise of little labour and of finding 'rest'. It is only an allusion, and some scholars doubt any reference to wisdom at all.[10] But if Jesus did make that allusion and some of his hearers picked it up, its claim is truly shattering. It is saying that what the law and wisdom were to Israel, Jesus is to the citizens of the kingdom. This metaphor was not forgotten in the church. The early Christian document, the *Didache*, calls Christ's commandments 'the yoke of the law'.[11] His yoke is gentle, but not in the sense that it is less demanding than Judaism. In some ways it is more demanding. But it is the yoke of love, not of duty. It is the response of the liberated, not the duty of the obligated. And that makes all the difference.

---

[9] E.g. *Aboth* 3:8; *Apocalypse of Baruch* 41:3; *Berakoth* 13a; *Psalms of Solomon* 17:32.
[10] Notably Stanton, ch. 16.   [11] *Didache* 6.

12:1–50
8. Human response to Jesus: for and against

Chapters 11 – 12 of this Gospel depict a good deal of rejection of Jesus. The dark shadow of increasing opposition falls upon the page, and it centres on the Pharisees. This follows appropriately from 11:28–30, contrasting Jesus' 'rest' with the Pharisees' legalism. Why was it, why *is* it, that so many people reject the most wonderful person who has ever walked this earth?

What makes people reject the claims of Jesus? (12:1–45)

There are many reasons why people reject him. John rejected him, or at any rate had the most serious doubts (11:1–6), because he was undergoing hard times and his expectations were not being fulfilled. A deadly combination. Korazin rejected him (11:20–24) because he was too straight for them. The city was set on a course of compromise: the bas-relief of the sun-god found in the black basalt ruins of its synagogue says it all. What the trouble at Bethsaida was we cannot even hazard a guess; the town lies under the waters of the Sea of Galilee.

The crowd rejected Jesus out of lack of seriousness (11:16–19). They were like children playing weddings and funerals, impulsive, petulant, irresponsible. They simply did not take him seriously. But the most serious opposition to Jesus comes from the Pharisees, and it is one of the main themes of chapter 12. Why did the Pharisees reject Jesus? They were good men, religious men. Why were they so set against him?

This is not an easy question to answer – partly because we have become prejudiced against the Pharisees over many centuries. It is no compliment to call anyone a Pharisee. But it is mainly because we are short of information about them. What we have comes from Josephus, the Gospels and the rabbinic tradition after AD 70. Josephus is prejudiced in favour of the Pharisees, the Gospels on the whole are against them, and it is hard to date the rabbinic material.

There is an irenic chapter in Jacob Neusner's book *Judaism in the Beginning of Christianity* which shows that the Pharisees stressed the minutiae of cultic law because they yearned for salvation, whereas the followers of Jesus were confident that in him they had found it. This perspective on Pharisaism has been developed by E. P. Sanders in his exhaustive work on Judaism in the time of Jesus.[1] He maintains that we have a wrong understanding of Pharisaism. The Pharisees, he believes, were 'covenantal nomists'. That is to say, they were passionate about details of behaviour because they wanted to keep their side of the covenant that God had made with his people. They were prepared to die for the law of God, trusting him to bring them resurrection.

Nevertheless, it cannot be denied that the Pharisees shared in Jewish responsibility for Jesus' trial and execution. Inevitably, therefore, they were seen as 'the opposition' by Christians, and Matthew was very interested in them – not only because of their activities in the time of Jesus but also because they continued to be influential in the synagogues of Matthew's own day. After the destruction of Jerusalem in AD 70, when the separation between church and synagogue was taking place, Sadducees and Essenes were gone: the only party of the Jews to survive was the Pharisees. They exercised great influence on the emerging rabbinic tradition, and helped to determine its later development. So the Pharisees in this chapter probably represent not only Jesus' opponents but those of Matthew's churches. His readers could find them in the synagogue down the street. But not exclusively so: the characteristics Matthew records are all too often to be found within the churches as well.

The Pharisee spirit can be legalistic about Scripture (12:1–8)

The Pharisees chided Jesus because his disciples, who were hungry, picked *some ears of corn* as they *went through the cornfields*, and ate them. That was a perfectly permissible act. It is expressly allowed in Deuteronomy 23:25. What was wrong, in the eyes of the Pharisees, was doing it on the Sabbath. Scripture had bidden the Jews keep the Sabbath holy, but the Pharisees had developed that healthy principle into a farrago of prohibitions. They made long lists of types of work people must not do on the Sabbath,[2] and the disciples were doing several of them. They were reaping, winnowing, and preparing a meal on the Sabbath! Like many legalists after them, the Pharisees were so anxious to study what Scripture said that they could not hear what Scripture meant. The Sabbath was meant to be a day for

[1] See the first three of his works listed on p. 18.
[2] They categorized thirty-nine areas of work forbidden on the Sabbath, according to the Mishnah (tractates *Shabbath* and '*Erubin*).

worship and recreation, not for bondage. The disciples were not breaking the law of God. They were simply breaking the Pharisaic regulations, and for the Pharisees this was almost worse.

So Jesus responded with two stories from the Old Testament itself. He reminded them that David once went into the tabernacle (the holy place which antedated the temple) and *ate the consecrated bread*, that is to say, twelve loaves set out in the Holy Place as a thank offering to God the giver. This was not allowed, but human need took precedence over ritual custom. Maybe a greater than David was here!

His second point was this. Offerings in the temple were doubled on the Sabbath day,[3] so the priests had more work to do than on weekdays. They broke the Sabbath rules, but the temple worship of God took precedence over the regulations about the day. Could it be that *one greater than the temple* was here?[4]

Finally, he quotes Hosea 6:6, as he had done earlier, in 9:13: '*I desire mercy, not sacrifice.*' God looks for the loving allegiance of the heart rather than the ritualistic precision of the cultus. Matthew, like Hosea, is not against ceremonial observance, but is against giving it priority. As Son of Man, Jesus does not abrogate Sabbath law, but has the right to interpret it – which he does in a way that undercuts Pharisaic legalism. He puts compassion above ritual.

The Pharisee spirit can be desperately conservative about religious customs (12:9–14)

Jesus had not actually broken Sabbath law in healing *the man with a shrivelled hand*, but he did break the Pharisaic code. The Mishnah's tractate *Yoma* 8.6 allows medical help on the Sabbath only if a person's life is in danger. This man's clearly was not. So Jesus takes on the Pharisees with his eyes open. God desires mercy rather than ritual. Not so the Pharisees, who allow the rescue of *a sheep* that has fallen into *a pit on the Sabbath* day,[5] but not the rescue of a human being. The Pharisees are determined to do nothing, in order to honour the Sabbath: Jesus is determined to do good. It is clear that a major clash is brewing. The Pharisee spirit loves custom rather than spiritual life, and is often to be found among reactionaries in churches. They place their hope in ritual performance, not in Christ. And for the first time we are told they determined to *kill* him (14). The clash had become inevitable.

[3] E.g. Num. 28:9.
[4] In Judaism the temple was the focus of God's presence; a greater embodiment of that presence is in the Messiah – who will, in fact, create a new temple, as much of the New Testament emphasizes.
[5] *Shabbath* 128.

The Pharisee spirit can sometimes attribute to Satan what is God-given (12:22–32)

They were wilfully blind over the Beelzebub issue. Their attitude was rather like Satan's in *Paradise Lost*, 'Darkness, be thou my light.' There was in some of them a deeply rooted antipathy to goodness as seen in Jesus. This attitude can still be found, even in high religious circles. I have known a bishop on one occasion close a church rather than allow an evangelical clergyman to go there. And here, so determined were the Pharisees to damn Jesus for his breaches of their Sabbath regulations that they attributed Jesus' healings to the devil. His answer is sharp and devastating. If he were indeed effecting cures through demonic agency, then Satan's kingdom would be divided against itself and would be in ruins. This is far from the case. Satan is very much in business and he does not self-destruct. Therefore Jesus does not effect his cures through the devil. Moreover, if he did, how would Jewish exorcists defend themselves from the same charge? That they did exorcise is clear from the *Magical Papyri* and Josephus, who describes a Jewish exorcism at which he himself was present.[6] The allusion to *the Spirit of God* by which Jesus drives out demons takes us back to Exodus 8:15. In the rabbinic commentary on this passage Moses is contrasted with the Egyptian magicians, and the finger of God with the power of the demons.

There remains one probable verbal allusion here which is both subtle and devastating. The Pharisees prided themselves on being separate. As we have seen, the very name 'Pharisee' means 'divided off', 'separated'. Could there be a word-play in *'If Satan drives out Satan, he is divided . . .'?* Jesus answers the Pharisees according to their folly, and refers back to the dramatic incident in Daniel 5:25–28: 'MENE, MENE, TEKEL, PARSIN.' Has Satan's kingdom gone Pharisee? Is the writing on the wall?

The Pharisee spirit can mask a rebellious heart under intellectual scepticism (12:38–42)

Replete as they were with signs, they asked for another! Unwilling to accept what they had seen, they still asked for more. Their *heart*, Jesus said, was *adulterous*, but rather than admit it, they pretended they did not have enough evidence on which to make a decision. Underneath intellectual doubt there is sometimes (but not always) a heart that does not want to know the answer.

A *sign*, as we have seen, can always be otherwise interpreted. The

[6] *Antiquities* 8.46–48.

Pharisees spoke against the signs that Jesus did, and gave them another interpretation.

The Pharisaic opposition was very serious. It began with suspicion (1–8). It moved into hostility (9–14). It brought about blindness (22–32) and it issued in a sinister conspiracy to do away with Jesus altogether (14). There is a clear link between chapter 12 and the passion of Jesus. The Pharisaic opposition, stirred into fury here, proved implacable. Jesus must go.

It is interesting to see the response of Jesus in this chapter as a whole. It has four aspects.

First and foremost he boldly takes on the Pharisees. He does not pander to them on the one hand, or keep a low profile on the other (9–14). He warns them with the utmost clarity (25–37) that if they persist in calling good evil they will insulate themselves from the mercy of almighty God, and put themselves beyond the pale of pardon. For sinning against the Holy Spirit is doing what the Pharisees did, ascribing to Satan what they knew perfectly well came from God.[7] Against such bigoted misinterpretation there is no remedy. That is not at all the situation of most of those who come to pastors fearing that they have committed the sin against the Holy Spirit. Those who fear they have committed it cannot have committed it! For those who sin against the light, against the Holy Spirit, deliberately ascribe to evil what they know comes from God. And it is unforgivable not because God will not forgive, but because those who practise such deliberate self-deception cannot bring themselves to the requisite repentance.

A second way in which Jesus meets this assault is by his reiterated claims: to be greater than David (4), greater than the temple (6) greater than Jonah (41), greater than Solomon (42). There is nothing in the spiritual history of the world than which he is not greater!

Thirdly, Jesus met the opposition of the Pharisees by urging that his kingdom teaching was essential (43–45). Without it people would be open to reinfestation by evil spirits, however thorough the moral and spiritual reformation had been previously. The gospel can do for people what the law can never do.

And finally, Jesus invites all and sundry, including his Pharisaic detractors, into the intimacy of family ties with himself. They can be closer than physical flesh and blood if only they will. The choice is theirs (46–50).

So much for the Pharisaic opposition and Jesus' way of dealing with it. The chapter has another most important area to deal with: demonization. The subject is introduced because of the hardness of

---

[7] 'The gravity of the blasphemy against the Spirit depends upon the Holy Spirit as the dynamic that stands behind and makes possible the entire messianic ministry of Jesus himself.' Hagner, 1, p. 348.

heart of the Pharisees. Such overt and palpable rebellion can open the way for infection by evil forces.

The Pharisee spirit can open the way for infection by evil forces (12:22–29, 43–45)

The whole area merits some attention if only because of the massive concentration on the occult which we have seen in our own day, and which was certainly a feature both of the Jewish and of the pagan world in the time of Christ.

First, the grip of evil forces on a life is a real phenomenon, and is different from disease. Diseases are regularly said to be 'healed' in the New Testament, while demons are said to be 'driven out' (cf. 15, 27). It is fashionable among theologians influenced by the assumptions of the Enlightenment to laugh at the possibility of demonization, but our culture is riddled with the effects of occult involvement. Perhaps Jesus and the culture of his day were not so naïve after all.

Secondly, the word used in the Gospels is generally *daimonizomai* (22). It means 'be demonized', 'be affected by demons'. It does not allow us to adopt the common distinction, made in some circles, between those who are 'oppressed' by the demonic and those who are 'possessed'. All are simply afflicted by that malign power, wherever it is situated.

Thirdly, certain instances of physical conditions may be demonic. Verse 22 speaks of a particular case of blindness and inability to speak as demonization. The boy with seizures in 17:18 is said to be demonized. So are the two deranged men in 8:28. Today too, occasional instances of physical conditions can be demonic, and when the evil spirit is addressed in the name of Jesus and driven out, the patient is immediately and permanently set right.

Fourthly, these evil spirits are organized under *Beelzebub* (24). The name means 'Lord of the house or dwelling', and it is one of the names of Satan in the Scriptures – a very significant one. He wants to be master of the house in people's lives.

Fifthly, Satan is compared to a *strong man*, a robber baron, who guards his ill-gotten possessions undisturbed, until someone stronger than he comes upon the scene to bring liberation (28–29). Notice what needs to be done. The strong man must be driven out (28) and tied up (29), and this is done by the power of *the Spirit of God* (28).

Sixthly, there is a danger of falling under demonic influence if you deliberately shut your eyes to good and call it evil, as some of the Pharisees were doing with Jesus at this point (22–32). That is one way in which it is easy to fall prey to forces one cannot control.

149

Another, not mentioned here, is to engage in any traffic with the occult.

Seventhly, there is a danger of demonization in a generation where there is widespread apostasy and rejection of the light of God (43–45). Despite the extensive influence of religion, the first century AD was one such period. It has not been the last.

Eighthly, a demon may well be driven out, but there is a danger that the person concerned may be 'reinfected' if the deliverance ministry is not properly handled, and if the person is not filled with the Holy Spirit (43–45). Negative religion, or even good intentions and moral effort, will never keep a heart free. Only the expulsive power of a new relationship will do that.

Finally, Jesus sets forth deliverance from demons as one of the marks of the breaking in of the kingdom (28). To discredit the possibility of the demonic is as foolish as to go overboard on it. It does occupy a great deal of Jesus' attention in the Gospels, and however difficult it is for us to cope intellectually with the possibility of evil forces affecting the lives of human beings, we would be unwise to rule it out and thus to ignore the plain text of the New Testament.[8]

Who is the real family of Jesus? (12:46–50)

Decision is imperative. Neutrality is impossible. 'He who is not with me is against me, and he who does not gather with me scatters' (30). There is an interesting contrast there with Mark 9:40, where we read the opposite: 'Whoever is not against us is for us.'[9] This latter saying restrained disciples from rejecting one who drove out demons in the name of Jesus but was not of their particular circle. The verse here in Matthew 12 challenges readers as to whether they are scattering with Satan or gathering with Christ. As so often in this Gospel, we are presented with a straight choice: no middle ground. 'He who is not with me is against me' is, accordingly, a test we should apply to ourselves. Where do I stand with regard to Jesus? But 'whoever is not against us is for us' is a test we should apply to others, rather than glibly write off those whose theology or practice differs from our own.

By the end of this chapter it is clear that the Pharisees have made their decision. They are not with him. They are against him. The religious Establishment is ranged in opposition.

---

[8] Those who wish to take the matter further may be referred to John Richards, *But Deliver us from Evil* (Darton, Longman and Todd, 1974); my *I Believe in Satan's Downfall* (Hodder and Stoughton, 1988); and John Woolmer, *Healing and Deliverance* (Monarch, 1999).

[9] See also Luke 9:50.

But so, it seems, is his family. It is one of the very painful things to note in the life of Jesus that members of his family seem constantly to have misunderstood him and opposed him. We read in John 7:5 that his brothers did not believe in him. Mark 3:21 is even more emphatic: they thought he was mad. And here *his mother and his brothers* are poignantly described as *outside* (46). The situation was wonderfully changed by the beginning of Acts, where we find his mother and his brothers gathered with his disciples in the upper room in prayerful fellowship, waiting for the gift of the Holy Spirit.[10] James, one of his brothers, was clearly converted by the resurrection[11] and became the leader of the Jerusalem church, in which, after his death in AD 62, he was succeeded by another brother, Simeon. So it came good in the end, but during his ministry Jesus was closer to his disciples than he was to his natural family. It must have given him deep and lasting pain that his nearest and dearest stayed outside the kingdom.

However, this incident of the family outside the door enables him to teach who his real family are, and enables Matthew to bring the importance of decision about Jesus to a climax. It is possible to be religious like the Pharisees, and still not be part of the kingdom of God. It is possible to be physically related to the Messiah himself, and still not be part of the kingdom of God. Religious practices and religious pedigree are utterly inadequate to bring anybody into the kingdom. There needs to be an acknowledgment of who Jesus is, and a determined decision to follow him. That brings a person into the most intimate relationship with Christ, closer than physical mother or brother. That decision and ensuing discipleship are nothing less than *the will* of the heavenly *Father* (50). And the chapter that has had so much darkness in it ends on this note of light in relationship with Jesus and obedience to God. It makes a great deal of difference how people decide.

---

[10] Acts 1:13–14.   [11] 1 Cor. 15:7.

13:1–58
9. The third discourse:
the parables of the kingdom

Chapter 13 brings the first half of Matthew's Gospel to an end. The person of Jesus has been brought very clearly before us, together with a variety of responses to him. And those responses have been sharpening in intensity. At the end of this section on accepting or rejecting him (11:2 – 12:49), Matthew brings together seven parables to form the third great teaching block of the Gospel. They reinforce the need to decide about Jesus, which is, of course, the burden of the previous two chapters. Fittingly, this, the middle teaching block of the five contained in the Gospel, is all about response to Jesus, and skilfully brings to an end this whole section about commitment which began in chapter 11.

Matthew has clearly grouped these parables together in one remarkable chapter. We shall need to examine them with some care, but Jesus' very use of parables prompts three initial questions.

1. *What is a parable?*[1] It is the comparison of two subjects for the purpose of teaching. It proceeds from the known to the unknown. It is an everyday story with a spiritual meaning. It is not an allegory, as if every detail in the story had deep spiritual significance. There is generally (but not universally) one salient point. It is, as the

---

[1] The parables have given rise to an enormous volume of literature throughout the history of the church. For centuries they were taken as allegories, with a hidden meaning for every detail. In reaction to the exegetical indiscipline this produced, Adolf Jülicher, C. H. Dodd, Joachim Jeremias and others in the last hundred years or so have argued that parables normally make only one point, though I agree with Blomberg that this is unnecessarily restrictive: 'But all elements viewed as symbolic must be given interpretations that could have come readily to the mind of a first-century Galilean, Jewish peasant audience. If there is doubt about whether a certain detail in a parable is significant, interpreters should err on the side of caution and not read in meaning that may not be present' (p. 212). His book *Interpreting the Parables* (IVP, 1990) and David Wenham's *The Parables of Jesus* (Hodder and Stoughton, 1989), are among the most readable recent books on the parables. Some of the most helpful recent criticism draws attention to the multivalence of meaning in these parables and the importance of the reader's own situation in understanding and applying them. See Hagner, 1, pp. 364–365.

Hebrews put it, a *mashal*, 'a riddle'. The Greek word gives another nuance: it is a *parabolē*, a comparison (literally 'a throwing together' – maybe for similarity, maybe for contrast, maybe for sheer surprise). The parable form is flexible. It can mean anything from a riddle like 'Out of the eater, something to eat; out of the strong, something sweet'[2] to an advanced comparison such as the parable of the sower. Such a teaching method has enormous advantages: storytellers are popular all over the world, and Jesus was the world's greatest master of the short story. It holds the attention, enables people to see themselves, and, while dealing with the well known, it always introduces that extra, subtle twist that fascinates and makes the hearer reflect. It is a brilliant instrument in skilled hands.

2. *Why did Jesus teach in parables?* That question was asked – and answered – in 13:10–17, 34–35. There are at least three good reasons. First, look at verse 1. The move from the synagogue to the seashore is significant. As the leaders of establishment religion turn increasingly against him, we find Jesus moving more and more out into the open air, where the common people hear him gladly. So the teaching in parables comes after widespread rejection of his message and his person by the rulers.[3] Its use enables him to continue to hold and intrigue the hearers at a time of great opposition. It enables him to fascinate without alienating. No doubt he had spoken in parables before, but now, against a background of sharpened claims and consequent polarization, the parables form an ideal vehicle for his continued ministry.

Secondly, Jesus valued parables because they were an instrument of revelation (35), but only for those to whom it is given to see (11, 16–17). The parable revealed truth to those who were hungry, and concealed it from those who were too lazy to look for it, or too blinded by hatred and prejudice to discern it. The law of atrophy is at work. '*Whoever has will be given more, and he will have an abundance. Whoever does not have, even what he has will be taken away from him*' (12). It may seem unfair, but that is life. If you do not use your muscles you eventually lose the use of them. If you do use them, they increase in size and strength. It is the same at the spiritual level. The parables bring light for those who look for it, and for those who do not the darkness intensifies. Matthew contrasts the crowds, for whom everything happens 'in riddles', and the disciples, who see and understand the mystery of the kingdom (16–17). This may well point respectively to the 'crowds' of ordinary churchgoers

[2] Judg. 4:14.
[3] But this should not be taken to extremes, and does not justify the dispensationalist claim that Matt. 13 was the turning-point of Jesus' ministry, when he withdrew his offer of the kingdom from Israel. Positive and negative responses to Jesus continue throughout the Gospel.

(who, by the time Matthew wrote, were growing in numbers if not in understanding), and to the leaders, the inner circle, who really need to know the revelation of God so that they may communicate it effectively to their congregations.

The third reason Jesus taught in parables was that they were a spur towards decision. The kingdom cannot be understood from outside. In the parables there is no direct relation between the analogy and the thing signified. This holds good for the parables just as it does for the sacraments. Both share in the hiddenness of Jesus. No human eye could pierce his incognito. There was a givenness of revelation when a person understood who Jesus was. As he would say to Simon Peter, 'Blessed are you ... for this was not revealed to you by man, but by my Father in heaven' (16:17). To be a historical contemporary of Jesus did you no good without the eye of faith. Likewise, hearing the parable gave you no insight without that 'click' which enables you to cry, 'I see!' And that is *given* to those who are ready to receive it. Otherwise, '*Though seeing, they do not see; though hearing, they do not hear or understand ... for this people's heart has become calloused. Otherwise they might see ... hear ... understand ... and turn, and I would heal them*' (13–15). The *Otherwise* does not mean that Jesus does not want people to turn to him and be healed. It is the cry of frustrated love and longing on his part. He quotes, with heavy irony, the condemnation Isaiah had issued to the people of his day.[4] The parable was meant to challenge people to think again. It was meant to be a mirror in which they could see what they really looked like. It was intended to draw the hearers to decision, and to give them room to do so – precisely like the incarnation itself. T. F. Torrance has some wise words of explanation: 'Jesus deliberately concealed the Word in parable, lest men against their will should be forced to acknowledge the Kingdom, and yet he allowed them enough light to convict and convince them.'[5] Or as Professor C. F. D. Moule once put it to me, 'You can't teach by spoon-feeding. You must let people puzzle it out for themselves.' That is part of why Jesus taught in parables.

3. *Why does Matthew group them together here?* He groups them, as so much else in this Gospel, for the purposes of clarity and simplicity. Seven[6] parables are brought before us. Three of them are particularly significant to him, and he gives us Jesus' interpretations of them. He gathers them here as a powerful pictorial climax to the

---

[4] Is. 6:9–10.

[5] 'A study in New Testament communication', *Scottish Journal of Theology* 3 (1950), pp. 304–305.

[6] Eight, if we follow David Wenham in seeing v. 52 as a short concluding parable. He sees them skilfully arranged in a chiastic order. 'The structure of Matthew xiii', *New Testament Studies* 25 (1979), pp. 517ff.

first half of his Gospel. Chapter 13 is the hinge on which the whole Gospel turns. At the end of this chapter we read: *'only in his home town . . . is a prophet without honour'* (57), and Jesus sets forth from Galilee towards Jerusalem and his death. And so there is something powerful and evocative at the end of the first half of the book, something that summarizes both the self-disclosure and the opposition we have met hitherto, and that echoes the great themes of who Jesus is, what he can do, and the need to respond to him. The parables are Christocentric. They point in all their hiddenness and revelation to the Jesus who both reveals and conceals. As people hear them, they are made to see where they stand in relation to the kingdom that he brings in.

How is it that this same message of the kingdom so polarized people? As Christians pondered this, they came to see that the kingdom itself, like the Jesus to whom it pointed, is a great mystery. The response to that mystery is what separates the crowds from the disciples – a division made very plain in verse 36. And the Christian scribes, men like Matthew himself who were in leadership in the church, needed to understand that mystery if they were to minister effectively. They had to teach with insight and with faith, not like the teachers of the law who often taught with literalistic pedantry and perhaps even in unbelief. Running through these central chapters, there may well be a fear lest the Christian scribes, who brought out of their storeroom treasures new and old (52), should relapse into the woodenness and coldness of some of their Jewish counterparts.

This collection of parables, then, provides a fitting end to the first half of the Gospel, and each one of these seven parables faces the reader in one way or another with the question, 'What will you do with Jesus?'

But of course it would be boring if this was simply repeated time and again. While therefore it is true that each parable is challenging, and that at the centre of that challenge is Jesus himself, each one has a particular nuance which may well be an answer to one or other of the pressing questions and needs of the early church. I may well have discerned that nuance wrongly, but I offer it here for what it is worth.

The parable of the soils (13:1–9, 18–23): what is your response now?

The first of the parables is the most significant of all.[7] It is not just 'a

---

[7] It has been fashionable to dismiss the interpretation of the parable given in vv. 18–23 as a construction of the early church. This is decisively rejected by B. Gerhardsson, *New Testament Studies* 14 (1997–8), pp. 165–193; and by P. B. Payne, 'The authenticity of the parable of the sower and its interpretation', in R. T. France and D. Wenham (eds.), *Gospel Perspectives* 1, pp. 163–207 (JSOT Press, 1980).

farmer' who went out to sow his field. It is (literally) '*the* farmer', and he comes bringing the precious seed which can transform the soil. The kingdom comes when the soil and the seed get together. It is a marriage of seed and soil. The seed is the word of God proclaimed by the Sower of God. And the kingdom begins to come in a life when the 'soil' receives the seed of the word for itself. Then it begins to germinate and shoot.

So those who hear with faith ask themselves a series of questions as the story progresses. 'Has the word bounced off me, like seed off the hard track that traverses the field? Has it begun to grow in me, so that I could face pressure, laughter from business associates, expulsion from kosher circles? And our children are growing up now. We must not be so ascetic; it's not fair on the kids. We must be a bit more like everyone else, with the cares, the riches and the pleasures of life! Or am I just a very ordinary church member, but in my small corner producing some fruit, albeit only thirtyfold? Maybe God has given me a rather wider ministry and I can see growth sixtyfold? Maybe he has put me in responsible leadership; does he see hundredfold growth in me?'

Those were the sorts of questions the original hearers and readers of the parables would have been asking themselves.[8] The Sower is the same. The seed is the same. The different results depend on the soils, how we respond to the Sower and his seed. What fruit we produce will depend entirely on that. In this first parable we have a reflection of what was happening in the mission of Jesus, and the varied responses to which it drove the hearers. The parable is a mirror: it shows people where they stand. It is held up to the faces of Jesus' hearers. It was held up to Matthew's readers. And it is no less challenging today.

The parable of the weeds in the wheat (13:24–30, 36–43): why does evil persist?

If the first of these parables of growth was intended primarily to press the questions 'What is your response now? Where do you stand?', this second parable wrestles with the problem of why evil is so persistent in a world that is supposed to be the kingdom of God. It has normally been explained as applying to the church, in which true and false believers coexist until the final judgment. But this will not do, for two reasons. For one thing, the problem of nominal Christianity did not yet exist, and for another we are explicitly told

---

[8] It is interesting that modern 'reader-response' interpretation of the parables proceeds in much the same way.

that *The field is the world* (38). David Wenham[9] is surely right in seeing that the field rightfully belongs to the Sower (24) who sows in it *sons of the kingdom* (38). But the evil one encroaches on it, and *the sons of the evil one* (38) have to be weeded out of the kingdom in due course (41). Yes. The world belongs properly to God as king,[10] and the kingdom movement that Jesus is initiating is the restoration of that rule.

Four things are said about those who belong to the kingdom. They are the *seed* sown by the Sower (37). They owe their position in the revolutionary kingdom of God entirely to his initiative. Secondly, they have God as *their Father* (43). Membership of the kingdom means adoption into the very family of God. Thirdly, they are called *righteous* (43), not only right in relationship to God but righteous in behaviour among their fellows. Fourthly, they will one day *shine like the sun* (43). The glory of the Lord, so often presaged in the Old Testament,[11] will be reflected in and from them.

By way of contrast, *the sons of the evil one* are described in three ways. They are seed sown by *the devil* (39). Strong language, but it is a clear New Testament perspective.[12] The usurper prince of this world (4:8–9) has claimed their allegiance. They *do evil* (41), or, more literally, lawlessness. They are rebels against God's kingly rule. And their destiny is ultimately destruction (42). All this is very unacceptable to people today: we do not treat evil with great seriousness, and many do not even believe in a future life, a heaven and hell where the great separation will be finalized. But it is an undeniable part of the teaching of Jesus. Are we going to claim to know more about it than he?

In the excitement of the kingdom's invasion, it would have been all too easy to be impatient. Why does not society change? This parable speaks of the silent revolution. It speaks of the different origins and different lifestyles of members of the community. It speaks of their ultimate separation and the final vindication of God's purposes. There is a strong contrast between the present hiddenness of the church and its future vindication. Though now scarcely distinguishable from one another, one day, at the final judgment, the sons of the kingdom will shine like the sun in the kingdom of their Father.

[9] *The Parables of Jesus*, pp. 57ff.
[10] Notice how the kingdom is at one moment said to belong to the Father (41) and at the next to the Son of Man (43). It reinforces the claims that have been made throughout the previous two chapters.
[11] E.g. Is. 40:5.   [12] See John 8:44; 2 Cor. 4:3–4.

The parable of the mustard seed (13:31–32): why is the kingdom so insignificant?

In comparison with the massive edifice of pagan religion, and the age-old splendour of Judaism, the infant Christian church must have felt very small and insignificant: the semiliterate first disciples of Jesus must have felt even more so. Why is the kingdom so insignificant, if Jesus really is the King? His answer is that it is like a mustard seed, as tiny as the end of a pin. But when it grows, it becomes *the largest of garden plants* – a sizeable bush about 4 metres tall. Compared with the microscopic seed from which it sprang, that is phenomenal growth. Moreover, the birds of the air come and roost in its branches. The image of the birds coming to roost would have been eloquent – if rather ominous – to those reared on the Old Testament. They found it in Ezekiel 17:23 and Daniel 4:12, 20–22. It is the Gentiles who are in mind. Jesus is hinting not only that this apparently tiny seed will grow to a remarkable size, but that it will spread beyond the narrow confines of Judaism and provide a home for the Gentiles. It may look insignificant. At present it is. But it will not stay that way. Judaism itself had been insignificant. It sprang from one man. But it grew into a multitude that nobody could number, as numerous as the stars of the Milky Way. Nor should we forget that great things can sometimes be achieved by just a tiny cell of believers. Think of what the Clapham Sect did in England in the eighteenth century. Think of the influence the microscopic church in Japan is exercising today in reform and social justice. Significance cannot be measured in terms of numbers.

The parable of the yeast (13:33): why is the kingdom so hidden?

Ah, yes, it may be hidden. But so is yeast when you put it in your dough. Hidden it is, but it will permeate the whole loaf. So with the kingdom. Obscure and hidden, it will pervade society and permeate the whole world. It is remarkable how Jesus takes for his parables things that every Jewish peasant would regularly see: a farmer at work, a field where weeds battled with corn, a fishing-net, a mustard bush. But none is more ordinary and domestic than this parable of the leaven. Just a little bit of fermented dough, and it transforms the whole.

Leaven had a bad press in Judaism. All leaven had to be scrupulously removed from the house before Passover. So the hearers would be surprised to find Jesus using leaven as an image of the kingdom. Yet, on second thoughts, that is just what his followers must have seemed to respectable Jews. Common, uneducated fishermen and farmers, carpenters and women, tax collectors and disreputable characters – it would all seem rather distasteful. But God is like that. He takes distasteful characters and transforms them, and then transforms society through them. Despite its appalling failures and sins, it is beyond question that down the ages the church has had an amazing record in medical care, social work, education, liberation of women and slaves, and the defence of prisoners, the aged, the helpless, and those whom society neglects. The first institution for the blind was founded by Thalasius, a Christian monk. The first free dispensary was founded by Apollonius, a Christian merchant. The first hospital was founded by Fabiola, a Christian woman. Hidden and obscure the kingdom may be, but it has had and continues to have an undeniable effect upon society. It is yeast in the flour.

What an encouragement these parables must have been to Matthew's despised and struggling churches! They address with enormous confidence three questions that pressed upon them. Why is the response to the gospel so mixed? Why does evil prevail? Why is the kingdom of Jesus so insignificant and hidden? The Lord reigns!

At this point we bid farewell to the crowds (34). The remaining parables in this chapter are addressed to the disciples. Matthew knows that in teaching through the medium of parables, as in so much else, Jesus is fulfilling hints given long ago in the Old Testament, and the point is made formally through one of his celebrated formula quotations (35).[13] The crowds have plenty to think about. Since the coming of Jesus the field is not empty. The tree is growing. The dough is rising, even though its effect is at present small and hidden. How will they choose? For him or against him?

The treasure and the pearl (13:44–45): how do people find the kingdom?

These two little gems of parables go together. Both stress the incalculable value of the kingdom: it is worth any sacrifice. Both stress the cost of gaining it: it will cost all we have.

The treasure is found by a poor man. He came across it by accident. There he was, engaged in his daily toil, expecting little, rather bored as he ploughed the field. And then, suddenly, his ploughshare hit a box. He dug it up, opened it, and precious jewels cascaded from it! He was thrilled to bits, and quickly hid it again until he could go and buy the field. Ethically dubious? Not by Jewish law. 'If a man finds scattered money, it belongs to the finder,'

---

[13] From Ps. 78:2. The message and mission of Jesus were the outworking of God's plan of salvation from the beginning.

said the rabbis. The point of the parable is clear. Some people discover the worth of the kingdom by accident. They are ploughing the familiar furrow of life when suddenly, against all expectation, they find treasure. What a marvellous picture of discovering Jesus! He is worth any sacrifice to secure.

The pearl *of great value* is found by a rich man. He came across it after a long and patient search. A pearl fancier by profession, he knew perfection when he saw it. And he never had seen it until he discovered this pearl. A most illuminating picture of the kingdom and the King. There are other pearls in the market. There are other things of great value. But none is to compare with the pearl of great value. That is how some people find the kingdom of God. They try many faiths, many ideologies, and they gain much from them. But one day they find the loveliest thing in all the world (which was how the ancients rated a really fine pearl), and they give all to gain it. One thinks of Justin in the early second century, a brilliant professor who had tried all the philosophical schools and remained unsatisfied. One day he met a little old man in the fields who told him about Jesus. He immediately started reading the Scriptures to see if this was so. He was convinced, and he became a joyful Christian, even though later on it led to his martyrdom. After a long search, he had found the pearl of great value.

So the message of these twin parables is clear. People find the kingdom in many ways. Some come upon it by accident, some after a long and patient search. But it is immensely worthwhile, however we come on it. It is treasure. It is a beautiful pearl. It is worth any sacrifice. Do the disciples of Matthew's day realize this? Do they teach it?

The net (13:47–52): what will be your response then?

A dynamic parable brings this memorable series to a conclusion. If the first one had challenged the hearers to reflect on what their response to Jesus was now, this one challenged them about their perseverance until the last day. Where will they stand then? For this parable is all about judgment, about separation. There is no trace in Matthew of any doctrine that we can have instant salvation apart from constant perseverance. We must be righteous in order to live with the Righteous One. There are no short cuts. Within the church we shall always find good and bad, real and unreal. And although we have been told in the parable of the weeds not to expect a pure world or church on earth and not to make our judgment now, the day will come when God will make his final separation. It is not yet. It will be when the net of the kingdom is drawn to the shore. And it will be God who does the sorting then, not people now. Let the Christian 'teachers of the law' in Matthew's church remember that. It is not for them now to determine who are 'the real Christians' in the mixed church in which they inevitably live and work. That task belongs to God in the future.

It may well be that Judas is in the back of Matthew's mind here. His defection caused an enormous trauma in the early church. That someone who was so close to Jesus could so terribly betray him was almost unthinkable. 'If you think you are standing firm,' Paul was to say soon afterwards, 'be careful that you don't fall!'[14] The case of Judas was the standing warning against presumption. At the end, when the Lord calls for me, what will be my response then? That is the question. And the series of parables which began with rejection of the word by human souls ends with the rejection of human souls by God.

'*Have you understood all these things*?' asks Jesus at the end of this series of parables (51). Do you understand – or are you at one with the crowds? How vital it is for leaders to know what they believe, and to understand the mysteries of the kingdom if they are going to instruct others and further the kingdom's cause! The leaders in Matthew's church were like scribes who drew from the *storeroom* of their Christian and pre-Christian knowledge *new treasures* and *old* (52). Christ does not come to erase all that we gained in life before we met him. He comes to enrich it. And this description of a teacher of the law who has become a Christian leader is perhaps the best picture we could have of the man who actually penned this Gospel. He shows all the characteristics of a Christian scribe, very Jewish, but very un-Jewish too. The new and the old blend marvellously in this wonderful book. And what Jesus did for its author he can do for anyone. A rabbi is one who 'will seek out the hidden meanings of proverbs and be at home with the obscurities of parables'.[15] So should Matthew's leaders be, as they seek to hold together the old *torah* and the new.[16] But such teachers are no independent originators of truth. They remain disciples, learners to the end.

Rejection in Galilee (13:53–58)

The concluding narrative unit, or 'pericope', of this chapter is very significant. *When Jesus had finished these parables* (53) he went to his own *patris*, his own country. This word is deliberately ambivalent. For at one level Matthew means Nazareth, and he is

---

[14] Cor. 10:12.   [15] Sirach 39:3.

[16] The faithful teacher is one who can juxtapose the old (i.e. the *torah*) and the new (i.e. the kingdom teaching). This is the key to understanding not only the parables but also Christianity. See Hagner, 1, p. 402.

writing of the rejection of Jesus in his own *home town* (57) where he was a boy (always the hardest place to witness; everyone knows you and your family!).[17] At a much deeper level his *patris* is Judaism. As John put it, 'He came to that which was his own, but his own did not receive him.'[18] But at an intermediate level Galilee is meant.

Up to this point Matthew has been giving an account of Jesus' ministry in Galilee, his own country. And the conclusion of it is that Galilee has rejected him. Not completely. And he will not immediately leave it. But an unmistakable indicator is raised that his days in Galilee are numbered, and from now on his direction is towards Jerusalem and his death. There is a powerful parallelism here, too. The first part of the Gospel ends with this note of rejection in Galilee. The second part of the Gospel brings us to his crucifixion in Jerusalem. The lesser prepares the reader for the greater. But there is an overtone here which it is important not to miss. The implication of a prophet not being recognized in his home area is that he *is* recognized outside it. And that of course took place. The hint of Gentile expansion at the end of the first half of the book is made explicit with the Great Commission to the Gentile mission at the end of the second half. The proximate rejection of Jesus in his *patris* leads forward to his ultimate recognition universally throughout the world. The balance of the book is complete.

---

[17] Familiarity bred contempt. Jesus and his family were well known in Nazareth, so its people found it almost impossible to evaluate him in terms of his message and his deeds. They failed to see who he was because of their preconceptions.

[18] John 1:11.

Part 2

To Jerusalem
(Matthew 14 – 28)

D. SHADOWS (14 – 18)

14:1 – 17:27
10. Shadows of the future

Elizabeth and Ian Billingham, in their breakdown of the pattern of the Gospel, make much of chapter 13 as the linchpin on which the whole movement of the Gospel turns. It is the hinge of the book. Part 1 is complete. We move now into Part 2. And that has three panels, just as the first half had. The middle panel on judgment is the centerpiece, just as, in effect, it had been in Part 1, where the central theme had been discipleship. It takes that theme further and gives it added shape. And just as in Part 1 we had beginnings, pointing forward to the main theme of discipleship, so here in Part 2 we have shadows, pointing forward to the central feature of judgment.

Now it must be confessed that nobody seems to have made a wholly satisfactory analysis of chapters 14 – 17, so when the Billinghams say it is a foreshadowing of the future, we may be mildly sceptical. However, with some emendations the pattern is as good as any other that has been suggested, so tentatively I shall stick with it.

Clearly, what complicates the issue is that Matthew is following the central part of Mark here, and his own tidy structure is much less in evidence because of that. Mark 6:1 – 9:32 reappears here with only slight modification. So the whole of this panel follows Mark, right up to the fourth great discourse, on the church, in chapter 18. We shall examine it in four sections.

The future of the story (14:1–12)

The death of John the Baptist opens this section. It is of the utmost importance. It is parallel to the death of the innocents at the start of Part 1 of the Gospel. It looks forward to the death of Jesus at the end of Part 2. The start of Jesus' ministry had been linked with John's. And now John's death points to the way the story of Jesus is going to end, with his passion. It may even be a premonition of the death by martyrdom that awaited so many of the followers of Jesus in the first century and ever since.

What courage John had in the face of the capricious tyrant, Herod! He dared to impugn Herod's marital life. Nobody likes to hear such criticism. And if the object of it happens to be an oriental despot with a difficult wife and a guilty conscience, then the outcome is predictable. John was executed, but little good did it do Herod. Indeed, he got nothing but ill from the divorce of his wife and subsequent marriage to Herodias. Aretas, king of the Nabatean Arabs, inflicted a great defeat on Herod, enraged as he was by Herod's rejection of his daughter for the sake of Herodias.[1] People, so Josephus tells us, regarded this defeat as divine retribution for his murder of John the Baptist. A little later Herod went to Rome at Herodias' instigation to seek the title of 'king'. Instead of gaining it, he lost both fortune and realm and was sent in exile to Gaul. The sins of Herod emphatically came home to roost.

John the Baptist holds the centre stage in this story, and it is not only his courage but his faith that is hinted at. No more doubts and fears! He is clear where he stands. He faces Herod unafraid. And fittingly his disciples first bury the body and then come and tell Jesus. Maybe that spoke volumes to sad Christians in Matthew's day who were enduring hardship and persecution.

The future of the Jewish church (14:13 – 15:20)

The death of John is the frontispiece to Part 2. It is a flashback to the beginning of the story, and a premonition of its end. It prepares us for a major theme in this second half of the Gospel: the suffering and death of Jesus. But now we come to what we might see as the future of the Jewish church. No more than a glimpse, of course, but there seems to be a futuristic tinge to the three incidents recorded here, set as they are within Jewish country, just as the next trio are set in a pagan context and point to the future of the Gentile church.

First comes the feeding of the five thousand (14:13–21). This is perhaps the most famous of all Jesus' miracles, and is the only one recorded in all four Gospels. It was seen to be typical of the mighty power of Jesus just as the parable of the sower was typical of his wonderful teaching. Jesus is the one who comes to make the messianic feast. He takes the resources, pitifully inadequate, provided by his disciples. He multiplies them over and over again, and there is more left over at the end than there was at the beginning. Such is the power of the Messiah. And that is good news.

The Jews believed that the messianic age would see the return of

---

[1] For an exhaustive study of Herod Antipas, and the details of this terrible incident, see H. W. Haehner, *Herod Antipas* (Cambridge University Press, 1972). Antipas governed Galilee from 4 BC to AD 39.

the bread from heaven, God's gift of manna to their ancestors in the wilderness. Food in the desert was a highly allusive strain in biblical revelation. Moses had fed the Israelites with manna in the desert. Elijah had been nourished by the ravens in the desert. Elisha had fed a hundred men on twenty loaves in the desert.[2] Bread in the desert was very significant to Israel. It is hardly surprising therefore to find in 2 *Baruch* 29:8, which dates from around the same time as Matthew's Gospel, the expectation that food in the desert would characterize the days of the Messiah. 'It shall come to pass at that time that the treasury of manna shall again descend from on high, and they will eat of it in those years, because these are they who have come to the consummation of the ages.' Such was the expectation in many Jewish circles in the first century AD, and Jesus fulfilled it.

By feeding the multitude in this desert place, Jesus is making a statement and a claim. He is making a statement about who he is and what he has come to do. He is indeed the Messiah, and he has come to usher in the days of salvation. He has every right, therefore, to their allegiance. The King is coming to and for his kingdom. No wonder that in John 6:15 we read that the multitude wanted to take him by force and make him king.

But the feeding of the multitude does not only look back to Jewish expectations and fulfil them. It looks forward in anticipation of the eschatological banquet that Jesus would institute for his messianic community. Matthew's church, and the church ever since that day, cannot read this story without being reminded of the Lord's Supper. The very terms of eucharistic liturgy have been influenced by the language of this passage. The holy communion nourished the members of the messianic 'synagogue' in which the author of this Gospel worked. Several feedings of penurious people are recorded in the Gospels: the feedings of the five thousand and of the four thousand, the Emmaus meal, the meal with the disciples in Jerusalem after the resurrection and the meal on the seashore by the lake.[3] They all stem from and reflect the institution of the Last Supper which looks both back to the Passover and to all the feedings of God's people throughout history in the desert, and forward to the messianic banquet which it anticipates. John is therefore in line with early understanding of the meaning of this miracle when he connects the feeding of the five thousand with the eucharistic discourse on the bread from heaven in chapter 6 of his Gospel. It is one of the great ways in which the people of God are nourished in the wilderness of their existence, and given hope of the future fulfilment of the kingdom.

[2] Exod. 16; 1 Kgs. 17:1–5; 2 Kgs 4:42–44.
[3] Matt. 14:15–21 = Mark 6:35–44 = Luke 9:12–17 = John 6:5–13; Matt. 15:32–38 = Mark 8:1–9; Luke 24:30–31, 41–43; John 21:4–14.

Next comes the walking on the water (14:22–32). This is fascinating both in what it says and in the undertones it suggests. Jesus has gone away to pray after the feeding is over; that indicates what it had taken out of him, and maybe even the temptation that he felt in the desire of the crowds to declare him king.[4] At all events, the disciples were left to row alone across the lake, and one of its notorious squalls blew up. They were terrified. It had happened once before (8:23–27), but this time Jesus is not with them. The undertones for the Matthean church are clear enough. But all is well, says Matthew, despite the storms: Jesus is praying for them (14:23). Jesus will come to them. Jesus will enable the trusting disciple to do the impossible, and walk on the water to go towards him (29). But they have to trust the Son of God (31, 33), who alone controls the storms of life and enables his followers to counteract the forces of gravity that would otherwise overwhelm them.

We have already seen Jesus stilling the storm. The new development here is that Jesus comes to them *in* the storm. Jesus walks *on* the storm. Jesus invites the trusting disciple to share that victory parade with him. And when Peter gets out of the boat to go to Jesus, he finds it works. He can walk on the storms of life. And then he wonders what he is doing. He takes his eyes off Jesus. He looks at the wind and the waves. And he begins to get engulfed. But then Peter, the prince of the apostles, shows the way of overcoming failure for others to follow. *Beginning to sink*, he *cried out, 'Lord, save me!'* (30). He did not wait until he was drowning. As soon as he felt himself sinking he called out to the Lord. And at once Jesus reached out his hand to him and caught him, saying, *'You of little faith . . . why did you doubt?'* (31).

It is not possible to question the value of this story to the Christian community for which Matthew wrote. It was a pattern both of unbelief and of faith. They were called to go to Jesus, to direct their lives to the walk of faith. But storms often beset them, and fear chilled them. In his power they could for a while do what would otherwise have been impossible – until they considered what they were doing and reflected on the size of the waves. Then, of course, they would begin to sink -- until they cried out to the Son of God for his powerful hand to catch them and hold them up. That is what the story would have been used for, and still is. So those who were struggling to build a church of largely Jewish believers in the northern part of Palestine in the 70s could take enormous encouragement from these two stories. The Jesus they worshipped both fed them in the eucharist and preserved them in the storms of life. Their part was to trust. His part was – and is – to save. No

---

[4] See John 6:14–15.

wonder the disciples acclaim him afresh as *Son of God* (33) in the light of both the feeding and the stilling of the storm.

This is picked up at the end of chapter 14. When the people recognized who he was (33), they longed for their *sick* friends just to *touch the edge of his cloak* (36). And as many as touched *were healed*. Those who merely touched a crust of bread during the feeding were filled.[5] Peter, who simply touched the outstretched hand of Jesus on the water, was held up. Faith is touch. It is making contact.

The third strand in this glance ahead to the future of the Jewish church comes in 15:1–20. It concerns the worship God wants. The setting is controversial. The Pharisees come to Jesus with their perennial query: '*Why do your disciples break the tradition of the elders? They don't wash their hands before they eat!*' (15:1). In the way Jesus responds to them, two main things emerge, both highly significant not only for Jesus' controversy with the Pharisees of his day, but also for Matthew's controversy with the Pharisees of his.

The first point Jesus makes is this: God's word, not human tradition, is the basis for authentic worship. The Pharisees had many ritual laws, among them the ceremonial washing of hands before meals. E. P. Sanders[6] doubts whether it was expected of lay people like the disciples to follow these Pharisaic ceremonial rules for handwashing. However, Jesus was seen as a rabbi, and his followers would have been under his tutelage. In any case, Sanders fails to explain why Judaism after AD 70, derived as it was, on the whole, from Pharisaism, has a whole tractate on hands and the various rules for washing them.[7]

The main point of controversy was this. The Pharisees had developed a whole 'fence' of traditions and additions to protect the law. They regarded their modifications, 'the tradition of the elders' or 'the oral law', as of equal value to the Torah, since they claimed that both the written and the oral law derived from Moses on Mount Sinai.

Jesus does not reply directly to their complaint. In typical rabbinic style he comes up with a counter-question: '*And why do you break the command of God for the sake of your tradition?*' (3). He is challenging the validity of the oral law. And he gives a powerful example. The fifth commandment, to honour parents, was originally backed up by the death penalty. Yet the Pharisaic *korban* laws overrode it! Here was a straight case of human traditions clashing with the law

---

[5] Matthew here highlights the very positive response to Jesus by large numbers of Jews, in contrast to the opposition he has recounted earlier.

[6] *Jesus and Judaism* (Fortress, 1985), p. 265.

[7] Mishnah tractate *Yadaim*. It has extremely detailed regulations for how much of the hand is to be washed, when, and with water from what part of the jug.

of God. '*You nullify the word of God for the sake of your tradition*' (6). This was no idle charge. The *korban* practice meant vowing property and finance to the temple[8] – a vow so sacred that it could not be revoked, even in order to care for your parents in their old age. But it was agreed that you could continue to use *korban* money during your lifetime! There is a whole tractate on *korban* practice in the Mishnah, *Nedarim*, much of which is taken up with informing worshippers which vows they need not keep. This was a pious fraud which invalidated the will of God as expressed in the fifth commandment. Jesus is very blunt. He calls it hypocrisy (7).

It is this totally different attitude to worship that separates the Pharisees from Jesus. Both believed in the prior grace of God. But the Pharisee response to this was a passion for detailed precision in worship. For Jesus it meant loving obedience, resulting in an intimate relationship with God, whom he called Abba, 'dear daddy'. For the Pharisees it was possible to honour God if the services were properly rendered. For Jesus it was impossible unless people's hearts were turned to God (8–9). Let us not persuade ourselves that this attitude to worship, which characterized the Pharisees, died in the first century. It is alive and well in many a parish church and chapel. We do well, as William Barclay reminds his readers, to take to heart Archbishop William Temple's description of worship, and seek to live by it: 'To worship is to quicken the conscience by the holiness of God, to feed the mind with the truth of God, to purge the imagination by the beauty of God, to open the heart to the love of God, and to devote the will to the purpose of God.'[9]

The second point Jesus made in this passage is that inner purity, not external ceremony, is what matters. The Pharisees, with their emphasis on ablutions, held the view that what entered into them could defile them (10–11). They had good reason for their view. It was not only substantially representing the scribal tradition, but it was heavily dependent on the purity laws in the book of Leviticus.[10] This saying, as Mark perceived in his Gospel's account of the incident,[11] had the effect of doing away with the ceremonial law and rendering all meats 'clean'. This was revolutionary.[12] No wonder the Pharisees were livid. Jesus quite firmly and deliberately sets himself up against the Old Testament ceremonial law. God had given those commandments to his desert people for health reasons as well as for religious ones. They had been kept with passionate zeal, while the great imperatives that the prophets were always calling for – justice, mercy, love for God and so on[13] – were deemed secondary and even

---

[8] Num. 30:2.   [9] Quoted in Barclay, 2, p. 117.
[10] E.g. Lev. 7:22–27; 11; 17.   [11] Mark 7:19.
[12] Even if its implications were not clearly understood until after Acts 10.
[13] E.g. Mic. 6:8.

optional. Judaism had almost become a religion of 'works' designed to win the approval of God. And Jesus says, 'Never!'

Judaism had not started out that way. It was a religion of sheer unmerited grace from God to Abraham. It flowed with love and trust and obedience. The commandments, which had been given as kerbstones along the path of that loving obedience, had in much later Judaism been taken to be the path itself. And that is an attitude Jesus powerfully repudiates. 'Works' are a beggar's refuge. For one thing, we could never keep every letter of the law day and night all our lives, and so we could never earn the coveted reward. Secondly, even if we could, the whole principle is sub-personal. One could do it all without a living relationship with God. And thirdly, just think how abominably arrogant we would become. 'Alone I did it!' To follow that path is blindness. In this sense the Pharisees are blind guides. They do not represent the plant of faith that God planted, and *every plant he has not planted will be pulled up by the roots* (13).[14] As Jesus went on to explain to Peter, defilement is far deeper than Pharisaism ever understood. It does not consist merely in external things. Unclean foods could not defile people. They go into the stomach and pass out the other end. What defiles people is the stuff that comes from within: *evil thoughts, murder, adultery, sexual immorality, theft, false testimony, slander* (19). These are what defile people; but *eating with unwashed hands* does not defile people (20). The human heart is 'deceitful above all things and beyond cure'.[15] No palliatives will heal it.

Those two characteristics are what God is looking for in his worshippers. His word is not to be emasculated by human rules. And inner purity, not external rectitude, is what delights the heart of God. Jesus had declared war on Pharisaism. This evaluation of true religion by Jesus sounded the death-knell first of Pharisaism, then of Jewish Christianity in so far as it clung to Pharisee tenets, and finally of all types of legalism to be found in Gentile churches where love for God is absent and dead ceremonialism present.

Each in its own way, all three of these pericopae have given an insight not only into Jesus and his times but also into the future of the Jewish church.

---

[14] This deeply polemical saying marked the parting of the ways with Judaism that was happening in Matthew's churches. Jesus had now explicitly contravened three of the four main badges of identity of a first-century Jew: temple, circumcision, dietary laws and Sabbath-keeping (12:6, 8; 15:10–11). By implication the place Judaism enjoyed is to be given to a new people (21:41, 43).

[15] Jer. 17:9.

The future of the Gentile church (15:21 – 16:12)

Here again we have three pericopae. The first is about the healing of a Gentile girl (15:21–28). Jesus had gone north to Gentile territory, Phoenicia, beyond the extremities of Palestine. He had gone to get some peace and quiet, hard to come by at home. The crowds were always round him, and now the Pharisees seemed to be dogging his every step. He needed to get away. Moreover, before long he would have to face the cross, and that demanded time for personal reflection and seclusion, and for the opportunity to prepare his disciples for what it would mean to him and to them. He has already withdrawn from Israel ideologically. Now he does so geographically.

A local woman came to ask his help. She was a Gentile, and her discussion with him fits marvellously as a sequel to the incident we have just been thinking of. For defilement is the issue in both stories. In the first, Jesus and his disciples are thought to be defiled because they do not keep the Jewish food or handwashing laws. In the second, they are thought to be defiled by speaking to a Gentile woman.

The purpose of the story is obvious. It points to the outreach of the gospel beyond Judaism. It is another of those hints we have already met in the Gospel, of the Gentile mission which would soon prove so widespread and so successful. It is a half-way house between 10:5 and 28:19: 'Do not go among the Gentiles' and 'Go and make disciples of all nations' (or 'Gentiles').[16]

Here we see Jesus struggling with his calling. The woman comes to him with a severe problem, and with words of amazing faith (words, indeed, of Christian confession) on her lips: *'Lord, Son of David, have mercy on me!'* (22).

He says nothing, as he wrestles with what to do. His disciples encourage him to send her away. And then Jesus gives his reply: *'I was sent only to the lost sheep of Israel'* (24). At least, that is one way of punctuating it. But punctuation was inferred, not written, in Greek manuscripts. So it may well have been a question, as Jesus mused half out loud: 'Was I sent only to the lost sheep of Israel?' I believe this was a soliloquy of Jesus. He had a clear limitation in his goals during the ministry: he was sent to Israel. But should he make an exception in the case of pressing need? It is one of the marks of greatness to allow compassion for people to overrule premeditated programmes.

And so he soliloquizes again: 'Is it fair to take the children's bread

[16] The Greek word is the same: *ta ethnē*.

and give it to the pups?' (26, my translation). And immediately, brilliantly, she picked up the half-derogatory, half-affectionate description (*kynaria* means 'puppies', thought of as waiting for scraps at table – of course, Jews thought of Gentiles as 'dogs'). And she came out with a riposte full of humour and faith. 'Yes, Lord, even the pups *eat the crumbs that fall from their masters' table*' (27). And of course Jesus did as she requested, and her daughter was made well – at a distance.

This story is full of subtle points. We see the greatness of Jesus. He has a clear objective for his ministry, and he regularly keeps to it. He is sent to rescue Israel. But on an occasion like this, when met with extravagant faith from a Gentile, is he to turn away – particularly after the Pharisees had just been arguing with him about washing hands? People matter more than things, and Jesus knew it. Consistency can be the vice of small minds.

The delayed response to the woman may even have a point. It could be hinting at the delay before the good news of the kingdom was spread in that northern tip of Palestine, and into the Phoenician seaboard, and up into Syria. Again, the wit and humour of this delightful woman are a joy to read. But the central thing in the story is the faith of a Gentile woman, who shows up many an Israelite – many a Pharisee for that matter – by her warm and wholehearted faith. Like the centurion in chapter 8, this Gentile woman exhibits the faith that God honours wherever he finds it.

Of course, in the background of the story, it is hard to forget the Gentile mission, and the perplexity Matthew's church leaders would inevitably be feeling in the 70s of the first century about the mysterious way in which the good news was snapped up much more enthusiastically by the Gentile 'pups' than by the Jewish 'children'. This passage helped them understand the success of the Gentile mission. Had not Jesus himself commended the faith of a pagan woman in these very parts beyond northern Palestine where we are probably right in supposing the Gospel to have been penned?

The second cameo of the future of the Gentile church consists in the feeding of a Gentile crowd: the feeding of the four thousand (29–39). Some think this is a duplicate account of the feeding of the five thousand. Such people think it was probably not miraculous anyway: Jesus simply managed to inspire people to bring out their packed lunches and share them. Such comment is jejune. This is not a duplicate of the five thousand. On that occasion the grass was green;[17] it was early spring. There is no such indication here: they sat on the hard ground (35). It was clearly after Jesus had undertaken a long and circuitous journey north. Moreover, much of the language

---

[17] Mark 6:39.

and detail is different in the two stories. But the most significant thing is that the five thousand were Jews and the four thousand were not. This is hinted at strongly in Matthew's account: *they praised the God of Israel*; but it is explicit in Mark's account,[18] which Matthew both followed and assumed throughout this section. The feeding of the four thousand took place, Mark tells us, in Decapolis, that is to say, a group of ten independently governed Greek cities in Transjordan. And the wonderful thing about this miracle is that Jesus is making available to non-Jews the same blessings as he had offered to Jews.[19]

It is as if Matthew is keen to gather together here a number of incidents in the life of Jesus which point forward to the primarily Gentile church that he knows and serves. A strongly Gentile flavour is present throughout. First the Jewish food laws are annulled. Then Jesus journeys up into Gentile country and heals a Gentile girl. Gentile crowds are taught and cared for, healed and shown the signs of the Messiah's presence as prophesied long ago in Isaiah 35, just as Jews had been earlier on. And now Gentiles are fed with the same heavenly bread that Jesus had made available to the Jewish 'children of the kingdom'. Once again, it is hard not to detect an allusion to the eucharist, the bread of heaven by which Matthew and his church were nourished. They will have seen the holy communion as a continuation of these miraculous feedings of tired and careworn followers which Jesus had generously provided during his ministry, and as a foretaste of the messianic banquet in heaven.

Why were the disciples so perplexed about what Jesus would do, when faced with this hungry throng in the wilderness? They had, after all, seen him feed five thousand people from a few bread rolls. Their obtuseness accords well enough with what we know of them at this time. But is it not very natural? Is it not like us? We see some marvellous display of the Lord's power, and yet we are full of doubts when we are thrown into another situation of need that casts us back on him. We simply do not expect him to act the second time! They were like that, it seems. And it may be that they did indeed remember the feeding of the five thousand, but they also remembered occasions when they were in real need and those needs remained unmet. And so their faith burned low, and expectancy shrank. Is it not so with us? Lack of trust often springs from forgetfulness of past blessing.

[18] Mark 8:1–9.

[19] It is fascinating and perhaps highly symbolic that whereas twelve basketfuls were taken up after the feeding of the five thousand (twelve is highly appropriate in this Jewish feeding of the twelve tribes of Israel), seven basketfuls were taken up after this Gentile feeding of the four thousand – and seven is the number of completeness. It may fittingly symbolize meeting the needs of the entire world: *all ate and were satisfied* (37).

And thirdly in this section, Matthew records Jesus' warnings against blind unbelief (16:1–12). That seems to be a reasonable way of grouping the material here. The Pharisees turn up again,[20] seeking a sign again! The people who throughout this Gospel have represented unbelief are now characterized by blind unbelief. They do not see, they do not understand, and they do not want to understand. They may be all right at weather forecasting (and that is a gift not to be sniffed at!), but they have no insight into the situation where the kingdom has broken in.

Actually, the text of verses 2–3 is very dubious in the manuscript tradition. It may be right to read from verse 1 straight to Jesus' reply in verse 4: '*A wicked and adulterous generation looks for a miraculous sign, but none will be given it except the sign of Jonah.*' The trouble with the Pharisees was that they sought the gratification of signs without the obligation of obeying the God who gave them. The miracles, of which there have been plenty in this Gospel, are indeed signs to all but the wilfully blind. They are meant to induce repentance (11:2, 20–21), but that is a response the Pharisees had refused to make. And therefore their darkness grew in intensity.

There are a couple of interesting details here. The first is that the Pharisees and the Sadducees came together to test Jesus by asking him for a sign. That is remarkable. They would not normally be seen dead in each other's company! Their theological views and political ideologies were diametrically opposed. It was opposition to Jesus that drew these most unlikely partners together. It is like the occasion when Jesus was given a testing question about paying taxes to Rome.[21] The Pharisees and the Herodians (again, sworn enemies) made a joint approach to him. It seemed impossible that he could avoid the trap set for him, but he did. A similar sinister combination met him here, and after giving his response he simply walked away. There are times when that is the best way to treat hypocrisy.

The other point of interest is the very compressed allusion to *the sign of Jonah*. What was the sign of Jonah? It was not his rescue from the bowels of the great fish. They had seen nothing of that. No, the sign of Jonah was Jonah himself, the preacher of repentance to Gentiles in Nineveh. And that is the sign of Jesus. It is not so much his resurrection, which none of the Pharisees and Sadducees would see, and which they later strenuously strove to discredit. It is his own person. He is the sign, the validation of that same repentance-preaching that Jonah delivered. If they will not listen to the teaching of Jesus and respond to the love and truth of Jesus, they will not

---

[20] This time, since 3:7, with the Sadducees. Enemies unite to deal with a teacher who in different ways threatened both of them.

[21] Matt. 22:15–22; Mark 12:13–17; Luke 20:20–26.

believe though one were to rise from the dead.[22] Jesus is the validation of his message. He is the sign that cannot ultimately be spoken against, and his resurrection will demonstrate that truth.

The section ends with a puzzling discussion about *the yeast of the Pharisees and Sadducees* (5–12). What is it that Jesus was warning them about? The answer is not entirely clear to us, any more than it was to the disciples. But verse 12 is the key: *Then they understood that he was not telling them to guard against the yeast used in bread, but against the teaching*[23] of the Pharisees and Sadducees. It was an evil disposition that wilfully rejected light and called it darkness.

There was a great deal of difference between the attitudes of the Sadducees and of the Pharisees. The Sadducees were against rocking the boat: they were the priestly party, the wealthy landowners who wanted to keep the Establishment going and to maintain good relations with the Romans, who were the occupying power. Wealth, comfort and expediency were their watchwords. The Pharisees were politically more radical, but, as we have repeatedly seen, tended to see religion in terms of outward observance and rules. Both types of yeast were disastrous for the life of faith which Jesus had come to inculcate. Both were utterly alien to the kingdom of God. And the trouble about yeast is that it permeates and raises the whole lump of dough with which it is mixed. That is what their respective branches of unbelief had done. It had become all-pervasive, blind unbelief. And that is something Jesus warns us against with all solemnity. Hardness of heart and unbelief take over like yeast. Although many Jews were blind to that truth, many Gentiles, like the Caananite woman, were well aware of it. If her attitude was typical in the Gentile church, Matthew seems to say, its future is assured.

The future of the Jewish-Gentile Messiah (16:13 – 17:27)

What is the future of this one who brings such polarization into the world? A life like that of Jesus is inevitably headed for trouble in a world like ours, and Jesus knows it. This section of the Gospel looks at seven different strands in that poignant future that awaits him.

The Messiah's recognition (16:13–17)

In the parallel passage in Mark,[24] the recognition of Jesus at Caesarea Philippi is the hinge on which the whole Gospel turns. In the verses immediately following it, he coins a whole new vocabulary about

[22] Cf. Luke 16:31.
[23] As Blomberg observes, 'There may well be an underlying play on words in v. 12b, given the similarity between "teaching" (*'amîr'ā*) and "yeast" (*hamîr'ā*).'
[24] Mark 8:27–33.

the suffering Son of Man. It is hard to exaggerate its importance in the scheme of the book. It is not quite so central here, because Matthew has already shown us unambiguously who Jesus is. But it is important, just the same, in a section where he is gathering together matters of great significance about Jesus the Messiah. Who he is would naturally come high on such a list.

It seems to me that in this confession of Jesus' status by Simon Peter three aspects are particularly remarkable.

The first is where it happened. Jesus had gone north again, probably in search of some privacy in which to teach the disciples all that they badly needed to learn in the comparatively short time he would be able to remain in their company. This time they came to a place some twenty-five miles northeast of the Sea of Galilee in the domain of Herod Philip, which he had renamed Caesarea in honour of the Emperor (it paid to do little things like that!). It has since returned to its ancient name of Banias. It was an amazing place. The name was derived from the fact that a grotto under the mountain there was reputed to be the birthplace of the god Pan, the most famous fertility symbol in ancient paganism. He was the legendary god of nature, and his worship was important in this town which bore his name. That same mountain saw the source of the River Jordan, while all around the land was filled with the temples of classical pagan religion. Towering above them, resplendent in its white marble and massive dimensions, was the new temple to the emperor from which the city derived its changed name. This was the place Jesus chose to see if any of his disciples really understood him. It was against this backcloth that he, wandering carpenter that he was, pitched his claim. '*Who do you say I am?*' (15). It is as if most of the rivulets of various ancient religions converged here. And calmly, as his due, Jesus accepts the adoration fit for the Son of God! It is a perfectly astonishing setting.

Today, when the world is a global village, and when the multiplicity of faiths is regarded as a fatal objection to the Christian claim of the uniqueness of Jesus, it is easy to forget that the seductions of syncretism in religion were every bit as attractive in the world where Christianity was born, and they were steadily and consistently resisted. Millions died for their quiet conviction that in the world of the relative the Absolute had arrived. Christianity cannot renege on that claim without a total denial of her Lord. Willem Visser 't Hooft, the first General Secretary of the World Council of Churches, was once asked what he thought would be the greatest peril facing the church in the near future. And he replied with prophetic insight: 'Syncretism. It is a far more dangerous challenge to the Christian church than atheism is ever likely to be.'

If the place was remarkable, so were the titles Peter accorded to

Jesus. They are all the more so when seen against the syncretistic tendencies of the place. Jesus is seen to be *the Son of Man*, the Messiah (*Christ*) and *the Son of the living God* (13, 16). None of these titles is new in this Gospel. But the collocation of them in one place most certainly is. *Son of Man*, as we have seen,[25] is a form of Aramaic speech that could be no more than a periphrasis for 'I'. But it could equally allude to the Son of Man to whom are given the everlasting kingdom and power and glory.[26] The ambiguity of the title matched the ambiguity of the person of Jesus. That is why he liked it. It could mean nothing – or everything. 'Messiah' (or *Christ*, the Greek equivalent for the Hebrew term, meaning 'anointed one') was soon so firmly associated with Jesus as to become almost a surname. In Judaism it meant the one who would come and fulfil the hopes of the nation. Traditionally, three sorts of people had been anointed with oil: prophets, priests and kings. And Jesus in fact did fulfil the expectations of all those three roles. Like the priest (only perfectly) he put people in touch with God. Like the prophet (only perfectly) he showed people what God was like. And like the king (only perfectly) he exercised God's rule over God's people while himself being uniquely the Servant of the Lord.

A remarkable place. Remarkable titles. And third, we find here a most remarkable insight. Simon Peter comes to recognize who this carpenter-teacher really is. No category of human exaltation can embrace him. He surpasses them all. Peter is here the spokesman for the conclusion to which he and the band of disciples had been driven by all they had experienced. Jesus is the Messiah, *the Son of the living God*. It is clear from the collection of messianic texts found at Qumran that some in Judaism were already dreaming of the longed-for deliverer as 'Son of God'.[27] The disciples had once already, under pressure of extraordinary circumstances, hailed Jesus as 'Son of God' (14:33). But now, coolly and thoughtfully, Peter does so again, and calls him Messiah too. This is the first time anyone directly addresses Jesus as Messiah in this Gospel. Going far beyond the populace, who gave a high place to Jesus and recognized him as one of the figures associated with the end-time (Jeremiah, Elijah and John the Baptist), Peter acclaims him as God's final self-disclosure. Here was the fulfilment of 2 Samuel 7:14, predicting one who would establish David's throne for ever. Here was the fulfilment of Psalm 2:7, the king who really was Son of God. There were no higher titles than these.

In response to Peter,[28] Jesus declares that no human insight gave

---

[25] See above, p. 40.   [26] Dan. 7:13–14.   [27] 4Q *Florilegium* 10–14.
[28] *Son of Jonah* (17) could equally well be translated from the Aramaic as 'Son of John', as in John 1:42; 21:15.

him this knowledge. Only God can reveal God; and God *had* revealed it to Simon Peter. It takes revelation from above to see as Son of God and Messiah a despised working man, one who was dismissed as crazy by his family and would be condemned as a criminal by his enemies. The principle of grace remains paramount. Nobody can pierce through to Jesus' identity by his own cleverness. That insight must be given by God himself.

This confession is very important in the scheme of the Gospel. Jesus had already been called 'Son of God' in an emotional reaction to rescue from a storm (14:33). This second confession is much more considered, and leads into the revelation that Jesus is called to suffer and die. And the third occurrence, again bringing together the two titles 'Messiah' and 'Son of God', appears on the lips of the high priest at his trial (26:63).

The Messiah's church (16:18–20)

Few passages in Scripture have attracted such acrimony among interpreters as this. What is the rock on which Christ will build his church? Catholics see the rock as Peter: Peter is empowered to control entrance into heaven; Peter is empowered to forgive sins. They see him as the first bishop of Rome and his authority transferred to succeeding popes. Protestants, by contrast, have maintained with equal passion that it is not Peter but Peter's faith that is the rock on which the church is to be built.

Maybe excessive heat has dimmed light on this matter. Peter is the spokesman of the Twelve, for good or ill. Nowhere is it clearer than here. At one moment he is commended as the recipient of divine revelation (17): the next sees him rebuked as the dupe of Satan (23). The Catholics have the more natural interpretation of the passage, up to a point. It is more probable that Peter (*Petros* in Greek) is the rock (*petra* in Greek) on which the church is to be built than that anything else, such as his faith, is given that role. The word-play is irresistible. The rock is not just Peter, however, but Peter *in his confessional capacity*. Peter, full of trust in the Son of God, is the one who will become the rock-man for the early church. He did become just that, as the early chapters of Acts reveal. It is Peter who preaches the first evangelistic sermon, but Peter as representative of the Twelve. And if the Catholics are right in thinking it is primarily Peter, albeit the believing Peter, who becomes the church's rock-man, the Protestants are surely right in pointing out that the passage contains no hint that this role should devolve on any successors in Rome or anywhere else. It affords no grounds for the claims preferred by the papacy; in fact, this verse was not attached to those claims until long after they were first put forward. The point is this:

Jesus had found in Peter a real believer, and on that foundation he could build his church.[29]

The reference to 'church' here and in 18:17 (the only occurrences in the Gospels) has often been thought to be an anachronism. But this is not so. The Messiah was always seen *with his people*. He was not going to be a solitary phenomenon. He would be the head of the renewed Israel. He would be accompanied by his *qāhāl*, his congregation, those who acknowledged him. Nothing could be more natural than the mention here of the Messiah's people just after he has been plainly hailed as the Messiah. They spring from confessing who he is.

The power to *bind* and *loose* (19) derives from rabbinic usage. It meant to allow or disallow conduct, based on interpreting the *torah*. For Matthew, Jesus is the true interpretation of *torah*, and will pass on that interpretation and indeed extend it. Peter has just confessed Jesus as the Son of God, the Messiah, greater even than the *torah*, and to him is given the responsibility of interpreting to others the person and teaching of Jesus. Nor was this role confined to Peter. 'I tell you the truth,' says Jesus, addressing all the disciples, 'whatever you bind on earth will be bound in heaven, and whatever you loose on earth will be loosed in heaven' (18:18). The power to bind and loose is given not to Peter alone, but to him as representative of the Twelve, to whom it is expressly committed in this second passage. They are to be the authorized interpreters of Jesus to succeeding generations. Hence the normative nature of their teaching for future generations of the church.

The power of *the keys of the kingdom of heaven*, here entrusted to Peter, goes further.[30] It means that Peter, along with the other disciples, can make access to the kingdom of God available or unavailable through their witness and preaching. They can admit people into the kingdom or exclude them. A similar passage in John 20:21–23 sheds light on what is meant. There the risen Christ declares: 'As the Father has sent me, I am sending you ... Receive the Holy Spirit. If you forgive anyone his sins, they are forgiven; if you do not forgive them, they are not forgiven.' This is clearly not intended to be arbitrary action on the part of Peter or anyone else. Jesus is sending out his disciples for world mission. He is equipping them with his Spirit. They go in his name and as his representatives, and are naturally bound by the terms of their commission. If people respond to the conditions of the gospel, and repent and believe, then they can be confidently assured that God has indeed forgiven them. Jesus made that very plain. If they refuse those conditions, their sins

[29] *The gates of Hades* (18; cf. Is. 38:10; Wisdom 16:13) means 'the gates of death'. Jesus means that the community built on Peter's confession will never perish.
[30] *Pace* France (1985).

are emphatically not forgiven by God. Jesus made that very plain, too. And of course we find the apostles doing just that in Acts. They confidently announce divine pardon to all penitent believers on the day of Pentecost and thereafter. They clearly remind Simon Magus that he is still in the prison of sin and has not yet met the Liberator. His sins are not forgiven.[31] That is the proper exercise of the power of the keys.

We must always remember that this passage is influenced by what was happening at that time in Judaism. The school of Shammai bound: that is to say it issued strict ceremonial and moral enactments. The school of Hillel, by contrast, loosed: that is to say, it was more flexible and sympathetic. Binding and loosing, and the power of the keys, were well understood among the rabbis. It means legislating and excommunicating. And Jesus is indicating that his messianic community, the church, would inherit powers similar to those of the Jewish rabbis. They interpreted the *torah*. The apostles would interpret Jesus and carry forward his mission and his message. All the forces of evil and destruction (*the gates of Hades*) would not be able to prevail against that church. And so it has proved down two thousand years.

The Messiah's contest and sufferings (16:21–28)

There is a battle on. That strain comes over strongly in the passage. It was particularly important for leaders in Matthew's church to remember this. To follow Jesus meant conflict with ease and comfort. It would involve following him in suffering and hardship (21). It would involve following him in self-denial and forfeiting their lives (24–25). It would mean taking on the forces of unbelief that refused to accept Jesus as Messiah. Jesus means his followers to share in Peter's confession: to share too in the suffering and power of the Christian life. Verses 21–22 show that they are not too willing to undertake that. Verses 24–25 show, however, that this is precisely what they are called to. No fight, no victory; no cross, no crown. Followers of Jesus must not forget that there is inevitably a lifelong battle to fight. They are called to follow their Master in suffering, but are promised a share in his triumph (24, 18).

That note of spiritual struggle is often absent from the contemporary church, but it is a mark of authentic Christianity. And in that war there will inevitably be casualties. Peter fell, and, instrument of revelation though he was, he became a mouthpiece for Satan. It is much to the credit of the Roman Church that the record of Peter's fall is depicted above the entrance to his great basilica in Rome.

---

[31] Acts 20:20–23.

Whatever spiritual experiences we may have had, we remain just as fallible and weak as ever before. There is no plateau of spirituality to which we can ascend and be for ever thereafter raised above the weaknesses that assail others. Sin and failure are to be found in all the saints. In this lifelong spiritual battle, victory is achieved only through ceaseless vigilance.

The prospect of Jesus' suffering begins to take on prominence in this chapter. It will increasingly dominate the story as it unfolds. It was hard for Jews to imagine that their Messiah, the crown of the nation's development and the fulfilment of its history, was destined to suffer ignominy, rejection and death. After all, the Messiah was intended to usher in God's victory. No doubt the land would at last be rid of its Roman invaders. Peace and justice, resurrection and rejoicing would be the order of the day when God brought in his Messiah! Well, that was not entirely short of the mark. There were those strands in the Old Testament hope.[32] But the whole conception was too small, too nationalistic, too materialistic and earthbound. No wonder *he warned his disciples not to tell anyone that he was the Christ* (16:20). They would have been sure to get it wrong, and the message would have been warped from its inception. No, his messiahship, as the baptism had hinted, involved taking on the role of the suffering Servant. Son of Man he was, but the Son of Man must suffer.

Why? Because how else could he empathize with poor, suffering humanity? How else could he understand what his followers, and indeed all humankind, have to go through? How else could he enter into the pain of the world and share it vicariously? How could he get to the root of the evil in the world, which lies even below the pain? How could he overcome the deadly disease of human sin and cosmic disorder? Only by taking upon himself all the assaults of evil, allowing them to crush him, and at the Father's bidding being raised to a new dimension of life, a life that will never end, for it shares the nature of God himself. That is the programme Jesus increasingly perceives to lie before him.

He outlines it in the three passion predictions which come with increasing intensity and with increasingly vivid detail here (21), in 17:22–23 and in 20:17–19. As soon as Peter comes up with this confession of Jesus as Messiah and Son of God, Jesus makes it plain to him what sort of Messiah he is confessing. It is the Lord who stoops to conquer, one whose suffering transcends human imagining, and whose victory will outstrip any social or political dimensions. *'On the third day* he will *be raised to life'* (21).

---

[32] And in some strands of intertestamental hope, e.g. the seventeenth *Psalm of Solomon.*

In addition, suffering will be the lot of Messiah's people. Inevitably they will share in his pain (24). An identity of destiny awaits Master and disciples alike.

No wonder Peter was aghast. This did not fit in with his idea of messiahship at all. Where was the political deliverance of Israel from the Romans? Where was the glorious future? Then, as now, the followers of Jesus have been very slow to accept the necessity of sacrifice and suffering. Those who seek to have life on their own terms will lose it. Those who are prepared to sacrifice, even their own lives, will find it. 'This dying to self makes possible the radical love and service that are the essence of discipleship' (Hagner). Taking up the cross, death to self-interest was far from Peter's mind when he acclaimed Jesus as Messiah. Jesus amazes them by his redefinition both of messiahship and discipleship.

Jesus then reinforces his challenge by pointing them to judgment. They will be accountable for the lives they have led (27). He concludes, '*I tell you the truth, some who are standing here will not taste death before they see the Son of Man coming in his kingdom*' (28). Does this refer to his 'coming' at the resurrection? Or at the destruction of Jerusalem? Does it refer to the parousia? If so, it raises the same problem as 10.23, an apparent prediction of the parousia within the first century. Was Jesus mistaken? The passage has been much debated. Matthew (like Mark) gives an immediate chronological link to the transfiguration ('After six days', 17:1). This is unlikely to be what Jesus meant (note the *some*), and he may well have been looking forward to the cross and resurrection (21), which will demonstrate that the King has entered on his kingly rule. There will indeed be a final 'coming' of the kingdom at the end of history, but the cross and resurrection would be a substantial first instalment[33] and would challenge people to make the decision that would settle their destiny.

Caesarea Philippi marks a very significant turning-point of the Gospel story, encompassing the recognition of the Messiah, the church that is built on that recognition, the battle in which it is locked, and the suffering and the triumph that will befall the people of God. It all begins to take shape. Caesarea Philippi is a watershed. After it come the passion predictions, and Jesus is seen as the Christ, the Son of God who must suffer. So must they. *Per ardua ad astra*, 'through trials to triumph'.

There are several important lessons to be learnt from Caesarea Philippi, and we are meant to learn them. Rarely in the Gospels is a saying of Jesus tied to a particular locality, as his sayings in this chapter are. The place is clearly important.

---

[33] France (1985) is succinct but very suggestive on this difficult verse.

First, this incident tells us we have to choose between world religions, sensuality, Caesar-worship and Jesus.

Secondly, we are called to public confession of what God reveals to us, supremely of who Jesus is.

Thirdly, we shall constantly be liable to fall into the comfortable error of the Pharisees, who looked for a Messiah that would fit in with their preconceptions, and who would be validated by signs and wonders, constantly successful, and the perquisite of the learned.

Fourthly, we shall be engaged, if we follow Jesus, in constant spiritual battle.

Finally, it will be costly to follow him. It will mean suffering. It will mean taking up the cross. It will mean losing our lives – but then, that is the only way to find them.

Yes, Caesarea Philippi marks a significant development in our understanding of who the Messiah is, where he is bound, and what it costs to follow him.

The Messiah's glory (17:1–13)

Just as the mention of a place name, Caesarea Philippi, is unusual and important in the narrative, so is the precise note of a time sequence that we find in 17:1 and in the other Synoptic Gospels, linking the first prediction of the passion with the foretaste of the Messiah's glory afforded by the transfiguration. The suffering Servant and the glorious Messiah are blended. Jesus had just asserted that some of those standing there with him would not taste death until they saw the Son of Man coming in his kingdom. That is a puzzling prophecy, but, as suggested above, it probably means that many of the bystanders would still be very much alive when the events of Good Friday, Easter and Pentecost showed clearly that the Son of Man was indeed King. The resurrection will have vindicated him. The coming of the Spirit will have pointed to a worldwide dominion, and Gentiles as well as Jews would be pouring into the kingdom of God. Nor was that the end. The kingdom was largely future: it would lead into God's heaven. Now, just six days later, Peter, James and John had a foretaste of that glorious future in the transfiguration, a mountain-top experience indeed.

We have read of the mount of temptation and the mount of the Sermon, and now this event on the mount of transfiguration sheds a shaft of light on who Jesus is, and vindicates the one who knew he must tread the path of rejection and crucifixion. God will not fail him. In Isaiah 53, where Jesus found the clearest delineation of the fate of this suffering Servant, unjustly condemned, executed with wicked men, identified with the guilt of the people, incarcerated in a rich man's tomb – in that very chapter, he would have read the triumphant conclusion: 'Therefore I will give him a portion among the great, and he will divide the spoils with the strong; because he poured out his life unto death, and was numbered with the transgressors. For he bore the sin of many, and made intercession for the transgressors.' Again, 'See, my servant will act wisely; he will be raised and lifted up and highly exalted.'[34] Such was the prediction, as Christ taught the disciples after the resurrection: 'How foolish you are, and slow of heart to believe all that the prophets have spoken! Did not the Christ have to suffer these things and then enter his glory?'[35] The transfiguration, coming as it does here after the bleak predictions of rejection, emphasizes the link between self-sacrifice and glorious vindication in the economy of the God who reigns and yet suffers.

It is highly probable that the amazing vision accorded to these three close disciples in the transfiguration took place on Mount Hermon, the highest mountain in the whole area. It was 2,814 metres high, and only a few miles away from Caesarea Philippi. Jesus had gone there to pray,[36] taking only these three trusted intimates with him. He was clear now that some people, at least, really understood who he was and what he had come to do. He must spend time with God to make sure that he had not made a mistake, and that the path to the cross really was God's way of victory. The transfiguration provided that assurance in the most concrete way, not only for Jesus, but for his closest associates. As at his baptism (3:17), the role of Son and Servant is reinforced by *a voice from the cloud* (5).

But this time Jesus is joined by *Moses and Elijah* (3). They were recognized as the supreme representatives of the law and the prophets of Israel. And here they were, in this vision, talking with Jesus who had come to fulfil what both law and prophets had looked forward to. Their significance was even greater than that, however. In Scripture, both Moses and Elijah are connected with the end of time. Both had something uncanny about the way they had left this life. Moses was never found: it is assumed that God took him.[37] Elijah was removed from his colleague Elisha in a chariot and horses of fire.[38] The expectation was that a prophet like Moses would arise in the last days, and the Israelites were instructed: 'You must listen to him'[39] – a phrase picked up here in the final words of the voice from heaven, *'Listen to him!'* (5). As for Elijah, as we have seen, there was persistent Old Testament and intertestamental expectation that he would return before the Lord at the end, as the herald of his coming.[40] Now, in this astounding vision, both expectations were coming true. The Lord was coming. The prophet like Moses was in

[34] Is. 53:12–13.   [35] Luke 24:25–26.   [36] Luke 9:29.   [37] Deut. 34:5–6.
[38] 2 Kgs. 2:11.   [39] Deut. 18:15.   [40] Mal. 4:5.

their midst! Both men stand round Jesus, as if pointing to him, the culmination of all that the law and the prophets had stood for in the unfolding story of Israel. And then they fade away and leave Jesus only (8). The forerunners have done their task. They can disappear into the background now that the principal figure is here.

So much here is allusive: the cloud, betokening the divine majesty; the voice from heaven, as at the baptism; the mixture of Psalm 2:7 and Isaiah 42:1 with overtones of Deuteronomy 18:15; the disciples' awe before the unveiled glory of God, just as Moses and Elijah had fallen down in awe before the Lord on Carmel and Sinai; the title *agapētos*, 'Beloved' (NIV *whom I love*, 5), already a messianic designation in pre-Christian Judaism; the divine affirmation of Peter's confession. Notice how Peter is once again tacitly corrected. In his amazement he blurts out the suggestion that they should make three shelters, one for Moses, one for Elijah and one for Jesus (4).[41] The prophets and the rabbis after them were sensitive to the fact that God dwelt with Israel in tents in the early days of the nation; he would do so again in the days of salvation.[42] If Peter had this notion in his mind he is swiftly disabused of it, for Moses and Elijah fade away, and Jesus alone remains. The heavenly voice underlines the point: '*he* (alone) is my unique Son: hear *him*' (cf. 5). The representatives of the law and the prophets yield place to the author of the new dispensation that fulfils them both. The whole incident has set the seal of the Father's approval upon the passion teaching Jesus has just given, and asserts the divine nature of the person who gave it.

Just as the disciples were bound to silence at Caesarea Philippi, so they are here. They would not be understood until after the cross and resurrection, which are now seen to be God's will and to be inevitable. But they are still puzzled about Elijah, and Jesus takes their question, '*Why ... do the teachers of the law say that Elijah must come first?*' (10) and makes it a further teaching point to summarize much of what has gone on in the previous pericope. Verse 11 should be read as a question: 'Is Elijah to come first and set all to rights? *I tell you, Elijah has already come, and they did not recognise him, but have done to him everything they wished*' (12). It is as if Jesus is saying that the most realistic interpretation of Malachi 4:5 and the scribal expectations is not the vision they have just had but the hard facts of recent history. John the Baptist has fulfilled the role of Elijah *redivivus*. Like Elijah he withstood the powers that be, and paid the penalty. The same fate would befall the Son of Man (12). But that would not be the end of the story. The Son of Man will be *raised from the dead* (9), and the transfiguration has been the pledge of it.

---

[41] Perhaps this was an honorific gesture. But perhaps Peter wanted to prolong, even institutionalize, the encounter, as Moses set up the tent of meeting in Exod. 33:7–11.

[42] E.g. Ezek. 37:27; 43:7; so Rev. 21:1–3.

The Messiah's frustration (17:14–21)

A high spiritual experience is often followed by a crashing anticlimax. And so it is here. As the three come down the mountain with Jesus and return to the everyday world, they are met with tragedy, need and failure. Someone has come to the other disciples and asked them to heal his epileptic son. They are unable to help. And Jesus, descending from this exalted time of communion with God, is faced with the problem not so much of the illness of the boy as of the ineffectiveness of his followers. Red-faced disciples, distraught father, epileptic son: chaos reigns. The man is like many today: he longs to get behind the representatives of Jesus, with whom he is disappointed, to the Master himself. The disciples are like many Christians today – powerless.

What is needed from the presumably Gentile father? Faith. What is needed from the Jewish disciples? Faith. That is the one thing Jesus must have if he is to use his mighty power among us. And the disciples tried his patience sorely because they were so weak in faith. The placing of this story after the transfiguration shows that the Son of God can do anything if only people, Jew and Gentile alike, can trust him. It must have been both an embarrassing and an encouraging story as it was read in Matthew's church. For Jesus had permanently ascended a mountain, and had left them to carry on his work. Were they powerless? It was attributable to lack of faith. So often when knowledge about God grows, actual dependence on God shrinks. Matthew goes out of his way to stress the danger of lack of faith. He has had a lot to say about the failure of the disciples in this department already. It is an important lesson, and the more settled and established a church becomes, the more it needs to learn afresh that it can achieve precisely nothing without sincere dependence on the Lord, a point highlighted by the many manuscripts that add after verse 20, 'But this kind does not go out except by prayer and fasting'[43] – a marvellous rebuttal, incidentally, of the charge that Jesus performed exorcisms by magic. Instead, they happened as a result of implicit faith in the power of the Lord, claimed by prayer and from time to time reinforced by fasting.

One additional point: what does Jesus mean by 'You can say to this mountain, "Move from here to there" and it will move' (20)? This seems to have been a proverbial image for resolving great problems.[44] Despite its aptness in the proximity of Mount Hermon, the phrase is clearly metaphorical: whoever would want to move a literal mountain? But it would have been possible for the disciples to

[43] See NIV mg. This reading is taken (wrongly) from Mark 9:29.

[44] Cf. 1 Cor. 13:2, and the rabbis used it thus. See *b. Sanh.* 4a, *b. Sota* 9b, *b. B. Bat.* 3b.

have overcome the difficulty of exorcising the boy if only they had trusted God. It is not the amount of faith that matters (even. a mustard-seed amount will do), but where it is located. No doubt that was an important lesson for Matthew's church, and for ours. When confronted with a case that calls for deliverance ministry, I know how impossible it can feel that one can accomplish anything. But afterwards one looks back on the 'mountain moved' with joy and gratitude.

The Messiah's obedience (17:22–27)

The chapter draws to a close with a marked emphasis on the death of the Messiah. He was no political messiah, full of blood and fire against the political leaders of the day. He was obedient right along the line, even to the distressing end of death on the cross.

This obedient attitude of his is stressed by the next story concerning the temple tax. This story is unique to Matthew, who was, of course, very interested in tax matters: it had been his profession. *'Doesn't your teacher pay the temple tax?'* asked the tax men. Although rabbis were exempted from the *two-drachma tax* which all other male Israelites had to pay for the upkeep of the temple, Jesus was not an official rabbi. Therefore he was due for tax. If he refused, there would have been ample grounds to accuse him. Jesus comments that *kings* do not tax *their own sons* (25).[45] After all, taxes were imposed for the upkeep of the royal house. Very well, the temple tax was for the support of the house of God. Jesus was the Son of God. Why, then, should he pay tax for his Father's house? A son in the royal house does not pay tax. Nevertheless, he proposed to pay, in order to avoid putting a stumbling-block (*skandalon*; NIV *offend*, 27) in the way of the collectors.

The situation was not merely contemporary but prophetic. For after AD 70, when the temple had been razed to the ground, the Romans reassigned the temple tax to the upkeep of the temple of Jupiter Capitolinus in Rome. This infuriated the Jews, and after repeated complaints it was revoked under the Emperor Nerva in AD 96. But when Matthew was writing, perhaps early in the 80s, the temple tax, reassigned to Rome, was an exceedingly contentious issue. Men would sometimes be stripped in the streets to see if they were circumcised and therefore liable to the tax! Christians saw themselves as distinct from Judaism: they were no longer the servants of the Lord, but his sons. They felt they had no need to

---

[45] The Greek word for *sons* can also, by extension, mean 'citizens'. Some translations take it this way here. But the point is then obscured. Kings do tax their own citizens, and they did in the ancient world, too.

contribute towards the Jewish temple, still less its Roman replacement! But lest their refusal to pay should set a bad example to others and spark off a major confrontation with the Roman authorities, which would do great harm to the cause of the gospel, let them go the extra mile and pay the tax. Had not Jesus done the same?

That seems to be why the story was so prized that it could not be left out of this rather Jewish Gospel. It spoke to a need that remained pressing in Matthew's day. But it derived, of course, from a real incident in the life of Jesus. He was free of the law, and yet, so as not to give offence, he was subject to the law in every way. 'Submit yourselves for the Lord's sake to every authority instituted among men,' wrote Peter, the other main actor in this story.[46] Jesus did just that. The temple tax would go into the treasury of the very Establishment that would betray him to death. Yet he did it. He refused to use his freedom as an excuse for claiming personal immunity and escaping obligation. Jesus set an example in the voluntary abnegation of his rights, and this provided a great challenge and stimulus in the developing life of the church. He did it, even though such obedience was part of the path which led him to the cross.

What are we to make of the miracle of the coin in the fish's mouth? Many people have taken it as either a folk tale (Herodotus has a similar story) or as a vivid form of saying that a day's fishing will solve the tax problem. However, the story as it stands is far from impossible. As any fisherman knows, a fish is attracted by a bright, flashing object – that is how millions of trout and salmon are caught every year. Why could not a fish have pounced on a silver didrachma which fell from someone's hand into the waters of the lake? Once in the fish's mouth it would have had to stay there, for the musht fish, one of the main species to be found in the Sea of Galilee, has an over-developed mouth into which the small fish rush for safety when a marauding cannibal fish attacks. The fish then spits them out when the coast is clear! I have myself placed a silver coin, much larger than the didrachma mentioned here, in the mouth of a musht fish caught in the Sea of Galilee. The only remaining problem, if this is accurate, would be how Jesus knew that Peter would catch that particular fish. But how did Jesus know, on two other occasions in the Gospels, where a massive catch of fish was to be had? How did he know how many husbands the woman of Samaria had had?[47] When Paul is recounting some of the spiritual gifts he mentions the gift of knowledge:[48] sometimes God does give supernatural disclosures about a situation to one of his servants. If that happens today, and it does, why should Jesus not have had this gift of knowledge as a highly developed part of his own spiritual equipment?

[46] 1 Pet. 2:13.   [47] John 4:18.   [48] 1 Cor. 12:8.

189

11. The fourth discourse: relationships in the kingdom

We come now to the fourth of the five great teaching blocks in the Gospel. It is all about personal relationships within the kingdom of God, and is therefore important as a quarry for Christian ethics. Once again the tidy-minded author arranges this material about church relationships[1] in seven sections for easy memorization. Chapter 10 concerned the outward orientation of the kingdom. This chapter, the next great collection of teaching, is properly devoted to its internal relationships. They make or mar churches. What are the qualities which the Master looks for in his disciples? They are a remarkable collection.

Humility (18:1–4)

If we were to stop and think what was most important in church relationships, I do not think many Christians would come up with this quality, which Jesus wants to see as the first and foremost characteristic of his disciples: humility. 'Who is the greatest in the kingdom?' ask the disciples (1). Alas, Christians ancient and modern are often preoccupied with that question. And, in sharp contrast to the disciples' fascination with status and position, Jesus takes a little child – and they were of little account in antiquity – and declares that greatness is to be found precisely there. The kingdom upturns secular values. Real greatness is not to be found in seeking to be praised and served by others, but in seeking others to serve, especially those who have no rights. Significantly, the first mark of Christians in the church is the supreme mark of the Son of Man himself, humility (17:22–23). If the Son of Man goes humbly as it is written of him, how much more should his followers?

We can be fairly sure that when Jesus called the little lad to him,

---

[1] Matthew has brought together in this compact form much of Jesus' teaching on relationships among disciples, now clearly seen as separate from Judaism.

he came promptly, and stayed where he was put. That child was accounted great by Jesus. Is that not a clue to what real humility means? It means coming when Jesus calls us and staying where Jesus puts us. So humility is not a matter of suppressing our drive and hiding our gifts. Humble people are quite unself-conscious about it all, like the lad. They claim no right from others, or from their Master. They follow where Jesus calls and stay where Jesus puts them. That is humility.

Archbishop William Temple unself-consciously displayed that humility in his own character. 'I have never sought and never refused a position of greater responsibility,' he said. That shows how humility can quite naturally accompany great positions of leadership. It is a quality that is imperative among Christians. Others may need to 'keep face' because they have no ultimate security to fall back on. Christians should never need to do this. They know they are accepted in Christ. They should be willing and able to take their masks off, lay no pretence to greatness, and be utterly at the disposal of Jesus. The American preacher S. D. Gordon, not himself highly educated, once advised, 'Get every qualification you can and then use it for God.' The trouble is that those who are not humble spend much of their lives hunting wealth, possessions and qualifications for their own sake, hoping that they will give them the status and self-esteem they crave. But no. God has already given us the highest status in the world. We are his *paidia*, his 'children'. But in Greek (as in Aramaic) the word also means 'servants'.

Welcome (18:5–6)

It is not clear in these verses whether Matthew is still thinking of the children in his church, or whether he uses the word in a secondary sense to mean 'unimportant people'. The phrase *little ones* (6) recurs in verses 10 and 14. It seems to be used ambivalently to denote both little children and the 'little people', those whom others regard as insignificant, but on whom God looks in a very different light. The church should be a place where both are honoured. Children matter. They mattered to Jesus. They matter in any congregation. The services should be arranged with their needs in view. They need to be befriended, understood and taught. The way we behave to children is one of the indicators of the way we behave to Jesus. That is quite a thought!

It is the same with the apparently unimportant people: the visitors, the strangers, the poor, the elderly, the odd. Do we bother more about the rich and monied than about the poor and ignorant? James, the brother of Jesus, may well have had this thought in mind when he launched his scathing attack on prejudice and favouritism in

191

church life.[2] The church should be the place, above all others, where the children and the leftover people can be sure of a warm, unjudging and unpretentious welcome. And what an encouragement for those who particularly care for the poor or for children, or do some similarly unspectacular job! As they receive one of those 'little ones', they are in fact receiving Jesus. They not only welcome the child or needy person; at times they can see something of the Master in him or her. The Lord comes to us through all sorts of people and circumstances, but in none more clearly than through the 'little people' and the way we treat them. Here again is a devastating criterion of church life, yet it is not one we would ever have dreamed of inserting.

Wholeheartedness (18:7–9)

A lot is made here of causing people to stumble. *The things that cause people to sin* is literally 'stumbling-blocks'. We put these in people's way if we are not wholehearted in our discipleship of Jesus, and if we are not serious in our commitment. In that case we also put stumbling-blocks in our own way: indeed, we *are* stumbling-blocks. But if we are wholehearted – not necessarily greatly gifted – we can instead be stepping-stones, leading others to God rather than hindering them. The previous two verses told disciples to be tough with themselves so as not to cause children to stumble. These verses are telling disciples to be tough with themselves so that their own effectiveness in the kingdom of God will not be nullified. The vivid language about millstones round the neck[3] and cutting off parts of the body is obviously intended to be figurative (though, as we have seen,[4] the early church father Origen castrated himself out of literal obedience to these verses in order to show his seriousness with regard to lustful thoughts). This teaching nerved Christians to face torture in the days of Nero and of Stalin, believing that it was better to *enter life maimed* than to go whole into final and irreparable alienation from God.

This chapter is all about the church, and the teaching about the cutting off of limbs was very early seen as referring to the amputation of an individual from the Christian body when it was plain that a 'limb' was gangrenous. If there is within a church someone who is guilty of unrepented sin which is affecting the whole church, that person must be disciplined, however difficult it is to do. The member must not be allowed to ruin the body of Christ.

[2] Jas. 2:1–13.
[3] Galileans drowned Herodians in Jesus' day by fixing millstones to their necks: Josephus, *Antiquities* 14.15.10.
[4] See above, on 5:29–30.

We cannot leave the application of this to the martyrs and to the body of the church. The challenge comes to us all as individuals. Does your hand cause you to sin – the hand raised in anger or grasping at money? Does your foot cause you to sin, taking you to places where you should not go, and declining to undertake Christian service? Does your eye cause you to sin – the never-satisfied eye of the consumer society? Be single-minded! Deal ruthlessly with whatever causes you to stumble in your walk with Christ in the body of his church.

Pastoral care (18:10–14)

A parable very much like this one about the lost sheep is to be found in Luke 15:3–7. But the context is quite different. There it forms one of three stories that show how much the Son of Man is willing to undertake in order to bring lost people, lost coins and lost sheep back to himself. The purpose there is evangelistic. The purpose here is clearly pastoral. Jesus is talking about relationships within his church. He is speaking to his disciples, those who were later to become leaders in the community. He has been telling them not to put stumbling-blocks in the way of the apparently unimportant, and to be utterly ruthless with sinful tendencies in themselves. And now he encourages them to care for the lonely, the lost, the sick and the discouraged. They are sheep without a shepherd, and God cares enormously for each one. That is symbolized by the fact that *'their angels in heaven always see the face of my Father in heaven'* (10).

This would have immediately rung a bell with his Jewish listeners, for there was a highly developed angelology among the Jews of that day. Nations have their angels.[5] Churches have their angels.[6] Here, individuals have their angels. The rabbis believed that even the flowers had angels to represent them before God. It is a delightful way of expressing the unceasing love and care of the Creator for his creatures, and there is a strong note of accessibility as well. The 'face' of the eastern ruler was hard to approach. He was a busy and important person. But the angels always see God's 'face'. They have unrestricted access to his presence. God cares very much for the little members, the stray sheep of his flock. Do the leaders care? That is the thrust of this passage.

The eastern shepherd has a remarkable accord with his flock. He knows each one individually in a way that is inconceivable to most western minds. He immediately knows which, out of *a hundred sheep* (12), is not there at the end of the day. He goes out to seek it,

---

[5] Dan. 10:13, 20–21; *Testament of Daniel* 5–6; *Testament of Levi* 5.
[6] Rev. 2:1ff.

and is full of joy when he rescues it. That is the attitude of the Father. It should be the attitude of the church leadership.

It is very hard, the sociologists remind us, to relate effectively to more than 150 people. Therefore members of larger churches are in great danger of being under-cared-for. Access to the minister is rare. The leaders are busy. Contact gets increasingly shallow. People become increasingly frustrated. Nobody in leadership really knows them, what their needs are and what gifts they could contribute to the church. Therefore it is imperative to break the congregation down into small, caring units, fellowship groups, where love is the universal language, where the dozen or so people in the group meet regularly for enjoyment, Bible study, prayer over each other's needs, celebration and acts of service. Such groups are a marvellous substructure in any church. They are an outstanding feature in the cell-church structure of Singapore, where the gospel is advancing so fast. Group leaders play a vital role, and they should be properly trained and continuously supported by the central leadership of the church. This results in high-quality pastoral work. All members of the 'cell' have a sense of belonging. All are known by name and cared for. All have the opportunity to offer talents and ask for support. Members learn from one another, and the *little ones* and the lost ones are no longer hurting. This is a radical expedient, and a simple one. It means that everyone can be cared for by the others and by the leaders of the group. People need to be noticed, to be loved. Jesus asserts that God cares for such people: he protects them, he will vindicate them, and he will judge those who offend them.

Openness (18:15–20)

We all make mistakes, and we are criticized for them, justly or unjustly. But either way it is a fact of life, and churches are often full of criticism and gossip. How are we to handle it? This remarkable pericope tells us how. In fact it breaks down the matter of response to criticism into three questions.

First, what do we do with criticism? When a member of the church has done something which offends us, we are to go and tell him direct (15). Letters, e-mails and even phone calls are less personal means of communication and are always second best. Rather, we should go and see the individual personally. There is no need for Christian brothers and sisters to dread confrontation. After all, we are all accepted by God. We do not need to feel that our standing may be destroyed by criticism. Our foundation is Christ, and that is solid rock. So why fear confrontation? '*Go and show him his fault, just between the two of you … But if he will not listen*', it may be necessary to '*take one or two others along, so that "every matter may be established by the testimony of two or three witnesses"* ' (15–16).[7] That was important in Jewish law; it is important still today.

A Christian business I was associated with had steadily been losing money. We were able to trace the losses to one person on the staff of the business. He was seen alone. He strenuously denied any wrongdoing. So I as Rector and three others saw him. He confessed what he had done when faced by incriminating evidence in the presence of witnesses. Sometimes even that does not suffice. It is necessary to tell the church. That is a painful last resort. I have once or twice had to take it. It simply will not do to conduct these things behind closed doors. If the wrongdoer will not listen to the church, he or she must be removed from it and become an outsider, like *a pagan or a tax collector* (17). We must be open with people, and with the church of which they are members.

Secondly, how do we make the initial visit to this brother or sister with whom we are in contention? Attitude is vital in the handling of these testing issues. We are to remember that this person is a fellow-Christian – not just a pain! We therefore go in charity; we go alone, so as not to embarrass the person; we go with a background of prayer (19). Those three ingredients may well make an entirely different mix when we have to perform the unpleasant task of criticizing the faults of others. The attitude is all important. In the case mentioned above, although it was painful and the offender had to leave our employment, the love and integrity with which he was confronted did in fact win our brother over (15). He got another job, and was restored to love and full acceptance in the church he had wronged. That seems to me to be a practical vindication of what Jesus is inculcating here. In secular employment he would have been sacked at once, and in all probability brought to law for reparation of what he had stolen. But we would never have gained his continuing affection and retained his membership of the church. The whole thing would have been much messier and destructive of personality all round. Attitude matters.

The third question is this: what do you want? You do not necessarily want the accused person to agree, when you have a criticism to raise. After all, he may be right and you may be wrong. What you want him to do is to *listen*. Three times here the word is used (15, 16, 17). You want him to weigh what is said and to consider it dispassionately, as if it concerned someone else rather than himself. If contestants come with that attitude within the church, the resolution of problems will be speedy.

[7] Quoting Deut. 19:15.

Three further points are worthy of mention before we leave this important passage.

A word about discipline. When a person has to be ejected from leadership or, temporarily at least, from membership of the church, he or she is to be treated like *a pagan or a tax collector* (17). Is this pure vitriol on the lips of Jesus? Some commentators think so. Are Matthew's old prejudices coming out? This is how he would have thought in his pre-conversion days.

I believe the answer is both simpler and more profound. There is realism and there is hope in that phrase *a pagan or a tax collector*[8] – the realism of recognizing that there is at present an impenetrable barrier separating us from him; and the hope of forgiveness and a new start. The person will not *listen*, we are told three times. It takes two parties to make reconciliation; and therefore exclusion must follow and the barrier must stand. But what did Jesus do with tax collectors and sinners? He loved them into repentance and new hope. Matthew had good reason to remember that. He had been one of them. So this instruction is saying that love and patient caring for the straying individual should always accompany Christian discipline. As Paul subsequently put it, 'hand this man over to Satan so that the sinful nature [literally, "flesh", the self-centred life] may be destroyed and his spirit saved'.[9] The aim should always be restoration.

A word about binding and loosing. As we have seen,[10] this is a rabbinic phrase to describe community regulations. Jesus gives that authority to leaders of his church, but woe betide them if they exercise it amiss. Church regulations affect immortal members of the body of Christ. They can do great good or harm. It is a responsibility that requires the greatest love, tact and thoughtfulness.

And a word about prayer. In verses 19–20 Jesus gives a beautiful promise about answered prayer. But we must remember the context in which it comes: Jesus is talking about the handling of disagreements in the church. Such things need to be bathed in prayer. It helps enormously to have a group of people praying while an act of discipline of this nature is being carried out. They do not need to have all the details: confidentiality can and should be preserved. But they do need to pray. That makes all the difference, for so often these disagreements are spiritual battles, not merely human failings and misunderstandings. Prayer will assuredly be answered in such a context. Here again, it is not a blanket promise that anything we ask

[8] This was a traditional Jewish expression of distaste for outsiders, such as Gentiles and tax collectors. While Jesus did not treat people like that (8:5–13; 9:9–13), he can still use the expression metaphorically for someone to be ostracized.

[9] 1 Cor. 5:5.   [10] See above, on 16:19.

will be granted. The promise is more limited by its context than that. It is telling them that prayer offered for reconciliation is utterly part of God's will and never falls on deaf ears in heaven. *For where two or three come together in* the *name* of the Messiah, he himself is *with them* (20). What encouragement that would have brought to the leaders and membership of Matthew's church! Imagine them hard pressed by powerful synagogues all round: it would be so easy to get discouraged. And the rabbis had a saying that when 'ten people sit together and occupy themselves with the *torah*, the *shekinah* abides among them'.[11] Amazing! The *shekinah*, the glory of God, which was absent from the second temple, was manifest when Jews were gathered around studying and obeying his Word. Now Jesus replaced the *torah* by himself. When disciples are gathered praying in the name of the Messiah,[12] he is in their midst (28:20); the *shekinah* shines among them and from them. Think of the Christology implicit in such a claim! Think of the encouragement to struggling believers!

Forgiveness (18:21–22)

Forgiveness is another of Jesus' hallmarks for authentic church life. There are bound to be failures and breakdowns between Christian brothers and sisters. Forgiveness is the way to handle them. The Christian life is born in forgiveness, and it must characterize us all the way through our relationships. Naturally, we may find it hard to forgive. Peter did.[13] He wanted to know how few times he could *forgive* his *brother* (poor Andrew!). He suggested *seven times*, and must have felt he was offering the moon: the rabbis reckoned that three times was enough![14] But Jesus' reply will have shattered him. *'Not seven times, but seventy-seven times,'* better, seventy times seven.[15] It means 'Go on and on and on forgiving.' Not, of course, 490 times, but constantly. God's pardon is like that. Ours must mirror it if we are in his family. And because we are forgiven people, we will be able to summon the motivation and the power to forgive. To say 'I forgive you' is not enough. It needs to be repeated whenever we feel the sense of grievance rising up in us afresh. It is

[11] *Aboth* 3.2.

[12] This cannot mean that any and every prayer will be answered affirmatively; it is prayer for the sinner of verses 15–18. The community prays according to God's will – as in the Lord's Prayer.

[13] This is the last of five key texts in chs. 14 – 18 where Matthew inserts references to Peter that are not found in any other Gospel (14:28–31; 15:15; 16:17–19; 17:24–27; 18:21). [14] E.g. *b. Yoma* 86b, 87a.

[15] NIV mg. These words of Jesus contrast sharply with the 'seventy-seven times' avenging of Lamech (Gen. 4:24); and McNeile comments: 'The unlimited revenge of primitive man has given place to the unlimited forgiveness of Christians.'

primarily a matter of the will. As we determine not to hold the grievance against our brother or sister, but to accept his or her penitence wholeheartedly as God does, gradually the heart catches up with the head, and forgiveness, repeatedly reiterated, becomes part of us and enters deep into the wounded feelings. We are at last able to say, 'It is finished.'

There is no doubt that these two areas on which Jesus has put his finger are singularly apt for most churches. Church life is bedevilled by failure to be open over wrongs that are committed, and by failure to forgive. As Christians, we are called to openness with those we feel have wronged us, and to frank forgiveness when apology is sincerely made. Hidden grievances and unwillingness to forgive are two things that make shipwreck of personal relations. Jesus warns us against them.

Freedom from resentment (18:23–35)

Resentment is a deadly disease, and it is very common. It can even have physical results. It certainly carries severe spiritual consequences. Our relationship with God becomes strangled by it. Counselling often reveals this as the basic problem behind dryness or spiritual decline. 'Is there someone you will not forgive?' can be a most revealing question. And this story of the unforgiving servant drives home the message of the last two pericopae like a pile-driver. It does not add anything very new. But it is one thing to be told a truth, and quite another to hear a brilliant short story in which you side with the underdog and then find yourself accusing not the man in the story but yourself! It is a powerful application of the parable. It drives you to take sides. And you end up by taking sides against your own actions. One is reminded of the parable Nathan recounted to King David, culminating in the devastating accusation, 'You are the man!'[16] And so this astonishing story brings to a climax this chapter on relationships. If these are not right in a church, nothing else will go right.

The *king* in the story found one of his debtors who could never, in many lifetimes, pay the debt he owed. That is the point. The debt was incalculable. And against all expectation the king forgives him freely, when he asks for mercy. Astonishing grace, but that is what God is like to us who are broken before him and could never begin to repay what we owe. *'Be patient with me ... and I will pay back everything'* (26) is pitifully untrue, as threadbare as our own excuses and palliatives: 'I will try a bit harder. I will come to church. Surely that will do?' But it won't. The debt is phenomenal: a

[16] 2 Sam. 12:1–7.

thousand times the annual revenue of Galilee, Judea, Samaria and Idumea put together! Totally beyond imagining. And the king forgives him the lot. The parallel is plain. That is what God has done to the sins of the disciple – any disciple. They have been piling up for years like debts: every day, every hour adds to them. They can never be paid. And God says, 'I release you from that debt.'

What did the man do? Behave towards others with the generosity that he had received? No. He exacted the last copper coin from a *fellow-servant* who owed him a comparatively trifling debt. He must have been brooding over that unpaid debt for years. Resentment had taken hold of his attitude towards his fellow-servant. Resentment is a horrible thing. It is wicked: *'You wicked servant'* (32). It is an attitude that captures us, enslaves us. It is fatal. If we do not forgive, we shall not be forgiven.

Once again we see how opposed Matthew rightly is to cheap grace. It will not do to claim to be forgiven and then to prove by our actions that our lives have not been changed. The pardon of God is dynamic, life-changing. We cannot go through heaven's narrow door if our lives are bulging with resentments. Heaven is for penitent sinners only, those who know themselves freed from a debt they could never pay, and who prove their gratitude by their lives. God puts his precious gift of forgiveness in our hands – but only if we open them up to him, not clench them in anger against our brethren. We have already seen this principle taught after the Lord's Prayer (6:14–15). Now it comes again, in brilliant colour in this wonderful story. The point is underlined. There is no escaping it by pious platitudes about God's willingness to forgive us whatever we do. His forgiveness is indeed inexhaustible, but it can be received only by those who repent. And resentment has to be repented of. It utterly blocks us from receiving and enjoying the forgiveness we long for. When someone says 'I cannot forgive So-and-so for what he [or she] has done to me,' the answer is clear: 'You *must* forgive, or you will never be forgiven by God. You will exclude yourself from his presence now and from his heaven later if you do not repent of this attitude. How can God forgive you if you will not forgive?'[17]

We are not responsible for the reaction of the other party in all this. If he or she will not accept our apology we cannot help it. We cannot do more, apart from reiterating it when appropriate. What we are responsible for is rooting out resentment in our own hearts and taking it to the cross where it belongs.

---

[17] Carson (p. 407) helpfully comments: 'Jesus sees no incongruity in the actions of a heavenly Father who forgives so bountifully and punishes so ruthlessly, and neither should we. Indeed, it is precisely because he is a God of such compassion and mercy that he cannot possibly accept as his those devoid of compassion and mercy.'

Consider those seven things. Hardly any one of them would feature in our own top priorities for the progress of our church. We would probably not have rated relationships that high in order of importance. If we did, I am reasonably sure that we would not have come up with a list of seven attitudes so searching, so painful, as these. Maybe that shows how far we are from the Christianity Jesus taught and exemplified, and which Matthew thought so vital for the life of his church.

E. JUDGMENT (19 – 25)

19:1 – 20:34
12. Judgments on issues

Let us remind ourselves of where we are in the pattern of Matthew's Gospel. If the Billinghams are right in their conviction that the Gospel hinges on chapter 13, and that each half is split into three corresponding panels, we have now completed the first panel of Part 2. We have seen the shadows on the wall for Israel, for Judaism, for Jesus and for the church. And, as ever, this section has ended with a block of teaching by Jesus to his disciples, this time about relationships in the kingdom of God.

Now follows the central panel of Part 2 of the Gospel. It parallels the central panel in Part 1 on discipleship, but it goes further. Its major concern is judgment: numerous judgments against Jesus in the first place, followed by judgments by Jesus against his opponents, and the climax is the final judgment of the sheep and the goats. This will bring the fifth block of teaching in the Gospel to an end, and accordingly complete the Christian *torah* which the new Moses left to the people of God.

The final judgment lies in the future. It is, however, preceded by many other judgments in chapters 19 – 20. They show the upside-down nature of the kingdom. In seven important areas human judgments are reversed by the breathtaking newness of the teaching of Jesus. We must prepare for shocks.

Jesus' judgment on marriage and divorce (19:1–12)

Jesus now leaves Galilee for the last time, and the Pharisees come to test him on a hot contemporary issue, divorce. We have already had a preliminary look at this subject in the Sermon on the Mount.[1] But now it is brought before us in a conflict situation. They were out to trap Jesus in front of the large crowds that followed him.

As we have seen, Judaism had a high understanding of marriage,

[1] See above, on 5:31–32.

but all schools within Judaism recognized the fact of divorce. Moses had made reluctant legislation to control its worst excesses, which allowed a man to divorce his wife on account of a trifling disagreement. Indeed, he could do so while drunk! To have to write a bill of divorce at least meant he had to wait until he was sober. Difference in Jewish schools arose over interpretation of 'something indecent',[2] which Moses had conceded could justify divorce. Shammai interpreted it as adultery; Hillel saw it as embracing a multitude of much less serious things. The Pharisees were therefore seeking to get Jesus to side with either Shammai or Hillel, and to show himself as a conservative or a liberal in sex ethics. Jesus refused to be drawn. Instead of talking primarily about divorce, he goes behind that regulation of marriage's failure to the purpose of marriage itself. He took them straight back to the Maker's instructions, in Genesis 1:27; 2:24, and he made six strong points about marriage.

First, it is designed by God. *'The Creator . . . said . . .'* (4). Actually, that quotation from Genesis 2:24 is not ascribed to God in the Old Testament. These are the words of the narrator of Genesis. But it was common ground among Jews that what the Old Testament said, God said. Marriage was no mere social contract. It was a God-given ordinance.

Secondly, marriage was meant to be complementary: God *'made them male and female'* (4). It is not a unisex world. There is a God-ordained difference and complementarity between the sexes. That is so obvious that it only needs to be stated today when homosexual relationships have come to be seen as an equally valid alternative to marriage. The basic trouble about it is that it contravenes the complementarity that God has built into the sexes.

Thirdly, marriage was intended to be permanent: *'the two will become one flesh'*. The bonding is meant to provide a permanent relationship that will not be broken by anything 'indecent', whether interpreted by Shammai or by Hillel. Here again, in an age of immense marital dissatisfaction and breakdown, we see God's judgment on what we think acceptable. Marriage is intended to be permanent, and any deviation from that is a declension from his purpose. Incidentally, the very physical words used to describe the union, *one flesh* and *united* (literally 'glued'), affirm the goodness of sexuality, one of God's most gracious gifts to his people, and not something that Christians should affect to disparage.

Fourthly, marriage is exclusive. The man is *'united to his wife'* (5). He becomes *one flesh* with her. No way is he permitted to have a little flutter on the side, any more than she is. Each is pledged to find fulfilment in the other, and so to discover on earth a model, however

[2] Deut. 24:1.

inadequate, of the permanent relationship between God and the believer which nothing can break.

Fifthly, marriage is nuclear. It means 'leaving' as well as 'cleaving' (5). It represents a fundamental transfer of allegiance from parents to spouse. There has to be a substantial measure of distancing from the old generation in order to create the new. A fresh family unit is in the making. Of course, the new couple will in many instances draw a lot of support from their parents. But the fact remains: they are a new unit, and need the freedom to behave as such.

Sixthly, marriage is not for everyone. This is the plain meaning of verses 10–12. The disciples were amazed at the rigour of Jesus' exposition of the purpose and nature of marriage. It was far tougher than Shammai had ever been. There seemed no way out, then, of a disastrous union. If so, *'it is better not to marry'* (10). But Jesus is not legislating. He is setting forth God's purpose in marriage. He is going behind the casuistry on divorce that was so beguiling then as now. He is telling them what God wants in marriage, and what befits the kingdom. If that seems tough, it is because marriage is a gift. It is something by which God joins people together. It is not his gift to everyone. Who can demand gifts? They are not rights. Some people are precluded from marriage because of some congenital inability to consummate. Some have been emasculated and turned into court eunuchs. So marriage is an impossibility for them too. But Jesus is interested in the third class he mentions, those who for the sake of pleasing the King have been willing to offer to him this prized area of their sexuality, and have been willing to stay single as their Master did. Not everyone can do that. Most are not able to sustain that pressure on so basic an instinct as to marry. *'The one who can accept this should accept it'* (12). There is such a thing as a call to celibacy. And it is a very beautiful thing when it is embraced and gladly followed through.

Marriage creates the most profound bond between two people. It is the basic cell in all society. And Jesus stresses that God invented it and wants to preserve it. He does not want divorce. 'I hate divorce,' says God.[3] But it happens. In Moses' day it was so common that he made this concessive regulation requiring something in writing before a divorce was valid. Jesus goes further in restricting it, and he does so by returning to the original purpose of marriage. If you break the 'one man, one woman' commitment, you break the will of God. You are not acting in the way of the kingdom. You commit adultery if you remarry. It is not the worst thing you could do. It may even be the least of all the evils under the circumstances, but you can never bear witness by your second or subsequent union to

[3] Mal. 2:16.

what marriage was intended to be. It is simply impossible. For the ideal of marriage was embodied in Genesis 2 between Adam and Eve. Divorce was not just inadvisable or regrettable. It was impossible! There was no possibility of dissolving the marriage bond. And that is Jesus' point when he takes the case back to the beginning. He is showing God's ideal for marriage: an indissoluble and exclusive union between two people for life. Divorce simply does not enter into the divine plan at all.

But it happens. And what is Jesus' teaching when it does? As is well known, Matthew modifies the absolute prohibition of divorce recorded in Mark and Luke[4] with the clause *except for marital unfaithfulness* (9). There are many problems concerning this clause. For one thing, it appears only in Matthew. For another, an unusual word, *porneia*, is used. This word was not restricted to adultery, but denoted sexual licence in a variety of circumstances, including with prostitutes. Is the exceptive clause to apply to infidelity after marriage as a ground for divorce? Or does it refer to previous sexual activity before marriage, which subsequently comes to light? Does the clause indicate that a fresh marriage is possible for the 'innocent party', as Paul seems to hint in 1 Corinthians 7:12–14, and as was universal in ancient divorce law, both Jewish and Gentile? The whole issue bristles with problems, and there is no unanimity among commentators.

Which did Jesus actually say? It makes a great deal of difference. And we cannot duck out of it – there is a straight contradiction between Matthew on the one hand and Mark and Luke on the other.[5] It is probable that Jesus gave the absolute form of the prohibition. Why? For one thing, because the disciples were so shattered by his words (10). If he had given an escape clause, they would not have been so amazed; after all, that is what Shammai allowed. For another, because Jesus has forcefully drawn their attention to the original purpose of marriage (6), and has taken his hearers back to the Garden of Eden. There was no divorce then, before the fall, and accordingly there should be none for members of the kingdom, in whom the ravages of the fall are being restored.

But we must understand that Jesus is not giving us a law here but an ideal, a goal. Marriage in the kingdom should be indissoluble, loving and exclusive. God hates divorce, and so should we. But it would seem as though Matthew takes the principle and turns it into a law. The ideal of 'one man, one woman, for a lifetime' turns into

---

[4] Mark 10:1–12; Luke 16:18.

[5] Unless Mark and Luke do not bother to mention the exception for adultery because, if a husband discovered previous adultery in his wife, he was not merely permitted but commanded to put her away. They simply take it for granted. If so, there would be no contradiction between them and Matthew; but I have a feeling this is too easy an answer. See Blomberg.

legislation that one man shall remain married to one woman for life. And that is a very different thing. As soon as you have legislation, you need exceptions to cover hard cases. And here in Matthew we probably see the earliest attempt of the first Christians to be loyal to the thrust of Jesus' teaching but making an exception for a manifestly difficult situation, post-marital infidelity. That seems to be the meaning of Paul's permission in 1 Corinthians 7, where he is clear on the absoluteness of Jesus' teaching, and then specifically says that when he makes exceptions he is speaking not from the Lord but on his own authority.

Difficult though this is, we must remember two things. It is not possible for the ethics of the kingdom to be articulated in anything less than ideal terms. And yet the Lord is consistently compassionate to those who fail, repent, and come back to him for restoration. This passage follows hard on the heels of one that expresses the unbounded mercy and forgiveness of God. So legalistic rigorism is as inappropriate for the Christian community as is casual divorce.

Clearly, Jesus taught that God's will for humankind is the indissolubility of marriage, and the equal partnership within that marriage bond. For Christians, his teaching is normative. Nevertheless, the whole thrust of his teaching is against legalism. What is more, he is replying to a hostile question and operates within the constraints of that context. And he is giving an ideal, not laying down the law. For these three reasons it is not possible to give a compelling answer to whether Jesus would allow remarriage after divorce in some circumstances – adultery, and maybe others, such as insanity? What is manifest is that he is in principle against divorce and remarriage, and would be appalled at the ease and frequency with which it takes place today. One of the most powerful Christian witnesses possible these days is the eloquent example of a warm, forgiving, hospitable, united and happy Christian home.

Jesus' judgment on children (19:13–15)

If Jesus caused consternation by the revolutionary attitude he displayed towards marriage and divorce, what he has to say about children is no less staggering. Children in ancient society, Greco-Roman and Jewish alike, were there to be seen and not heard. They had no rights, no status. They did not matter very much until they grew up. So when the disciples shooed away people who were bringing little children to Jesus for his blessing, they were acting in a typically Jewish (and for that matter Gentile) manner.[6] But that is

---

[6] However, on the Day of Atonement it was necessary to bring children to the elders for prayer and blessing: Mishnah tractate *Sopherim* 18.5.

not the attitude Jesus wants to see in the kingdom. Children matter, and have much to teach us. They are usually more sensitive to the things of God than adults are. Their attitudes of trust, simplicity, inability to put forward their own achievements, and dependence, all characterize true disciples. Those qualities are priceless in the kingdom of God, and therefore children can provide a signpost towards life in the kingdom style. So Jesus stands their assumption of the irrelevance of children on its head. His response reveals several things.

First, Jesus welcomed little children. He did not drive them away. He was irresistibly attractive to children – and that is one of the marks of a great person. Secondly, Jesus rebuked those who wanted to keep the children away from him. He was not too self-important to bother with them. It is interesting that the phrase *do not hinder them (mē kōluete)* became part of a baptismal formula for children in the second and third centuries.[7] The welcoming attitude of Jesus to children was one of the indicators that led Christendom to baptize children, though of course this passage had no original connection with baptism. Thirdly, children can actually receive a blessing from the hands of Jesus, even when they are too young to understand. Moreover, they can enter the kingdom. '*The kingdom of heaven belongs to such as these*' (14). And most important of all, children can and do model the conditions of entry into the kingdom of God. Their unself-consciousness is a paradigm for us all.

These are among the reasons that have led the majority of Christians to baptize the children of believers.[8] That is reasonable, and in line with the Old Testament recognition of the place of children within the covenant: boys were given circumcision, the mark of initiation, at seven days old. But that is not the main purpose of the passage, which is designed to show the reversal of human judgment once we allow Jesus to dominate our attitudes. To him the children are not to be despised or kept away; they are important, and indicate the way into the kingdom.

Jesus' judgment on religion (19:16–22)

The story of the rich young man is one of the most famous and poignant stories in the Gospels. This rich man, whom Matthew tells us was *young* (22), and Luke tells us was a ruler, comes to Jesus and asks a question which is typical of the religious attitude. It was seen in the Pharisees of that day, and is alive and well among churchgoers

[7] See the evidence in J. Jeremias, *Infant Baptism in the First Four Centuries* (SCM, 1960), pp. 53–54.

[8] For a contrary view, see Kurt Aland, *Did the Early Church Baptize Infants?* (SCM, 1961), and G. R. Beasley-Murray, *Baptism in the New Testament* (Eerdmans, 1962).

and many others today: *'Teacher, what good thing must I do to get eternal life?'* (16). The man is patronizing: no disciple in Matthew's Gospel ever calls him 'teacher'. He is self-confident – sure that eternal life is something that lies within his own power to attain by doing the right things.

Mark and Luke also record this story,[9] and there the man calls Jesus 'Good teacher'. Jesus replies, 'Why do you call me good? No-one is good – except God alone.' There is considerable textual variation in the manuscripts at this point, but Matthew seems to transfer the 'good' from Jesus to the deeds the man is so proud of, perhaps in order to emphasize that good works provide his ticket to heaven.[10] Matthew has been accused of making the change for reverential reasons: he does not want anyone to question the goodness of Jesus But Mark and Luke were just as certain of Jesus' divinity as was Matthew, yet they recorded the phrase. No doubt Jesus wanted to probe beneath the man's bland exterior, and point him to the source of absolute goodness, God himself, from whom he was actually running away while seeking to establish himself by his good deeds. Matthew's form of expression is not to avoid a seeming irreverence, but to lay stress on the good deeds this man was so proud of and to force him to recognize that they come from the one good God. Behind the good commandments that the man tries to keep, there is a good God – and what is he doing about God? His relationship with God is in disarray.

Just as Jesus punctures the man's patronizing attitude, so he deals with his self-satisfaction by underlining four important things.

First, Judaism does not, and never did, see law-keeping as the way to life. Law-keeping is the way those who have been given spiritual life behave. Law-keeping is the kerbstone on the path of loving loyalty. The Ten Commandments themselves were laid down for people who had experienced God's rescue and wanted to respond worthily.[11] They were not virtues to flash in the face of God Almighty.

Secondly, Jesus challenged the man with God's revelation. It is as if he said, 'Why do you come to me asking the way to life? You will find the answer to that question in the Scriptures.' That was the point of his response, *'If you want to enter life, keep the commandments'* (17).

'Which ones?' asks the man. Jesus directs his attention to the second half of the Decalogue, but with two very significant alterations. To point him in that direction is vital because Jesus realizes

---

[9] Mark 10:17–31; Luke 18:18–29.
[10] On Matthew's alterations here, see N. B. Stonehouse, *Origins of the Synoptic Gospels* (Tyndale, 1964), ch. 5.
[11] Exod. 20:2.

that the man is proud of his social and religious achievements. Jesus is determined to allow the law of God to have its convicting effect where the man was most proud. Notice how deftly Jesus hints at where the man's greatest weaknesses lie. He puts *honour your father and mother* out of order at the end of the Decalogue. It looks as though the man's relationship with his parents is a weak area that Jesus wants to point out.

Then Jesus adds, ' ... *and "love your neighbour as yourself"*.'[12] This addition was common in the Jewish catechism, but particularly apt here. Weak in his relationship with God, the man is weak in care for his neighbour. The ancient, non-canonical *Gospel according to the Hebrews*[13] records this story with an illuminating expansion here. Although Jesus did not say these words, they may well indicate the point hidden beneath the surface in Matthew: 'And the Lord said to him, "How sayest thou, 'I have kept the law and the prophets?' For it is written in the law, 'Thou shalt love thy neighbour as thyself'; and lo, many of thy brethren, sons of Abraham, are clad in filth, dying of hunger, and thine house is full of good things, and none of it goes out to them." ' The man was selfish through and through. He was in bondage to possessions, and no doubt he shared the common Jewish illusion that wealth was a mark of divine favour on the recipient. It would just be nice to have eternal life as icing on his already delightful cake! And Jesus cuts to the heart of that selfishness. He must sell his possessions! Not, as the *Gospel according to the Hebrews* thought, because the poor needed the money (though they did), but because he needed to get rid of it. Some have inferred that all Christians should give away all their possessions, but that is not what Jesus says or means. Money was getting in the way between this man and the kingdom. He had to deal ruthlessly with the stumbling-block if he was serious in wanting to enter into life. He failed the test.

And Jesus put the challenge in another way. Instead of pleasing himself and pursuing his own route to goodness, he needed to come and follow the despised teacher whom he had greeted so patronizingly. If he really wanted to gain the perfection he professed to desire, let him do what the law indicated, and follow the one to whom it pointed. Incidentally, note the high Christology, all the more significant because it is so artless and uncontrived.

Sadly, this man missed *zōē aiōnios*, eternal life. The primary meaning of this phrase is not quantity but quality of life. It is not so much life that goes on and on, as a new quality of life, life released from materialism and selfishness to share the loving and self-giving life of God. John's Gospel puts it so clearly: 'This is eternal life: that

---

[12] Cf. Lev. 19:18.   [13] Recorded in Origen, *Commentary on Matthew* 15:14.

they may know you, the only God, and Jesus Christ whom you have sent.'[14] Instead, he went away with his possessions intact, but missing life. He went sorrowfully. To prefer riches to Jesus, our way to his, does not bring happiness. The thrust of the story is to teach that we gain eternal life only in the kingdom. And, as we have seen, the kingdom makes absolute claims on the disciple's life. For this man the stumbling-block was his money. What is it for you?

Jesus' judgment on riches (19:23–30)

It was a commonplace in Judaism, not a little reinforced by the book of Job, that riches were a mark of God's favour. Many Christian sects and individuals have both taught and acted on the same assumption. But once again Jesus springs a surprise. Instead of it being hard for a poor person to enter the kingdom, as they would have thought, Jesus says *it is hard for a rich man to enter the kingdom* (23). Indeed, it is harder than it would be *for a camel to go through the eye of a needle* (24). Various attempts have been made to mitigate the toughness of this saying: does *the eye of a* needle mean a narrow gate that a camel, laden with rich possessions, would have difficulty pushing through? Is the Greek word *kamēlos* (camel) a misunderstanding of *kamilos* (*rope*), and is it harder for a rich man to enter the kingdom than it is to thread a rope through a needle? No. The literal meaning is to be preferred. It is frankly impossible for a camel to go through the eye of a needle. And it is *impossible* (26) for a rich man to enter heaven. It can't be done. And why not? Because money tends to make us selfish, materialistic, independent of God and of our fellows, and distracted with methods of retaining our wealth. Wealth leads to an overconfidence which is the very antithesis of the childlike spirit of trusting dependence on the goodness and mercy of God. It is perfectly evident. It had just happened in front of their eyes, in the person of the rich young man. Wealth was something Jesus set his own face against. Christians who have great possessions are in great peril.

The disciples were *greatly astonished*, once again. This kingdom teaching was the very opposite of all they had ever thought. It was indeed an upside-down kingdom. It is not surprising that they asked, '*Who then can be saved?*' (25). Jesus' reply sets the whole of the foregoing discussion in perspective. He says plainly that no-one can be saved. It is utterly impossible for a religious person, a rich person, indeed anyone to be saved. Nobody can earn his way or pay her way into the kingdom. With humanity it is impossible. Not difficult: impossible. '*But with God all things are possible*' (26).

---

[14] John 17:3.

Jesus knows how to bring believers into the kingdom. It cost him everything he had to come and seek us. If there had been any other adequate way, he would have taken it. Because we could not save ourselves from our sins, Jesus came to do just that. Jesus' answer is based on strict monotheism and divine grace. Without grace nobody can enter the kingdom. This is the death knell to 'justification by works', a theme Paul takes up in a major way in his letter to the Romans.

That theme is continued here in chapter 20, but in the meantime Jesus pauses to answer a legitimate, if rather self-centred, query from Peter: 'What do we get out of giving up so much to follow you?' (cf. 27). It is easy for us to sneer at the question, but which of us has given up what the disciples had? Perhaps that is why Jesus gives no rebuke but rather great encouragement to the Twelve. Christians who have given up all for him will share his victory (28). In the new world,[15] they will also find that they gain far more than they lose. Believers find enhanced relationships, and profit from the beautiful generosity of brother and sister Christians in the loan of homes and in the quality of relationships. And they will one day enter into the new world beyond the grave, where they will find many surprises (30). Christ is no-one's debtor, and those who sacrifice to follow him will find it abundantly worthwhile.

Jesus' judgment on merit (20:1–16)

Jesus picks up and expands the last verse of chapter 19, 'Many who are first will be last, and many who are last will be first.' How can it be that poor fishermen are up with the first, and rich young men rejected? On what principle does God work? The answer lies in the parable of the vineyard, and 20:16 picks up the 'first and last' saying to stress the linking.

The story is very Jewish. From time immemorial the vineyard had been an image of Israel. A moving passage in Isaiah 5 likens God to a vineyard owner, and is distressed that, after all the trouble he has taken over Israel his vineyard, it produces only wild grapes instead of cultivated ones. It is not hard to see Israel in the vineyard of this parable. It is obvious who the employer is: God. The details are the sort of thing that happened time and again in any Jewish village at grape harvest. Storms could ruin the crop; timing is of the essence. So in many ways this parable would be familiar; in other ways, totally astonishing. The working hours are right, from dawn to sunset. The wage is right, indeed very generous, for a full day's

---

[15] *Palingenesia, renewal*, literally 'rebirth', occurs elsewhere with a personal application in Titus 3:5. Here it speaks of the new order associated with the messianic age (cf. Is. 65:17; 66:22).

unskilled labour. The unemployment background is right, and was all too familiar. Actually, *standing in the market-place* was the equivalent of attending the Job Centre. It was all very familiar, as was the payment of the labour force at the end of the day, lest the working man should go home with no money for the evening meal.[16]

Despite its familiarity, the parable is a total reversal of normal values, and is certainly no recipe for industrial peace! The unions would be up in arms if any employer acted like that today. But of course the story has nothing to do with industrial peace. It was intended to show the principles on which God receives people into his kingdom.

Three surprises await us in this picture of the upside-down kingdom. First, there is something strange about this employer. He really cares about the down-and-outs. He could have sent an employee to the Job Centre. Instead, he goes out himself. Indeed, he goes out repeatedly to seek them. They are hungry, unemployed and, as the day wears on, increasingly hopeless. He cares about that. He wants to give them a job of work and a reward. An unusual employer.

A second surprise comes at the end of the day, when he pays them off. That is the normal time; and, as was the normal custom, he begins with the last arrivals. But he gives each of them a full day's pay. The last, who have worked only one hour, are paid the same as those who have been working all day long. Such is the amazing generosity of this employer.

While his hearers were reeling under the impact of an employer like this and a pay structure like this, Jesus tossed in a third surprise: the reaction of the 'shop steward'. A spokesman for the labour force complains: 'This isn't fair. Why should those who have *worked only one hour* get the same as me and my mates who have worked all day in the boiling sun?' (cf. 11–12). Jesus replies, *'Friend (Hetaire) ...'* That should alert us. It is an ironical term in the Gospel. In each of the three cases in which it is used, the recipient of the title is in the wrong. That is so here. It is so in 22:12, where it is addressed to the man who was not wearing wedding clothes and still wanted to come to the wedding, and in 26:50, where it is addressed to Judas, arriving with the soldiers to betray Jesus. So here the thrust of Jesus' reply is this: 'Friend, may I show you a document you signed this morning? A little contract? How much was it for? One denarius? Yes, I thought so. It is a very good day's wage. What are you complaining about? Are you demanding, in the name of justice, that I break the contract you willingly entered, and which I have fulfilled to the letter?'

---

[16] Lev. 19:13: Deut. 24:15.

The worker wants the employer to break the contract that both sides have signed. He is in the wrong. Far from being unfair, the employer totally fulfils his contract and then displays uncalled-for generosity to latecomers.

And so this familiar vehicle of country employment in Israel suddenly becomes, in the hands of Jesus, charged with the most staggering reversals of the normal. The point of the story is plain. Length of service and long hours of toil in the heat of the day constitute no claim on God and provide no reason why he should not be generous to those who have done less. All human merit shrivels before his burning, self-giving love. Grace, amazing grace, is the burden of this story. All are equally undeserving of so large a sum as a denarius a day. All are given it by the generosity of the employer. All are on the same level. The poor disciples, fishermen and tax collectors as they are, are welcomed by God along with Abraham, Isaac and Jacob. There are no rankings in the kingdom of God. Nobody can claim deserved membership of the kingdom. There is no place for personal pride, for contempt or jealousy, for there is no ground for any to question how this generous God handles the utterly undeserving. He is good. He sees that the one-hour workers would have no money for supper if they got paid for only one hour. In generosity he gives them what they need. Who is to complain at that?

The Pharisees might complain. They were pleased with themselves and contemptuous of the 'amme hā'āreṣ, the common people.

Jews in general might complain. After they had been punctiliously trying to keep the law of God for two millennia, the despised Gentiles are welcomed on equal terms with them into the kingdom.[17]

The disciples might complain. They had given up all to follow him, as Peter insisted in 19:27. It would have been easy for them to begrudge the free welcome accorded to those who had denied Jesus during his earthly ministry and become his followers only when the movement spread after Pentecost.

The church members of long standing in Matthew's church might complain. They had built the church, modelled it, slaved away in it. Now here were all these new believers crowding in and wanting to make changes and take office. They did not know their place!

To one and all this parable presents a firm rebuttal. One's standing in the kingdom of God does not depend on human merit in any way whatsoever. Matthew is as clear on this as ever Paul was. It depends on the sheer unmerited favour of the only one who is ultimately

[17] Matthew's church would almost certainly have identified those who worked all the day with Israel, and the latecomers with Gentiles. Both are equally welcome in the employment of a God of grace. The parable underlines passages like 9:13, 'I have not come to call the righteous, but sinners.'

good (19:17) and who accepts those who could never be good, in order that this free grace may produce in them genuinely good works. These good works are not meritorious deeds for life: they are responsive, grateful behaviour springing from the life that God in his generosity has given them. We find exactly the same message in Ephesians 2:8–10. And people try to tell us that Paul has misunderstood the teaching of Jesus! Both are crystal clear that when sinful men and women are faced with a holy, good God, they have no clothes to hide their nakedness. Merit is excluded. All depend on grace alone. Without it they would not have a chance.

So, as we look back on the way this parable springs out of 19:23–30, we see that, although Jesus is gentle and understanding with the disciples, he does not endorse their plea, 'We have left everything to follow you! What then will there be for us?' (19:27). The whole idea of merit in leaving all, and of reward in 'What will there be for us?' is alien to the kingdom. That is why so many who are last will be first and the first last. Many Christians who have worked hard for God over a long period will have a lowly place in the kingdom because their motives were not purged of the ideas of merit and reward. Many poor Christians who came to faith only at the end of their life will be high in the kingdom because they knew they had done nothing to boast of, and never gave rewards a thought. They just responded to the unexpected love that sought them and accepted them. That is the attitude that brings joy to the heart of God, the great lover.

Jesus' judgment on greatness (20:17–28)

Greatness is measured by service. That is the heart of this next element in Jesus' judgment on contemporary attitudes. Peter had been thinking about greatness in the kingdom (19:27) and Jesus followed it with his parable of the vineyard. Now the sons of Zebedee with their mother come to discuss top seats in the kingdom (20). The other disciples are angry, not because they have a different attitude to greatness, but because they want the top seats themselves (24)! Achievement, merit, is a very difficult root to weed out. And so Jesus delivers some arresting teaching on the subject. First, he deals with his own fate, then with the fate of James and John, and then with pagan ideas of greatness, which lead him to reflect on its true nature. All three assert the same thing: the royalty of service. '*The Son of Man did not come to be served, but to serve, and to give his life as a ransom for many*' (28). Service is the mark of greatness in the Master. It must characterize the disciple too. '*Whoever wants to become great among you must be your servant, and whoever wants to be first among you must be your slave*' (26–27).

First of all, Jesus applies this principle to himself. He must practise what he preaches, and he will. *'The Son of Man will be betrayed to the chief priests and the teachers of the law. They will condemn him to death and turn him over to the Gentiles to be mocked and flogged and crucified. On the third day he will be raised to life'* (18–19). There you have the ideal expression of the nature of greatness: service of others, endurance of hardship, opposition, even agonizing death for those you serve. And God will vindicate such an attitude. It is the very life of heaven. *'On the third day he will be raised to life!'* (19).

This third prediction of the passion is a little more specific than either of the first two (16:21; 17:22–23). It was a time of increasing strain for Jesus. Mark tells us that he was walking ahead of the disciples on his own, and that they were amazed and afraid as they sensed the turmoil in his soul.[18] He now sensed that he was to be betrayed, condemned by the leaders of his own people, turned over to the Gentiles, mocked, flogged and crucified. It was a horrific filling in of the picture sketched on the other two occasions. How much of this growing awareness came from spiritual insight, how much from musing on the Old Testament, how much from political wisdom and an understanding of what Romans did with messianic pretenders, it is impossible to say. It is not given to us to penetrate the mind of Jesus. But his greatness stands out in clearer relief against so dark a background, an outcome he realized would happen and still went to meet: *'We are going up to Jerusalem'* (18).

We begin to glimpse what that ghastly concentration of rejection and pain on the cross will achieve. Why should it happen, and to one as good as he, of all people? The answer is that he was about to *give his life as a ransom for many* (28). A ransom is the money paid to gain the liberation of those in captivity. Usually that captivity is alienating and dangerous. Jesus clearly sensed, from his reading of the prophets, if from no other source, that there was to be something special about his death. It would not only entail the pain of betrayal, of unjust condemnation, of surrender to an alien power, of mockery, of the ghastly cat-o'-nine-tails shod with lead, and the shame and excruciating agony of crucifixion. It would actually *do* something. It would rescue a world of people in chains, like hostages on a hijacked aircraft – not perished yet, but in imminent danger of perishing. His death was the price God paid for sinners to go free.[19]

No image is perfect. If we go round asking to whom the ransom

---

[18] Mark 10:32–34.
[19] The closest analogy is Is. 53. The unexpected 'many' is a quotation from Is. 53: 12–13, and the preposition *anti* (in the place of) clearly indicates the vicarious suffering of Jesus for sinners. This is one of the plainest descriptions in the New Testament of the meaning of Christ's death.

is paid, we get into big trouble, as the church fathers found.[20] It is simply a powerful image to say that sin is dangerous and hard to deal with; that it cost nothing less than the sacrifice of God's Son; that it achieved the rescue of a whole world that was out of touch with God; and that his greatness was never seen more clearly than when he was hoisted up in degradation on that cross.

In the light of this reflection on his own impending fate, it is easier to understand the following section about the desire of James and John, accompanied, to their embarrassment, by their over-demonstrative mother, for seats at Jesus' right and left in the kingdom. Only Matthew mentions their mother's part in it. If their mother was Salome, Mary's sister, they were cousins of Jesus[21] and might expect special treatment in the kingdom. But here are two of the 'last' wanting to join the ranks of the 'first' and thus displaying the selfish ambition that made the others 'last'! Jesus' reply is that his own calling, albeit to suffering and rejection, is the highest to which anyone could conform. He has come to serve, to give, to suffer and to die. Dare they face that? *'Can you drink the cup I am going to drink?'* (22). They thought they could. The cup meant judgment and retribution,[22] and drinking it, as Jesus realized full well (see 26:39), meant suffering and rejection. James in fact was executed by Herod,[23] and John seems to have lived to an old age in Ephesus and to have endured the hardship of banishment to the mines of Patmos.[24] Jesus' own cup would, of course, be drained to the bitter dregs at Calvary.

One cannot help being struck by the patience of Jesus as he stared death in the face while his followers, on whom he had expended such efforts, were still thinking in terms of earthly ambition. But unfortunately that attitude is common in the church. Equally, one cannot help being struck by the courage and loyalty of the disciples, despite all their failings. When Jesus tells them clearly that the future is bleak and that suffering and death await them, they do not turn tail. They stay with him. But they still have much to learn about greatness, and so Jesus draws to a conclusion the lessons on the subject which have emerged from his prediction of his own passion and the request of James and John.

Jesus contrasts greatness in the eyes of the world with greatness in the kingdom of God. Greatness in the world is determined by status; in the kingdom by function. In the world greatness is shown by ruling; in the kingdom by serving. In the world's eyes the great are

---

[20] For a clear and readable account of the patristic discussions of the idea that on the cross Jesus paid a ransom to the devil for the lives of humankind, see G. Aulén, *Christus Victor* (SPCK, 1931).

[21] See p. 307 below.   [22] Jer. 25:15ff.; Is. 51:17–18.   [23] Acts 12:1.

[24] If he is the John who wrote Revelation. See Rev. 1:9.

those who can order others about; in the kingdom they are those who endure hard times and injustice without complaining. How slow the church has been to learn the lesson! We are status-ridden. We talk in terms of promotion in the work and ministry of the church. Generally clergy leave the menial tasks to others, instead of sharing in the washing-up! We love honorific titles like 'Right Reverend' and 'Venerable', whereas Jesus came to be, and to be seen to be, the Servant. *'The rulers of the Gentiles lord it over them, and their high officials exercise authority over them. Not so with you. Instead, whoever wants to become great among you must be your servant, and whoever wants to be first must be your slave'* (25–27). In the upside-down kingdom, greatness is measured in terms of service, and that is a severe judgment from Jesus on estimations of greatness both outside the church and, regrettably, in it.

Jesus' judgment on outcasts (20:29–34)

As Jesus and his friends leave Jericho for the last time on the journey that will culminate in Jerusalem, both Luke and Matthew stress the fact that he went out of his way to bring the good news of the kingdom to the outcasts, in contrast to the religious leaders, with whom much of the Gospel is concerned. In Luke, Jesus confronts Zacchaeus and transforms his life.[25] Here, in Matthew, two blind beggars[26] see who Jesus is, despite their blindness; they trust him, they call on him. They are healed, and at once they follow him.

There are many significant details here. These blind men have a lot to teach us. They refused to accept discouragement when the crowd wanted to silence them. They were specific in their request, and took the only chance they would ever get of being healed: Jesus would not pass that way again. Their faith, though earthbound (Jesus did not encourage cries of *Son of David*, because it gave an entirely wrong impression of messiahship, as if it meant earthly rule), was firm and centred in Jesus. As we have seen,[27] it is not the amount or theological correctness of faith that matters, but where it is placed. Weak and confused faith, if placed in Jesus, can bring the believer into healing contact with his grace. The grateful surrender of their lives to following Jesus (surely the statement that they *followed him* [34] is meant to indicate more than that they became part of the procession!) is clearly meant as an example. All of this is worthy of reflection.

The most profound point here is the judgment, the reversal of

[25] Luke 19:1–10.
[26] For Matthew's two blind men, compared with one in Mark and Luke, see the discussion of the demoniacs, above, on 8:28ff.
[27] See above, pp. 187–188

values which we have seen throughout the past two chapters and to which this story fittingly supplies the climax. It is very subtly drawn. The request of the disciples (for top places in the kingdom) shows their blindness: the request of the blind men shows their vision – of who Jesus is and what he can do. The blind men see Jesus as great David's greater Son. The crowd, who can see, are blind to who he is, as are the Pharisees. The counterpoint is poignant. The judgments are complete.

21:1–27
13. Judgment on Israel

In the preceding seven narrative units, Matthew has shown us seven ways in which the kingdom of heaven reverses human judgments. The judgment theme has clearly been central, and it will remain so during the next two chapters. Chapters 21 – 22 continue with God's judgment on Israel in and through the kingdom claims amid controversies that form the subject matter of these chapters. Then the section ends (chs. 23 – 25), as have all the other four panels in the Gospel, with a major collection of sayings from the mouth of Jesus. This time, naturally, they bring to a climax the theme of judgment that has dominated this section of the Gospel.

It may not be immediately apparent that judgment continues to be the thrust of chapter 21, because it begins with the familiar story of the triumphal entry. But as we look beneath the surface, it becomes clear that judgment is the focus: judgment that Jesus brings on the unbelieving, or judgment that the unbelieving bring on Jesus.

God's judgment on the temple: no worship (21:1–13)

The theme of judgment colours the whole narrative between now and the passion. One could call the triumphant entry 'The King comes in judgment to his capital'. So he does, but in a most unexpected way, acting out the principle of humble service which he has just enunciated in the previous chapter. The suffering Son of Man, who comes to Jerusalem to give his life as a ransom for many, enters the capital not as a messianic figure on a warhorse but, as Zechariah had anticipated in his prophecy centuries before, *gentle and riding on a donkey, on a colt, the foal of a donkey* (5).[1] There may be an allusion to King David's return by the same route after the defeat of Absalom's rebellion.[2]

---

[1] This is the only time we read of Jesus travelling in any other way than on foot.
[2] 2 Sam. 15:30.

The burden of his entry is clear. He wants to make the people of Jerusalem see that though he is their rightful king, his reign is one of peace and service;[3] he is not the political messiah they were expecting. He has come to rule over the hearts and lives of men and women, not to kick the Romans out; but this reversed most contemporary ideas of what the kingdom should be. So while the people cried, *'Hosanna!'*, 'Lord, save now!' (9), and *the blind and lame came to him* (14), the leaders were furious.

As we look more closely at this story, it becomes apparent that the occasion of Jesus' entry had strong links with the Maccabean feast of the Rededication of the Temple after it had been desecrated by the Greek ruler Antiochus Epiphanes, who offered pigs' flesh to Olympian Zeus on the altar and turned temple cubicles into a brothel. This was an important festival, celebrating as it did the shaking off of the invader's yoke through the wonderfully successful Maccabean uprising. The temple was in fact rededicated in 164 BC, three years to the day after Antiochus defiled it. 2 Maccabees 10 tells us about it. They sang 'Hosanna!', waved palm branches, and looked forward to redemption, having once tasted something of it under Judas Maccabaeus. This was the time when the pagan yoke had been broken, and this would be the time when the Son of David, both king and high priest (a combination that was not allowed in Old Testament times)[4] would come and set the whole world free of sin for ever.[5] Is not this what the prophets had suggested?[6] Is not this the confidence the people expressed as they came singing the Hallel,[7] chanted regularly in worship, and particularly by pilgrims as they approached Jerusalem)? Now it was all happening, albeit in a perplexing manner. But Israel was too blind to see, so God had to judge their culpable blindness. This chapter indicates four such judgments.

The first is here, against the temple itself.[8] It was the very centre of Judaism, and yet its worship was hollow. To the piercing eye of Jesus it looked more like *a den of robbers* (13)[9] than a house of prayer. Worshippers needed a special sort of temple money to buy their sacrifices, and the money-changers were cheating the pilgrims left, right and centre. The dove market was a particular racket. The whole thing was totally dishonouring to God, who had set that

---

[3] Here we have another of the 'formula quotations' to show how Jesus fulfilled Old Testament prophecies, in this case Zech. 9:9 with overtones of Is. 62:11.
[4] Cf. 2 Chr. 26:18   [5] *Psalms of Solomon* 12:23.
[6] Zech. 3:8; 6:12; 13:1.   [7] Pss. 113 – 118. See below, p. 277 and note 18.
[8] The cleansing of the temple was as provocative a messianic claim as the entry into Jerusalem. It was a fulfilment of Scripture, a public demonstration, a critique, and a sign of the future worship in the Messiah's church.
[9] Jer. 7:11.

temple there not only for Judaism but with an emblem of universalism at its heart, the court of the Gentiles. And all the Gentiles met was corruption in the very place where they were intended to be able to draw near to God! So, like Judas Maccabaeus, Jesus strode in to cleanse the temple, a bold prophetic act such as the Old Testament prophets loved to use in order to draw attention to their message and make it memorable. But it was rather ironical. The almost contemporary *Psalms of Solomon* expressed the belief that 'he shall purge Jerusalem of Gentile defilement, making it holy as of old'.[10] In point of fact, Jesus comes to cleanse the court of the Gentiles from Jewish defilement! The temple has not served the purpose for which it was built. It has not manifested the glory of God, but has rather succumbed to corrupt practices. And *the prophet from Nazareth* (11)[11] comes not so much to purge the temple (it is too late in the drama of salvation for that) but to overturn it. The temple will no longer play a significant part in God's purposes. A greater than the temple was present, and the people half-recognized it as they waved palm branches, and cried, *'Hosanna to the Son of David!'* For he came to the temple in fulfilment of Malachi 3:1–5, and therefore it constituted a messianic claim for those who had eyes to see. But if Christians could see that Jesus' prophetic action was profoundly fulfilled in the destruction of the temple by the Romans in AD 70, there was little cause for self-congratulation. For it would not be possible for Matthew's leaders to hear this story without realizing its implication: *God will judge bad churches*. His severest judgment will be reserved for those churches whose worship is hollow, where corruption and dissension are rife, and which repel rather than attract 'Gentile' outsiders. There is a moving and humbling account, in one of Israel Abrahams' books, of the corruption he saw around the Church of the Holy Sepulchre as trades-people swindled pilgrims, and vendors sold sacred and irrelevant relics. He wondered, rightly, whether Jesus would not overthrow these false servants of his, were he to return today, just as he overthrew the false worshippers in Israel long ago. Many a church needs to take that message to heart.

There is so much more in this story. The timing of it is one problem: in John's Gospel[12] it comes at the outset of the ministry; in the Synoptics it comes at the end and contributes to his death. An acted claim like this must have had enormous repercussions. Probably the Synoptic dating is right, and John uses it near the beginning of his Gospel to highlight what the ministry of Jesus really set out to

---

[10] *Psalms of Solomon* 17:3.

[11] That may seem an inadequate title, but it looks back to the promise of the eschatological prophet in Deut. 18:15.

[12] Ch. 2.

do. Quite likely the story was well known and circulated independently of any dating. It was shortly before Passover, and it was in Jerusalem. The precise year was not remembered. Indeed, we are not sure whether Jesus was executed in AD 30 or 33. The sequence, not the year, is what matters.

Commentators make extraordinarily heavy weather of verse 7, *Jesus sat on them*. Matthew has just mentioned that the disciples brought from nearby Bethany a donkey with her colt for the Master's entry into Jerusalem. The other evangelists mention only the colt. So scholars think Matthew misunderstood Hebrew parallelism in the quotation from Zechariah 9:9, and imagined two animals to have been present when in fact there was only one. The evangelist is then supposed to have had the crass stupidity to make Jesus sit *on them* (*epanō autōn*, 7). To which one can only reply that Matthew knew his Hebrew a lot better than the said scholars, and that it makes excellent sense to bring the mother along if you are going to seat your leader on a colt that had never been broken in. The *on them* refers, of course, to its immediate antecedent in the Greek, that is, the *cloaks* which people were, with nationalistic fervour, throwing on to the animals.

None of this must, however, obscure the fact that there is one main point to this story. The allusions make it plain that this is a covert messianic gesture from Jesus, as he enters Jerusalem and conveys the sense of God's righteous judgment upon the temple and its hollow worship.

God's judgment on the priests: no praise (21:14–17)

If the worship of the temple brought no joy to God, the same must have been true of the attitude of the priests. *The blind and lame came to him at the temple, and he healed them* (14).[13] The children came to the temple and shouted, *'Hosanna to the Son of David'* (literally 'Save now', a traditional cry for assistance to God or his representative). But the priests were indignant. They could not bear these non-regulation happenings and new songs in the temple. Nor can some clergy these days!

And God's judgment will always be on the adherents of the Christian religion who pig-headedly resist change and try to box the Spirit of God into what has always been done, what is safe, and what is uncontroversial. God will judge the priests who do not lead the praise with heartfelt worship, and who do not rejoice when unconventional new voices worship Jesus and broken lives are

---

[13] The blind and lame were excluded from the temple (2 Sam. 5:8), but the Son of God welcomes them in this, the only miracle he is recorded as performing in the temple.

healed by his mighty power. 'Scribes of the kingdom', Christian leaders, bear a great responsibility. They are not to dampen the enthusiasm of others, however naïve or ill-informed it may be. Perhaps they will need to channel it. But if they pour scorn on it, or damn it with faint praise, they will face the same judgment that Jesus brought upon the priests and teachers of the law in the Jerusalem of his day.

After this incident, Jesus leaves the temple and spends the night at nearby Bethany.

God's judgment on the fig-tree: no fruit (21:18–22)

The fig-tree, like the vine, is one of the classic symbols of Israel in the Old Testament. If you wanted to be a characteristic Israelite, you sat under your fig-tree. Such is the background. Now for the action. *Early in the morning, as he was on his way back to the city* (many pilgrims at the great festivals had to camp in 'Greater Jerusalem', the area outside the city, because of the vast crowds), *he was hungry. Seeing a fig-tree by the road, he went up to it but found nothing on it except leaves. Then he said to it, 'May you never bear fruit again!' Immediately the tree withered* (18–19).

An immense attack has been brought against this action of Jesus: he is accused of petulance, selfishness and loss of temper. It is regarded as unworthy of him, and many scholars think it was originally a parable that has 'become' a miracle. The truth seems to me to be relatively easy to discern on this particular issue. It is an acted parable, just like the entry into Jerusalem on the donkey, and the cleansing of the temple, that precede it. Jesus longs to find some fruit in God's people Israel. Unfortunately, all he finds is leaves! What good is that to him?[14] The meaning is plain. Instead of the fruit of righteousness, of response to the Messiah, of entry into the kingdom, Jesus had been met by narrow and legalistic religion that refused to listen to his message and his claims. His action when he said to the fig-tree, *'May you never bear fruit again!'* was the action of God's frustrated hunger for true religion. If that fruit was not going to be produced, the days would soon come when the leaves would be stripped from the fig-tree of Israel, and the land would be sacked by the Romans. It happened with terrible thoroughness and unimaginable slaughter in the years AD 66–77. As so often elsewhere, Matthew has greatly shortened the account given by Mark, which has the cursing and the withering separated by a night. Mark's story is both more difficult and more comprehensible. He is interested in the particular days of this Holy Week, and sandwiches the cleansing

---

[14] See Mic. 7:1 for the fruitless fig-tree, applied to Israel's religious failure.

of the temple[15] between the two halves of the cursing of the fig-tree that he records.[16] It is plain therefore that Mark sees the judgment on the fig-tree and the judgment on the temple as correlated. He is in no doubt about the prophetic symbolism in both.[17] Judgment is coming to the temple and the nation alike. But the difficulty in Mark's account is that he says, 'It was not the season for figs.'[18] If so, was it not highly unreasonable of Jesus to expect to find figs, and to be so disappointed when he did not? No. Fig-trees bear an early crop of bitter and immature male figs called *taksh*, which precede the leaves and drop off before the proper fruit forms. Bitter though this crop is, it is often eaten by impoverished peasants. This tree was in full leaf (it was March), but the time for figs was not yet: that would normally begin in June. But Jesus could tell that the tree was barren because it had no *taksh* on it. There was therefore nothing unreasonable in his hope of finding something edible on the tree (the bitter *taksh*), and in his disappointment when the absence of that immature fruit showed that the tree was barren.

To the intense sorrow and frustration of Jesus, there was little but nominal religion in Israel. And God always judges it. He judged it in Israel's case in AD 70, but Matthew's church leaders need to take note, for dead religion in Christian churches will fall under his judgment just as surely as Israel's failure evoked it. God is no more bound to Christian churches with a long pedigree than he was to Israel with an even longer one. If there is no fruit (in prayerfulness, in evangelism, in love and ministry to the community), God will judge such churches and they will die. True, God has no heart for the splitting of churches and the forming of new ones, which is so common in some parts of the world. His preference is to renew, not to start again. But if the new life is not welcomed in the old fig-trees, the day may come when those old fig-trees are cut down. If there is no fruit in our church life, it will shrivel and die like the fig-tree.

Immediately (19) emphasizes the certainty that Jesus' judgment was fulfilled. Since, unlike Mark, he does not recount the story in two parts, this is Matthew's way of saying that what Jesus predicted took place. The axe was laid to the root of the tree, as John the Baptist had predicted (3:10). It was decisive. Nominal religion cannot stand beside the kingdom of God.[19]

---

[15] Mark 11:15–19.   [16] Mark 11:12–14 and 20–25.
[17] See W. R. Telford, *The Barren Temple and the Withered Tree* (JSOT Press, 1980).
[18] Mark 11:3.
[19] The 'mountain-moving' faith of Jesus (cf. 17:20) evokes the amazement of the disciples. Note that this promise of answered prayer is only for those who have faith. 'And "faith" is always in Matthew not a quality of the one praying, but a relationship of practical trust in the one to whom prayer is offered (8:10; 9:2, 22, 29; 15:28; 17:20).' France (1985).

God's judgment on the leadership: no integrity (21:23–27)

Throughout the Gospel we have seen the growing unwillingness of the religious leadership of the Jews to countenance Jesus and his claims, although these have been validated before them in both word and deed. The Jewish leadership of his day had plenty of 'leaves' (to pursue the imagery of the previous pericope), but not much fruit. This part of the book records considerable controversy between them and Jesus, and this will intensify. It is an important matter to Matthew, for he is anxious to equip the leadership in the churches of his day, and it was all too possible that they could go the way of the Pharisees and teachers of the law. The same dangers threaten religious people, be they Christian or Jewish.

Verses 23–27 condemn the religious authorities for lack of integrity. Naturally, after the remarkable teaching and healing he has been giving, they come and ask him by what authority he does these things. He had been to no scribal school and had received no formal authorization to give spiritual leadership in Israel. What right did an unordained carpenter have to make such a nuisance of himself? Jesus replied to their question by asking them another in turn. This is a wise expedient, which Christians should exploit rather than give unconvincing answers when they are attacked for their faith. To force opponents to examine their own presuppositions is an effective way of proceeding. Jesus no doubt adopts this regular rabbinic tactic here because he senses that a straight answer would precipitate the final crisis before he has completed his work. But he also wants to show up the lack of integrity that underlies their question.

So he asks them about John the Baptist. What authorization did he have? Had he the official recognition of the Jewish leadership, or did he come clothed with the authority of God's voice, crying in the wilderness? That is an extremely painful dilemma for them to be impaled upon. If they admit that John's authority came from God, Jesus will want to know why they did not go and get baptized by him, and why they have not responded to Jesus himself, the one to whom John pointed forward. If they say that his authorization came from human sources, what is it, and who has given it him? Moreover, to diminish John in this way would be a dangerous thing to do. The festival crowd is in full flow. To them John was a martyred prophet of the highest repute. Accordingly, the priests lamely reply, 'We don't know' (27). That feeble escapism is a transparent covering for their duplicity. They know perfectly well that John came from God, but they do not dare admit it because their own lives would come under such justifiable criticism. Theological agnosticism can cover moral disobedience. There is a distressing lack of integrity among these leaders of the temple.

Jesus is not just asking them a difficult question which he knows would unmask their dissimulation and cause them embarrassment. His question is highly apt. Jesus is emphasizing the eschatological dimension of his cleansing of the temple. He is 'the Lord ... suddenly come to his temple',[20] and John was his messenger, sent to prepare the way. They will never understand who he is until they recognize who John was. John's message, 'Repent', is the precondition for Jesus' message, 'Believe'. If they have not done the one, they cannot do the other. They must face up to who John was. To take refuge in agnosticism is no excuse. Even their failure to answer does not evade the dilemma that Jesus' question poses them. Because of their admitted inability to assess John, they implicitly confess their incompetence to judge Jesus, whose mission and ministry are intertwined with John's. Their lack of integrity has boomeranged.

Having made this penetrating exposure of his priestly questioners, Jesus now tells three parables to hammer the message home. Each of them reveals God's judgment on the leaders of Israel for rejecting God's spokesmen. But each brings a particular charge. We shall examine them in the next chapter.

[20] Mal. 3:1–2.

21:28 – 22:46
14. Parables and controversies on judgment

Matthew now brings before us three parables which drive home this matter of human responsibility in the face of divine judgment, and follows them with three stories of controversy between Jesus and his opponents which make the same point. Finally, Jesus brings the series to a conclusion by asking his interlocutors a question they dare not answer. As ever in this Gospel, the plan is beautifully designed and orderly.

Three parables

The parable of the two sons (21:28–32)

This, the first of a trio of 'controversy parables', impugns the Jewish leaders for their lack of obedience. If the main charge his question about John raised was 'no integrity', this parable complains of 'no action'. Like the first son in the story, the leaders of Israel made all the right noises, and promised to work for God and obey him in his vineyard (Israel), but they *did* nothing. The second son was rebellious, but afterwards, *changed his mind* (29; literally 'repented') and went to do the father's work. Which was the obedient one? The answer was so evident that the priests could not evade it by the plea of ignorance this time. And Jesus hammered home the implications. The despised tax collectors and defiled sinners were crowding into the kingdom of God because they repented and believed John's teaching; but the religious authorities, on the whole, stood well clear, not only when John was operating but afterwards: *'even after you saw this, you did not repent and believe him'* (32). Once again Jesus co-ordinates his own ministry with that of John. Once again he charges the leadership with lack of repentance, lack of faith, and rank disobedience in rejecting God's call to work effectively in his vineyard.

A couple of details are worth noticing. The first hints at the degeneracy of Israel, which her leaders were called to rectify, but about which they did nothing. While it is true that Israel is often seen under the figure of the vine in the Old Testament, it is also the case that when she is so described there is generally an allusion to her degeneracy.[1] Israel's state is parlous. The priests and leaders are called to work, but they have declined, and their disobedience is heinous.[2]

The second hints at a last chance for Israel, in the goodness of God. If he waited for the harlots and tax collectors to repent and believe, and they had responded, might the priests not follow suit? The arms of divine mercy are still open.

The parable of the wicked tenants (21:33–46)

Another controversy parable is brought forward in this increasingly hostile situation. If the thrust of the last one has been the failure of the religious leaders to obey God, the problem here is their lack of loyalty to the God who entrusted them with their privileged position.

This parable shows how restrictive it would be to assume that a parable always has one point. The word 'parable' means 'a throwing together' for comparison. Very often, as we have seen,[3] there is one main point in the comparison, but there may well be more. In this case there clearly is. The *landowner* who *planted a vineyard* is God. The *vineyard* is Israel.[4] *The tenants* are the religious leaders of the nation. The messengers (*servants*) are the succession of prophets whom God has sent to them. Last of all he sends *his son*, who stands in succession to all the other prophets God has sent to Israel but is nevertheless on a different level – the difference between the servants in a household and a son. The background of the story as Jesus sketches it is very much an everyday affair. It was a procedure with which everyone was familiar. It would be easy to 'read' the parable and make the identifications. The *chief priests and the Pharisees* did just that (45)!

This parable unveils the flagrant disloyalty of the leaders of Israel. God had given them a wonderful vineyard to cultivate; he had given them all the necessary equipment to do the job (*winepress, watchtower* for shelter and burglar control, *wall* to keep out wild pigs and other trespassers; 33). He had put his trust in them. And what did they do? The history of Israel tells the story starkly. In

---

[1] E.g. Ps. 80; Is. 5; Jer. 2:21; Ezek. 15:1–8; 19:10; Hos. 10:1–15; cf. 2 Esdras 5:23–30.
[2] Matthew substitutes 'kingdom of God' for his regular 'kingdom of heaven' in order to emphasize their personal failure before God to recognize his saving action in Christ.
[3] See above, p. 152.   [4] Cf. above, p. 210, and Is. 5:1, 7.

brief, they appropriated his goods, rejected his prophets, denied his rightful claims on them, and killed his Son. They were given freedom as well as trust, but the day of reckoning is at hand: they will be held accountable for the way they have exercised that freedom. A very solemn message indeed, and highly controversial.

Just as controversial is the claim of Jesus to be the Son, compared with all the previous prophets, who were servants. The collision course is plain. Jesus knows that he will be thrown *out of the vineyard* (i.e. to Roman executioners) and *killed* (39). He asks the hearers what they think the day of reckoning will bring. Drawn into the movement of the story by its sheer power, they blurt out, almost against their will, the obvious answer: they knew what happened to bad tenants on estates – it was not an uncommon situation in those days. '*He will bring those wretches to a wretched end ... and he will rent the vineyard to other tenants, who will give him his share of the crop at harvest time*' (41). Indeed he will. God will not be mocked. He will take from Israel the position of responsibility which they had abused, and will give it to other tenants, that is to say the Gentiles. By the time Matthew wrote, the transition was in full flow. Verse 43, unique to Matthew, emphasizes the 'new people' who inherit the position and promises of apostate Israel, a people composed of both Jews and Gentiles, who will be loyal to the Vineyard Owner and his Son.

Could Jesus have called himself *the Son* in this absolute sense (38)? In the Old Testament, 'son of God' is used in four ways. First, for the angels.[5] Secondly, for the king.[6] This was given a messianic flavour by the men at Qumran a little before the time of Jesus.[7] The king was thought of as adopted 'son' of God. Thirdly, 'son of God' was used for certain righteous men.[8] Fourthly, it was used of Israel, God's 'firstborn'.[9] In all four usages, obedience was the hallmark of election. All four failed, but God kept sending messengers with the good news of God's anointed (not adopted) king, the unique Son, the Righteous One, the true Israel. And now he stood before them, the tenants who had so abused the terms of their commission. What a poignant encounter!

Jesus drives the point home by using another text common in messianic discussion, Psalm 118:22–23.[10] It is a tremendous claim to finality, and to God's way of reversing human evaluations. The image is fourfold.

First, *the stone the builders rejected* (i.e. himself) has become under God's hand the capstone of the corner, the keystone that holds everything together. This takes up and reverses the theme of his

---

[5] E.g. Gen. 6:1–4; Job 1:6. [6] E.g. Ps. 2:7; 2 Sam. 7:14. [7] 4Q *Florilegium* 1:11.
[8] Sirach 4:10; Wisdom 2:18; Matt. 27:43. [9] Exod. 4:22; Hos. 11:1; Sirach 36:12. [10] See Acts 4:11; 1 Pet. 2:4–7.

rejection, in the parable. God will vindicate the Jesus whom Judaism has rejected. This emphasis provides the element in the three passion predictions which is missing in the parable, the theme of resurrection. Jesus Christ is foundational. That is the point.

The second image is more composite. The idea is of a mighty rock over which people would stumble if they walked into it, and which would crush them if it were to fall on them. In Isaiah 8:14 the Lord would be both sanctuary and stumbling-block, depending on people's response to him. Jesus applies that to himself.

Thirdly, in Isaiah 28:16 we are told that God lays in Zion a foundation stone, tested, and precious, a sure foundation: 'The one who trusts will never be dismayed.' Very well, that foundation stone has been laid, in the person of Jesus. He is tested (23–27), precious (37) and a sure foundation (9). That provides a powerful contrast with the perishable, false, human foundation of disobedient Israel.[11]

The fourth passage Jesus must have had in mind is the 'stone' passage from Daniel 2:34–45, where the stone is the apocalyptic kingdom that will destroy the greatest empires of the world and fill the earth. Strands of all four passages are woven together into this powerful claim that Jesus is the *capstone* (42), the only proper foundation for life. To disobey his way is to hit our shins and break our bones against God's foundation for life. To defy him is to have the life crushed out of us.

It was easy for Semitic people to move from the idea of 'son', which dominated the first part of this controversy story, to 'stone', which has dominated the second. For in Hebrew *bēn* means 'son' and *'eben* means 'stone', and they loved plays on words. Interestingly enough, the targum (Aramaic commentary) on Psalm 118:22 reads: 'The *son* which the builders rejected …', and that was certainly not influenced by Christian exposition! It does, however, show how closely linked the two words 'son' and 'stone' were. This made the passage congenial to Christians expounding the Old Testament, and rather difficult for those who were not Christians to repudiate, since their own exegetes interpreted it in the same way!

I have spent some time on the use of Psalm 118 made here because it is a prime and rich example of early Christian exegesis.[12] Two further things ought to be added before we leave it. The first is that in Psalm 118:22 it is Israel that is exalted as the stone the builders (the nations) rejected and which has nevertheless become the

---

[11] Is. 28:15; cf. Matt. 21:30.

[12] See E. E. Ellis, 'How the New Testament uses the Old', in I. H. Marshall (ed.), *New Testament Interpretation* (Eerdmans, 1977), and Stanton's rather unusual exegesis: 'The Pharisees are rejected in favour of the *ethnos* [people] whom they themselves have rejected' (pp. 151–152).

capstone. Jesus turns that claim upside down. This time it is Israel that does the rejecting: he is the capstone they have refused. Secondly, people would never be able to forget this teaching, for Psalm 118 was sung at all the great festivals. It would be indelibly inscribed on their memory. And it would underline the disloyalty of the 'builders', the finality of the 'Son' or 'stone', and the sovereign hand of God over the roller-coaster of history. Matthew's Christian leaders would take all this to heart, and would read it as a warning to themselves as well.

God expects his leaders, whom he trusts, and whom he equips so richly, to be utterly loyal to him. They must not make their position an excuse to 'keep the fruit' and feather their nest. They must not fail to listen to God's prophetic messengers in their congregations (albeit unordained), and they must above all else beware of 'crucifying the Son of God all over again'.[13] If God had been compelled to change tenants once, he could, if provoked, do it again.

The parable of the wedding feast (22:1–14)

Still Jesus is speaking to and about the Jewish leadership (14–15). Still he is castigating them for their lack of integrity. That main charge (21:23–28) is fleshed out in the parable of the two sons, which points out their inaction in the vineyard of Israel, and in the parable of the tenants, which points out their disloyalty in that same vineyard. Now he goes further, and tells them plainly that they have no standing in the kingdom of God.

In this story we have a generous king who gave a marriage feast for his Son. Again note the sovereignty of the king, the unique position of the son, and the nature of the kingdom; it is not a funeral but a feast. Following eastern custom, the king sent out his servants at the time of the wedding feast to tell them that the moment had arrived; they should be in attendance. *But they refused to come* (3). The intransigence of the original recipients of the invitation, that is to say the Jews, is stressed when Jesus tells of the second and more pressing invitation.[14] ' *"I have prepared my dinner: My oxen and fattened cattle have been slaughtered, and everything is ready. Come to the wedding banquet." But they paid no attention and went off – one to his field, another to his business'* (4–5). Indeed, Matthew (maybe even Jesus) goes outside the bounds of the story[15] and predicts the implication. Luke simply tells us the excuses people

[13] Heb. 6:6.
[14] It was an oriental custom to issue an invitation to an event without specifying a precise time until later. See Kenneth E. Bailey, *Through Peasant Eyes* (Eerdmans, 1980), pp. 88–113
[15] Compare the parallel in Luke 14:16–24.

made and states that they had missed their chance and were excluded from the banquet. Matthew, using the Jewish *pesher* method of interpretation, of which we now have ample evidence in the Qumran literature, interweaves the text of the story Jesus told with the application he has observed in his own day.[16] So Matthew goes on: '*The rest seized his servants, ill-treated them and killed them*' (6). That had happened to many Christian missionaries on Jewish soil in the four decades or so since Jesus told the original story. '*The king was enraged. He sent his army and destroyed those murderers and burned their city*' (7). This is a graphic description of what happened in the fall of Jerusalem to Titus, the horrors that were perpetrated, and the destruction that followed. It would be hard for the Christians not to see this as, in part at least, a judgment from God on the nation that had rejected their Messiah when he came to them.[17]

The wedding feast proceeds regardless, even though so many from the chosen people have declined the invitation. Many from the *street corners*, the highways and hedges have come into the wedding feast of the kingdom. The invitation goes out to all and sundry. Indeed, we catch a whiff of the evangelistic fervour of Matthew's church in the very phraseology: '*invite to the banquet anyone you can find*' (9). The *wedding hall was* indeed *filled with guests* (10).

What about the man who had no *wedding clothes* and was ejected (11–13). It seems clear that the generous king not only provided the feast free for the wedding of his son; not only invited everyone to it; but also provided beautiful festal robes for all to wear.[18] In this way the poor need not be ashamed of their rags, and the rich no right to be proud of their dinner jackets or gowns. All came in on the same footing, just as in the parable of the workers in the vineyard. There is room neither for embarrassment nor for pride in the feast of the kingdom. Both attitudes ruin the enjoyment.

But one man pushed his way in without wedding clothes. No doubt he thought his own were good enough. Of course, he stuck out like a sore thumb. The king noticed him as soon as he came in. '*Friend*,'[19] he asked, '*How did you get in here without wedding clothes?*' There was no answer to that; the man was thrown out *into the darkness, where there will be weeping and gnashing of teeth* (13).

---

[16] This is not playing fast and loose with the text. It was a reputable method of Jewish exegesis.

[17] However, this does not demand a date after AD 70 for the Gospel. This was a standard way of describing the destruction of cities in war. Cf. Is. 5:24–25; 1 Macc. 5:28; *Testament of Judah* 5:1–5.

[18] For examples of festal dress being offered to guests, see Gundry.

[19] Again there is a sinister note in that word, as on the other two occasions when Matthew uses it. See above, on 20:13.

The punishment is ludicrously severe for having come to a wedding improperly dressed. But the point goes far deeper. The man who scorned his host's provision of wedding clothes insulted the host and showed personal complacency. His best was good enough for God! And God says that it is not. The king in the story has the man thrown out. God will do the same to anyone who relies on his own fancied goodness to gain entry into the kingdom. There are overtones of Isaiah here. 'All our righteous acts are like filthy rags.'[20] That is the human predicament: we are literally not fit to be seen before God, let alone to enjoy the feast of his kingdom. But the prophet had already found the solution: 'I delight greatly in the LORD; my soul rejoices in my God. For he has clothed me with garments of salvation, and arrayed me in a robe of righteousness, as a bridegroom adorns his head like a priest.'[21]

So the meaning of this parable is clear. God has provided the feast of the kingdom. It is the wedding feast for his Son. The invitation goes out far and wide. If you reject it, you miss the party. If you think you can get in relying on your own fitness, you will be thrown out. *Many are invited*, but few show, by their response, that they *are chosen* (14). In the Old Testament, the word translated 'chosen' was originally used as a synonym for Israel, but the failure of the nation to fulfil its destiny led to its being reinterpreted as those who share the inheritance of the chosen covenant people.[22] And there is a double nuance to it; both divine call and human response. Without the latter we do not show ourselves to be among the elect. So Jesus means that many had received the call, but few had shown themselves 'elect' by responding to it. Alas, the Pharisees on the whole fell into the category of the *many* who were called but did not respond.

Three controversy stories (22:15–40)

The theme of judgment is still to the fore. The breach between Jesus and the rulers of his nation yawns wide. We have just had three controversy parables to underline the charge Jesus brings of the lack of integrity in the religious leadership in Israel. Respectively those three parables impugn the inaction, the disloyalty and the standing of the Jewish leadership. They could not have been best pleased. Indeed, the anger runs so high that Pharisees and Herodians, nationalists and quislings, join forces to bring Jesus down, with the Sadducees at their heels (15–16, 23). They prepare their positions with passionate care and set out to *trap him in his words* (15). The

---

[20] Is. 64:6.   [21] Is. 61:10.

[22] See J. Jeremias, *New Testament Theology* (SCM, 1973), p. 131.

controversies they initiate are each packed with high explosive, but Jesus takes them on.

Controversy for the truth is an aspect of Christian leadership which is widely neglected today, since tolerance seems to be almost the only virtue. But Christ was a controversialist, and so should his disciples be as need arises, especially when they are in positions of leadership and truth is dragged in the dirt. So Jesus engages robustly in these three controversies, and ends by asking his opponents a controversial question which they cannot answer.

The first controversy, about politics (22:15–22)

The tribute money or poll tax paid to the Roman emperor was a contentious issue. It was bitterly resented in the province of Judea. The question was very cunning: if Jesus said, 'Refuse the tax', he would immediately be liable to arrest. If he said, 'Pay it', he would immediately forfeit popular support. And with the improbable coalition of *the Herodians* (who advocated paying) and *the Pharisees* (who did not like it at all) watching every word and gesture, Jesus was in an exceedingly difficult situation; his opponents were itching to exploit it.

Three things strike me particularly in this remarkable incident.

First, the sheer poverty of Jesus. He who was heir to the whole universe had to ask for *a denarius* (19). Here was one who was desperately poor and yet supremely happy.

Secondly, after robustly exposing their hypocrisy (for the Pharisees heartily disliked the tax, yet cheerfully used the offending money!), Jesus asked them an embarrassing question: *'Whose portrait is this? And whose inscription?'* Reluctantly, they spat out the one word, *'Caesar's'* (20–21). The coin bore the legend 'Tiberius Caesar, Augustus, son of the deified Augustus, chief priest'. The use of Caesar's coinage acknowledges his authority and, with it, the obligation to pay taxes. They could not benefit from imperial roads, education, justice and freedom from invasion without making their contribution. Far from imperilling the socio-political structure, Jesus was saying that those who enjoy Caesar's benefits should pay Caesar's taxes. Jesus' response is a reminder that, instead of being quick to attempt answers, we should give more attention to asking the sorts of question that provoke thought and penetrate to the deepest levels of the people we are with.

In the third place, Jesus gives his own answer. *'Give to Caesar what is Caesar's, and to God what is God's'* (21). Jesus was here cutting at a fundamental conception about the state in antiquity. The cult of the gods and the power of the ruler go very closely together. Indeed, our word 'religion' comes from the link, *religio*, that binds the king or emperor to the king of the gods. It goes back as far as Numa, the first king of Rome, who struck a bargain with Jupiter, the king of the gods. He would supply the god with sacrifices, and Jupiter would give strength to his armies. But if civic life was separated from the cult of the gods, disaster could overtake, as it had done in a century of civil war before Octavian won the battle of Actium in 31 BC and named himself Augustus. In his *Res Gestae*, the prestigious (and very public) version of his will, he prided himself on having restored no fewer than eighty-two temples that had fallen into disrepair. The agreement was on again! He reverenced the gods, and the gods smiled on his empire.

Jesus refused to accept this widely held view. He said 'Yes' to paying Caesar taxes, but 'No' to giving Caesar worship. That disjunction had the most profound consequences, and was one of the reasons the Roman Empire was so jittery about the Christians. Peaceful and law-abiding though they were for the most part, they refused to give Caesar the customary worship, and they had a loyalty higher than to the emperor. All very disturbing. The reply of Jesus hit deep into the memory of the early church[23] and was form-ative in developing Christian social and political ethics. The Pharisees and Herodians have comprehensively failed in their plot.[24]

One delightful touch comes through in the Greek word translated *give* (*apodote*), which means 'give back'. The coin bears Caesar's image: give it back to him. You bear God's image: so give yourself back to him!

When we do give ourselves without reserve to the God who gave us everything and formed us in his own image, and when we set out to give Caesar what is Caesar's and to give God what is God's, then we have within ourselves a spring of action which is always questing, always seeking integrity in a world of compromise. We must wrestle to discern the areas where Caesar has no right to dictate. These areas must be handed back to God.

The second controversy, about life after death (22:23–33)

Life after death fascinated the Jews. In the intertestamental books it is one of the prevailing subjects for conjecture and discussion. It therefore furnished an ideal area for another trick question designed to trap Jesus.

The *Sadducees* were the aristocratic priestly families of Israel,

---

[23] See Rom. 13:7; 1 Pet. 2:13.

[24] This brilliant answer, confounding both Pharisees and Herodians, would not of course satisfy the militant Zealots. Although in this story Jesus so clearly distances himself from the popular Zealot option, he was, ironically, executed as a Zealot. On Jesus' politics, see J. H. Yoder, *The Politics of Jesus* (Eerdmans, 1972).

pragmatists about the Roman power, and earthbound in their theology. They accepted only the Pentateuch among the sacred books of the Old Testament. 'The doctrine of the Sadducees is this: souls die with bodies.'[25] There were constant debates between Pharisees and Sadducees over life after death. The Pharisees not only held to it strongly, but believed in a physical resurrection at the last day. So now the Sadducees come with a question which, they hope, will show how ludicrous it is to believe in a physical resurrection. The story is not only ridiculous; it is also hypocritical, for it is put forward by people who do not believe in any form of resurrection.

The Jews had a custom (how often was it observed?)[26] of levirate marriage, which obliged a man to marry his brother's widow and beget children for him so that the line and the name did not die out. So the Sadducees came with this story of levirate marriage in which *seven brothers* successively married the same woman, and all of them died childless, and so were on a par. Whose wife would she be in the resurrection?

Jesus' reply to this catch question was dynamic. First, he told them bluntly that they were wrong. Then he told them why they were wrong. They were ignorant of *the Scriptures* and of *the power of God*. They prided themselves on knowing the *torah* inside out, but rejected much of the Old Testament Scriptures.[27] What is more, they knew nothing of God's power to raise the dead (contrary to their convictions) and to raise them in such a way that their cavilling criticisms fall by the wayside. For in the future life, marriage is a thing of the past (contrary to the convictions of the Pharisees). The intimacy that a human being shares with one other person in marriage is universalized in the joy and love of heaven. Believers will be spiritual beings like the angels (in which the Sadducees did not believe). And angels can no more marry than they can die. They are eternal children of God.

So the Sadducees get egg on their faces. The power of God changes us[28] and gives to believers 'resurrection bodies'; that is to say, the means of expression and identity that are appropriate to their changed situation. The Sadducees know nothing of that life-changing power. They are also ignorant of the Scriptures. For Scripture attests the resurrection, and not only in Daniel 12:2 ('Multitudes who sleep in the dust of the earth will awake'). If only they look beneath the surface they will find it implied in the Pentateuch itself (where they were certain there was no trace of it.)

[25] Josephus, *Antiquities* 18.16. See Acts 23:8.
[26] However, see Mishnah tractate *Yebamoth*, which shows that levirate marriage was still a lively issue after AD 70.
[27] Including passages that speak of resurrection, such as Is. 29:16; Dan. 12:2.
[28] Cf. 1 Cor.15:51.

Jesus then quotes Exodus 3:6 as God's pronouncement: *'I am the God of Abraham, the God of Isaac, and the God of Jacob.'* Not 'I *was* the God of these patriarchs', but 'I *am!' 'He is not the God of the dead but of the living'* (36). This may seem a somewhat Jesuitical argument to us, but it must have struck the Sadducees powerfully, using precisely their own method of exegesis[29] against them. In point of fact it is a profound argument for life after death. Jesus does not, like Socrates, infer it from some supposed inherent part of us which will survive death. He hangs the hope of life after death totally upon the generosity of God, who stoops to win our hearts upon this earth, and cannot bring himself at death to scrap what is precious to him. Exodus 3:6 not only suggests the reality of life after death through the generosity of God when we had no claim on him at all; it hints at the nature of this life: unbroken fellowship with him and with his people for ever. We do not read that Jesus convinced the Sadducees. We do read that he silenced them (34). At all events, *the crowds* recognized the impact of *his teaching* (33; cf. 7:28–29).[30]

The third controversy, about priorities (22:34–40)

The Pharisees were delighted with Jesus' rebuff of their enemies, the Sadducees, but one of them wanted to test Jesus' attitude to the law itself. Was he orthodox? *'Which is the greatest commandment in the Law?'* (36). Jesus' answer was orthodoxy itself. *'Love the Lord your God'* was taken from Deuteronomy 6:5, part of the *Shema*, the *credo* of Judaism. *'Love your neighbour as yourself'* was taken from Leviticus 19:18.

It is not certain whether Jesus was the first to isolate these two commands and put them together as the heart of God's require-ment.[31] It is certain that no teacher of the law could have faulted him for doing so. The summary is exceedingly powerful and disturbing, for it takes the questioner from the area of achievement, which he might conceivably fulfil, to that of attitude, where nobody can boast fulfilment. For people who, like this *expert in the law*, were strong on ethics and weak on relationships, this strongly relational teaching was a revealing mirror of the heart. Nobody has ever loved God with all his being. Nobody has ever loved her neighbour as herself. So nobody can possibly merit eternal life. Once again, it brings us

---

[29] And from that part of the Old Testament whose authority they *did* accept.

[30] 'Throughout this dialogue with the religious leaders ... this "crowd" is an important though silent participant (cf. 21:46; 23:1). Much of the teaching is intended for public consumption.' France (1985).

[31] See R. Banks, *Jesus and the Law in the Synoptic Tradition* (Cambridge University Press, 1975), pp. 165–166, and Blomberg, for Jewish debates on which laws were the most important.

back to grace. If we are to have any place in the kingdom of God, it will be due to the unmerited grace of God for sinners who could never make it by themselves.

What a marvellous definition of true religion this is! If there is real love for God, there will inevitably be real love for neighbour; God's overflowing love is infectious. The criterion of whether love for God is real is whether or not it is reflected in our relationships with others. And it will not do to say, as many do, 'I don't do any harm to anyone.' That is not only negative, but it neglects the first and great commandment, to put God as number one in our lives. With God first and neighbour second, all else in the law is commentary.[32]

Postscript (22:41–46)

At the end of this chapter of controversies, in which the would-be judges are judged, Jesus asks the combined opposition a question that summarizes both his claims and their discomfiture. '*What do you think about the Christ? Whose son is he?*' '*The Son of David,*' they reply (42). They take the mainline expectation in Judaism at that time, as seen in the Pharisaic *Psalms of Solomon*, which look for a descendant of David's line to arise, gather the people in revolt, throw off the Roman yoke and restore independence and theocracy. There were other expectations in Israel in those days, but this hope was the most common. Their reply was unexceptionable. They saw the Messiah as primarily a political deliverer, though they did not entirely neglect a spiritual dimension in that hope, as the seventeenth *Psalm of Solomon* shows. So Jesus, in his turn, asks them a question. '*How is it then that David, speaking by the Spirit, calls him "Lord"? For he says, "The Lord said to my Lord: 'Sit at my right hand, till I put your enemies under your feet.'"* If then David calls him "Lord", how can he be his son?*' (43–45).

It is often argued in scholarly circles that Jesus is repudiating a Davidic origin for the Messiah. Nothing could be less probable. He knows full well that the Messiah is to come from David's stock. The prophecies in the Old Testament are explicit on that point. But he knows, too, that the Messiah is so much more than the sort of deliverer the Jews were hoping for. He wants to make them examine their easy assumptions and inherited prejudices. He wants to make them *think* at this time when their minds are almost closed and they reckon they know what to make of Jesus and his claims. So he presses them with this further question. If the Messiah is no more than David's descendant, how do they explain Psalm 110:1, which

---

[32] The whole of the Law and the Prophets depends on this double love commandment. For New Testament ethics in general, see R. E. O. White, *Biblical Ethics* (Paternoster, 1979), and A. Verhey, *The Great Reversal* (Eerdmans, 1984).

they admit to be both Davidic and messianic? In it Yahweh, God Almighty, addresses this descendant of David as 'Lord' and offers him a share of his throne until all opposition to his rule is banished. How could this merely be David's son? If David calls him 'Lord', how (*pōs* – in what sense?) can he be his son? The Messiah is indeed David's son, but he is also David's Lord. That does not fit their notion of a merely earthly and political Messiah. Jesus is trying to open their eyes to the futility of a messianic hope which does not rise beyond the human level. 'Son of David' is not an adequate title for him. He is Son of God, whom Matthew knows to be exalted to the right hand of God, where he shares God's reign over the world. No lesser concept is big enough to embrace one who is both David's son and David's Lord.

In this, the last of the controversial judgments in these two chapters, Jesus really puts his opponents on the spot. How could they possibly answer him? His claim to be both David's son and David's Lord is clear. The grounds on which that claim has been put forward are equally clear: the Gospel has been tabulating them since chapter 4. Why do they not believe him when the testimony of his words and works is so powerful? The answer is that they have chosen to believe a lie. They have blinded their eyes to the truth. They have wilfully turned away from the one who came to reconcile them with God. Woe has come to the leaders of Israel, and that is the subject of chapter 23.

23:1–39
15. The fifth discourse:
(1) judgment on dead religion

These three chapters of sayings of Jesus (23 – 25) bring the central panel of Part 2 of the Gospel to an end. It has been concerned throughout with the subject of judgment, seen from many aspects. And in this collection of sayings of Jesus the judgment theme is brought to a climax, as Matthew gives us his last book of the Christian *torah* taught by the new Moses. It consists of two parts: first, a series of woes on the leaders of Israel (23), and second, five parables about his return at the end of history (24–25), culminating in the final judgment of the sheep and the goats, which is entrusted to the wandering carpenter who is Son of Man. We can be sure that this is a pattern Matthew intended us to perceive, for in 26:1 we find the tell-tale formula that follows all the five teaching blocks in this Gospel, 'When Jesus had finished saying all these things . . .'

Three notable factors

As we begin to examine these chapters, three things ought to be borne in mind. First, the fact that there is great *balance* in the structure of the book. Just as Moses, the great rescuer from Egypt, ended his life by giving a swan song to the Israelites,[1] so does Jesus, the great rescuer from sin. Moses was looking into the future for his people, and that last will and testament of his became a pattern for others. We have the *Testament of Levi*, the *Testament of Dan*, the *Testament of Judah* and so forth in the intertestamental books. Now Jesus takes up the same model and gives his final testament to his church. These chapters are much the same length as chapters 5 – 7, and so there is a careful balance between the first and the last of the five great collections of Jesus' teaching in this Gospel. Indeed, like the Sermon on the Mount, this material is addressed to the disciples and the crowds alike. And the woes against the Pharisees

[1] Deut. 32:1–43.

are a studied parallel with the Beatitudes about the disciples in chapter 5.

Secondly, their *audience*. Jesus addresses *crowds* and *disciples* alike (1). So often in Matthew we have seen that the crowds represent the Christians at large, while the disciples represent the church leadership; so there is more than one level of meaning here. It is applicable to Christian leaders, because they too love prestige and position, for which the Pharisees are being rebuked. It fits Christian leaders as well as Jewish. It is equally apt for ordinary churchgoers. They are particularly in mind in verse 3: '. . . obey them and do everything they tell you. But do not do what they do, for they do not practise what they preach.' Clearly the congregations are in mind as well as the leaders, and Christians are in mind as well as Jews.

Thirdly, their *'anti-Semitism'*. Shamefully, western civilization has a long history of abusing the Pharisees, and undeniably this has been influenced by material in the Gospels, particularly this twenty-third chapter of Matthew. In recent years, however, scholars have gone a long way towards rectifying this, and the work of D. Farbstein, E. P. Sanders, Jacob Neusner and others[2] helps us to see a more rounded picture. Sanders is widely regarded as having destroyed the picture of Pharisaism that we find in the Gospels and Paul, and yet I am far from persuaded by his approach. In his large book *Judaism: Practice and Belief*, he does not even refer to the challenges presented by Matthew 23, let alone answer them. In *Jesus and Judaism*, he resorts to the normal liberal tactic of rejecting unpalatable evidence: 'The Jesus of Matt. 23.5–7, 23–26 is not the historical Jesus,' he writes.[3]

What these writers have done, however, is to show that Pharisaism at its best had a godly passion to keep the law in its entirety as the people's part of the covenant between God and Israel (what Sanders calls 'covenantal nomism'). It included love, faith and obedience. All this is important, but the problem that Matthew focuses on is not so much Pharisaism as a whole but those Pharisees whose lives belied their profession – a critique with which the best Pharisees concurred. The heart of the matter is the question of who is the true interpreter of the *torah*. Is it Jesus, or is it the Pharisees, with their understanding of righteousness in terms of increasingly rigorous legal prescriptions, a tendency which could obscure the whole meaning of what it means to please God and be right with him? Consequently, it is too naïve to regard this chapter as anti-Semitic. After

---

[2] D. Farbstein, 'Waren die Pharisäer und die Schriftgelehrten Heuchler?' *Judaica* (1952), pp. 193–207; Hagner 1, pp. lxxi–xxiii. See J. Neusner, *Judaism in the Beginning of Christianity* (SPCK, 1984), and the works by E. P. Sanders listed on p. 18 above.

[3] E. P. Sanders, *Jesus and Judaism* (Fortress, 1985), p. 276. See S. Westerholm, *Israel's Law and the Church's Faith* (Eerdmans, 1988), for a critique of Sanders' whitewashing of the Pharisees.

all, it comes from the most Jewish Gospel of the four.[4]

In fact, the anti-Semitism is more apparent than real. Matthew is plagued by a deep fear that the leadership of his own churches could go the way of the Jewish leadership, and succumb to the ever-present danger for religious leaders of a Pharisee spirit. It is all too easy to lapse into blindness, hypocrisy, and fussing about minor ecclesiastical details while allowing the major matters of the faith to go by the board. One of the weaknesses of the modern church is that we major on minor matters and leave pressing issues unaddressed. That is a profound expression of the Pharisee spirit. Matthew did not want it in the churches with which he was associated. So the 'anti-Semitism' is not directed towards the Jews in particular: it is an assault on all forms of Pharisaism wherever they are found. No, this Gospel is not anti-Semitic. The Jews are not singled out for blame for Jesus' murder. But Matthew is very anxious that his own leadership cadre should not absorb the poison that he saw to be current, in some areas at least, in the Pharisee party. That is what makes this chapter of abiding importance.

The curse of Jesus on Pharisaism, Jewish and Christian (23:1–39)

A graphic description of Pharisaism (23:1–12)

The teachers of the law and the Pharisees have, says Jesus, a God-given teaching authority: they *sit in Moses' seat* (1), and are to be respected for their teaching role in the synagogue. The same applies to Christian ministers, in Matthew's day or our own, but there is a great danger that the spirit that infected the Pharisees may creep into subsequent leadership. We are to beware.

Here are five characteristics for which the Pharisees were rebuked. They are ever-present dangers for Christian leaders. First, they may *not practise what they preach* (3).[5] Secondly, they may be unwilling to undertake themselves what they prescribe for others (4). Thirdly, they may love to show off (5).[6] Fourthly, they may revel in honorific titles and in being paid respect (6–10).[7] Finally, they may misunderstand ministry (11–12). They may see it less as an opportunity

---

[4] *Pace* S. van Tilborg, *The Jewish Leaders in Matthew* (Brill, 1972), who believes that the Gospel originated from an Alexandrian Gentile!

[5] The Pharisees themselves denounced six types of hypocritical Pharisaism (*b. Sota* 22b), just as Jesus does here.

[6] *Phylacteries* (5) were small prayer boxes containing Old Testament texts and worn on the brow and arm. *Tassels* (5) on prayer shawls were intended to remind one how far one had got in one's prayers.

[7] Notice how Jesus moves from speaking about *them* to *you* (7–8) – those among the crowds and disciples who intend to follow him. Christianity, too, has an unhealthy delight in honorific titles, and Jesus discourages it.

for service than as a sphere of management or a chance to gain recognition. Are these weaknesses confined to Jewish leaders in the first century AD? Are they not always contemporary? If Christian leaders fail in these five ways, their failure is comprehensive indeed.

Seven curses or woes on Pharisaism (23:13–32)

These woes are very instructive. Woes were really a funeral lament, a mix of music and literary convention for mourning the dead. How apt! That is what we find in Isaiah 5:18–23 and in other places in the Old Testament. The very word for 'Woe', *ouai*, has a mournful sound, and Jesus utters this wailing lament seven times over these Pharisees who appear to be religious but are dead inside.

Why has woe come to them? First, they are arraigned for rejecting the kingdom themselves, and blocking the way for others who want to draw near (13).[8] They reject God's kingly rule in their own lives – they have their own programme. And by their priorities, their example, and their scorn of those who display simple faith, they prevent others going into the kingdom.

There is a distressing amount of cynicism in some clerical circles, which shows itself in laughing at people who turn to Christ in simple faith. I have known university chaplains attempt to undo the work of student missions after undergraduates have professed faith. The Pharisee spirit is not dead. In thousands of churches the leaders do not honour Jesus as Lord. Their worship is a formality. They do not seem to know anything of the joy of the kingdom, and they offer no encouragement to anyone else to enter into it.

Secondly, they are condemned for a legalistic approach to mission (15). They had enthusiasm, but it was misdirected. They wanted to enhance the numbers and prestige of the Pharisee party.[9] Accordingly they sent out people to secure converts to Pharisaic Judaism through proselyte baptism, circumcision, sacrifice and adherence to the law. But it was not just the law that they advocated: it was the plethora of Pharisaic additions which they erected as a 'fence for the law' and which they made mandatory for their disciples. Hidebound and legalistic as they were, they turned converts into replicas of themselves. Jesus is condemning sectarian growth that writes everybody else off. It flourished in Pharisaic Judaism. It is even more common in church circles today where co-operation is so often at a discount, and the only thing that matters is our particular church and its particular stance.

Thirdly, Jesus condemns them for breaking solemn oaths (16–22).

---

[8] Verse 14 is omitted by the best manuscripts, and in NIV (see mg.).

[9] See S. McKnight, *Light among the Gentiles: Jewish Missionary Activity in the Second Temple Period* (Fortress, 1991).

The oath is a significant feature in this Gospel of Matthew. The first of the discourses has warned us against the danger of taking oaths (5:33). The same theme is taken up here in the last discourse. It has influenced the Gospel. John the Baptist was murdered because of an oath (14:7). Shortly the high priest will misuse the oath of testimony (26:63). Peter will deny Jesus with an oath (26:72). And in this passage Jesus returns to the cynical casuistry of the Pharisees who are not really interested in the temple, but are very interested in the gold of the temple; they are not interested in the altar but very interested in the gifts on it. They waive the binding nature of the former in order to enforce the latter – to their own advantage.

On the whole, the rabbis accepted with professions of regret the need for oaths in a fallen world, and then set to work to find ways round them. But there were differences between them on this matter, not surprisingly. Hillel allowed ways out of a binding oath. Shammai did not. What the Lord wants in leadership is solid reliability: people who say what they will do, and whose word is their bond; people who are dependable, and do not say one thing to one person and give a somewhat different version to another. Some people make an undertaking to one person and, under pressure from others, do not go through with it. Unreliability in leadership is disastrous for a congregation. Woe to the weak ministers who dare not carry out what they have promised because of fear! Woe to sceptical ministers who promise at their ordination to accept and teach the faith of the Bible and do nothing of the sort!

Fourthly, Jesus accuses the Pharisees of misconstruing God's revelation (23–24). They commit monstrous, camel-sized sins while taking every precaution against allowing an unclean gnat to bring ceremonial impurity to their drink! They strain out a minor impurity and swallow a major one.[10] Blind guides indeed! It will never do to follow them. The gnat is a tiny insect that breeds during the fermenting process, so here we get the picture of these worthies, no doubt dressed in their ministerial robes, putting their wine through gauze strainer after strainer to ensure that they are not infected by any impurity, while at the same time swallowing the biggest unclean object in the world![11] The church is full of clergy who insist on bowing to the altar but are agnostic about the deity of Christ or the fact of his resurrection.

Fifthly, the Pharisee spirit always goes for externals (25–26). Often, church meetings have 'parish pump' agendas, all about the drains or when Mrs Jones's memorial vase should be dedicated.

---

[10] Jesus attacks not their meticulous tithing but their neglect of the big things: justice, mercy and faith.

[11] The ironic humour is even sharper in Aramaic. There is a pun on *qalma* (gnat) and *gamla* (camel).

When did they last put pastoral care for the whole congregation on the agenda? When did they last discuss evangelizing the thousands of people without Christ in the vicinity? It is all too easy to miss the main things in God's purposes, to be blind to the great highway signs in his revelation, and to get lost in byways and country lanes. Are we passionately striving for justice? Where does mercy for the needy come in our priorities? And where is the primacy of faith in the planning of the leadership? These are the big things: the Pharisee spirit neglects them.

Jesus cannot abide the attitude that rests content with externals. It is the heart of the Pharisee spirit (25–26). Ritualism has replaced living relationship with God. So long as it looks good on the outside, it does not matter what lies beneath the surface. That attitude may suffice for the person who 'looks at the outward appearance, but God looks at the heart'.[12] 'Blind Pharisee!' he says, turning directly on the individual listener or reader. *'First clean the inside of the cup'* (26). It is interesting that in Luke's account of this woe[13] he seems to have mistranslated the underlying Aramaic and produced something very like nonsense: literally 'give alms from the inside', confusing *dakki* (purify) with *zakki* (give alms). Matthew, with his expertise in Aramaic, does not make that mistake. Small verbal points like this take us back almost within earshot of Jesus himself in his native language. But how relevant this message is to ordinary church life! The congregation may be split over the colour of the choir robes, but nobody minds whether they have any faith or not – they are there to sing! And so it goes on through so much church life. Blind Pharisee indeed, Christian and Jewish alike!

Sixthly, Jesus assails the hidden decay in Pharisaism (27–28). These men looked good on the outside but inside they were full of decay; they were the walking dead. There is nothing so repulsive as dead religion, and there is a lot of it about. When the pilgrim season began in Israel they used to paint the tombs with whitewash to make them very obvious, so that nobody brushed up against them and got ceremonially defiled by accident.[14] The contrast therefore is between the fair-seeming exterior of these men and the corruption that festered in spiritual death below the surface. But the subsidiary message was also clear: don't get too near these people – you will get defiled. Spiritual death under a religious veneer is no less a possibility today than it was then. It is to be avoided at all costs.

The last woe Jesus calls down on the Pharisees has another most contemporary ring about it. They are monument-keepers (29–32)! The prophets were greatly respected in Judaism, and the Pharisees

---

[12] 1 Sam. 16:7.   [13] Luke 11:41.
[14] See Mishnah tractate *Shekalim* 1.1 for this practice.

had taken upon themselves the task of building ornate tombs for them, out of respect. They wanted to give the impression that if they had lived in the days when that prophet was hounded to death, they would have been on his side and would have had nothing to do with his persecution and murder. They saw themselves as heirs to the prophets. Jesus saw them as heirs to those who killed the prophets. By building the tombs, they were finishing off the job of those who killed them. He concludes: 'Go on, then. Finish what your ancestors started!' (cf. 32). How right he was! They were at that very moment planning his own murder, and in a few days were able to see it carried out. And where could this challenge more fittingly be offered than in the temple? This was the jewel in the crown of Judaism, but it had become a monument. It encouraged the 'museum-keeper' attitude that is so common among many ministers today. But Jesus did not leave his disciples to be keepers of aquaria, but fishers of men and women. The trouble is that so many churches are rafts to which people cling for safety in the rough seas of life, not trawlers to catch people for Christ. Such churches are into maintenance, not mission.

How deep those seven indictments bite, and how dangerously up to date they are! Are we rejecting the kingdom ourselves and obstructing the entrance of others? Do we have a legalistic approach to church growth, interested only in our own neck of the woods? Do we break solemn promises if convenient or if the heat is on? Do we misconstrue God's revelation by neglecting the central and going for the peripheral? Do we go for external things and ceremonial precision, but remain indifferent to the attitude within? Are we walking around as a living lie, a spiritual tomb, highly decorated, maybe, on the outside, but inwardly full of corruption and dead men's bones? And keepers of ancient monuments? What a list! How important for Christian Pharisees to take it to heart, and for us all to note the tendencies to Pharisaism that lie embedded in each one of us!

The grounds for Jesus' critique

Jesus himself gives two main grounds for so castigating the Pharisee leadership of his nation. The first is that they are *blind*, and the second that they are *hypocrites*.

Five times here they are called *blind*. They do not understand the important things in God's revelation. They do not go for inner purity, but rest content with externals. They are faultless in their ceremonial observance, but the primary matters which the prophets had stressed – justice, mercy and faithfulness – were in short supply. Blind guides who act and teach like this are a great danger to any synagogue or church.

Six times in this passage the Pharisees are called *hypocrites*. The word comes from the Greek for 'actors' in a play. That is the trouble. They act the part of the godly person, but their own hearts are far from him. There is therefore a yawning gap between their claims and their behaviour. They do not actually carry out the law of which they are guardians. Because of the spiritual death within, they do not even begin to see that gap diminished, that law carried into obedience.

Blindness to what really matters in spiritual things, and an air of godliness that masks inner decay, are still two major viruses that can easily infect Christian leaders. We must be on our guard against them.

We have seen the description of the Pharisee spirit, the woes Jesus calls down on it, and the reasons for his accusations. It is highly contemporary and painfully near the bone.

The love of Jesus in the face of AD 70 (23:33–39)

This is a lovely piece of writing, and takes us to the very heart of Jesus. He realized that the constant bubbling of insurrection against Rome could not but lead to a massive retaliation which would crush the nation before long. Jewish zealotry would inevitably invite the heavy heel of Rome. Disaster stared Judea in the face, and any intelligent person could see it. So, in the light of that imminent catastrophe, Jesus interjects into this most painful chapter a wonderful ray of his love. His love for the nation is brought home to us in four graphic ways, two negative and two positive.

First, on the negative side, he unmasks the Pharisees. He takes up John the Baptist's pungent words (3:7) and calls a spade a spade. They are a *brood of vipers* (33), but he loves them, and so he has to tell them to their face. He strips the masks off these play-actors so that they may be seen as they really are. They are on the road to political and spiritual destruction.

Secondly, he leaves them (24:1). His departure is the fitting conclusion to this terrible assessment he has in honesty felt driven to give of the contemporary spiritual leadership of his country. Leaving the temple is a significant gesture, for the temple was the centre of worship, the focus of Israel's hopes, the place of divine revelation, the location of some of his own most famous teaching, where the leaders of his nation confronted him and were driven to make up their minds about him. They have made up their minds: he must die. And when love is denied, it withdraws. The Messiah leaves his temple. A few years later it would come crashing down, when their *house* was left forsaken and *desolate* (38).

On the positive side, Jesus loves them. Verses 37–38 are among the warmest and most loving words he is ever recorded as using. Incidentally, the exclamation *how often I have longed to gather your children together* indicates that Jesus probably taught in Jerusalem more often than during this one trip which Matthew, like the other Synoptists, records; John tells us something of those other visits. Despite the resistance and disobedience of the Pharisees and of the people in general, Jesus loves them and goes on reaching out to them. He longs to gather them to him *as a hen gathers her chicks under her wings* – a marvellous image of the mother-love of the Lord.

Jerusalem has a history of killing the prophets. *From . . . Abel to . . . Zechariah* (35) means 'from A to Z'. *Zechariah* the Old Testament prophet was the son of Berekiah,[15] and it may be he who is meant, for an old targum tells us he was slain in the temple. However, another Zechariah, the son of Bariscaeus, an eminent Jewish citizen, was cut down by two Zealots in the courts of the temple in AD 68,[16] and he was the last *'righteous* man' to be martyred in Israel before the city fell to the Romans. There is variation in the textual tradition, too, and probably we should with some manuscripts simply omit *son of Berakiah*; it is an incorrect gloss. Jesus will then simply have referred to Zechariah, who was killed between the altar and the Holy Place: that is how Luke recounts it.[17] That murder is recounted in 2 Chronicles 24:20–21 – and Chronicles is the last book in the Hebrew canon of the Old Testament, so it fits in very well with this 'A to Z' scope of Jesus' words.[18]

Jesus' final words of frustrated love embody both judgment and mercy: on the one hand, *your house is left to you desolate* if you continue in this way; on the other, it may still be possible at this eleventh hour to repent and cry, *'Blessed is he who comes in the name of the Lord'* (39).[19] They must choose.

Jesus loves them, yes, and he reaches out to them. That is the last point Matthew makes. *'Therefore I am sending you prophets and wise men and teachers . . .'* (34). That word 'Therefore' is significant. Because they are full of 'woe', because they continue to resist, because they are in a dangerous position – that is why Jesus goes, and authorizes others to go, on a mission to the Jews. The very hostility of Judaism in general and of the Pharisees in particular is all the more reason for the Christian mission among them. Let Matthew

---

[15] Zech. 1:1.   [16] Josephus, *Jewish War* 4.5.4.   [17] Luke 11:51.

[18] But see J. M. Ross, 'Which Zechariah?', *Irish Biblical Studies* 9 (1987), pp. 70–73, for the view that this is an otherwise unknown Zechariah, martyred just before the time of Jesus.

[19] Those words, of course, echo 21:9 from Ps. 118:26. Could Jesus be looking down the centuries to the hope of Israel's ultimate salvation, as Paul did after him (Rom. 11:25–26)?

and his fellow-leaders never forget their obligations to the synagogue down the street. It will be hard. The fate Jesus envisages for them (34) is the same as that predicted for the disciples in 10:17, 23. The form of expression is amazing: '*I am sending you ...*', says Jesus. He is the author of that stream of godly people down the ages, prophets, martyrs and apostles, who have come to an untimely end through obedience to the call. *He sends them!* If he had said that the Father, or God, sent them, that would be natural enough. But quite unself-consciously, and all the more powerfully for that reason, he claims the position of God himself as the author of the mission. Luke's account attributes the sending to the wisdom of God,[20] and that probably preserves the original flavour of Jesus' words. The Christian disciples must never forget the Jewish mission, tough and unrewarding though it would be. It was hard for Jesus, and it would not be easier for his followers. Perhaps one of the reasons Jesus concentrated on the mission to Israel during the days of his public ministry was in order to set an example that would burn itself into their consciousness. The Jewish mission might not be very successful. It would lead to persecution and not infrequently to death. But it must be undertaken, or the heart of the Saviour would burst. He loved them so much.

The time was short. The crisis of AD 70 was not far away. After that, if not altogether too late, it would be immeasurably more difficult. For their *house* would have been left to them *desolate*, just as it was in Jeremiah's day.[21] '*Therefore I am sending you prophets and wise men and teachers ...*'

---

[20] Luke 11:49.   [21] Cf. Jer. 12:7.

24:1 – 25:46
16. The fifth discourse:
(2) the end of Jerusalem and of history

This section's links to the previous chapter are strong but elusive. Chapter 23 ended with Jesus predicting the destruction of the temple. Yet here it stands, large and imposing, before the eyes of the disciples. It looks as if it is built to last for ever. What could Jesus mean? Jesus had also spoken of the end of all things. When might that be? The Pharisees had repeatedly asked for a sign, and now the disciples decide it is time for them to make a similar request. *'Tell us . . . when will this happen, and what will be the sign of your coming and of the end of the age?'* (24:3).

Judgment imminent and ultimate (24:1–41)

So now, seated like a rabbi to teach, just as he was when giving the Sermon in chapters 5 – 7, Jesus gathers his disciples around him privately and speaks to them about the future. In the middle distance is the judgment at the fall of Jerusalem. In the far distance is the judgment at the end of the world. They are connected. The one sheds light on the other. And the intertwining comes out in this remarkable prophecy that follows. Verse 2 of chapter 24 speaks plainly of the fall of Jerusalem. Verse 3 speaks equally unambiguously of the end of the world. Jesus sees the kingdom coming in judgment in AD 70 and closing the Jewish era with immense finality; he sees his own return at the end of the age as bringing to a close the universal history of humankind.

In his commentary on Matthew's Gospel, William Barclay points out how varied are the elements that occur in this chapter, looking as it does both at the destruction of Jerusalem and then through that lens, so to speak, at the end of the world. Some verses foretell the terrible days of the siege of Jerusalem, one of the most gruesome in history (15–22). Some speak of the destruction of the temple at Jerusalem (1–2). Some verses are coloured by the picture of the 'Day of the Lord' given by the Old Testament prophets, marked by sudden destruction, terror, cosmic disarray, civil war and moral chaos (6–8, 29–31). Some verses deal with the persecution the followers of Jesus will have to endure (9–10); others indicate the threats that will develop against the life and purity of the church (4–5, 11–13, 23–26); and others speak directly of the return of Christ at the end of the world (3, 14, 27–28). Barclay then examines the chapter by developing each of these six strands.

I propose to handle 24:1–41 rather differently. It is a deep and difficult chapter: prophecy always is. Rather than go through it verse by verse, I shall look at some themes that stand out.

The end of all history

Perhaps the most important thing of all in this chapter should be underlined at the outset. It is primarily about the end of the world's history.

Matthew has a tremendous amount of teaching in these two chapters about the return of Christ, or 'parousia'[1] as it is often called. Why is this important? Because it is all of a piece with his emphasis on the kingdom of heaven. The kingdom has come with the first coming of Jesus. It has been inaugurated, but it has not yet been consummated. Disciples are citizens of two countries. They belong both to this age and to the age to come. They live at the intersection of the ages. Hence the glory and the shame of the Christian life and the Christian church. Hence the ambiguity of Christian experience. We are not what we were, but equally, we are not yet what we shall be. The kingdom inaugurated at the first coming of Jesus will be consummated by his return at the end of history. Then his will shall be done on earth as it is in heaven. History is not 'a tale / Told by an idiot, full of sound and fury, / Signifying nothing'.[2] It is, in a real sense, his story. He made this world. He came to dwell in it. He will return at the end of history to wind it all up. That is the Christian hope. History is moving steadily towards that grand day. We shall not go out like a light. We shall not be blown sky-high in a nuclear holocaust. We shall not destroy the Earth by our environmental vandalism. This world will not, however, go on for ever. Jesus will come again, not this time to suffer but to reign. And his coming will settle the future destiny of all people (39–41). That is the central point of this chapter. At the end we shall see Christ as he is. It is not a question of rewards and punishments. Matthew does nothing to encourage detailed millennial expectations or speculation about the rapture. He steadily fixes our eyes on the King, who is one day

[1] This Greek word, which could mean both 'presence' and 'arrival', was used of the visits of gods or rulers.
[2] Shakespeare, *Macbeth* V. v.

coming back to be crowned. And that is something to look forward to. That is something no vision of the future, in any religion or philosophy, can match. It is good news.

The fall of Jerusalem

Jesus clearly foresees this terrible event as the anticipation in their lifetime of the end of all things (34). Verses 15–22 are particularly concerned with the fall of Jerusalem. It was a terrible siege, lasting nearly four years, and it involved unimaginable hardships. The city was hard to capture, and was defended with fanatical zeal. The Romans made a sustained attempt to starve its inhabitants into submission. Parents were reduced to cannibalism. There was indeed unparalleled affliction, as Jesus had predicted (21).[3] In AD 70 the troops determined as a last resort to storm the city and the temple, and so they did. The temple, one of the greatest architectural masterpieces of antiquity, made of marble and faced with gold, was smashed to pieces. The city was reduced to rubble. The carnage and slaughter were terrible. More than a million Jews died in the operation, and Josephus, who was there,[4] tells us that more than 97,000 Jews were taken captive. The Romans were so pleased and relieved at the satisfactory solution of the Jewish problem (as they thought) that they erected Titus' Arch in the Forum at Rome to celebrate the victory.

Just as Antiochus Epiphanes had brought *the abomination that causes desolation* (15)[5] into the temple in 168 BC when he sacrificed swine's flesh on the altar and turned the rooms of the temple into brothels in a determined attempt to stamp out the Jewish faith, so history would repeat itself. Titus would desolate the holy site even more efficiently by razing it to the ground, and *the reader* would *understand* (15) how thoroughly Daniel's prophecy had been fulfilled.[6] That is the time to flee the city and make for the hill country of Judea (16).[7] They should pray that their flight be not impeded by its taking *place in winter* storms *or on the Sabbath* day (20; the law allowed only a very short journey on the Sabbath; moreover, gates would be shut and provisions unobtainable).

[3] Blomberg observes that all nine of the preliminary events outlined in vv. 9–14 in fact occurred before AD 70, and continues: 'This fulfilment will explain how 24:34 can be true. It demonstrates that everything necessary for Christ's return was accomplished within the first generation of Christianity, so that every subsequent generation has been able to believe that Jesus could come back in their times.'

[4] He records its horrors in his *Jewish War*.   [5] Better, 'the desolating sacrilege'.

[6] Eusebius (*Ecclesiastical History* 3.5.3) tells us that just before the siege of Jerusalem some Jewish Christians, responding to 'an oracle given by revelation', fled the city and made for Pella in Transjordan.

[7] Dan. 9:27; 11:31; 12:11.

Pregnant women and *mothers* with young children would face particular traumas (19), as television pictures of refugees in Kosovo, Chechnya and Mozambique brought home to us. And the air would be thick with talk of messianic pretenders and their marvellous credentials (4–6, 23–26), and of *wars and rumours of wars*, with *nation* rising up *against nation, and kingdom against kingdom* (6–7). They must not be alarmed (6). They must not be deceived (23, 26). They must not be surprised: this *must happen* (6) before the longed-for return of the Son of Man.

All this came true. The years AD 68–70 saw the Roman world tottering on the edge of total ruin from internal wars and rumours of wars. After the death of Nero in AD 68, the next year or so saw no fewer than four contestants for the supreme office of emperor fighting it out. It was a period in which, so Roman writers tell us, people were widely expecting the end of the world. That is what was happening on the broad international front.

On the Jewish front, there were the siege and capture of Jerusalem, accompanied by false messiahs, horrors and devastation. But even this was not the end of the world, though many thought it would be. There is a link between *this* (the events of v. 2) and *the end of the age* (3), but it is not the link of straight chronological sequence. '*The end is still to come*' (6). Rather, the cluster of events around the fall of Jerusalem form a cameo of what will happen at the end of all things. The coming of Titus in retribution on Jerusalem will be a miniature of the coming of Christ in judgment at the final hour of human history. How we are to envisage this we cannot tell; it has not happened yet. And prophecy is not intended to give us a detailed picture of the future, but to lift up our hearts in expectancy so that we make ourselves ready for what is to come. And that is what the fall of Jerusalem should do for the followers of Jesus. It is an anticipation of the end. It is one stage in the progressive 'coming' of the kingdom which will not fully come until the last day when Jesus offers it up to God the Father, and God is all in all.[8] That seems to be the meaning of the obscure verses 27–28. The final coming of the Son of Man in glory and judgment will be no hole-in-the-corner affair. It will not happen as Jehovah's Witnesses claimed it happened, in obscurity and ambiguity in 1914. No, it will be the most public event in all history. It will be impossible to miss it, for it will be like sheet lightning from one side of the sky to the other. It will be as obvious and unmistakable as the gathering of vultures to a carcass; from many miles away you can see the birds concentrating on the one spot (28). The primary reference here is manifestly to the end of history and to the return of Christ (apparently with his angels,

---

[8] 1 Cor. 15:24–28.

swooping upon a 'dead' world, rotten with evil). But many must have seen a secondary allusion as the Roman legions with their 'eagles', the legionary standards, closed in for the kill on Jerusalem.

The return of Jesus Christ

The dominant theme in this chapter is the return of Christ at the end of the age, and the fall of Jerusalem and the events surrounding it anticipate that return. His return will be personal, and that is tremendously significant. It means that we shall not be confronted at the end of all things by one who is alien to us and does not understand us, but rather by one who has such intimate understanding of us that he has shared our existence, within our very skin. We shall in the end be confronted by what it means to be really human, and that is both our shame and our hope.

The return of Christ has another important facet to it, which this chapter underlines. *History is going somewhere.* It is not meaningless. It is not random. It is not eternal. There will be a real end just as there was a real beginning. And at the end we shall find none other than Jesus Christ.

The return of Christ also speaks of *triumph*: the triumph of good over evil, of God's purposes over human and Satanic rebellion, of God's will in human hearts, in human society and in the natural world.

The return of Christ spells *restoration*. The Jewish expectation of the Day of the Lord, which has influenced the language of this chapter a good deal, spoke of cosmic disaster in sun and moon and stars, and of supernatural darkness. It spoke of social disasters in *earthquakes, famines, wars and rumours of wars.* It spoke of moral disasters in the growth of evil and the loss of love.[9] Verses 6–8, 29–30 make use of this traditional language, but the new and wonderful hope that has dawned through the coming of Jesus is that when the Son of Man comes there will be restoration – social, cosmic, personal and moral. There will be a new creation, 'a new heaven and a new earth, the home of righteousness'.[10]

The return of Christ spells *judgment*. It will be a time of separation. Some *will be taken* and some *left* (40–41). What has been hidden in the human heart over the years will emerge into the clear light of day, and all will be shown in their true colours. This will not be a matter of degrees of goodness, but of whether they come running to him with arms outstretched at his coming, or shrink away in fear and hatred. The return of Christ will be the day of judgment. It will reveal what has been going on unseen all the time.

---

[9] See e.g. Joel 2:1–11; Amos 5:18–20; Zeph. 1:14–2:3.   [10] 2 Pet. 3:13.

The return of Christ will be *decisive*. There will be no more chance to repent, no more opportunity to change (37–39). It will herald the final breaking in of the kingdom of God. Until then, business as usual. After that, all shops close – and many reopen to an entirely new future!

The return of Christ will be *sudden and unexpected*. It will be as sudden as a flash of lightning in the sky (27). It will have an immediacy that Matthew (the only evangelist to use this word) represents by *eutheōs* (29, *Immediately*). It will be as unexpected as the flood in Noah's day (37 – though there were signs for the discerning). It will come out of the blue upon a heedless world.

The return of Christ will come *at a time known only to God the Father* (36). The disciples did not know. Preachers do not know. Millennialists and postmillennialists do not know. Not even Jesus knows: the conditions of the incarnation meant his laying aside his full divine foreknowledge. The repeated attempts to fix a date for the end of history are illusory. It will come; that is sure. But nobody knows when; that is sure too.

In the light of that teaching about Christ's return, speculation on dates is inappropriate, indeed blasphemous (36). Our priorities must be a steady endurance of hardships (13), a balanced wisdom in seeking to read the signs of the times (28–33) and a watchfulness so that his return will not find us idle or abusing our privileges (44–51). Those seem to be the main strands in Matthew's collection of Jesus' teaching in this chapter. A good deal more will unfold in the parousia parables that follow.

The place of signs

The teaching of Jesus about whether or not there will be signs presaging the end is not easy to discern. There seems to be an ambiguity about it. The entire chapter responds to the request of the disciples for a sign of his coming (3). On the whole Jesus discourages them from seeing the decline in the church (9–13), the state of the world (6–7), the claims of those who profess to know (5, 23–26) or the spread of the gospel (14) as a definitive sign of the approaching end. Such things are significant but not decisive. The coming of the kingdom can be predicted as little as where lightning is going to strike (23–27).

Nevertheless, his final coming will be preceded by signs. The fall of Jerusalem, the spread of the gospel, the cooling of love in the church, chaos in society and the vindication of Jesus' words (35) are factors that will precede the end. Indeed, there may be two more hidden in this chapter.

One comes in verse 32, and we shall be looking at it below. Some have seen the sprouting of the fig-tree as indicating the resurgence of the Jewish people, and this has certainly been an important element in world history since the restoration of the State of Israel in 1948. It is, however, exegetically very questionable to read so large an inference out of so slight an allusion in a parable.

The other concerns the mysterious verses 30–31. What can they mean? They are normally applied – uneasily – to the return of Christ at the end of history, but this accords ill with Matthew's phrase *Immediately after the distress of those days* (29), which seems to point to an event connected with the destruction of Jerusalem. But what if we look at it a different way? What if the language about *the sun* being *darkened, the moon* withholding *its light, the stars* falling from *the sky* and the *heavenly bodies* being *shaken* is poetic and refers to the universal panic, distress and imminent collapse of the world in the cataclysmic 'year of the four emperors', AD 69? Tacitus' description of the scene as Jerusalem was about to fall is very reminiscent of Matthew's words here.[11] It was an apocalyptic time. Not till the year of the four emperors, not till the year of the fall of Jerusalem, would the world recognize the fact that the Son of Man had ascended to the right hand of God, and was even now in control of the world that seemed so volatile. When the old order ended, when Jerusalem fell, the new order could be heard like a trumpet throughout the world (31). If so, *the Son of Man coming on the clouds of the sky, with power and great glory*, will refer not to the parousia at all, but to the 'coming' of the Son of Man to the Ancient of Days which in Daniel 7:13–14 is certainly an ascension, not a descent. In other words, the climactic time of AD 69–70 would show to a shaken pagan world and a devastated Jewish nation that world power did not lie with the big battalions or with fanatical religion, but with the Christ, who had returned to his heavenly Father and was even now reigning. The *angels* of verse 31 would then have the normal meaning of the Greek *angeloi*, messengers. And the gathering of *his elect from the four winds* would mean the winning of people to the gospel all over the world as his emissaries go out with the good news.

Nobody can prove that this is the right interpretation of these difficult verses, but it is more than possible. It yields good sense. It does not make Jesus guilty either of self-contradiction or of false prophecy. And it would make excellent sense of verse 34. There were indeed some present in AD 30 who would not die until they had seen all these things come to pass. They would see Jerusalem destroyed, a worldwide Gentile mission, a spiritual harvest reaped, the evidence of the spiritual sovereignty of the Son of Man, and the gathering of

[11] Tacitus, *Histories* 5.13.

255

the elect through all the world to his allegiance. If this is so, it would provide an additional 'sign' that will precede the coming of the Son of Man at the end of time.

They – and we – are not to go overboard on signs. They should look for the Son of Man. Josephus records that the Jews who perished in the siege of the holy city all died looking towards the temple, so glorious but so soon to be destroyed. Christians should look towards the Son of Man, hidden and inglorious during his time on earth, but coming in unimaginable splendour. And when he comes, it will be sudden (37), unexpected (44) and unmistakable (27).

The folly of date-fixing

Jesus predicted both the fall of Jerusalem and the end of the age. Significantly, he himself did not profess to know the date of either (36). He specifically disclaims knowledge of when the end will be: that secret the Father has locked in his own breast. Christians need have no embarrassment about admitting that there is something Jesus did not know. That is a very different matter from saying that he was wrong on particular things. Limitation of knowledge is a necessary condition of a real incarnation. He did not just appear to be one of humankind: he was truly human.

Although Jesus professed not to know the date of his return, there have never lacked those who think they do know it. Amid the scores who have made confident prophecies and got it wrong (and history is white with the bones of such people), names such as J. N. Darby, C. I. Scofield and Hal Lindsey stand out. These writers have given a highly detailed account of how and when it will be.[12] It would take us too far afield to look at their opinions, influential though they are. I believe them to be misguided. 'He who announces the messianic times based on calculations, forfeits his share in the future,' said Rabbi Jose. It was a wise word.

Those who disobey Jesus' warning about attempting to fix dates for his return generally rely on one or more of three bases for their speculations.

The first is the prophecy game. The doomwatch brigade was particularly active as the year 2000 approached. Not long ago all the main newspapers in Western Europe came up with a full-page advertisement announcing the return of Jesus Christ on a particular day, courtesy of a nameless gentleman who predicted it. Needless to say, it did not happen. He was just one in a long line of false prophets, against whom Jesus warned in verse 24. An earlier

[12] For a wise and charitable but astringent review of their views, which are known as 'dispensationalist', see Stephen Travis's fine book *I Believe in the Second Coming of Jesus* (Hodder and Stoughton, 1982).

one was Maximilian, one of the leaders of the Montanists, an apocalyptic Christian sect in the middle of the second century. 'After me', he said, 'there will be no more prophecy: only the end of the world.'

The second line of argument plays the numbers game. It usually has recourse to abstruse areas of the prophecy of Ezekiel and the book of Daniel. There was tremendous excitement and fear in some Christian circles as the year AD 1000 approached: it would herald the end of the world. But it did not. In the twelfth century the monk Joachim of Fiore calculated that there would be an apocalyptic climax to world history in 1260. Before that date, and leading into the messianic period of bliss that would follow, the Emperor Frederick II would remove the papacy, the empire itself would fall to the Saracens, and the Tartars would destroy the ten kings from the east. Of course it did not happen. But precisely the same sort of speculation was applied to what was then the Common Market when it grew to ten members! More recently, equally baseless speculation attached to the year 2000. The moment such speculations are falsified by events, the advocates say that there has been a mistake in the calculations, and the game goes on. This is neither reputable nor honouring to God. Jesus did not tell us to get out our calculators and polish our crystal balls, but to live a holy life in preparation for meeting him.

The third approach to date-fixing comes from playing the signs of the times. Luther confidently expected the parousia in 1530, 'for it is certain from the holy Scriptures that we have no more temporal things to expect. All is fulfilled. The Roman Empire is at an end, the Turk has reached his highest point, the pomp of the papacy is falling away, and the world is cracking on every side as if it would fall apart.' Yet three years later he was to be found hammering an opponent called Stifel for predicting that the parousia would happen at 8.00am on 19 October 1533!

The whole approach is utterly mistaken. All such attempts have proved wrong, and they will continue to do so. They are not only unhelpful, but positively dangerous in Christian circles. On the one hand, they preoccupy people's attention and detract from living usefully and responsibly in this world now; on the other, they breed the disillusionment that springs from disappointed hopes and unwarranted predictions. Jesus said he did not know. We can be sure that nobody else does.

The purpose of prophecy is not to give us history written in the future tense, but, like film previews and hazard warning lights on a motorway, to lift our hearts in expectation or in warning. The date-fixing approach neglects this, and, by its mixture of literalism and speculation, militates against patient faith and social involvement.

The return of Israel

'But', you may say, 'what about the return of Israel to their land? Is this not a sign that the return of Christ is at hand?' Some see this indicated in the image of the fig-tree in verse 32: '*Now learn this lesson from the fig-tree: As soon as its twigs get tender and its leaves come out, you know that summer is near. Even so, when you see all these things, you know that it is near, right at the door.*' Hal Lindsey, and a lot of American opinion, saw the return of the Jews to Israel as a clear sign of the imminent coming of Christ. Lindsey has gone on record as saying that, taking verses 32 and 34 together, the second coming had to happen before the year 2000, during the lifetime of the generation that saw the Jews return to their land. Writers such as Lindsey rely on verses such as Genesis 17:8; Ezekiel 37:11; and Jeremiah 29:10. But these prophecies were fulfilled either in a few years, when the Jews returned to their country from the Babylonian exile in 539 BC, or in Christ.

Any deeper fulfilment that there may be will be found not in Judaism and its history, but in the church. That is the point of Acts 15:16–17. Amos' prediction that David's fallen tent would be restored one day has found fulfilment, James there asserts, not in Herodian Judaism but in the emergence of the church. Always in the New Testament the church takes over the role of Israel in the Old. Jesus gave no political predictions whatsoever for Israel. Therefore the physical return of Israel (or a fraction of Israel; there are more Jews in New York than in the State of Israel!) is theologically irrelevant. Either God's promises to Israel are taken up into and fulfilled in Israel's Messiah Jesus, or they refer to the spiritual return of Israel to Christ at the end of time.[13] We are not to politicize the promises made to Israel in the Old Testament. The promise to Abraham that in his seed all the nations of the earth would be blessed finds its fulfilment through Christ in his church,[14] not in Israel's return to Palestine in 1948, fascinating though that is.[15]

We must not be sidetracked. Jesus will return. We must be ready. The timing lies with God. In the meantime we have some general intimations which should help to keep us alert.

Five parables of the parousia (24:42 – 25:46)

The world is headed not for ultimate chaos and disaster but for the return of the King and his coronation. We do not know when it will

[13] Rom. 9 – 11.

[14] 1 Pet. 1:3–5 emphasizes the fulfilment of Israel's hopes in the church.

[15] For the many – and conflicting – interpretations of this chapter, see the literature cited in Hagner, 2, p. 708, and Gundry.

be, but it is certain, as certain as the fall of Jerusalem. This hope is not pie in the sky. It is based fairly and squarely on the cross and resurrection of Jesus to which the Gospel story inexorably leads. That is the ground for Christian optimism. He took the full weight of evil, pain, and death, and it was not sufficient to hold him down. God has raised him from the dead, and there, at the mid-point in history, we see in Jesus crucified and risen the pledge of the final triumph. It is the trailer of the main film. Christian hope rides high, because the grave was not able to hold down the author of life.[16] But what difference does such hope make to daily life? Jesus shows us the difference in five powerful parables, which form the crown and climax of his teaching ministry.

The nocturnal thief (24:42–44)

Jesus' assertion of his second coming concludes on a very practical note: *'Therefore keep watch, because you do not know on what day your Lord will come'* (42). And the first of his parousia parables builds on that.

Christians are to be watchful. *If the owner of the house had known at what time . . . the thief was coming*, he would of course have waited up and *not have let his house* be ransacked. This small parable is a call for *expectancy*: 'Watch!' This 'thief' saying had an enormous impact on the early Christians. We find traces of it in parts of the New Testament as diverse as 1 Thessalonians 5:2, 4; 2 Peter 3:10; and Revelation 3:3; 16:15. Christians are to watch: not like astronomers through a telescope, or guards watching a CCTV screen, but like lovers who can't wait for another glimpse of the beloved, or captives in a labour camp longing for the day that will allow them home. God can guide expectant Christians. They are open to direction, ready for the unexpected. But those devoid of expectancy are very hard to shift.

The disorderly servants (24:45–51)

Jesus pursues the theme of watchfulness, but now gives it a different nuance. He is looking for servants he can rely on, who will act in the same way when he is absent as when he is present. In this story *the master* delays his return for a variety of reasons of which *the servants* know nothing (an echo of the sense of delay in the return of Christ that was so deeply felt among the early Christians). Delay can breed bad behaviour. Nobody appears to be in charge, and the servants do their own thing. Their baser passions are given free reign.

[16] Acts 2:24; 3:15.

The outcome will be disaster. Holiness is called for. That is to be one of the main distinguishing marks of Christians in the time between the two advents.[17] It is indispensable. Without it we shall land up with the hypocrites – outside the kingdom (24:51). This is a solemn warning to us if, like Augustine, we tend to say, 'Lord, make me holy – but not yet.' 'Without holiness no-one will see the Lord.'[18]

The ten virgins (25:1–13)

Once again the theme of division is to the fore, as in the previous story. The background to this parable is Jewish wedding custom. The wedding is not only a joyful but a protracted affair. The couple would not go away on honeymoon, but stay at home and welcome all comers. It was a relaxed affair; there was no set time when the bridegroom would come to the house of his bride, either to eat the wedding feast there or, more frequently, to take her to his own home for the wedding feast. The festivities lasted for a week or even two,[19] and were marked by great joy, feasting and music. The *virgins* waited to escort the bridegroom into the house. Once he arrived and went in, the door was shut, and there was no possibility of late access. So the *foolish* virgins will have missed the whole week, not just one supper, in being shut out.

So much for the customs. How did Jesus use them for his purposes as he looked to his return?

It is not difficult to 'read' the main thrust of the parable. Jesus is the bridegroom.[20] He will come one day – nobody knows when – to take his bride and celebrate the marriage supper.[21]

The virgins are Christian people. Half of them were prepared for his coming: they had the lamps required for any night-time wedding, and had taken the trouble to put oil in them. The other half were not prepared, should the bridegroom choose to come at night. The message, in the light of the return of Christ at the end of time, is clear: 'Be prepared.' Most of the Jews were not prepared when Jesus came, and have not gone in with the bridegroom. But Jesus hopes for better things in his church.

There are three surprises awaiting us here, as so often in the parables. The girls all looked the same, but they were not. Only half of them were ready for the feast and went in to enjoy the festivities with the bride and groom. And then the door was shut! What a warning! It tells us that it is all too possible to be often in church and

[17] See Titus 2:11–13, which makes the point plainly, and 2 Pet. 3:11, 14.
[18] Heb. 12:14.   [19] Gen. 29:27; Tobit 8:20.
[20] Cf. 9:15. He takes over the role of God in the Old Testament: Is. 54:4–6; Jer. 2:2; etc.
[21] Rev. 19:9; 21:2, 9.

in Christian company and yet be a stranger to the Holy Spirit. It is possible to have a lamp that looks good, but has no oil in it.[22] It is possible that one day Jesus may have to say, 'I never knew you' (7:23). All that is a great surprise to churchgoers, in Matthew's day and ours.

The second surprise is to discover that there are some things you cannot borrow. You need to possess them for yourself. It simply is not possible to rely on anyone else for them. Holiness is one of those things. It cannot be traded. If you are not what you profess to be, nobody else can help you or stand in for you. The bridegroom will come. And then it will be too late.

And that is the third surprise. There are some times when it is too late. 'Too late' is a terrible verdict. The job has been lost; it is too late now to say you will try harder. The divorce has come through; it is too late now to make amends. The examination starts today; it is too late now to prepare for it. And those terrible words are never more awesome than when applied to the parousia. Make sure you don't miss the party! That is what Jesus means. Readiness is the key.

The varied talents (25:14–30)

Here the key word is *faithful* (21, 23).[23] The master has gone into a far country, and will return (14). He has given *talents* to his servants to trade for him in his absence. These are not abilities (a talent is a weight, which later became a large unit of money). They are, rather, the responsibilities the Lord gives his people in the light of their abilities and opportunities. So it is not a 'talent' in the way we would use the word. It is not a gift, as if we control it. It is not an ability, of which we might boast. It is actually an investment which the Master makes in us his servants. He wants to be able to rely on us in its use.

This parable hovers on the edge of allegory, the 'comparison' (*mashal*), is so multi-faceted. To be sure, the main point of the story is faithfulness towards an absent master who will one day return and will want to know about the business we have conducted. But there are subsidiary features which are not to be missed.

The most notable is the man who did nothing with his talent but *hid* it *in the ground*. That was reckoned a safe place to hide something in the ancient world – as long as the spot was marked with some care![24] It looks as though the original application was to the Pharisees. They received the *torah* and oral law with great care from their predecessors, and ultimately from God. They preserved

---

[22] It is best to take this broadly, rather than be dogmatic about the nature of the oil.
[23] This parable shows how the 'waiting time' before the parousia is to be used – in practical service for the Lord.
[24] 'Money can be guarded only by placing it in the earth.' *Baba Metzia* 42a.

it unchanged. They buried it where ordinary people could not get at it. And they did not use their responsibility well. They wanted a religion without change and without risk. And they are heartily condemned for it. They are *worthless* servants, who will have their prize possession, the law, taken from them, and will find themselves outside the kingdom, in the *darkness* (30). The application also goes wider than the Pharisees: it applies to all who are determined to retain the status quo and to avoid risk and change in their religion – to all who refuse to trade with the responsibilities the Master gives them. But nobody fits the description better than the Pharisees.

There is a fascinating parallel between spiritual and natural laws. If we develop our muscles, our reward is that we can carry heavier burdens and still feel good. To those who have, more is given (29). And if we lie in bed and do nothing, atrophy takes over, and we find we can do less and less. We lose even the pathetic muscles we once had. It is like that in the spiritual realm. When we act faithfully under the responsibilities the Master has entrusted to us, our capacities will grow. If we do nothing with them, our ability to respond and be useful will diminish to vanishing point. The image is dynamic and organic. It is a powerful spur to responsibility in the service of the Master, and a warning against sloth, whether that is induced by laziness, fear of change or unwillingness to take risks.

Both the five-talent man and the two-talent man made full and responsible use of what had been entrusted to them. Both received the identical commendation when the Master returned: 'Well done, good and faithful servant! You have been faithful with a few things; I will put you in charge of many things. Come and share your Master's happiness!' (21, 23). Both found their opportunities doubled. It is not the quantity of talents that matters: it is how we use them. If we deploy them responsibly, we have the Master's commendation and his renewed and enlarged commission. It is those who will not try who are condemned.

The sheep and the goats (25:31–46)

This parable[25] (actually, it is not really a parable) has been endlessly discussed. People who reduce the gospel to social action love it, because it seems to have no theology in it and a great deal of care for the poor and needy. It gives the impression that to serve the poor is necessarily to serve Christ in them. People with a strong Reformed

---

[25] The four parables of 24:43 – 25:30 have all alluded to judgment. This one concentrates on the judgment itself. S. W. Gray, *The Least of my Brothers* (Scholars, 1989), gives a full history of the interpretation of this parable. See also G. E. Ladd, 'The parable of the sheep and the goats in recent interpretation', in R. N. Longenecker and M. C. Tenney (eds.), *New Dimensions in New Testament Study* (Zondervan, 1974).

theology have problems with it. It looks dangerously like justification by works, the very antithesis of Paul, Augustine and Luther.

On closer inspection, the passage does not warrant either of these attitudes. There is much here that goes uncomfortably with a social gospel: the exalted Son of Man executing the final judgment of God is hardly a theme you would expect in those circles. Equally, it is hardly about justification by works: our relation to the kingdom and the King is at the heart of it, and it is upon that relationship and its outworking that judgment is meted out.

Let us look at it afresh. A number of features, many of them uncomfortable, stand out.

It tells me that I am accountable. I am free to live my life just as I please, but at the end I shall have to give account to the one who gave me my life.

It tells me that judgment awaits everyone. There will be no exceptions. There will be no favouritism. There will be no excuses. It will be totally fair.

It tells me that we are not all going in the same direction though by different roads, as we would dearly love to think in this tolerant and pluralist age. We will not all end up in the same place. It is possible to be utterly lost, and Jesus warns us of that possibility here.

It tells me that there will be great surprises on that day. Lots of people who were very confident of their condition will be undone. Lots of people who rated themselves very lowly will be astonished by their reception.

It tells me that the heart of Christianity is relationship with Jesus himself, which shows itself in loving, sacrificial care for others, in particular the poor and needy.

It tells me that people who have never heard the good news (and it is they, the pagans, *ta ethnē*, who are primarily in view here) will be judged by their response to what light they had, and in particular by their response to the *brothers* (and sisters) of Jesus, whether these be Jewish or Christian.

But most of all this great parable brings us face to face with our Judge, and we need to be clear about three great realities which it underlines.

First, *the Son of Man will return* in glory (31). His coming will be sudden, unexpected, decisive. It will be the end of human history. It will determine human destiny. What should his people be doing when he returns? They should be caring for the poor, those who lack clothing, strangers, the prisoners and the sick. In this way they express the love of God that they talk about. It has to be tangible to be real. Such caring is the express command of Jesus the Messiah. He lived like that. He expects his followers to do the same. In places such as Singapore, where lay Christians major on imaginative ways of loving service, this makes an enormous impact in drawing people to Christ.

Secondly, *the Son of Man has come* – in disguise. He has come already. The point is not stressed in the story, but it underlies it. He came and identified with the poor and needy. He spoke our language without a trace of a foreign accent. He took our nature upon him. One of the meanings of 'Son of Man' is simply 'human being'. And when he was on earth, with whom did he mix? For most of the time it was with the diseased, the mourners, the outcasts, the lonely and the tax collectors. What was he, anyhow? Poor and outcast, and he ended in utter disgrace.

Thirdly, *the Son of Man will judge*. To this despised working man is committed the judgment of the whole world. Before him will be not just Jews and Christians, but *ta ethnē*, the pagan nations, *and he will separate* them *one from another just as a shepherd*, having run his flocks of *sheep* and *goats* together all day, separates them after the evening watering, because the goats have to be kept warm at night. This Son of Man will judge us. He will separate sheep from goats.

This is not really a 'judgment' scene. There is no debate. No witnesses are called. A person's destiny is written all over him or her before coming to the judgment. Jesus has met everyone before, and has asked for a response: '*Whatever you did for one of the least of these brothers of mine, you did for me*' (40). Both those who had cared for the needy, and those who had rejected them, are surprised to find that it was Jesus they were reacting to. 'When, Lord? We did not know it was you.' People did not recognize him at his first coming, and, although it will be so public, there is a sense in which people will not recognize him at his second. And in between the advents we are blind to the Christ who judges us in and by our reaction to the poor and needy, the hungry, homeless and oppressed. It will not do for Christians to sing hymns and keep ourselves pure. In the needy world in which we are placed between the advents, we must be known by our Christian love and service. We must realize that in failing to care for the poor and unemployed we are failing to care for those with whom Jesus identified himself. '*Whatever you did not do for one of the least of these, you did not do for me*' (45).

The more we learn to discern Christ challenging us through the poor, the more prepared we shall be to face him on the day of judgment. For on that day all will be disclosed. There will be many surprises. Many who were famous in Christian circles will be on the very edge of the crowd in the kingdom. Many who have never been heard of outside their own neighbourhood will be very near the throne. Why? Because they showed their love for Christ, they showed their readiness to meet him, their watchfulness to serve him on every occasion, their reliability. They did what the four preceding parables have been urging. And they gave themselves in generous service without a thought of reward, simply because of the need of the people they met and the love of God flowing in their hearts.

In this, the last and most awesome of his parables, Jesus is holding up to us the pattern for practical, Calvary-like love. There is nothing like it in the whole world. It is the supreme hallmark of the disciple of the kingdom. There is one test, and one only, of the extent of our love for him, and it is a very uncomfortable one. How have we treated the poor?[26]

William Barclay closes his comments on this passage by giving two moving stories. They are worth a world of theory, and they help us to see what Jesus is getting at by this insistence on practical love.

Francis of Assisi, wealthy and high-born, was out riding one day and met a man disfigured by leprosy. Francis was moved to dismount and hug the poor man. As he did so, the face of the leprosy sufferer changed into the face of Christ.

Martin of Tours was a Roman soldier and a Christian. One freezing day a beggar asked him for alms. Martin had no money, but, seeing the man blue with cold, he ripped his soldier's cloak in half and gave one part to the beggar. That night he had a dream. He saw Jesus in the courts of heaven, wearing half his cloak. He heard an angel ask, 'Master, why are you wearing that battered old cloak? Who gave it to you?' And Jesus replied, 'My servant Martin gave it to me.'

The return of Christ is the future dimension of the kingdom. It is of the greatest importance that citizens of that kingdom are ready to meet their King when he comes. These five parables which Matthew has gathered together here show believers what Jesus expects of us in the time between his first coming and his last. He looks for his servants to be watchful, holy, ready to meet him at any time, faithful in the use of their gifts and opportunities, and above all full to overflowing with his self-forgetful, self-sacrificing love. There is no higher calling. And it is open to the humblest disciple.

---

[26] David Wenham, *The Parables of Jesus* (Hodder and Stoughton, 1989), pp. 88–93, concludes: 'Jesus calls his followers to be a revolutionary, caring community, not comfortable conservationists protecting the status quo.' But he warns against supposing that to be a nice, caring person is all that will be required on the day of judgment. This would be to fly in the face of Jesus' teaching about loyal relationship to him and the heavenly Father. He links the 'blessedness' of caring activism here with the blessedness of confessing Christ as Messiah (16:17). This parable is designed to show how those who call Jesus 'Lord' (37, 44) should live.

F. FINALE (26 – 28)

26:1–16
17. A study in contrasts

We come now to the last of the six great sections that make up the Gospel of Matthew. The theme of judgment, seen from a variety of angles, has dominated the last seven chapters. We are about to embark on the denouement, where the judgment theme is focused most sharply. Just as the third panel in Part 1, on commitment, emerged naturally out of the theme of discipleship that occupied chapters 8 – 10, so here a similar thing happens. We see in this last great section of the Gospel how terrible was the judgment meted out to Israel's Messiah, and we are given a hint of how terribly that fateful decision would boomerang: 'Let his blood be on us and on our children!' (27:25). But God's purposes are not to be thwarted. The end was not the end, but rather the beginning of a new stage in the coming of the kingdom, when, with their sins forgiven, men and women from both Israel and the Gentiles could come and be disciples of the Risen One, and his good news could go out to all the world for which he came to die. Pilate's question, 'What shall I do . . . with Jesus who is called Christ?' (27:22), haunts the reader, and urges decision.

Part 2, therefore, ends in a challenge, just as Part 1 had done; but the intensity is far higher. Instead of a teaching block to conclude this section, such as has concluded all the other five sections of the Gospel, we are given the story of the resurrection. The unique thing about the new Moses is that he is always contemporary. Death has not robbed us of him. The one who has enunciated his new *torah*, book by book, in the five blocks of teaching, confronts us at the conclusion as the living Teacher who is with us always, to the end of the age (28:19–20).

Such seems to be the plan of the final section of this book. It is all about the death and resurrection of Jesus of Nazareth. The account of his passion was clearly continuous before it came into the hands of Mark, and Matthew's account follows Mark's quite closely. Probably the heart of the story was regularly recited at the holy communion – and the communion was celebrated frequently. From the earliest times, on the first day of the week, Christians met to break bread in vivid recollection of the cross and the risen presence of Jesus; so it would have been natural for the story to have assumed a clear and continuous form very early. It is a story of contrasts, of royalty, of fulfilment and of new life for the world at the cost of the death of the Saviour.

It is introduced with a couple of verses, 26:1–2. Two things in those verses are important. The first is that Jesus has finished all his teaching. For the last time Matthew utters his concluding formula which has rounded off each of the five great blocks of teaching in the Gospel, but this time it has a slight change: the addition of the word 'all'. *When Jesus had finished saying all these things* ... (1). His teaching ministry is at an end. From now on he concentrates on the prospect of his suffering. Here Jesus initiates the subject of his death this coming Passover season (2). The notable thing about it, apart from the shock of its nearness, is that Jesus is seen to be in control throughout. He is going to his death, but he is totally free, unlike any of the other actors in the drama. Of his own will he goes to his death (42). He knows that his appointed time has come (18).

High priest and disciple: conspiracy (26:3–5, 14–16)

The plot to arrest Jesus has been imminent for some time. Now it reaches its climax. The account falls into two parts: first the machinations of Caiaphas and the chief priests (3–5), and then the complicity of Judas (14–16). Caiaphas and Judas: what a combination! The high priest and the intimate disciple join hands to extinguish the most perfect life that has ever lived.

The Jewish historian Josephus has left us a description of Caiaphas and his family. The plot to destroy Jesus was nothing out of character for them. Caiaphas was adept at political and ecclesiastical manoeuvring. He was a genius at keeping in with the Romans. When the Romans came to power in Palestine, the office of high priest changed from its lifelong status into something like an annual appointment. It was an obvious move: the Romans wanted to break the centre of Jewish power and influence. Yet Caiaphas managed to hold on to the job not for one year but for eighteen, from AD 18 to 36. He was a master of intrigue and duplicity. And now, at Passover time,[1] we see him plotting to arrest Jesus and get him killed.

---

[1] Passover lambs were killed on 14 Nisan: the Passover itself was eaten that evening, the 15th (Jewish days began at 6.00pm). The year was either 30 or 33. The Palestinian Targum on Exod. 12:42 looks forward to the Passover when the future Messiah would bring salvation.

Judas, *one of the Twelve* (14), was very different. Almost every reference to Judas in the New Testament defines him as 'one of the Twelve'. The sheer horror of his betrayal of Jesus reverberates through the phrase. He is prepared, at the last, to exchange his Master for *thirty silver coins* (15). There is an allusion to Zechariah 11:12: 'So they paid me thirty pieces of silver.' The early Christians were convinced that every detail of the passion was to be found in the Old Testament if you dug deep enough. But the poignant thing about the thirty silver coins was this. It was the amount a person had to pay, back in the days of Exodus, if his ox happened to cause the death of a slave.[2] Probably inflation would have shrunk the value of those thirty silver coins to one tenth by the time of Jesus. That paltry sum is what he was prepared to trade Jesus for!

Why did Judas do it? We can never know for sure. It may be that the love of money had eaten into his soul and he was prepared to do anything for cash, like a drug addict. If so,[3] it provides the clearest demonstration in all history that the love of money is a root of all kinds of evil.[4] It may be, though, that he had a more political motive. One of the possible derivations of his strange name, Iscariot, is that it is a corruption of *sicarius*, *sicarii* being the Latin name for the Zealots, who wanted to rid Palestine of Roman domination by force. Had he come to the conclusion that Jesus was not the deliverer he had looked for? Jesus was thinking of death, and therefore, *ipso facto* as far as Judas was concerned, of failure. He would never deliver Israel as Judas hoped the Messiah would. It was time for him to be liquidated. We do not know: but for whatever reason, Judas determined to betray his friend.

A woman: adoration (26:6–13)

In striking contrast both to the sustained hatred of Caiaphas and the Jewish hierarchy, and to the terrible treachery of Judas, we have, sandwiched between them, the story of the unnamed woman who made the offering of her costliest treasure to the Master she loved.

Mark and John both place this story at this particular juncture in Jesus' life. Luke omits it, because he records a similar anointing by a woman of the streets much earlier in the ministry.[5] If we may piece together the story from Matthew, Mark and John,[6] an amazing probability emerges. The host at this party is *Simon the Leper* (6). Had he been healed by Jesus? Or is 'leper' a mistranslation of the Aramaic word meaning 'jar merchant'? (The mistake would be easy, because

---

[2] Exod. 21:32.
[3] Clearly, John thinks this had something to do with it: John 12:4–6.
[4] 1 Tim. 6:10.   [5] Luke 7:36–50.   [6] See Mark 14:1–9; John 12:1–8.

the consonants are the same and vowels were inferred, not written.) The place is Bethany, just outside Jerusalem. And the guests at the meal include Mary and Lazarus. In the presence of this man, whom he had just raised from the tomb to new life, Jesus, the Lord of life, is anointed for his burial! The woman who does it is not named in Matthew and Mark, but from John it is clear. It was Mary, Lazarus' sister, who anointed Jesus. No doubt the jar of precious ointment was a family heirloom. It was certainly incredibly valuable, worth 'a year's wages'.[7] We are undoubtedly meant to contrast the extravagance of the woman's grateful love with the plans of Caiaphas and Judas to put Jesus to death. Indeed, the poignancy is made all the greater in John's account, for there it is Judas who is spokesman for the disciples: 'Why wasn't this perfume sold and the money given to the poor?' John tells us he said this because he was treasurer of the group of disciples and sometimes dipped his fingers into the common purse.[8] But in any case, what a statement from the man who was just about to betray his Master for thirty silver coins!

The anointing is also a solemn pointer to Jesus' death. Each of the paragraphs in this chapter has some such pointer. But like the myrrh which the wise men brought at the beginning of the Gospel (2:11), this offering of myrrh (*myron*, NIV *perfume*) is unmistakable in its significance. It is used in burial. It points to death. Jesus is on his way to die, and he is flanked on one side by hatred and treachery and on the other by adoring love.

There are a couple of thoughts here for our minds and a couple for our hearts. The rather self-conscious contrast between giving money to the poor and spending it in love for Jesus may owe something to the situation in which Matthew found himself. All around him were Jews, one of whose highest virtues was almsgiving to the poor. He and his fellows had no quarrel with that: but it was not so important as the sacrificial offering of loving and adoring worship to Jesus, who had gone to the cross for his followers. And it is interesting, too, to see how firmly the missionary vocabulary of the early Christians, *preached, gospel, throughout the world* (13), is rooted in the very words of Jesus.

But we must never forget that no offering lavished on Jesus is wasted (10). Of course it is crucial to care for the poor, and Matthew has made that abundantly plain in the parable of the sheep and the goats (25:31–46). But there is nothing that so delights the heart of Jesus as loving devotion from his disciples, something done expressly out of love for him. And the other *beautiful thing* (10) to remember is that no sacrifice made for Jesus is forgotten (13). It seems improbable that one woman's present to Jesus should be

[7] John 12:5.   [8] John 12:5–6.

recounted in the preaching of the gospel all over the world and all down the centuries, but so it has turned out. Those twin facts, that nothing done for Jesus is wasted, and nothing forgotten, should nerve disciples to take the cap off their alabaster jars of precious possessions and pour them out for Jesus.

26:17–56
18. Jesus' last evening

The Last Supper (26:17–29)

Jesus had come up to Jerusalem to celebrate the Feast of Passover. The feast had to take place within the walls of the city, though pilgrims spilled over into the surrounding villages for their own accommodation. Normally, some three million people would gather for it. No wonder Caiaphas did not want to arrest this high-profile and popular figure 'during the Feast' or 'in a festival crowd' (6)! Four things are especially significant in this section.

The Supper itself

Jesus and his disciples were celebrating the age-old Passover meal, eaten *on the first day of the Feast of Unleavened Bread*.[1] The whole festival was also termed 'the Passover'. The Passover meal reflected the deliverance of the Jews from Egypt, the land that had become associated for ever in their minds with cruel bondage. Exodus 12 tells the story of this meal. On a certain date, 14 Nisan, each Israelite household was to slaughter a lamb, put some of its blood on the doorframes of their houses, and eat the meat. That same night the Lord went through Egypt killing the firstborn of people and animals, except where he saw the blood; these households he 'passed over'. The meal, celebrated annually thereafter, presaged the deliverance of the whole people from bondage and death. It was at this special commemoration that Jesus decided to institute his meal which spoke of a deliverance far greater than from Egypt: it spoke of redemption from bondage to sin and spiritual death. No wonder he said, *'My appointed time is near'* (18). The Jews, at God's

---

[1] This feast, originally separate from Passover, ran from 14 to 21 Nisan. Passover itself took place on the first evening of the festival, after 6.00pm. See France (1985) for an important suggestion on the complicated issues surrounding the date of the Last Supper.

command, kept the Passover as 'a lasting ordinance'.[2] The followers of Jesus would keep his Passover meal until he returned in glory.[3]

It was the perfect feast to anticipate what Jesus had come to do. For the Passover in Judaism had three particular orientations. It looked back to the *past* and the deliverance from that terrible bondage in Egypt. It gave *present* strength for the journey; people ate it ready for the road. And the Passover always had a *future* look, towards the Promised Land. All down the ages the Passover liturgy, or *haggadah*, has retained that future hope. 'This year we eat it in the land of bondage: next year in the land of promise,' they recited; and they kept a chair at the meal for Elijah, that great prophet who would return at the end of time to prepare for the coming of the Lord.

Each of those strands would be taken up and fulfilled in the Last Supper Jesus was preparing to institute. It would look back on his mighty deliverance from the grip and doom of sin. It would give strength to pilgrims along the Christian way. And it would be a foretaste of the messianic banquet in heaven.[4]

And so Jesus sent his followers to prepare the meal for this Passover that would eclipse all Passovers. The preparations would take them much of that Thursday. The lamb had to be secured and ritually killed.[5] The room had to be got ready. Yeast had to be scrupulously excluded (partly as a reminder of the haste with which they left Egypt, with no time even to put yeast into their bread – it cooked much more quickly without; and partly because yeast had become a symbol of evil, and all evil needed to be swept away before that sacred meal of Passover). Bitter herbs had to be got ready, in memory of the bitter bondage endured in Egypt by their ancestors. Salt water was part of the ritual too, a memory both of salt tears shed in the days of slavery and of the salt of the Red Sea through which they passed. A paste made of apples, dates, pomegranates and nuts reminded them of the clay of Egypt which they had been forced to turn into bricks for their masters, and sticks of cinnamon in the paste stood for the straw which helped to make the bricks. All this had to be got ready, along with four cups of wine which were passed round at the feast to recall the four promises of Exodus 6:6–7: 'I will bring you out . . . I will free you . . . I will redeem you . . . I will take you

---

[2] Exod. 12:14.   [3] 1 Cor. 11:25–26.   [4] Matt. 8:11; 25:10; Rev. 19:9.

[5] No mention is made of any lamb at the Last Supper. Is this because, as many of the church fathers thought, Jesus himself was the lamb, and his death superseded all that the Passover lambs had stood for? Or is it the case that Jesus celebrated an anticipated Passover, a day early, a private meal with his disciples? This would explain why there was no lamb. They had to be ritually killed in the temple. It would also make sense of John's chronology (13:1; 18:28; 19:14), which seems to indicate that Jesus died in the afternoon at the end of 14 Nisan, when the Passover lambs were being killed in the temple – graphic symbolism indeed.

for my own people, and I will be your God.' Jesus had, it would seem, made previous arrangements to celebrate Passover in a particular friend's house: hence the injunctions to his disciples in verse 18.

The note of betrayal

The horror and the enormity of betraying Jesus are brought out in strong colours in this Gospel. The first thing Jesus is recorded as saying during the meal is, '*I tell you the truth, one of you will betray me*' (20). *They were very sad*, and each asked, '*Surely not I, Lord?*' (22). That is a question every disciple needs to ask, and Matthew may have good reason to know it. The temptation to return to Judaism and disown Christ was great in the 70s and 80s of the first century, but particularly as the siege of Jerusalem from AD 66 to 70 put almost unbearable pressure on every self-respecting man with Jewish blood in his veins to support the nationalist cause. Matthew's church in northern Palestine must have known many a defection under such intense pressure of public opinion.

Jesus tells them that he will be betrayed by one who has the closest ties of sacred table fellowship with him. '*The one who has dipped his hand in the bowl with me will betray me*' (23). To break that tie was anathema. Yet one of them would do it. '*Surely not I, Rabbi?*' asks Judas, and Jesus replies, doubtless in a whisper, '*Yes, it is you*' (25).[6] And if Jesus was able so to whisper in the ear of Judas, then Judas must have been reclining next to him on the couch on which Jews ate the Passover. And that was the most favoured place! Jesus did everything to show his love for Judas, but in vain.

The new covenant

Christians are over-familiar with the words Jesus used on this memorable night: '*Take and eat, this is my body . . . Drink from it, all of you. This is my blood of the covenant, which is poured out for many for the forgiveness of sins*' (26–27).

It is almost impossible for us to conceive of the astonishment and indeed horror with which this group of Jewish disciples would hear those words for the first time. To eat the flesh and drink the blood of a person is an abomination in almost every culture. To Jews it was utterly beyond the pale. Their amazement knew no bounds that night. For the president at Passover (and any ten men could celebrate Passover together) would take unleavened bread and say, 'This is the bread of affliction which our fathers ate in the wilderness.' It wasn't,

---

[6] NIV is inaccurate here. *Sy eipas* means 'You have said it' or 'The words are yours'. Comparing vv. 24 and 25, it is instructive to note that divine sovereignty in the death of Jesus does not abrogate Judas' free will in betraying him.

of course, but it represented it, and brought it vividly to mind. 'This the Almighty did for me when I came out of Egypt,' recited the celebrant at the Passover liturgy. Worshippers identified with the rescue long ago, which made them what they were.

Imagine, then, the atmosphere as Jesus takes bread and replaces the hallowed formula by these shattering new words, *'this is my body'* (26). This bread was so soon to be broken on the cross. This is 'the bread of life', which, if we eat it, means that we 'will never go hungry'.[7] Jesus was that bread. And both the discourse on the bread of life in John 6 and the Supper here point to the one who alone gives them meaning. His followers are to feed on him, just as the Jews fed on the Passover lamb and the unleavened bread of the first Passover. That is what he means, and it is amazing. For the separation of 'body' from 'blood' points to death, and a violent death at that. The disciples are to be nourished continually by depending on that death of Jesus. That seems to be the thrust of his words.

These words have been the cause of violent disagreement. When Jesus said, *'this is my body'*, *'This is my blood'*, did he mean that it literally *was* his body and blood, or that it merely *represented* his body and blood? Catholics have preferred the former under-standing; Protestants the latter. The ambiguity was there in the original, for Aramaic grammar does not require the verb 'to be' in such usages. Jesus would have said, 'This – my body.' Against the Catholic interpretation, we can say that such excessive literalism is somewhat bizarre and unlikely to be what Jesus meant: after all, he was reclining there among them. Against the extreme Protestant interpretation, we can say that the communion is far more than a bare memorial of what Jesus did on the cross. It is a means of feeding on him, just as it is a pledge of his return. So 'This represents my body' is altogether too shallow an interpretation. We have here a great mystery, as mysterious as the parables of Jesus and as the person of Jesus. We shall never plumb its depths. But we need to come with the utmost reverence, gratitude and expectancy to the feast Jesus instituted, to make him as real – no, more real – to his followers than the Passover made the rescue from Egypt real to Jewish worshippers. It speaks of the past rescue: it is a present feeding; and it brings the promise of future table fellowship with Jesus in the kingdom (29). But more than all this, it brings the Saviour to believing disciples, in all the power and beauty of his sacrificial love. The bread that comes down from heaven is Jesus, and this sacrament brings it before us as nothing else on earth can.

Where does the blood come in? Way back in Jeremiah 31:31–34 the prophet had a marvellous vision of the new covenant. The Old

---

[7] John 6:35.

Testament knows of many covenants, binding God to humankind, and from the days of Noah onwards they were all sealed in blood. The death of an animal was the pledge of the binding nature of the covenant. Indeed in early Hebrew religion one literally 'cut' a covenant, passing between two halves of a slaughtered animal.[8] It was universally recognized in Israel that 'without the shedding of blood there is no forgiveness'.[9] But when Jeremiah predicted the new covenant, no blood was mentioned. That is unique in the whole of Scripture. Now, with intense feeling, Jesus makes good the deficiency. For the new covenant would be sealed not with the blood of animals but, as the letter to the Hebrews insists so strongly in its central chapters, with the blood of Jesus. His life, no animal's, is the ultimate sacrificial offering. And it confirms and establishes the new covenant. *'Drink from it, all of you. This is my blood of the covenant, which is poured out for many for the forgiveness of sins.'*

Note well that phrase *for the forgiveness of sins*. Mark had it early in his Gospel.[10] He was describing the baptism of John, which was *eis aphesin hamartiōn*, 'with a view to the forgiveness of sins'. John's baptism did not confer that forgiveness, but it pointed forward to it. The coming deliverer, Jesus, would bring it into being. And he will do it tomorrow, on that terrible cross. That is where his blood will be shed, for the forgiveness of sins. So Matthew does not use the phrase in connection with John's baptism. He keeps it till now, when the new covenant is described. That is where the covenant blood belongs, for the forgiveness of sins.

What was this covenant? Jeremiah had foreseen it: he knew that it would enable a permanent relationship to be established between God and sinful people, who broke the old covenants with boring regularity. There were three weaknesses in the old covenant. First, the law was external. It stood over against people, commanding, accusing. But in the days of salvation to which Jeremiah looked forward, ' "This is the covenant that I will make with the house of Israel after that time," declares the LORD. "I will put my law in their minds, and write it on their hearts. I will be their God, and they will be my people." '[11] That is what was going to happen when the Holy Spirit took up residence in the hearts and lives of the disciples. The new Moses put his new *torah* in their hearts by means of his Spirit.

The second thing was this. In the Old Testament days the majority of Israel would never have professed to know the Lord. A few of the great ones, such as David and Isaiah, of course did. But not ordinary Israelites. They would go to consult God through prophet or priest. But the wonderful hope cherished by Jeremiah was that ' "No longer will a man teach his neighbour, or a man his brother, saying,

---

[8] See Gen. 15:9–10, 17–18   [9] Heb. 9:22.   [10] Mark 1:4.   [11] Jer. 31:33.

'Know the LORD,' because they will all know me, from the least of them to the greatest," declares the LORD.'[12] The chance to know God personally is one in which every believer revels. There is a world of difference between knowing about God and knowing him. Jesus came to make the Father known. Jesus came to enable us to know the Father. It is a priceless blessing of the new covenant.

All this is based on the third characteristic which Jeremiah saw would mark the new covenant. It would convey forgiveness of sins: 'I will forgive their wickedness, and will remember their sins no more.'[13] The Old Testament sacrificial system did not convey forgiveness of sins. It is important to remember that. It is not as if God decided that the death of animals would atone for sins in the Old Testament and then changed his mind. The death of Christ atoned for all the sins of all the sinners who had ever been or who ever would be, as well as those who were alive at the same time as he. The sacrificial system pointed forward to that sacrifice of Christ, but could not itself take away sins. The writer to the Hebrews is clear about that: 'The law ... can never by the same sacrifices, repeated endlessly year after year, make perfect those who draw near to worship. If it could, would they not have stopped being offered? ... But those sacrifices are an annual *reminder* of sins, because it is impossible for the blood of bulls and goats to take away sins.'[14]

Those three great blessings of the new covenant, foreseen by Jeremiah, but never hitherto achieved, were going to be brought to the world by the shed blood of Jesus: sins would be forgiven, men and women could know the Lord personally, and God's will would be written on their hearts by the indwelling Holy Spirit (as Jeremiah and Ezekiel had in some sense foreseen).[15] Universal pardon, universal knowledge of God, universal availability of his Spirit: these were the marks of the new covenant, and they were all going to be sealed in Jesus' blood the next day. The disciples must never forget it. The Last Supper must replace the Passover as 'a lasting ordinance'.[16]

The stress on the future kingdom

Jesus had come to bring in the kingdom. He went about preaching the kingdom, healing in the name of the kingdom and offering parables of the kingdom. But now we see that one of the most decisive moments in the coming of the kingdom is the death of the King. The legacy of the Supper is witness to the 'already' and the 'not yet' of the kingdom. The kingdom had already come: the

[12] Jer. 31:34. [13] Jer. 31:34. [14] Heb. 10:1–4.
[15] As well as Jer. 31:33–34, see Ezek. 11:19–20; 36:25–27. [16] Exod. 12:14.

broken body and the shed blood which are recalled at every communion service demonstrate it so graphically. But the kingdom was yet to come in all its fullness. Jesus longed for the day when the kingdom would be completely realized. And the holy communion bears testimony to that too. It anticipates the heavenly banquet, 'the wedding supper of the Lamb', as the book of Revelation puts it.[17]

Gethsemane – and arrest (26:30–56)

When they had sung a hymn, which would have been the Great Hallel,[18] they left the upper room and went across the Kidron Valley *to the Mount of Olives* (30). An incredible sense of peace descends upon Jesus. Just think of singing as you walk to Gethsemane! And what did they sing in the Hallel? 'I will give you thanks, for you answered me; you have become my salvation. The stone the builders rejected has become the capstone; the LORD has done this, and it is marvellous in our eyes. This is the day the LORD has made; let us rejoice and be glad in it. O LORD, save us; O LORD, grant us success.'[19] Isn't that amazing? And how does the psalm end? 'Give thanks to the LORD, for he is good; his love endures for ever.'[20] That is how Jesus sang as he walked towards the cross. And all the time his soul was racked with anguish at the approaching falling away of his disciples (31) and at Peter's grossly misplaced self-confidence (35); and he was sick at heart at the prophecy of Zechariah 13:7: 'I will strike the Shepherd, and the sheep of the flock will be scattered' (31). It would be fulfilled all too soon, as the good Shepherd was smitten to his death and his followers ran off like startled sheep.[21] These few verses suggest an astonishing picture of peace and serenity in the midst of the most ghastly turmoil. They suggest to us that we shall have tribulation in the world as our Master did, and yet that serenity is possible in the midst of it. It has happened. And it can again.

Jesus' destination on the Mount of the Olives becomes apparent to his followers. He is going to the garden called Gethsemane ('oilpress'). Some age-old olives, perhaps emanating from that era,

---

[17] Rev. 19:7–9.

[18] The Great (or Egyptian) Hallel was a group of psalms (113 – 118) with the theme of thanksgiving for deliverance, traditionally associated with the Passover.

[19] Ps. 118:21–25.   [20] Ps. 118:29.

[21] In Zech. 13:7–9 the shepherd who is 'close' to God is struck by God's sword, and the flock scatters. But later some of them, refined and restored, are established as God's people. So here the violent death of Jesus will lead to the dispersion of the disciples, but in due course they will be restored as the messianic community. There will be renewed fellowship with Jesus in Galilee (28:7, 10, fulfilled in 28:16–20). *Proagō* (32) could mean 'I will go (to Galilee) before you' or 'I will lead you (into Galilee)' – an ambiguity that has given rise to many theories.

still survive, and the atmosphere is drenched with history. Here Jesus prayed that night as no-one ever prayed. He prayed, Luke tells us, with an intensity which made blood drop from his brow. A few people in history have sweated blood. It is very rare. The blood is pushed out through the pores of the skin.[22] Jesus sweated blood in that time of prayer, intense and intimate beyond description.

What a lot there is to learn about prayer here in the example of the Master! First, it teaches us the necessity of prayer even when the hard times seem intolerable. When the most crucial and demanding action in the world's history was about to happen, it had to be rooted in prayer. Jesus knew it was essential.

Secondly, it teaches us the value of shared prayer. Jesus longed for the encouragement of sharing this prayer time with his disciples, but they were too tired, and they failed him. He had promised that 'where two or three come together in my name, there am I with them' (18:20). But when he himself needed them, no two or three were to be found.

Thirdly, it teaches us that there is value in repeated prayer. Jesus himself prays here three times for *the same thing*. He prayed with all his heart that the *cup* of suffering which he could see awaiting him might *be taken away* (39, 42, 44). Such prayer is not like the 'many words' of the pagans, who 'keep on babbling'; such repetition is condemned in the Sermon on the Mount (6:7). No, it is showing God we mean business. It is all too easy, shallow and cheap to pray and walk away and think no more about it. To keep on praying indicates both determination and confidence, and demonstrates a note of seriousness that is a vital part of intercessory prayer.

Finally, this account discloses to us something of the mystery of unanswered prayer. This prayer of Jesus himself, who enjoyed the most intimate relationship with the Father, was not answered. A remarkable passage in Hebrews tells us that Jesus 'offered up prayers and supplications with loud cries and tears to the one who could save him from death, and he was heard because of his reverent submission'.[23] He was heard. But the answer was not in the affirmative. Not for him the almost blasphemous suggestion that 'anything you ask' will be granted in prayer if you believe enough. He had utter trust, perfect relationship with God, passionate sincerity, and he was heard. But he was not answered in the affirmative. 'Although he was a son, he learned obedience from what he suffered and ... became the source of eternal salvation to all who obey him.'[24] That was it. The Father in his inscrutable wisdom had to say 'No' to the content of his Son's prayer. Otherwise there would have been no salvation

---

[22] A. Plummer, *St Luke*, International Critical Commentary (T. and T. Clark, 4th edition, 1901), pp. 510–511, gives examples.
[23] Heb. 5:7.   [24] Heb. 5:8–9.

for anyone, and the kingdom would have shattered in pieces. Jesus had prayed, *'If it is not possible for this cup to be taken away unless I drink it, may your will be done'* (42), and the Father took him at his word. The prayer of Jesus in Gethsemane shows that we can be close to God, live a holy life, and pray with faith, earnestness and expectancy, and yet not get what we ask for. It is a profound mystery before which we must bow.

Jesus prayed with a clear objective, which all his humanity longed for; but above even that, he wanted God the Father's will to be done. For prayer is not seeking to manipulate God. It is opening up to God. It is welcoming the 'good, pleasing and perfect will' of God.[25] That is the difference between prayer and magic. Magic seeks to control cosmic powers. Prayer seeks to surrender to the will of God.

We can never pierce the mystery of that prayer. Others have died with even greater bravery than Jesus: they have rarely sweated blood as they contemplated their violent end. But nobody has ever had to face a fraction of what he had to face as he took responsibility for all the evil in the world. It was not the prospect of physical suffering, or even the appalling torture of crucifixion, that caused him to sweat blood; it was the sinbearing that was so terrifying.

Such agony of anticipation would have been exacerbated by his betrayal. 'Even my close friend, in whom I trusted, he who shared my bread, has lifted up his heel against me.' Psalm 41:9 had literally come true. *Judas, one of the Twelve* (47),[26] comes up to him with a band of soldiers in the darkness, meretriciously calls him *'Rabbi!'* (49) and uses the mark of close intimacy, a kiss, as the token of betrayal.[27]

One of Jesus' companions (John tells us that it was Peter),[28] so misunderstands what Jesus is about that he draws a sword and hacks at a slave of the high priest. He misses his head, and severs an ear (51). How much Peter had forgotten! He had forgotten that it was God's purpose that Jesus should die; forgotten that Jesus was not without God's protection (53); and forgotten that violence always breeds violence and rarely proves anything – something our increasingly violent world very much needs to learn.[29]

[25] Rom. 12:2.   [26] This description highlights Judas' treachery.
[27] Jesus' response is obscure and ambiguous in the Greek. It may be a question: 'Why have you come?' It may be an exclamation: 'What an errand you have come on!' It may be a command: '. . . *do what you came for*', as in NIV.
[28] John 18:10.
[29] Peter had indeed misread the situation. Jesus was not a victim who needed protection. He steadily undertook the path of innocent vicarious suffering indicated by the Scriptures. He will not call on human or angelic assistance. He was determined to fulfil his calling to suffering and death, and he points out the folly of militarism as a way of solving problems (52). This observation that violence breeds violence is no more a call to undiscriminating pacifism than it is a justification, as Luther claimed, of militarism.

Jesus is alone. Neglected, misunderstood or betrayed by his friends, and later *deserted* (56), he faces the cross willingly (but at such cost). The sins of the world, ours included, cut him off like an obscene storm-cloud from the sunshine of his Father's presence. He tasted the hell of separation from God the Father as he hung on that cross. And in the Garden he got the first bitter taste of what our salvation was going to cost. The outcome he must face alone.

26:57 – 27:31
19. The trials of Jesus

The Jewish trial (26:57 – 27:10)

Jesus underwent two trials, one before the Jews and one before the Romans.[1] He was declared guilty in both, though he had done nothing wrong. In the Jewish trial there is a dramatic antithesis between the Jewish leaders with their power, their self-righteousness, their self-deceptions arising from the profound challenge to their own interests posed by Jesus – and a single, silent, 'false' prophet without position, prestige, supporters or any visible evidence of God's help.

The heart of this Jewish trial is the person of the accused. It is not what he has done but who he is that is the issue. That question has been relentlessly brought before the reader throughout the Gospel. *False witnesses* were sought who could provide evidence for a capital charge against Jesus, not in the sense that gratuitous charges were trumped up, for those who were caught doing that became liable to the death penalty themselves, but in the sense that Jesus' words were twisted. The two charges that looked the most promising (and two witnesses were needed for corroboration) maintained: '*This fellow said, "I am able to destroy the temple of God and to rebuild it in three days"*' (26:61), which was very like the claim of Jesus in John 2:19, 'Destroy this temple, and I will raise it again in three days.' But there is a clear difference. His accusers produced a version of the words of Jesus which would sustain a capital charge either for sacrilege (destroying the temple) or for magic. The actual way Jesus expressed himself in John 2:19–21 showed a profound dependence on the power of God to raise the temple of his body from the ruin of death: 'the temple he had spoken of was his body'. So the charge

---

[1] The trials of Jesus have attracted a great deal of attention. See D. R. Catchpole, *The Trials of Jesus* (Brill, 1971), and A. N. Sherwin-White, *Roman Society and Roman Law in the New Testament* (Oxford University Press, 1963).

would have been very convenient if it could have been made to stick. But it was not possible.

It seems that there was a substantial anti-Caiaphas party in the Sanhedrin, the council of seventy-one who led the Jewish nation at that time. Pharisees of the calibre of Nicodemus and Joseph would have been political opponents of a Sadducean high priest. They were prepared to tolerate the illegality of a night meeting and trial (only one of about fourteen illegalities which experts have detected in the way the trial of Jesus was conducted) but not the possibility of a false condemnation. Either they remembered well enough what Jesus had actually said, or they had too much perception to take it literally, as the common people did. It is interesting that at the cross itself one of the taunts from the crowd was on precisely this issue: 'You who are going to destroy the temple and build it in three days, save yourself!' (27:40). But even if Caiaphas could have got the Sanhedrin to accept the validity of this charge against Jesus, it would not have sufficed. The Romans would have laughed it out of court. And it was the Romans who, since becoming the occupying power, had the sole right of execution in the province. If the Jews deemed someone worthy of death, it had to be on a charge that the Romans would consider valid.

This was a difficult position for Caiaphas to be in, so he gambled on a last, illegal throw of the dice. He applied what was called the oath of testimony (26:63). This was a question under oath to which the prisoner was legally bound to reply – but it was illegal to pose it in a trial for life! The accused was never required to incriminate himself. Hitherto Jesus had kept silence in the trial, perhaps from disdain, but more probably because of the pattern of the suffering Servant of the Lord in Isaiah 53, which he knew he must fulfil: 'He was oppressed and afflicted, yet he did not open his mouth; he was led like a lamb to the slaughter, and as a sheep before her shearers is silent, so he did not open his mouth.'[2] Maybe Psalm 38:12–15 went through his mind, too. It was very apt.

> Those who seek my life set their traps,
>   those who would harm me talk of my ruin;
>   all day long they plot deception.
>
> I am like a deaf man, who cannot hear,
>   Like a mute, who cannot open his mouth;
>   ... whose mouth can offer no reply.
> I wait for you, O LORD;
>   You will answer, O Lord my God.

[2] Is. 53:7.

This was a crucial moment in the proceedings. Caiaphas could see the trial collapsing, and he could not afford that. If Jesus were released after being arrested, there was no knowing what the wave of popular support would do in a festival crowd. Whatever it was, it would not be good news for the Sadducees, the maintainers of the *status quo*. So he put to Jesus the illegal question which would, he hoped, lead the prisoner to incriminate himself: *'Tell us if you are the Christ, the Son of God.'*[3] Perhaps Caiaphas used the term 'Son of God' in the old sense of 2 Samuel 7:14 and Psalm 2:7 (the Christians would read it with a deeper understanding), but even so, if Jesus said 'Yes', he would be claiming to be a descendant of King David with a special relationship to God as his Father. It was as crucial a moment for him as it was for Caiaphas. What would Jesus reply?

The fate of the world hung in the silence before that reply. If Jesus said 'No', he would walk out of that trial a free man. If he said 'Yes', he signed his own death warrant. Which was it to be? Could he face the bitter cup that he was agonizing over in the Garden?

But then the decision was made. His reply was affirmative. But it was guarded: *Sy eipas*, 'That is your way of putting it' (cf. 26:64). Jesus had not denied the title 'Son of God' or 'Messiah' during his ministry, but he had courted neither. It was not his way of putting things. Both ideas were swathed in so much confusion that they were best avoided. But yes, he could not and would not deny it. He was the Messiah. He was the Son of God. And then Jesus puts it his way: just as incriminating, but in line with his own teaching and consistent with his claims to be the Son of Man. *'I say to all of you: In the future you will see the Son of Man sitting at the right hand of the Mighty One* (a reverential Hebrew periphrasis for God), *and coming on the clouds of heaven'* (26:64).

Here were two of his favourite ways of understanding himself and his mission. He was the Son of Man of Daniel 7:13–14, to whom all kingdoms would eventually bow and whose dominion would be everlasting and indestructible. He was that Son of David who was also David's Lord (as he had told them in 22:41–46), and whom God vindicated, set on his right hand, and with whom he shared his throne. That is how Caiaphas should think of him! The priests and leaders of Israel would very soon see facts and circumstances that would show beyond reasonable doubt that Psalm 110:1 and Daniel 7:13–14 had been fulfilled in the person and achievement of Jesus. As we saw earlier, Daniel 7:13–14 describes not a descent, but an ascent, to the Ancient of Days by the Son of Man. That is what is about to happen. The criminal's cross would prove to be the prince's throne. Jesus is claiming, as he stands there alone, bound and mocked among

---

[3] For the expressions 'Christ' and 'Son of God', see above, on 16:13–17.

his judges, that the glorious destiny that belongs to the Messiah of Israel and the Son of Man, although described in different ways by psalmist and prophet, will be seen to be his. This process would be set in train by the passion. The enthronement was imminent, whether you see that in the cross, as John certainly did, or whether you see it in God's vindication of his Messiah through the resurrection. The enthronement was imminent, but the parousia lay in the future of God's timing.

Christians would not be able to read and reflect on this passage without being stirred to a deeper recognition of what Jesus had done. The old order of Judaism with its temple and priesthood is fading away. It is being replaced by the new. The judges of Jesus are themselves judged, and they will before long see evidence, in the rise and meteoric growth of the church on the one hand and the destruction of Jerusalem and its temple on the other, which vindicates Jesus' claim. The temple of Christ's body, incarnate, crucified and risen, will replace the temple at Jerusalem. Caiaphas the high priest will go into oblivion. He will be replaced by the high priest for ever after the order of Melchizedek. This fascinating figure, combining the roles of king and high priest, who strides on to the scene in Genesis 14, is picked up in the messianic Psalm 110, which Jesus has just quoted, as the 'type', or foreshadowing, of the Messiah. Jesus, the Messiah, is the eternal high priest who makes all other priesthood irrelevant. He has offered the perfect sacrifice, and he is himself the perfect priest. The Melchizedek allusion is not expanded here as it is in Hebrews,[4] but it is explicit in Psalm 110. Jesus quotes it to explain to the Sanhedrin who he is.

Jesus' answer to Caiaphas implies this total reversal of roles. Caiaphas the judge is himself judged, and so is his mediatorial priesthood. The system of mediating priests is coming to an end. The enthronement of Jesus, the new priest who is also king, is at hand. It begins from now! Such is Jesus' last word to Israel, its leaders and its priesthood.

But Caiaphas understood none of this. He was simply astonished and overjoyed to find that his stratagem had worked. It looked as if he had got a watertight case at last, and that Jesus had implicated himself to such an extent that the Sanhedrin would deem him worthy of death for blasphemy,[5] and the Romans for claiming a kingdom. The Romans were very jittery about anyone claiming a kingdom; they were expert in eradicating messianic pretenders in Israel as they emerged during the half-century before the destruction of Jerusalem.

But Caiaphas was not quite out of the woods yet, and he knew it.

---

[4] Heb. 6:19 – 8:2.   [5] See Lev. 24:10–23.

Jesus had neither claimed nor abused the divine name. He had actually avoided it, using the reverential periphrasis *Mighty One*. He was not, strictly speaking, guilty of blasphemy. A Sadducean high priest could put a most damaging construction upon the claim to sit at God's right hand, but he knew he was on thin ice. So he *tore his clothes* in real or simulated horror, and cried out, '*He has spoken blasphemy! Why do we need any more witnesses? Look, now you have heard the blasphemy. What do you think?*'

'*He is worthy of death,*' *they answered*, and descended to abuse, mistreatment, punching and spitting. Jesus had made ultimate claims; if they were not true, they were positively blasphemous. The reader, like the Jewish leadership, must decide.

Peter (26:69–75)

Interwoven with the central figure there are two others, Peter and Judas. The leader of the apostolic band, the man on whose faith and courage Jesus was to build his church, crashes unceremoniously. *Three times* he fulfils Jesus' prediction that he would *disown* him (26:34, 75). First he denies that he was *with Jesus* (69–70). Then he denies that he knows him (72). Then he *curses* and swears that he does not know him (74).

Peter had followed the crowd of soldiers who arrested Jesus. He noted where Jesus was taken, and joined the motley collection of people who were hanging around the courtyard as the proceedings were going on in the house of the high priest. Peter's strong north-country accent gave him away in Jerusalem circles, and invited comment and the suspicion that he must be one of the followers of the Galilean prisoner. (Indeed, the Galilean accent was so marked and so disliked that the rabbis forbade a Galilean to pronounce the blessing in the synagogue service!)

It is a very poignant, painful and shameful story. Earlier that very evening, Peter had sworn that he would never disown Jesus (26:35). Death would not drag a denial out of him. Yet here he is denying that he is a disciple, denying that he even knows Jesus. He does so first *in the courtyard* where *a servant girl* notices him. He withdraws to *the gateway* area and is embarrassed at *another girl* noticing him and drawing people's attention to him. And then the crowd standing around presses the same accusation. Three times Peter denies his Lord.[6]

There are several undertones here. One is the contrast Peter's denials form with the threefold prayer of Jesus in the Garden, and

---

[6] Peter *began to call down curses on himself* (74). 'On himself' is not in the Greek. Did Peter pronounce a curse on Jesus, as later Christians were required to do as proof of their apostasy (see Pliny, *Epistles* 10.96)?

his strong injunction to them to 'watch and pray so that you will not fall into temptation' (26:41). One is the awesome parallel between Peter's *'I don't know the man!'* and Jesus' words at the last judgment to those who are not related to him: 'I never knew you' (7:23; cf. 25:12). If we do not confess him before others, he will not confess us before his heavenly Father (10:32–33). The cock's crow is ambiguous. It could mean the early-morning crow of a cockerel, or it could mean the 3.00am changing of the guard in the nearby barracks of Antonia where the soldiers were stationed. At that hour a trumpet was blown known as a *gallicinium* (cock crow).

At the cock's crow, *Peter remembered . . . and he went outside and wept bitterly.* The church that Matthew served would have felt keenly the guilt of the leader of the apostolic band. He had denied Jesus in his Master's hour of need. He had buckled at the knees. Hulking fisherman that he was, he had been afraid of a servant girl's words.

There are two brighter things to notice. The fact that the New Testament records such failures in its heroes is a remarkable testimony to its veracity and reliability. If the story had been made up, nobody would have dreamed of making Peter fail at so crucial a juncture. It was true, and that is why it was recorded. It was a warning to other leaders who might be in danger of promising more than they could perform and who, through failing to watch out against temptation and pray for God's strength, might succumb to denying Christ themselves in a hostile environment – which is what most of them lived in.

The other astounding thing is that this story must have originated from Peter himself. Matthew is following Mark's account closely. Mark was the 'interpreter of Peter',[7] and there is a great deal of evidence in the second-century writers to show that much of Mark's material is derived from Peter. It takes a big man to admit such comprehensive failure, and to be willing to have it published. That is one of the differences between the failure of Peter and of Judas. Judas did not allow his fall to drive him back to repentance and recommissioning. Peter did. Judas gave way to remorse and killed himself. Peter was brought back in deep humility and repentance to Jesus, was recommissioned (three times, as John tells us[8] – to compensate for his three denials), and became that rock-like man whom Jesus had longed for. But he could not become that rock until he realized how weak he was in his own strength. He could not bring in the kingdom with his sword or with his loyalty. God takes those who fail and makes them saints.

[7] Eusebius, *Ecclesiastical History* 3.39. [8] John 21:15–19.

Judas (27:1–10)

As for Judas, what a complex character he was! It may be that the devotion of the follower turned to hate (as happens sometimes among lovers) when, Zealot that he may well have been, he realized that Jesus was not going to fulfil the Zealot hope. It may even be that Judas hoped to force the hand of Jesus by betraying him. This would make him act. This would induce him to bring in the kingdom. Maybe even the kiss in the Garden (and the Greek word indicates an affectionate and repeated kiss) was not just a traitor's hypocrisy, but something real: he hoped that at that moment Jesus would call down the legions of angels to his aid and rout the enemy. Yes, it could just have been meant in good faith. If it was, it shows in the darkest colours the peril of trying to do God's work in our own way. For it came most terribly unstuck. Instead of a shattering denouement, Jesus meekly allowed himself to be led away, and Judas realized with the blinding light of terrifying recognition that he had ruined everything and delivered his closest friend to death. What hell he went through in the hours that followed we cannot know, but he certainly saw the horror of what he had done. He brought *the thirty silver coins* and tried to give them back to *the chief priests*. They did not want to know, and callously replied to his agonized admission of having *betrayed innocent blood*, '*What is that to us? ... That's your responsibility*' (3–4). So he strode through the court of the Gentiles, through the court of the women, through the court of the Israelites, and came to the court of the priests, called the *naos*, at the far end. In a gesture of blind despair he *threw the money* at them and their court – into which, of course, he was not allowed to go. *He went away and hanged himself*, so profound were his despair and remorse (5). He saw no other way out.

Remorse is destructive, repentance is creative. So Judas went to destruction and Peter became a new man whom Christ could use and rely on.[9]

Both Matthew and Luke[10] tell us about the death of Judas and the purchase of *the Field of Blood* (8). They are quite independent. Both wrestle with the treachery of one of the closest followers of Jesus. Both ransack the Old Testament Scriptures for light on this appalling thing. Luke says that Judas bought the field, that he fell in it and his intestines spilled out, and that it was called the Field of Blood for that reason. Matthew tells us that Judas *hanged himself*, that the *chief priests* bought the field with the *blood money* Judas had thrown back

---

[9] In line with Matthew's emphasis on fulfilment throughout his Gospel, Peter fulfils Jesus' prediction in 26:34, and Judas fulfils that in 26:24.
[10] Acts 1:18–20.

at them (using it to bury *foreigners* in), and that it was called *the Field of Blood* for that reason. It is not very difficult to reconcile those two accounts. Judas went and hanged himself: then either his corpse rotted and fell, or the rope broke and he fell and his insides were ruptured and gushed out. Either Judas had already acquired this field previously, or the priests bought the field in Judas' name with the money that was still legally his and which they could not receive back into the treasury because it was blood money (6). The field fittingly became a cemetery (the meaning of the Aramaic 'Akeldama' in Acts 1:19).

There were clearly two accounts circulating of why it was called Field of Blood: either because it was bought with blood money, or because it was the field where Judas' blood was shed. It may well be that both reasons coinhere. Perhaps it was the very field in which Judas died that the priests bought to use as a cemetery.

Where does the 'potter' fit in all this? Matthew has in mind one of his formula quotations, which enable him to see how God's revelation, outlined (often very obscurely) in the Old Testament has pointed to the events around Jesus' life and death. This one, which he uses to illuminate what happened to the thirty silver coins, comes in Zechariah 11:12–13. Zechariah says that he threw the money 'into the house of the LORD to the potter'. In Matthew, the chief priests use the thirty silver coins *to buy the potter's field* (subsequently renamed the Field of Blood), and so unconsciously fulfil the prophecy of Zechariah. But Jeremiah had also visited a potter and (separately) had bought a field,[11] and it looks here as if Matthew has conflated quotations from both Zechariah and Jeremiah and attributed the result to Jeremiah. We must remember that Scripture was written on large and cumbersome rolls, and people did not own copies of their own. They had excerpts containing important passages, and they learned other sections by heart. Thus it was easy for various Bible quotations to be conflated, and it is quite understandable that Matthew assigned the whole quotation in verses 9–10 to Jeremiah. A similar thing has happened in Mark 1:2–3, which conflates Malachi and Isaiah and is ascribed to Isaiah. We ought to thank God for printed Bibles and concordances!

These references back to Jeremiah and Zechariah merely underline the sense of inevitability and fulfilment which enshrouds the events of the passion. They were no disaster which ruined everything; ghastly they were, but they happened under the perfect control and guidance of God. Every detail of the passion tied in with some allusion in the Old Testament. It shows how these early Christians had a tremendous sense of reverence for their Old Testaments. It was

[11] Jer. 18:2–4; 19:1; 32:6–15.

here that the plan of God was revealed in direct teaching, allegory, typology or history. Jesus did not come to abolish the Old Testament (5:17) but to fulfil it. There is a wonderful unity about God's revelation. As Augustine put it long ago, 'The New is in the Old concealed: the Old is in the New revealed.' The Lord is in control of every detail of the passion and death of his Son.

The Roman trial (27:11–31)

Verses 1–2 of chapter 27 pick up the events of the previous night. It seems clear that the first trial had been an informal (and illegal, since it was after nightfall) gathering of the Sanhedrin, and that they met the next morning in formal council to ratify the verdict. Then they bound Jesus and led him away to Pilate to get the Romans to ratify the verdict if they could. The Mishnah tractate *Sanhedrin* tells us that the right of execution had been removed from the Jews since the Roman occupation, so it was imperative to get Pilate's agreement. Thus another trial was necessary.

The trials and execution of Jesus are seen, in the brilliant construction that characterizes this Gospel, as constituting his witness to the Gentiles. The silent witness of his suffering and death is the supreme exemplar of that endurance under persecution that he enjoined upon his followers.

Think back to 10:17–18: 'They will hand you over to the local councils and flog you in their synagogues. On my account you will be brought before governors and kings as witnesses to them and to the Gentiles.' That is what would happen to his followers later. But it would happen to him first. Or think of 24:9–13: 'You will be handed over to be persecuted and put to death, and you will be hated by all nations [or, Gentiles] because of me. At that time many will turn away from the faith and will betray and hate each other . . . but he who stands firm to the end will be saved. And this gospel of the kingdom will be preached in the whole world as a testimony to all nations [or, Gentiles], and then the end will come.'

Jesus was predicting that fate for his followers, but it was to befall him first. He was dragged before a governor, Pilate. He was dragged before a king, Herod. He was hated, flogged and put to death. That was his testimony to the Gentiles. His testimony to Israel had come through his teaching. For him, as for his followers, word and deed, proclamation and sacrifice had to go together. And so it has proved down the ages. The power of his teaching and of his cross has become a magnet to draw people of every background and nation to the Crucified.

Let us examine this Roman trial under seven heads.

A king's silence (27:11–14)

There is great stress on the royalty of Jesus running through this part of the Gospel. He is indeed King David's royal Son. *'Are you the king of the Jews?'* asks Pilate. *'Yes, it is as you say,'*[12] says Jesus, forcing the governor to think. But when he was accused by the chief priests, he said nothing. *He made no reply, not even to a single charge – to the great amazement of the governor* (14). Total injustice, met by total, silent suffering. Jesus is in control of the proceedings. It is Pilate, it is Caiaphas, it is the reader who is on trial. Jesus is the one with moral authority at his own trial, majestic in silence.

A woman's dream (27:19)

Only Matthew tells us about Pilate's wife. She comes upon the scene of history only on this one memorable occasion. She was Claudia Procula, the illegitimate daughter of Claudia, the Emperor Tiberius' third wife, and so she was a grand-daughter of Augustus. She was therefore much better connected than her husband, and it may be that it was due to her that in AD 26 he gained the appointment as 'prefect of Judea' (the correct title was discovered in 1961 on an inscription in Caesarea).

Claudia had had a dream about Jesus the night before. It would seem that on some occasion she had heard Jesus personally, and she could not get him out of her mind at this Passover feast. She tried to influence her husband to release Jesus by sending a message to him during the trial, telling him of her dream. Pilate had been dug out very early indeed in the morning, and no doubt she was still in bed, but she could not rest until she had passed on the warning of that dream. God used dreams in that day (there have been several earlier in this Gospel). God still uses dreams today. It is a mistake to profess to be too sophisticated to take any notice of them. How human history might have had to be rewritten if Pilate had listened to his wife's dream! But he did not.

A criminal's release (27:15–18, 20–21, 26)

There was, so three of the evangelists tell us,[13] a custom that at the Feast of Passover one prisoner was released, as a goodwill gesture. There is no independent evidence for this custom in Judea, but an

---

[12] *Sy legeis* means 'The description is yours' – just as Jesus had answered Caiaphas (64). The title 'King of the Jews' is used only by Gentiles in this Gospel (2:2; 27:29, 37). It has a political innuendo that Pilate is keen to exploit. Jesus is the King of the Jews – but not in the way Pilate fears.

[13] Matt. 27:15; Mark 15:6; John 18:39.

Egyptian papyrus of about AD 80 knows of a parallel, and so does Livy.[14] I have no doubt that Pilate made an annual habit of it; it would be a good way to try to ingratiate himself with the Jews, who hated him. Pilate therefore tried to evade responsibility for Jesus, whom he saw to be innocent, by offering the people a choice between Jesus and *Barabbas*, a notable prisoner who was doubtless a Zealot, captured along with two of his colleagues by the Roman security forces. He was a freedom fighter who had committed murder in an attempted coup. Contrary to Pilate's expectation, the crowd, egged on by the chief priests, asked for Barabbas, so Jesus went to die on the cross prepared for Barabbas.

The incident is full of irony. The one who refused to take arms as a freedom fighter was crucified on the cross of Barabbas, the freedom fighter. Not only that: the name 'Barabbas' means 'son of the father', so there were two 'sons of the father' in the centre of the stage that day. But nobody would simply be called 'son of the father': Barabbas must have had his own name, and a number of the ancient manuscripts tell us what it was – Jesus! 'Jesus' was a common name in first-century Palestine. It is almost certain that his name was Jesus Barabbas, but that the personal name was dropped from the majority of the manuscripts out of reverence: you couldn't have a criminal with the same name as Jesus! *But you could!* That is the point of Jesus' coming and identifying with sinners. Here stood two sons of the father; two men called Jesus ('God to the rescue'). One pillaged and killed. The other loved and suffered. People were called to choose between those two ideals, and still are. On that Good Friday, the one ended up on the cross intended for the other, and the guilty man walked away free. An amazing picture of what the cross of Christ really means! Jesus took Barabbas' place. He took ours, too.

A crowd's vacillation (27:21–23)

'*Crucify him!*' the people howled time and again (22–23). It wasn't just the chief priests and Pharisees any more. *They all answered,* '*Crucify him!*' And this was the same crowd which, less than a week ago, was celebrating the Son of David's entry into Jerusalem with cries of 'Hosanna!' and scenes of delirious joy. A crowd is often like that, vacillating and fickle.

The call for crucifixion is remarkable on Jewish lips. This hated form of execution was Roman. But it was the necessary outcome of the decision to impugn Jesus on a quasi-political charge that could carry the death penalty.

[14] *History* 5.13.

A governor's weakness (27:11–26)

It is perfectly plain from this account that Pontius Pilate found Jesus innocent of the charges preferred against him. He saw no good reason why this prisoner should die. He realized that the charges were trumped up, but he did not know how to handle it. He tried to release Jesus, but he feared for his career, which he had jeopardized by several bad decisions in the past. He dared not make another.

Pilate was prefect of Judea, a second-class Roman province, from AD 26 to 36. He was recalled and sent into exile in AD 36 and we do not know what became of him. Eusebius says he was forced to commit suicide in Gaul under the Emperor Gaius (AD 37–41).[15] We know a good deal about Pilate from Philo and Josephus. He was both weak and cruel, and was hated for the murders he continually perpetrated on untried people. He enjoyed the reputation of being corrupt and grossly inhumane, and he had a total lack of sympathy with the Jewish people and their sensitivities.

Four episodes in that decade of his government illustrate this graphically. The legionary ensigns had images of the emperor upon them, and this was anathema to the Jews. Other governors removed them before entering Jerusalem. Not Pilate! There was a major threat of civil disobedience, and he had to withdraw the ensigns, with a very bad grace.[16]

Then there was the matter of the votive shields. These were golden shields that Pilate erected in his residence in Jerusalem. They were inscribed with his own name and the emperor's. This seemed blasphemous to the Jews, who reported him to the emperor, and he was severely cautioned.[17]

On another occasion he raided the *korban*, the temple treasury, in order to raise funds for the worthy task of improving the city's water supply. He wanted to build an aqueduct from the Pools of Solomon to the centre of the city. The Jews were livid. So when Pilate came up to Jerusalem, he sent in his troops among the protesting crowds, and many were slaughtered.[18]

Finally, he massacred a peaceful crowd of Samaritans, some of whom had foolishly come armed in response to what turned out to be an impostor's claim to have found some sacred vessels from Moses' day in Samaria. This led to his dismissal by the governor of Syria, Vitellius, to whom the Samaritans rightly complained.[19]

Such was the man who was now required to make a decision about

[15] *Ecclesiastical History* 2.7.   [16] Josephus, *Antiquities* 18.5; *Jewish War* 2.169.
[17] Philo, *De Legatione ad Gaium* 299ff.
[18] Josephus, *Antiquities* 18.60; *Jewish War* 2.175; Eusebius, *Ecclesiastical History* 2.7. This is probably the occasion mentioned in Luke 13:1–2.
[19] Josephus, *Antiquities* 18.85–89.

Jesus. John records a shout from the crowd which profoundly influenced him during this trial. 'If you let this man go, you are no friend of Caesar. Anyone who claims to be a king opposes Caesar.'[20] There was a category of *Caesaris amici*, 'friends of Caesar'. Membership of this élite was highly valued and hard to achieve. Pilate must have got access through Claudia his wife, but he would lose this prized position if rumours got back to Rome that he had freed a pretender to political power. Reluctantly Pilate realized that it was Jesus or his career that had to be sacrificed. He made his choice, while hating every moment of it. He tried to wash his hands of the affair. Indeed, Matthew says that he adopted the graphic expedient of washing his hands in public, which was a Graeco-Roman custom as well as a Jewish one. It is hard, though not impossible, to envisage a Roman governor going to these lengths to avoid responsibility in a case brought before him.[21] But when the governor found himself so out of sympathy with the Jews and the case they were presenting, and when he despised them so heartily, such a grandiose gesture is not out of the question. At all events it is the act of a weak man.

A people's guilt (27:25)

It is hard to imagine the Jews crying out, *'Let his blood be on us and on our children!'* But in the heat of the moment, and given the passions and intrigue of that bizarre early-morning gathering, it is quite possible that the Jews present did take full responsibility for Jesus' execution even though they could not have it carried out without the governor's approval.

This verse has been grossly misunderstood. For centuries it has been the supposed justification for anti-Semitism. This does total despite to the text. Matthew records the cry of the 'rent-a-crowd' which the Sadducees had brought with them into the praetorium. He does not say that the Jewish nation killed Jesus, its Messiah. The Jewish nation did not. This is not an anti-Semitic verse or an anti-Semitic Gospel. There is no trace of hatred against those who nailed Jesus to the cross. For it was not the Jews who crucified Jesus. If we listen to Matthew, *we are all involved!* It was the refusal of the human heart to respond to the King proclaiming the kingdom that led to Jesus' death. In that refusal all sinful humanity is implicated. On a political level, it was not the Jews but the Gentile Romans who executed Jesus, and Matthew makes that perfectly plain. He

[20] John 19:12.
[21] Josephus (*Jewish War* 6.300ff.) tells of a later procurator trying another Jesus who was denounced by the Jewish authorities. He decided to declare the man insane and let him go. Pilate would cheerfully have done the same. If the Jews would not accept this, the responsibility must be theirs.

probably reflects the fulfilment of these terrible words in the destruction of Jerusalem in AD 70. The nation lost its privileged status as a consequence of its rejection of Jesus.

A soldier's game (27:27–30)

A macabre game was played occasionally in the ancient world.[22] At the spring festival they would dress up a prisoner as a king, pay him mock allegiance, grant all his last wishes for a night – and then scourge and kill him. It seems that they played 'the king's game' with Jesus. In Plutarch,[23] we read of pirates mocking a man who says he is a Roman, stripping him, scourging him and killing him. That is what the soldiery did with Jesus.[24] There were precedents for their behaviour.

Jesus was subjected to this treatment in *the Praetorium* (27), but what is meant by that term is not clear. The two possibilities are the Herodian palace, where Pilate normally stayed when he came up to Jerusalem for festivals, or the Roman Antonia barracks adjacent to the temple area. It is likely that with such a volatile situation on his hands, Pilate will have stayed at this fort. There is a fascinating inscription on one of the stones of the courtyard of that barracks, which has been excavated and lies beneath the Sisters of Zion Convent in Jerusalem. There are several graffiti of the soldiers' gambling games on the stone paving, and one of them is of the letter B adjacent to what looks like a crown of thorns. Could that stand for *basilikon*, the king's game? And could those stones have witnessed the howling of the mob and the pathetic manoeuvres of the governor, the cruelty of the soldiers and the silent suffering of the Christ? At all events, Matthew wants us to know that just as the Jews had mocked and abused Jesus, so did the Gentiles, only with greater violence and cruelty.

---

[22] As Dio Cassius, *History* 4.66, tells us.   [23] *Life of Pompey* 24.
[24] The *scarlet robe* is a soldier's red cape, and parodies the imperial purple. The *staff* imitated a sceptre, and the *crown of thorns* a royal crown. Homage follows, as to a king, before barbarity takes over.

27:32–66
20. The cross and the tomb

The crucifixion of Jesus (27:32–56)

The death of Jesus by crucifixion is without question the most famous death in all history. It was a very grisly method of execution, which the Romans took over from the Carthaginians. Cicero[1] affirmed that 'this most cruel and terrible punishment' was so degrading that it should not even be discussed by Roman citizens. It was reserved for the lowest of the low.

Th was the form of execution which the Romans used in Judea for capital offences.[2] There were various ways of carrying it out. The most basic way was to hang a man or impale him on a stake (*crux simplex*). Generally there was a crossbeam (*patibulum*) across the *stipes*, or upright. It could be fixed at the top of the upright, making the shape of a capital T (*crux commissa*). More often it was fixed a third of the way down (*crux inmissa*), and it is widely believed that Jesus was killed on a cross of this shape. The third variety was what we know as the St Andrew's cross, shaped like a capital X (*crux decussata*) on which the victim could be stretched either the right way up or upside down. Simon Peter was said to have been crucified upside down.

The condemned man was invariably scourged, and men were known to die under that punishment alone, so severe were the wounds inflicted by this cruel cat-o'-nine-tails inset with metal. If he survived the scourging he had to carry the *patibulum* of his cross, and was led out under an armed guard of Roman soldiers to die.

There were several ways in which a condemned man might be fixed to the cross. He might have his wrists tied or nailed to the

---

[1] *Against Verres* 2.5.165.
[2] For a detailed description of crucifixion, see M. Hengel's powerful monograph *Crucifixion in the Ancient World and the Folly of the Message of the Cross* (SPCK, 1977). Matthew does not concentrate on the physical agonies of Jesus, but on the significance of his death.

patibulum and then be hauled by ropes up on to the *stipes*, which was already firmly fixed in the ground. More commonly, the cross was put together on the ground, the condemned man bound or nailed to it, and the whole thing then erected by dropping its base into a pit that had been prepared to receive it. The degradation was made complete by the removal of all clothes from the criminal. He was crucified stark naked. Sometimes a draught of rough, drugged wine was offered to the condemned man to help dull some of the pain; rich Jerusalem women used to prepare it as a work of mercy. Jesus refused the drugged wine. He was in complete possession of all his faculties as he faced the full rigour of the most agonizing death known to humankind.

The physical effects of crucifixion were appalling. Of all deaths it is the most lingering. The suspension of the whole body on jagged iron nails (one dating from AD 50 has been discovered in Jerusalem), driven through the most sensitive nerve centres of the wrists and ankles, ensured constant torture. When it was deemed to have gone on long enough, the soldiers would perform the *crurifragium*, or breaking of the legs. This would ensure that the man, if still alive, could no longer hoist himself up to breathe and would soon expire.

That is the death which Jesus undertook for humankind. I shall not try to go through the story chronologically in my comments on this passage: that would diminish its power. Instead, I shall pick three great strands running through Matthew's account of the passion as he looks back, after thirty years and more, to that terrible day when the sun went black.

The royalty of suffering

There is a good deal of emphasis in this account on the kingship of Jesus.[3] Verses 11, 17, 29, 37, 40, 42 and 43 all point it up. Jesus is royal in his suffering. That is what Matthew is saying. He is also showing that Jesus is innocent in his suffering (4, 12–14, 19, 23–24). He has done nothing to deserve it, yet he suffers death in excruciating agony. In Jesus of Nazareth we see the most acute example in the history of the world of the problem of suffering. Why does God allow the innocent to suffer? Why does he allow such pain and agony in his world? That general question is focused with almost unbearable clarity in the specific question: why does he allow his beloved Son Jesus to suffer in unsurpassed horror on that cross?

In the Beatitudes (5:3–11), Jesus had said that suffering could be a path to blessing, and he was now demonstrating it in the manner of

---

[3] Indeed, some of the highest Christological titles are used in this narrative of the passion: King of the Jews, Son of God, temple-builder, etc.

his dying. It was hell to suffer like that. There was *darkness over all the land*, and darkness in his soul (45–46). Out of that darkness he cried, '*Eloi, Eloi, lama sabachthani*', a mixture of his native Aramaic and the Hebrew of Psalm 22. It would have been easy enough for the bystanders to misunderstand him as crying out to 'Eli', Elijah,[4] rather than 'Eloi', God. '*My God, my God, why have you forsaken me?*' He felt God-forsaken. He was God-forsaken.

Yet this passage is suggesting that though we can never experience what Jesus underwent, we too must suffer. Like Simon of Cyrene (32), a Jewish proselyte who had come up for the feast from North Africa and was conscripted by the soldiers to carry Jesus' cross when its intended victim collapsed under its weight, we too are called to carry his cross and share his pain and ignominy. Suffering is the ineluctable fate of all people, and Christianity is no insurance policy against it.

What, then, is there to hang on to in times of terrible trouble, such as Matthew's church was probably undergoing in the opposition that came their way, and such as Christians down the ages have faced? Four things seem to be suggested here.

First, there is *an answer to suffering*. There is no answer in words. Jesus remains the almost silent sufferer throughout the ghastly proceedings. The answer is that in Jesus God has come to share our pain. God is no absent academic who writes a book on the problem of pain. He is the caring doctor who comes alongside us as we lie in anguish. He has got involved. He has allowed pain at its most severe to strike him. We worship a suffering God: that is the best answer to the problem of undeserved suffering.

Secondly, there is *a fellowship in suffering*. There is some sort of fellowship with all fellow-sufferers, of course: Jesus had it with the thieves crucified alongside him. But I refer to the fellowship with Christ in suffering which has meant so much to believers down the ages and has nerved them to great endurance. Jesus understands. He has been through it, and he will not desert us. Paul was eagerly prepared for that fellowship of suffering with Jesus as part of his Christian calling: 'I want to know him and the power of his resurrection and the fellowship of sharing in his sufferings . . .'[5] Suffering need not separate us from the awareness of God's love and presence. In fact, Jesus endured that separation from the Father as an element in his suffering which need never be necessary for his followers. When our hearts cry out, 'Why does God allow it? Why has God turned his back on me?', the cross of Jesus tells us that God has not

---

[4] Elijah would return to usher in the 'day of the LORD' (Mal. 4:5). Perhaps, thought the bystanders, he is calling on Elijah to save him.
[5] Phil. 3:10.

turned his back on us. We are sharing in the sufferings of Christ, and will share, too, in his glory.

Thirdly, there is *a future to suffering*. Suffering is not blind, wanton and senseless. It is purposeful. It has a clear goal. Look what Calvary produced. Look what benefits flowed from that awesome suffering gladly undertaken. It is the same with the suffering of the Messiah's followers. That is not senseless and useless either. Many good things flow from it, mystery though it is. Character is formed by it. Inventions are stimulated by it. Compassion and care are evoked by it. Warnings emerge from it. And at the end, when this life is over, 'our light and momentary troubles are achieving for us an eternal glory that far outweighs them all'.[6]

Fourthly, there is *a royalty in suffering*. Jesus showed that it is possible to reign from a gallows. His royalty is not, so to speak, a reward after his suffering. It is part of his suffering, and it shines out through his suffering. He was regal on that cross. There is a royalty in suffering both for the Messiah and for his people when they follow him in innocent hardship and persecution. That was demonstrated very powerfully during the twentieth century, when there were more martyrs for the gospel than during all the preceding centuries put together.

The royalty of Jesus in his suffering is a major strand in Matthew's account of the passion. The King has come to Israel, and even the cross cannot mask his grandeur.

The one who took our place

The theme of substitution has been prominent throughout the Gospel, and it rises to a crescendo in this, the last act. This chapter gives us five cameos of how Jesus, in his death, took our place.

It comes out clearly in the Barabbas incident (16–17), at which we have already looked. The meaning of Jesus' death is brought out here by way of *contrast*. Jesus rejects the way of violence, yet he dies on the cross that has been prepared for that violent revolutionary. Jesus suffered a Zealot fate, though he had repeatedly repudiated a Zealot programme. Barabbas went free, because the other Son of the Father had a far more profound programme than the political messianism of Jesus Barabbas, and was prepared to implement it at the cost of his life. What a contrast! What a substitute!

The second way in which Jesus took our place in his death is brought out *by implication*. Every condemned prisoner had his charge sheet (*titulus*), which told why he was being executed. It was generally painted on a board which was carried round the prisoner's

6 2 Cor. 4:17.

298

neck, and then fixed to his cross, as a deterrent for others. Jesus carried the ironic *titulus* proclaiming his crime: THE KING OF THE JEWS (37). Matthew means us to see that people have crucified their King. His blood is indeed on us (25), for we are guilty. His blood is also on us for pardon; without that we have no hope. That *titulus* stuck in the minds of the early Christians. It is recorded by all four evangelists. We even have it in Paul, who says that Christ 'cancelled the written code, with its regulations, that was against us and that stood opposed to us; he took it away, nailing it to the cross'.[7] What he is saying is that God Almighty removed the *titulus* from Jesus, and replaced it with another, inscribed with the sins of the whole world. The writing in that accusing document is in our own hand; we cannot cavil at it in any point. And he cared so much for the fallen world that he took the responsibility for it himself. He took it out of the way and nailed it to his cross.

Thirdly, the note of *irony* is prominent in all four Gospels. It is strong in John, with Caiaphas' cynical comment, 'It is better for you that one man should die for the people than that the whole nation perish.'[8] It was expedient! Indeed, it was indispensable. Here too in Matthew the same device is employed. The things that are said in irony are profoundly true: '*You who are going to destroy the temple and build it in three days, save yourself!*' (40). The temple (of his body) was indeed destroyed, and it was raised in three days, and believers down the ages have become living stones within it.

'*He saved others ... but he can't save himself!*' (42) is another profoundly true piece of ironical mockery. If he was to save others, he could not save himself. '*Let him come down now from the cross, and we will believe in him*' (42). He could have come down, and they would have believed – for the moment. But how ephemeral that impression would have been! And the task for which he had come would have remained undone. His people would still be in their sins. The temptation of the devil in the wilderness, that Jesus should evade the destiny of sinbearing, must have been even more attractive now than it had been then. '*Come down from the cross, if you are the Son of God!*' (40). Precisely because he was the Son of God, he did not come down from the cross. Irony stresses the truth of life through death: it is the pattern for Saviour and disciple alike (16:25).

Memory, fourthly, plays its own part in interpreting what that death of Jesus meant. People could not forget the supernaturally chill darkness which came upon the land from noon till 3.00pm (45). The secular historian Thallus, writing about AD 52, records it in his

---

[7] Col. 2:14.   [8] John 11:50.

history of the world.[9] 'Will not the day of the LORD be darkness, not light – pitch-dark, without a ray of brightness?' said Amos.[10] This day of crucifixion was the day of the Lord, and dark it was. It recalled, no doubt, the three days of darkness in Egypt during the plagues before Moses led the people out of bondage, 'a darkness that can be felt'.[11] The great drama of redemption enacted in Egypt was re-enacted at a far deeper level at the cross of Jesus. It meant darkness for him, but light for us. It meant the destroying angel for him, but protection for us. It meant the fate of the Passover lamb for him, but life for us. And so that awful afternoon of darkness, an emblem of the utter darkness and desolation in the soul of the Son of God, was for ever graphically etched in the memory of those who were there.

Finally, Matthew uses *access* as a fifth way of helping us to have some understanding of what the death of Jesus achieved. *The curtain of the temple was torn in two from top to bottom* (51). That curtain separated the Holy of Holies from the rest of the Holy Place. It was 18 metres high, and made of thick material. It was an eloquent symbol saying, 'No access'. Access to God was restricted to one man, the high priest; once a year, on the Day of Atonement; and then only when he carried the fresh blood of animals sacrificed for his sins and for those of the rest of the people. This tearing of the temple curtain on Good Friday, and from top to bottom at that, suggests that it is God's work: human beings would have torn it from the bottom upwards. The perfect high priest has entered the Holy of Holies in God's presence. He went in, not with the blood of animals but with his own blood which he shed for the sins of the world: he had no need to atone for any sins of his own. He had none. Such is the implication.

And that torn curtain spelt access. God was no longer unapproachable. Anyone who trusted in Jesus could approach the divine presence with confidence. And who do we find doing just that, but the centurion who was in charge of Jesus' execution! The very man who has just presided over his death confesses, '*Surely he was the Son of God!*' (54). No doubt he did not have a full Christian belief in the deity of Jesus. His expression may have owed more to popular usage: 'a son of the gods' would be an exceptional person, maybe even a demi-god, the offspring of a human parent and one of the Pantheon of gods. The emperor, too, carried *divi filius* (son of a god) on his coinage and therefore in his propaganda. He was the son of his deified predecessor. The centurion would have coins bearing that

---

[9] In F. Jacoby (ed.), *Die Fragmente der griechischen Historiker* (Berlin, 1929), 11B, p. 1157.
[10] Amos 5:20.   [11] Exod. 10:21.

title in his pocket. The phrase in his mouth was, on any showing, an expression of profound respect. And Matthew's church would see in it the full Christian confession. The very man who killed the prince of life is seen going, as it were, through that split curtain, with his sins pardoned and his welcome secure because Jesus had made access to God possible for all who would, with the centurion, acknowledge Jesus as the Son of God. Moreover, the man was a Gentile, and a Gentile with blood on his hands. But he was no longer far off. He had drawn near, and he was accepted.[12] That would have been a great wonder and a great encouragement to Gentile members of Matthew's church, many of whom had doubtless got much blood on their hands and felt totally unworthy of acceptance by God. The one who died in their place had made it all possible.

These five pictures of the way in which Jesus met the needs of all humankind on his cross perhaps have something significant to say to a generation which has little time for God but a great deal of admiration for people who give themselves for others. Jesus supremely displayed what such self-giving meant, and by his living and dying he has spurred his followers to take the path of self-sacrifice. Such a lifestyle speaks eloquently to others of the Lord we serve.

The key to the future

In the cross itself, Matthew sees not only the royalty of suffering and these varied pictures of the self-oblation of Jesus, but the key to the future destiny of humankind. He sees people's hearts failing them in fear, as they look at the uncertainties of life – particularly the uncertainties of human destiny and the breakdown of human community. The 'year of the four emperors' (AD 69) and the destruction of the temple in the following year made an impact upon the whole civilized world which is almost impossible to exaggerate. The *Sibylline Oracles* give some idea of what it felt like to be alive at that time, and the fears about the imminent end of the world that were prevalent:

> When swords in the starlit heaven appear by night towards dusk and towards dawn, and straightway dust is carried from heaven to earth, and all the brightness of the sun fails at midday, and the moon's rays shine forth and come back to earth, and a sign comes from the rocks with dripping streams of blood, and in a cloud you shall see a battle of foot and horse, this is the climax of the war which God is bringing to pass.[13]

[12] See Eph. 2:11–13. [13] *Sibylline Oracles* 3.767–808.

It is against this background that Matthew presents Jesus the Messiah as not merely the sacrifice for sin but its conqueror. Christ the Victor is the key to the future.

First, what does the death of Christ say about human destiny? A remarkable group of happenings is associated with the death of Jesus in verses 51–54. The *curtain of the temple* was split *from top to bottom*. There was an *earthquake*. The *tombs broke open and the bodies of many holy people who had died were raised to life. They came out of the tombs, and after Jesus' resurrection they went into the holy city and appeared to many people*. And *the centurion* came to make the Christian confession of faith.

Those verses are saying something profound about human destiny. We do not go out like a light when we die. We do not look for any sort of resuscitation. We do not anticipate some shadowy existence in Sheol. We do not get reincarnated, or fall like a drop of water back into the ocean. We look for God's new life, the same life that was seen in the resurrected Jesus. No sooner does Matthew speak of the death of Jesus than he brings in this material about new life. It is certainly strange stuff, and peculiar to Matthew. But once again there is some shadowy corroboration in Josephus,[14] the rabbis[15] and Tacitus[16] which speaks of the temple being shaken and a lintel collapsing forty years before its destruction, i.e. in AD 30. The great bronze gates of the inner court opened of their own accord, there was a quaking and a noise, and a loud cry: 'Let us remove hence!' Earthquakes are not uncommon in the area: Jerusalem is on that seismic ridge in the Earth's surface which stretches down to the Great Rift Valley in Kenya, so these events are perfectly possible. But what does Matthew mean by them?

Surely he means that a new age is breaking in. The darkening of the sun, the tearing of the curtain, the earthquake and the shaking of the tombs is the sort of material we have met in the apocalyptic discourse in Matthew 24, pointing forward to the new age. A decisive stage in this new age (which is still largely future) has been brought about by the dying of Jesus on the cross, which makes it all possible.

Does Matthew mean us to take this literally? Does he mean that the tombs were broken open, and that the bodies were somehow clothed with flesh and brought to life, as in Ezekiel's vision?[17] It is possible but unlikely that this is how Matthew intended us to read it.[18] After all, he says that these bodies of the saints went into the

---

[14] *Jewish War* 4.5.4. [15] *Yoma* 43c. [16] *Histories* 5.13. [17] Ezek. 37.

[18] I agree with Hagner that in recording this story Matthew wanted, at the very point when Jesus died, to draw out its theological significance. A straightforward historical reading of these verses is hard to contemplate. Who were these people? Were they resurrected or resuscitated? Why did they go into the holy city? What happened

holy city *after* Jesus' resurrection. By that phrase he is guarding the primacy of the resurrection of Jesus, 'the firstfruits of those who have fallen asleep',[19] yet he presents us with these resuscitated bodies at the cross itself, long before the resurrection. If Matthew meant us to think of these people from a bygone age walking into Jerusalem that Friday evening, how would that accord with his plain insistence throughout this chapter (especially 40–50) that no compelling proofs of Jesus' deity were given at this time of his death any more than they were during his life?

No, Matthew seems to be giving us a profound meditation on what the crucifixion of Jesus means for the destiny of humankind. His death is an eschatological event: it is a foretaste of the end of the world. It is one of the great elements of the age to come that have broken into this age. The significance of what has happened is hidden from the bystanders mocking the dying Jesus. While they look on unmoved, the curtain is torn and the very rocks reel and shatter. The life and death of Jesus remove the curtain that has kept us alienated from God, ignorant of what he is like and unfit to enter his presence. The rending of the tombs is powerful symbolism for the victory over death which Jesus achieved. Because of his passion, the tomb has lost its terror and its finality. Because he lives, we shall live also. Many rabbis believed that the end of the ages would break in at Jerusalem, that the Mount of Olives would be split in two, and that the dead would appear and be raised to life again. Matthew seems to be alluding to this sort of expectation about the future. He is saying that at a profound level the end has come, the end of the old age of the tyranny of death and evil. Moreover, it is at Jerusalem that these stirring events have taken place. The rocks are split. The dead are raised. And it is all due to the prior dying and rising of Jesus of Nazareth.

But perhaps we are too earthbound in thinking of the holy city as Jerusalem. Maybe it means the 'Jerusalem which is above', the heavenly city.[20] And when Matthew speaks of the bodies of holy people entering into the holy city after the resurrection of Jesus, perhaps he refers to his conviction, maybe reinforced by a vision, that the cross and resurrection of Jesus have paved the way into heaven for God's people all down the ages. The passion is cosmic in its influence, retrospective as well as prospective.

Jesus Christ is 'the firstborn'[21] or 'the firstfruits'[22] from the dead. He is the firstfruit of the crop. He is the pledge that a crop will

to them subsequently? Indeed, what happens to the priority of Jesus' resurrection? And if they *appeared to many people* (53), why is there no reference to this event elsewhere, either inside or outside the New Testament?

[19] 1 Cor. 15:20. [20] Gal. 4:26; cf. Rev. 21:2. [21] Rev. 1:5. [22] 1 Cor. 15:20.

follow. As in John 6:25–29, Christ's death gives life to the dead. His crucifixion and resurrection in the midst of time give us our only firm assurance about the end of time and the outcome of human destiny. The decisive move in the game has been played at its mid-point. The end of the game will merely reveal and underline how significant that move was.

So in this strange passage Matthew is bringing out the hidden repercussions of Jesus' death. Because of that crucifixion which Matthew has just recorded, and the resurrection to which he will now turn, his readers may look even death in the face with equanimity. The gates of the tomb, locked since the primal disobedience of the first couple, have been burst open by Jesus' death and resurrection. The saints will be gathered into the heavenly Jerusalem, because the Saviour broke the back of death by dying outside the walls of the earthly Jerusalem.

The second great question that occupies human minds as they reflect on the possible nearness of the end and the decay in society is this. What holds human society together? In an age when the divorce rate is so widespread, the collapse of the family so great, and when alienation is growing on all sides, what could hold people together? There is a remarkable passage in Winston Graham's novel *The Sleeping Partner* where he maintains that it is worship that holds society together.

> Science, I suppose you would say, begins with observed facts, systematically classified. Right? Well, there is one fact about man that has distinguished him since his first appearance on the earth. That is, he's a worshipping animal. Wherever he has existed there are the remains, in some form, of his worship. That's not a pious conclusion; that's an observed fact. And all through history and pre-history when he has deprived himself of that, he has gone to pieces. Many people nowadays are going to pieces, or else they find the first convenient prop to tie their instincts on to. It's behind the extraordinary adulation of royalty. It's behind the worship of TV stars. If you don't give expression to an instinct you've got to sublimate it or go out of your mind.

Do we have a hint of all this in verse 40? For of all the charges brought against Jesus, this is the one which Matthew singles out. Clearly Jesus said something about the temple being destroyed and in three days being raised up. It was twisted at his trial and it was thrown in his teeth as he hung upon the cross. As we have seen, John 2:19 probably preserves the most accurate impression of what Jesus actually did say: 'Destroy this temple, and I will raise it again in three days.' His hearers thought he was referring to Herod's temple, a most imposing structure begun in 19 BC and never finished before it was destroyed in AD 70. But John remarks, 'The temple he had spoken of was his body. After he was raised from the dead, his disciples recalled what he had said.'[23] They did indeed, and the idea of the new temple became important in early Christianity. It is prominent in 1 Corinthians 3:16; 1 Peter 2:5; Ephesians 2:21 and other places in the New Testament. God has not given up on temples. But no longer is the building the important thing. 'Your body is a temple of the Holy Spirit' at an individual level.[24] Christians are indwelt by the Holy Spirit. But when they gather together for worship they corporately become the temple of God,[25] and he dwells in them and moves among them. The *shekinah* glory that filled the tabernacle but was absent from the second temple and from Herod's temple shines out in the body of Jesus the Messiah, as John emphasizes: 'And the Word became flesh and made his dwelling among us. We have seen his glory, the glory of the One and Only, who came from the Father.'[26] Significantly, the three consonants in the Hebrew word for 'glory', *škn*, are the central consonants in the Greek word for 'made his dwelling', *eskēnōsen*, related to *skēnē*, the word for 'tabernacle'. John's allusion to the *shekinah* is deliberate. The glory of the incarnate Jesus 'tabernacled' with his people, giving a foretaste of what Jesus would do worldwide as he 'tabernacled' with his followers, who would gather together in the 'new temple' of the church to worship him after the resurrection.

This seems to be why Matthew gives such prominence to the destruction and resurrection of the 'temple' of Jesus. He knew that the death and resurrection of the Messiah would usher in an era of worship that would unite Jew and Gentile in Christ. That is why he underlined the hint of the new temple at the very climax of his story, at the crucifixion. It gains all the more power being spoken in detraction at his trial and in mockery on his cross. But it was nothing less than the truth. The new temple would be founded by one who saved others by giving himself. And this idea of the new community remains the hope of the world. It is the community where differences of race and colour, of sex and age, are subordinated to Jesus Christ, and his people are bound to one another in worship, fellowship and service. And this is brought about by the glorious Spirit of the Lord, who indwells his people. That new community was constituted at Calvary. But, as with any of the fulfilment themes, where the church takes up and embodies one of the Old Testament hopes, the completeness lies in the future. The church is indeed the new temple,

---

[23] John 2:21–22.   [24] 1 Cor. 6:19.
[25] Rom. 12:4–13; 1 Cor. 3:16; 12:12–31; Eph. 2:11.   [26] John 1:14.

but, mercifully, not the final embodiment of it! That will be found only in the perfectly restored relationships and pure worship of heaven. On this earth it is possible to have only a partial anticipation of that perfection which remains for the city of God. But such anticipation, imperfect though it is, is better than anything else earth has to offer.

The burial of Jesus (27:57–66)

Jewish law forbade the body of an executed person to be left hanging all night. It had to be buried by sundown, when the Jewish day ended. 'You must not leave his body on the tree overnight. Be sure to bury him that same day.' This was particularly charged upon Israelites when one of their number had been hung upon a tree after his execution.[27] This, of course, applied to Jesus. His body needed to be taken down and buried, but none of his relations owned a property and a tomb in Jerusalem, since they came from Galilee.

Into this situation stepped a man who has not been heard of before now in the Gospel. Joseph of Arimathea was a rich man. He was a member of the Sanhedrin or Council, so Mark and Luke tell us, and, Luke adds, a good and upright man.[28] Matthew's emphasis on his wealth may draw our minds back to Isaiah 53:9, where the suffering Servant would be 'assigned a grave with the wicked, and with the rich in his death'. He came from Arimathea, which is unknown, but which some ancient commentators identified with Ramathaim,[29] the home town of childless Hannah, whose prayer for a son was answered, and the place where the prophet Samuel was buried. Matthew tells us that Joseph had been 'discipled'[30] by Jesus. Allusions like this show us how much material lies beyond and behind the Gospel story.

Jesus had made a personal disciple of this rich member of the Sanhedrin. Why then did he not stand up for Jesus at his trial? For all we know he may have done, but in all probability he was not there. It is fairly clear that Jesus was brought before a hastily summoned, illegal night trial of the Sanhedrin, and there is no reason to suppose that all seventy-one members were present or even informed. Caiaphas was determined to get a condemnation. He would not have been above packing the court with his followers, and failing to inform those whom he knew to be sympathetic to Jesus until the formal meeting for ratification of the sentence the next morning, when it would have been too late for them to affect the outcome. Maybe Joseph had protested, but in vain: Luke says, 'he

---

[27] Deut. 21:22–23; Josephus, *Jewish War* 4.5.2.   [28] Mark 15:43; Luke 23:50.
[29] 1 Sam. 1:1.   [30] *Emathēteuthē*, a rare word: NIV *had . . . become a disciple.*

had not consented to their decision and action'.[31] Clearly, fear played a part in his caution.[32]

At all events, this man stepped forward and courageously approached the governor, asking for the body of Jesus. Bodies of crucified people were normally thrown into a trench in a field: only one body of a crucified man has been found in Palestine, and that is because he was well connected and his bones were buried, complete with the spike through wrist and ankle, in an ossuary. He was executed some thirty years after Jesus. Joseph did a courageous thing. He braved the governor, who would have been in a foul mood at the end of that traumatic day. He was prepared to face the hostility of his colleagues in the synagogue, and he sided with a crucified criminal. What's more, he gave him his own grave.

Some faithful women saw where Jesus was laid. They had stayed loyal to the bitter end, even when the men had fled. They had followed him from Galilee. They had cared, as best they could, for his needs, and from afar they watched his grisly execution (55–56). Now they came to see what would befall their master after his death. But who were they? A little New Testament detective work is in order!

Matthew tells us of three women at the cross: *Mary Magdalene, Mary the mother of James and Joses, and the* unnamed *mother of Zebedee's sons* (56, 61). So Mary Magdalene was there; and she is mentioned in all four accounts. The woman whom Mark calls 'Salome', Matthew *the mother of Zebedee's sons* and John '[Jesus'] mother's sister' was there too.[33] The most natural explanation is that Salome was sister to the virgin Mary, married Zebedee and became the mother of James and John. If so,[34] this explains several things. It tells us why John is called 'the disciple whom Jesus loved' in John's Gospel. This apparently arrogant description makes perfect sense if it is simply saying that the cousins Jesus and John had been lifetime friends. And it explains why Salome had desired leading positions in the kingdom for her children, James and John. No wonder, if she was sister to Jesus' mother! Alas, now she saw what a bitter baptism he had undergone, and how he had drained the cup of suffering to the dregs. Was she still so keen that her sons should share his destiny?

The third woman present is called by Matthew *the mother of*

[31] Luke 23:51.   [32] John 19:38.

[33] See Matt. 27:61; 28:1; Mark 15:40, 47; 16:1; Luke 23:49, 55; 24:10; John 19:25.

[34] Certainty is impossible, particularly since many of these Jewish names had variations. 'Joses', for example, could appear as 'Joseph', and in the reconstructions suggested here, 'Clopas' is the same as 'Cleopas'. Although undemonstrable, however, the identifications made above and worked out in detail by John Wenham in *Easter Enigma* (Paternoster, 1984) make good sense of the varied accounts in the four Gospels.

James and Joses (56) and *the other Mary* (61). John tells us that she was the wife of Clopas.[35] The man who met the risen Christ three days later on the Emmaus road[36] was the husband of the woman who was present at his crucifixion and burial! Actually, his relationship with Jesus seems to have been very close. Hegesippus, a Jewish Christian from the second century, who is quoted by Eusebius in the fourth, tells us that 'Clopas, of whom mention is made in the sacred volume, was the brother of Joseph'.[37] So it looks as if Clopas and Mary were uncle and aunt of Jesus. No wonder Mary stayed to the bitter end and observed his burial!

The actual burial[38] is recorded with an economy of words, and is entirely in accordance with Jewish custom. People were buried outside the city (and there is good evidence that the Holy Sepulchre site in Jerusalem lay outside the line of the walls in those days) in tombs cut out of rock or in natural caves. Bodies were often placed on a shelf or in a recess, and then the tomb was closed until it was necessary to reopen it for further use. Joseph's tomb was a new one, and being so close to the city it would have been expensive to acquire. And since Jesus was executed on a criminal charge, the law forbade the tomb to be used again for anyone else. It was a costly gift to make. A number of tombs from this period are still to be seen in Israel today. Often a great millstone would be rolled along a groove cut into the rock to close the grave's entrance. No doubt the emphasis Matthew places on the closing of the tomb and the watch by the mourners is intended to remind readers that there was no mistake about the place or the events surrounding the burial of Jesus.

Next day, Sabbath though it was (62), and a high Sabbath at that, since it was the Passover Sabbath, the chief priests and Pharisees bearded Pilate in his den. This was an astonishing breach of the Sabbath law. No other incident in the Gospels shows so clearly how desperate the authorities were to eliminate Jesus. Having accused Jesus of breaking the Sabbath law in order to bring life and healing to a man with a shrivelled hand, and having got together afterwards to plot to kill him (12:9–14), the Pharisees themselves are now prepared to break the Sabbath law in order to ensure that Jesus is really dead and gone.

John Wenham, in his fine book *Easter Enigma*, gives three reasons which may help to account for this remarkable move on the part of the Jewish authorities. In the first place, it shows what a healthy fear they had of Jesus. They feared an uprising among the people because of Jesus' influence. But more, they feared the remarkable powers of

---

[35] John 19:25. [36] Luke 24:13–35, esp. 18.
[37] Eusebius, *Ecclesiastical History*, 3.11.
[38] On the crucifixion and burial locations, the most comprehensive study is by Peter Walker, *The Weekend that Changed the World* (HarperCollins, 1999).

Jesus himself. Their fears were to some extent quelled by the crucifixion: but the earthquake, the darkness over the land, and the torn curtain of the temple would have done nothing to add to their peace of mind.

Secondly, if the early second-century apocryphal *Gospel of Peter* may be credited (and its information is highly circumstantial), there was popular disquiet at the crucifixion and at the signs that accompanied it, and the murmuring of the people made the rulers afraid. Moreover, it states that a crowd gathered around the tomb on the Saturday morning. If this is the case, the Jewish leaders would have had little choice: the movement must be nipped in the bud.

Thirdly, they were worried about rumours that Jesus would be raised on the third day. Had not Matthew emphasized the words of Jesus about destroying the temple and in three days raising it again, both at the trial and as Jesus hung on the cross? The authorities would have been sure to know about the claim, and they were determined not to allow any grave-robbing coup by the disciples to add verisimilitude to it.

So they approached Pilate. The job of looking after the body would normally have been a Roman responsibility, but owing to the totally unexpected action of Joseph of Arimathea, it had become a Jewish one. They were therefore understandably anxious to transfer that responsibility back to the governor. Had there been a riot at Calvary, Pilate would have been responsible for quelling it, but now that the body was back under Jewish jurisdiction it would be they, the Jewish authorities, who would bear the blame. This accounts both for their willingness to approach Pilate while he was in a rage, and for their violent hatred of Joseph of Arimathea, as evidenced in the apocryphal Gospels.

The governor's reply was ambiguous. *Echete koustōdian* (65) could mean either 'You have a guard' – and they had, the temple police; or '*Take a guard*', that is to say, a Roman detachment. It is difficult to decide whether a Jewish or a Roman guard was detailed for this task, but it was an important decision. It showed who had won the psychological battle to put responsibility on the other party.

On the whole, it seems that Pilate, who had refused the first request of the elders to change the *titulus* over the cross,[39] was equally unmoved by their second. To be sure, Pilate uses a Latin word for a guard of soldiers, *custodia*: this need not indicate a Roman guard, but could simply be accurate reportage of a Roman governor's actual words. They had a temple guard, admittedly exhausted by the events of Thursday night. Let them use that!

[39] John 19:21–22.

Pilate's contempt for the Jews could be seen in that rebuff to their request, together with his refusal to reassume the responsibility that had fallen to them. Moreover, in the sequel the soldiers are made to plead falling asleep on duty (hardly likely if they were Romans; it was a capital offence) and to report back to the chief priests (28:11–15). So we are probably right in supposing that Pilate's meaning is 'You have a guard. Use that over the tomb. Make it as safe as you can.'

The irony of it is delightful. Try as they could, no guard could keep Jesus in the tomb. They might go away and make the sepulchre secure by sealing the stone and setting a guard, but neither they nor anyone else could imprison the Lord of life. And the next chapter tells of his breaking those bonds and rising in the power of an endless life.

28:1–20
21. The end of the beginning

The great awakening (28:1–20)

The philosopher and broadcaster, Professor C. E. M. Joad, was once asked who, of all past figures in history, he would most like to have met, and what question he would most have liked to ask. He chose Jesus Christ, and he wanted to ask him the most important question in the world: 'Did you or did you not rise from the dead?' That is the issue between Matthew's church and the synagogue down the street. You can almost overhear the debate in the undertones of this chapter. It was the critical issue, indeed it was almost the only issue, separating Christians from Jews in the first century AD.[1]

When faced by the story of the resurrection of Jesus, the first question that crosses our minds is, 'Is it possible?'

Is it possible?

Dead people don't rise. If we are asked to believe in the resurrection of Jesus, this must be something quite unparalleled. There is nothing comparable in Judaism. There is nothing comparable in the Græco-Roman world. Mythological stories of the raising of Adonis or Isis and Osiris are totally beside the point. They were just stories. Nobody believed they had happened. They concerned mythical figures of long ago who had never even existed. But the resurrection stories of Jesus concern a man whom they all knew. He was executed in a very public manner. He was seen to be alive and well, but in a

---

[1] For the evidence for the resurrection, and its relevance to life, reference may be made to my *The Empty Cross of Jesus* (Hodder and Stoughton, 1984). For a sustained and brilliant attempt to make sense of all the details of the five accounts of the resurrection to be found within the New Testament, see John Wenham, *Easter Enigma* (Paternoster, 1984), and Peter Walker's superb book *The Weekend that Changed the World* (HarperCollins, 1999). For academic discussions of the resurrection, see the authorities cited in Blomberg, p. 426.

strangely other mode of existence, three[2] days later and for the next six weeks before being finally parted from his infant church. That is unparalleled in the history of the world.

There is no parallel, but it might still be possible if God exists at all – if his Son came into the world he made, and lived the perfect life that the Gospel attests; if he faced and conquered sin, the most basic of all the foes of the human spirit, the foe that gives death its power over us. If that is the case, then why should it be deemed impossible that God should raise him from the dead?[3] Of course, we have seen no others rise from their tombs, but we know only broken, sinful, human nature. We have no idea of what might happen if a person never deviated from the perfect will of God throughout his whole life and took personal responsibility for the evil in the lives of all the world. Who can say that under such circumstances resurrection might not be possible? Jesus was different from anyone else: in who he was, in the perfection of his life, and in his victory over sin and Satan at every point. The resurrection is God's vindication of such a life. There is nothing impossible about it. It is no more impossible than for God to create us in the first place.

It is possible, but the question remains: is it true? 'Yes,' says Matthew. 'No,' says the Synagogue. We must examine the two sides in the debate in turn.

Is it true?

Matthew does not give exhaustive evidence for the resurrection, but he does give us a handle on six arguments for the truth of the resurrection which were widely deployed in the early church and down the centuries.

1. The female witnesses (28:1–10)

The two Marys go to the sepulchre *at dawn on the first day of the week*: chronological time, true, but highly symbolic, too, of the new age that is dawning. They do not see the resurrection. Nobody sees the resurrection in the Gospels. It is not until well into the second century, with its apocryphal Gospels, that anybody is said to witness the resurrection. The resurrection is God's witness to Jesus. As we have repeatedly seen throughout this Gospel, human witness cannot attest a divine person. Only God can do that. And he does, through two ways that traditionally indicate God's heavenly power breaking

---

[2] By our reckoning it would be two days later. Ancient enumeration counted 'today' as the first day, tomorrow as the second day, and the next day as the third.

[3] Never does the New Testament suggest that Jesus raised himself from the dead. Always it is the powerful, vindicating work of God the Father. Hence the passive *ēgerthē, he has* (lit. 'is') *risen*, or 'he has been raised'.

into human affairs: the earthquake and the angel (2). Characteristic-
ally, this divine action elicits from the human participants typical
reactions of fear, trembling, awe and bewilderment. God has acted,
and has revealed himself in the resurrection of Jesus. The angel opens
the tomb, not to let Jesus out, but to show the women that he is no
longer inside.

It is probable that the earthquake had happened a little before the
women arrived, and the guards were knocked to the ground with
amazement both at the repetition of the earth tremor that had taken
place on the Friday, and even more by the dazzling heavenly being
who appeared at the tomb. If I had been on guard then and had felt
an earthquake and seen an angel in awesome splendour, I would,
when I had recovered, have scurried back for dear life to report to
those who had appointed me! Matthew certainly does not want to
represent the enemies of Jesus as the first witnesses of the resurrection. It is reasonable, therefore, to suppose that the guard had gone
by the time the women arrived. They then receive words of comfort
(*'Do not be afraid'*), of understanding (*'I know that you are looking
for Jesus, who was crucified'*), of assurance (*'Come and see the place
where he lay'*), of command (*'go quickly and tell his disciples . . .'*),
and of encouragement (*'he . . . is going ahead of you into Galilee.
There you will see him'*).

All of this is brought to us through female witnesses! That is
simply astounding. As we have already seen, women counted for
little in both Jewish and Graeco-Roman circles in those days. They
were nobodies: they were goods and chattels; they could in some
circumstances be offered for sale; they could not bear witness in a
court of law. And God perpetrates the supreme irony of having two
women as the first witnesses of his Son's resurrection!

Jesus had been born in an obscure province that nobody had heard
of; his genealogy contains various disreputable females who might
be considered liabilities in any family; he worked as a jobbing
builder where nobody would have dreamed of looking for him; he
went to a cross, the place associated with God's curse, not his
approval; and now the last and greatest surprise is that God allows
the first witnesses of his resurrection to be women! If anyone was
going to fabricate the story of the resurrection, would they have
made the witnesses women? Of course not. Only God could have
dreamed up so remarkable a thing. But this is the supreme irony, the
supreme humour, the supreme surprise value of almighty God, that
when he does his greatest act since the creation of the world, in
raising his Son from the dead, he attests it through the lips of those
who were so widely discounted. Magnificent!

Paul probably found this rather trying: the women are significantly absent from his list of resurrection witnesses in 1 Corinthians

15. This is not the supposed Pauline anti-feminism at work. He is simply giving evidence for the resurrection that would stand scrutiny in a court of law.

2. The empty tomb (28:2–6)

Despite the stone, despite the guard, the tomb was empty on the first Easter Day. It had been emptied by divine agency, not by human activity. That is the claim. And that is the meaning of the *angel*[4] and the *earthquake*. God is at work in the resurrection of his Son, and the angel and earthquake are the symbols that say so. By the whole thrust of his account, Matthew seems to be indicating that it would not do to provide some naturalistic interpretation of the empty tomb. The enemies of Jesus were delighted to have him at last where they wanted him, dead and buried. They wanted nothing more than for him to stay that way. The friends of Jesus were utterly dispirited; it would never have entered their heads to perpetrate the fraud of removing his body and pretending he was alive, and then to die, if need be, for that deception. But even if it had entered their heads, the guard on the tomb and the continuous watch which Matthew attests show that it would have been impossible. Although by itself the empty tomb is not compelling evidence for the resurrection (there could be various reasons for its being empty), it is a powerful supporting factor in the case for the resurrection, and Matthew wants us to know it. It is impossible to imagine how the preaching of Jesus and his resurrection could ever have got off the ground in a Jewish milieu if his body had remained in Joseph's tomb. All Jewish ideas of resurrection involved the body of the deceased. They had no conception of merely spiritual survival or resurrection. As Professor C. H. Dodd put it: 'When they said, "He rose from the dead", they took it for granted that his body was no longer in the tomb; if the tomb had been visited it would have been found empty. The Gospels supplement this by saying that it *was* visited and it *was* empty.'[5]

3. The resurrection appearances (28:9, 16–20)

Many resurrection appearances are recorded in the Gospels and 1 Corinthians 15. Matthew records two: the first to the women (9) and the second to the eleven disciples in Galilee (16–20). This is another powerful strand in the evidence for the resurrection. It is undeniable that a large number of people believed that they had seen

---

[4] Angels indicate that God is at work. In Matthew an angel announces Jesus' birth (1:20) and resurrection, in both cases with the words *'Do not be afraid'*. In Mark it is a young man, and in Luke two angels. In all probability the women were so flabbergasted that they were not quite sure what they had seen. See J. D. G. Dunn, *Jesus and the Spirit* (SCM, 1975), pp. 126ff.

[5] C. H. Dodd, *The Founder of Christianity* (Collins, 1971), p. 166.

their crucified leader, Jesus, alive again after his death. It was upon this conviction and this witness that the early church was built. 1 Corinthians 15 quotes a piece of tradition recording the witness of the very earliest disciples to the resurrection of Jesus. It dates back to within a year or two of the events themselves, for it was 'tradition' by the time of Paul's conversion, which cannot have been later than the mid-30s. Jesus appeared to Peter (Paul actually uses his Aramaic name, Cephas), then to the Twelve, then to 'more than five hundred of the brothers'[6] at once, most of whom were still alive in the 50s, when Paul wrote to the Corinthians. Then he appeared to James, his brother, then to all the apostles, and last of all to Paul.[7] The resurrection appearances in all their variety are very strong evidence indeed for the resurrection of Jesus. No attempt to portray them as visions or hallucinations has been successful.

4. The transformed lives (28:8–9, 17)

The transformation of Jesus' followers is one of the wonders in the Christian claim for the resurrection. Those who put their trust in the risen Christ do experience great changes in their lives. This has been true all down the centuries. It was true of the first disciples. The two Marys had approached the tomb with deep mourning for a dead friend and teacher. They returned full of awe and an indestructible *joy* to tell the others about Jesus, who had both risen from the grave and greeted them. It was much the same when Jesus met the disciples at the hill in Galilee to which he had directed them through the women. Despite the rumour of his resurrection which they all heard, there was that mixture of worship and scepticism (17) that runs through all the resurrection accounts and has such a ring of truth about it. Of course, they could scarcely believe. Not only was a resurrection unprecedented, but Jesus' resurrection life, though continuous with his incarnate existence, was cast in another mould. The continuity between a caterpillar and a butterfly after going through the transformation of the chrysalis stage may give us some idea of the difference. It was Jesus, but he was not the same as before. There was a new quality to his existence. But they were in no doubt that it was he, and that he was alive for evermore. Death could never again claim him. His resurrection was irreversible. It changed everything. And not least, it changed their characters and personalities. James and John, those 'sons of thunder', became apostles of love. Simon Peter, that vacillating leader, became the rock-like man on whose fearless witness the early church was built. The eleven

[6] It is wonderful that, uniquely in this Gospel, Jesus should call his disciples, who had so let him down, *brothers* (10). The church is a brotherhood, portraying more equality than hierarchy.
[7] 1 Cor. 15:1–8.

were no more a frightened rabble; they became an apostolic task force.

5. *The fulfilled predictions (28:6)*

The note of fulfilment has been prominent in this Gospel and it is prominent at the end. Three times[8] in the Gospel account Jesus had predicted that he would rise again on the third day. This chapter shows the fulfilment of that prophecy. The chief priests and Pharisees had a shrewd idea that his disciples might attempt to fake a resurrection. That is why they had approached Pilate on the Sabbath for a guard on the tomb (27:64). And the angel underlined it again: 'He is not here; he has risen, just as he said' (6). The other Gospels suggest some hints of the resurrection in the Old Testament Scriptures.[9] There is very little foreshadowing of it in the Old Testament; certainly not enough for anyone to have set out from those predictions and postulated a resurrection to fulfil them. On the day of Pentecost, Peter quotes Psalm 16:8–11 and 110:1.[10] But Matthew does not quote them. He emphasizes the fulfilment of the words of the new Moses. Fulfilled prophecy is hard to gainsay.

6. *World mission (28:18–20)*

'Go and make disciples of all nations,' said Jesus (19). And what actually started the world mission? Nothing other than the resurrection. It is agreed among all New Testament theologians that it was the Easter faith that launched the church on its mission in and to the world. Of course, behind the Easter faith lay the Easter event. But the spread of the gospel is one of the indicators that Matthew adduces for the truth of what he proclaims. By the time he wrote, the gospel had gone into many parts of the known world, and hordes of new disciples were crowding into the church.[11] He wanted the synagogue across the street to take full note of this. Numbers do not, of course, validate truth. But something had happened to these many Jews and Gentiles who now found themselves fellow-worshippers. The Christians were sure what it was: the resurrection of Jesus, no less. What alternative explanation was plausible?

Is the resurrection true? Matthew has given six reasons why he believes it is. But the synagogue along the street did not believe it for a moment. They gave a very different account of what had happened that first Easter. A widely based Jewish belief and explanation was that the disciples of Jesus had come and stolen the body while the

---

[8] Matt. 16:21; 17:23; 20:19; there is also the more cryptic prediction in 12:40.
[9] E.g. Luke 24:25–27.   [10] Acts 2:25, 34.
[11] In Matthew, Galilee represents Gentile country (4:15). The references to Galilee in 26:32; 28:7, 10, 16 all have an eye on the Gentile mission.

guard had slept. Matthew is clearly sensitive to this rumour; he goes out of his way to say it is still current in his day (15). A hundred years later it was still current. Listen to Justin dialoguing with the Jew, Trypho:

> And though all the men in your nation knew the incidents in the life of Jonah, and though Christ said amongst you he would give the sign of Jonah, exhorting you to repent of your wicked deeds, at least after he rose again from the dead, and to mourn before God as did the Ninevites, that your nation and city might not be taken and destroyed, as they have been destroyed; yet, you have not repented after you learned that he rose from the dead.
>
> Moreover, as I said before, you have sent chosen and ordained men throughout all the world to proclaim that a godless and lawless heresy had sprung from one Jesus, a Galilean deceiver whom we crucified, but his disciples stole him by night out of the tomb, where he was laid when unfastened from the cross, and now deceive men by asserting that he has risen from the dead and ascended to heaven.
>
> Yet we do not hate you, or those who by your means have conceived such prejudices against us. But we pray that even now all of you may repent and obtain mercy from God, the compassionate and longsuffering Father of all.[12]

That passage is worth quoting in full, showing as it does the strength of the Jewish reaction to Christian resurrection preaching, the counter-mission they promoted, and their recourse to the hypothesis that Jesus did not rise from the dead but that the disciples came and stole the body away in the dead of night.

This, then, was the Jewish riposte to the preaching of the resurrection. Jesus did not rise: his disciples came and stole the body. So Matthew addresses himself to it. He does so with conscious artistry. From that grave two messages have gone back: one to the disciples, carried by the women, to the effect that Jesus is alive; the other to the chief priests, carried by the soldiers, to the effect that the body has been stolen. Nobody on that Easter day could deny that the body was gone and the tomb was untenanted. Nobody attempted to deny it. But what are we to make of Matthew's story? It is generally regarded as Christian apologetic, and quite unreliable. That is how most of the commentators see it. But as John Wenham says,

> The story of the setting of the guard is one of the most extraordinary pieces of Christian apologetic ever written.

[12] Justin, *Dialogue* 108.

It bristles with improbabilities at every point: the sabbath visit to the governor, the great earthquake, the flashing angel rolling back the stone, the reporting to the chief priests, the bribe to the soldiers to tell the tale *that they were asleep on duty* – everything invited not belief but incredulity. And how stupid, having introduced the useful apologetic idea of a closely guarded tomb, to give a handle to the opposition by even hinting that the guards did not do their job! It is a worthless piece of Christian apologetic at whatever date it was written, *unless it happens to be undeniably true!*[13]

To be sure, this story was a piece of Christian apologetic, but only because it was true. It could not have been made up to meet the situation of the empty tomb, as two words made plain, *hēmōn koimōmenōn*, 'while we slept' (13). No Christian would have made up those words and put them in the mouth of the guards. The story would have been of any use for Christian propaganda *only if the guards had stayed awake!* Had they slept, how could they have known what was going on?

The only possible reason for the story of the guard is that it was true. There had been a guard. It had not prevented the resurrection. Probably, when the earthquake dislodged the stone, the guard entered to ensure that all was well, found that the tomb was empty, saw the angelic presence, and fled to tell the chief priests, once they had sufficiently recovered to get to their feet. This disaster called for an explanation. So the chief priests bribed the soldiers, and circulated the story that the disciples had stolen the body while the guard was asleep on duty. Highly embarrassing, but not so embarrassing as admitting the truth of the resurrection. The authorities were simply making the best of a bad situation.

This is an interesting element of tradition, because it shows us three stages in its formation. First, the Christian proclamation of the resurrection is presupposed. Then comes the Jewish counter-claim that the body had been stolen, and then Matthew's assault on that argument. It shows what a central issue the resurrection remained in the mission both to Jews and to Gentiles in the latter half of the first century, and how fiercely the evidence was contested.

Does it matter?

The great awakening from the tomb happened. But what are its implications? Matthew's account gives five answers to that question.

First, the resurrection of Jesus is the heart of the good news. There

[13] *Easter Enigma*, pp. 78–79.

would be no good news to proclaim had it not been that Jesus was crucified, but is no longer in the tomb because he is risen (5–6). The gospel is nothing other than the resurrection of the crucified Jesus. On this hangs the truth of the kingdom and the supreme evidence for God's existence. Without the resurrection there is no good news.

Secondly, the resurrection of Jesus is the proof of his sonship. It is significant that both the resurrection appearances that Matthew records lead to worship. Mary Magdalene and the other Mary fell at his feet and worshipped him (9). The disciples, when they saw him, worshipped (17). No doubt that has importance for Matthew's church. The proper response to Jesus is worship, but only because Jesus shares the nature of God, who alone is to be worshipped. The claims to sonship throughout the Gospel are validated by the resurrection. As an old Jewish Christian creed put it, the gospel concerns God's 'Son, who as to his human nature was a descendant of David, and who through the Spirit of holiness was declared with power to be the Son of God, by his resurrection from the dead: Jesus Christ our Lord'.[14]

Thirdly, the resurrection of Jesus is the springboard for mission. The disciples can go and proclaim the good news (18–20) only because of the resurrection. Without it there would be nothing to declare. But because of it, how can they keep silent? It is the most exciting news in the whole world. It should be impossible for believers to refrain from mission.

Fourthly, the resurrection of Jesus means that his power and his presence are available. The risen one comes to them and claims *all authority* in the universe (18). He promises that he will be with them on their worldwide mission wherever they go, and until the *end of the age* (20). And disciples down the centuries have rejoiced, and still do, in the constant presence of the mighty, risen Christ, who is both the ultimate controller of all circumstances that can befall them, and the strength they need for moral victory and untiring service.

Finally, the resurrection of Jesus is the key to eternal life and the new community. We have already seen this truth in the comments at the end of chapter 27; but it must not be forgotten if we are to appreciate the implications Matthew draws from the resurrection. He has told us implicitly of the new temple that has been raised up, and explicitly of the new and eternal life made possible for 'the saints' by the resurrection (27:53).

It is important to hold together both the evidence for the resurrection and the implications and results that flow from it. Matthew does both in this, his final chapter.

---

[14] Rom. 3:1–4.

The Great Commission (28:16–20)

The book ends on a *mountain*, just as it had begun (after Jesus' birth and temptation) on a mountain, and just as its mid-point had been another mountain (5:1; 17:1). The mount of the Sermon reveals the lifestyle Jesus requires in the kingdom. The mount of the transfiguration reveals who he really is. And the mount of the Great Commission outlines his worldwide mission.[15] The pattern of the book is skilled, and it is complete. It is the end of the earthly story of Jesus. It is the end of the training of the Twelve. And the emphasis now shifts to them as the Lord undertakes to work with them and empower them. They are now to do the discipling (19), although they still remain disciples. In one sense their apprenticeship is over. The ball is passed to them and they must run with it. And now what has been given them in the earlier part of the Gospel springs into life and relevance. The manual for missionaries in chapter 10 is now seen to be so relevant for their mission. The five great sermons of the book, and the intercalated narratives, give them the agenda to be taught and to be obeyed. This last commission sets them over those they would baptize and disciple, but under Jesus in whose authority they would go. It is apparent here that the disciples are becoming the disciplers, and those among whom Jesus has been go now, with Jesus, into the world. They are his middlemen, and Christian leaders inherit their role.

The *authority* of Jesus is a major theme in this Gospel. Jesus appears on the scene as a teacher who has authority (7:29). The miracles in chapter 8 onwards denote his authority not simply in word but in deed. He even has God's authority to forgive sins (9:6). And in chapter 10 he imparted that authority of his temporarily to his apostles as they went out on their mission, a trial run for all that would await them after his death. Indeed, the authority of Jesus over against the contemporary interpreters of the law has been a major theme of this Gospel. And now his authority is emphasized by his resurrection. He is shown to be Son of Man, King of the Jews, Messiah, Son of God, the glorious risen one. And he imparts his authority to his followers. They are his empowered representatives. He gives them *all authority in heaven and on earth*, heavenly authority in place of the earthly authority offered him by the devil (4:8). The authority given him by God, and envisaged in Daniel 7:14, has been tested in the fire of controversy, suffering and death. And now, resplendent in his risen glory, he delegates that authority to his followers. They will need every bit of it if they are to fulfil the vision

---

[15] Perhaps there is an allusion to the theme of Jesus as the new Moses, issuing his instructions from a new Sinai.

of Daniel and exercise Christ's dominion worldwide.

This role of the disciples, becoming evangelists and teachers, is to be found in the other Gospels. It is the inevitable outcome of the revelation in Christ: once you have found it, you long to spread it. Thus in Luke's Gospel we read of what Jesus had begun 'to do and to teach' during his earthly life. Volume 2, Acts, is the record of what he continued to do 'through the Holy Spirit' in the disciples.[16] It is much the same in John's Gospel. The risen Christ commissions his disciples to go forth in the power of the Spirit and proclaim a message which, if received, leads to forgiveness of sins; if not, sins remain unforgiven.[17] Even Mark, with his truncated ending at 16:8,[18] makes the same point, albeit more allusively. Jesus' words, 'I will go ahead of you into Galilee',[19] are taken up by the 'young man' in Mark's resurrection account, which continues, 'There you will see him, just as he told you.' And the women to whom this angelic announcement came were 'trembling and bewildered', and 'fled from the tomb. They said nothing to anyone, because they were afraid.'[20] That is where Mark's Gospel, as we have it, ends; whether by design or accident is much contested. But, brief though it is, it is sufficient as it stands. God has acted in the resurrection, with his own unique power. And the only proper response is awe and wonder, trembling and astonishment, lips struck silent in worship. But there is still the hint of mission. For 'He is going ahead of you into Galilee.'[21] What is Galilee? Is it not, as in Matthew, 'Galilee of the Gentiles'? Jesus goes at their head into the Gentile mission, and it is as they launch out into mission that they will appreciate his presence.

How true that is! And it is the concluding theme of all four Gospels. The baton has been passed from the Master to the disciples. The power of the risen Christ is available for those disciples. The commandment of the risen Christ is given for those disciples: they must go and make disciples. And the promise of the risen Christ is their comfort and stay: nothing shall ever rob them of his presence.

The Gospel that began with the assurance that this baby to be born would be Immanuel ('God is with us', 1:23) closes with the assurance that he is with them still, and will be to the end of time. This promise is not merely for the individual, but for the group. Chapter 18 verse 20 assures them as they gather in his name that he is in their midst. Without his presence and empowering they could never even contemplate world mission. When the Lord commands, he enables. And his enabling is his presence.

The Great Commission to the unevangelized nations, *ta ethnē*,

---

[16] Acts 1:1-2.   [17] John 20:21-23.
[18] Mark 16:9-20 is not present in the earliest and best manuscripts.
[19] Mark 14:28.   [20] Mark 16:7-8.   [21] Mark 16:7.

who have appeared from time to time in a minor role thus far in the narrative, is now at the top of the agenda of Jesus for his followers. The last command of Jesus is: '*Go and make disciples of all nations.*'

The Great Commission is the response to meeting the risen Christ (17). It is not until the disciples have personally met with the risen Lord that they are consumed with a passion to go and tell others. If evangelism is at a low ebb in parts of the worldwide church (and it is), could it be because many churchgoers have never had a personal, life-changing encounter with Jesus?

And the Great Commission springs from worship (9, 17). It was as the Marys and the disciples fell down in total adoration of Jesus, and were lost in wonder, love and praise, that they were inspired to go on mission. It is still. Evangelism springs from worship. It is no individualistic enterprise. It flows from a Christianity where worship is vital.

Moreover, the Great Commission is the counterpart of the great commandment to love God and neighbour. Without that, evangelism will be cold and hard. It will alienate rather than attract. It will not embody the spirit of heaven, where love is the universal language.

The Great Commission is a matter of sheer obedience. Verse 19 picks up the repeated stress to go to Galilee (7, 10, 16). Galilee was of course the region where Jesus met them: there is one Jerusalem appearance and one Galilee appearance in Matthew's balanced account. But it has a deeper meaning, as 4:15 shows. It points to Galilee of the Gentiles, so that 'the people living in darkness may see a great light'.[22] Jesus does not recommend such a mission. He demands it. It is his final charge. How can his church fail to keep it? Yet evangelism is the Cinderella at the Christian ball. We Christians are guilty of flagrant disobedience to our Master, and the coming of his kingdom is delayed.

The Great Commission includes the baptism and careful discipling of new believers. Matthew is not satisfied, Jesus is not satisfied, with any hasty profession of faith, any perfunctory baptism. The apostles are called not to evoke decisions but to make disciples. And that is an altogether tougher assignment. Matthew has shown throughout his book how slow Jesus' disciples were to do and be what he wanted. The apostles would not have an easier ride as they set out to continue Jesus' mission. There would be much blindness, much failure and misunderstanding, much opposition. They must baptize into the name of the Trinity; and, astonishing as it is[23] to find the triune name here, the passage has not suffered any interpolation. Eusebius had exactly the same text before him in the

[22] Matt. 4:16, quoting Is. 9:2.
[23] Many scholars cannot believe that this trinitarian statement could have been made by Jesus, but its credibility is defended by Hagner.

fourth century. In the Acts there is often baptism into the name of Jesus, but that phrase may be a summary. Baptism has always involved commitment to the God who sent both Jesus and the Spirit who baptizes into Jesus. All three were involved in the baptism of Jesus. All three are involved in Christian baptism.

It is probable that the actual baptismal formula is assumed in Acts, and only the special new factor, Jesus, singled out for emphasis. Certainly those who baptize in the name of 'Jesus only' have no support from the words of Jesus himself in this Gospel. The apostles are to baptize and they are to nurture people in the Christian path so that they in turn can go and make disciples themselves. The Letters show the depth and intensity of that discipling, and show up our modern five-minute sermonettes for the pathetic things they are.

Finally, the Great Commission is always directed outwards, to the unreached. The Christian church must never degenerate into a comfortable club for the like-minded. It is always called to a discipling, teaching evangelism. And Matthew has provided not only for his own church, but for all time, a magnificent, well-organized tool for carrying out that Great Commission with which his Gospel ends.

That is a very comprehensive commission. It represents Christ's standing orders for his church. Unfortunately many churches in the West have to a large extent neglected it. Congregations and clergy seem committed to maintenance, not to mission. Happily, however, churches all over the developing world are providing a much-needed corrective. They show a passionate desire to fulfil this last command of Jesus, and to bring his kingdom nearer to its consummation. Those who obey the command to go and make disciples are the ones who can rightly lay claim to the promises of verses 18 and 20. The presence and the authority of Jesus are specifically attached to his command to fulfil the Great Commission. That is what Christians in hard places like China, Russia, South Korea, Sarawak and Peru are finding, as new believers flood into their churches. It is an outward thrust that would delight the heart of Matthew.

So ends this Gospel, which has very clearly depicted who Jesus is, what his message contains, how his kingdom comes, and the cost and challenge of discipleship. Jesus, revelling in his Father's company and authority, had come to bring outsiders into the kingdom. And now, at the climax of the Gospel, his disciples are called to follow his lead, and to go and make disciples of all nations. That task will be complete only when he comes again at the end of all history. Such was the glorious hope that nerved Matthew to give his all for his Master. May it inspire us!

Study guide

The aim of this study guide is to help you get to the heart of what Michael Green has written, and to challenge you to apply what you learn to your own life. The questions have been designed for use by individuals or by small groups of Christians meeting, perhaps for an hour or two each week, to study, discuss and pray together.

The guide provides material for each of the sections in the book. When used by a group with limited time, the leader should decide beforehand which questions are most appropriate for the group to discuss during the meeting and which should perhaps be left for group members to work through by themselves or in smaller groups during the week.

In order to be able to contribute fully and to learn from the group meetings, each member of the group needs to read through the section or sections under discussion, together with the passages in the Gospel to which they refer.

It's important not to let these studies become merely academic exercises. Guard against this by making time to think through and discuss how what you discover *works out in practice* for you. Make sure you begin and end each study by focusing on God in praise and prayer. Ask the Holy Spirit to speak to you through your discussion together.

Introduction (pp. 19–53)

1 Why can Matthew's Gospel be considered as 'the most important single document in the New Testament' (p. 19')?
2 What exactly is a 'Gospel' (p. 19)?
3 What problems are there in discovering who wrote Matthew's Gospel (pp. 19–24)?
4 In what ways is the external evidence for the authorship of

325

Matthew's Gospel contradicted by the internal evidence? How can this be resolved (pp. 21–24)?

5 What do we infer about the man called Levi or Matthew from what the Gospels tell us (pp. 24–25)?

6 What about the author of what we know as 'Matthew's Gospel'? What does what he has written reveal about him (pp. 25–27)?

7 What clues about its intended readership does this Gospel contain (pp. 27–29)?

8 What does Michael Green mean when he says that 'we must read the book at two levels'? Why is this important (p. 29)?

9 How does thinking about the structure of the Gospel help us to gain further insight into the author's thinking (pp. 30–36)?

10 How are we to explain the relative popularity of Matthew's Gospel in the early church (pp. 37–38)?

11 What needs to be taken into consideration when trying to work out when Matthew was written (pp. 38–39)?

12 What does Michael Green identify as Matthew's main concerns (pp. 30–50)? Which of these do you think is going to be particularly important for you as you study this Gospel?

13 What significance is there in the different titles Jesus is given in Matthew's Gospel (pp. 39–41)?

14 What is the relationship between God's revelation in the Old Testament and his revelation in Jesus (pp. 41–42)?

15 What do you understand by the phrase *the kingdom of heaven*? What do you think Matthew meant by it (pp. 43–47)?

16 How should we see the relationship between the kingdom and the church? What dangers are there in confusing the two (pp. 46–47)?

17 What particular features of this Gospel highlight the fact that the good news is for everyone (pp. 49–50)?

PART 1: IN GALILEE (MATTHEW 1 – 13)

A. *Beginnings (1 – 7)*

1:1–25
1. Jesus' pedigree and birth (pp. 57–64)

1 Why does Matthew begin with this 'great long list of names' (p. 57)? What impact would this have had on his original readers (pp. 57–59)?

2 What evidence of 'consummate artistry and care' (p. 58) is there

is this list? What significance is there in the names chosen – and in their gender (pp. 58–59)?

'At the very beginning of the Gospel the all-embracing love of God is emphasized' (p. 59).

---

3 How does Matthew tell us 'in no uncertain terms' who Jesus is (pp. 59–60)?
4 In what way is this passage 'strongly . . . trinitarian' (pp. 60–61)?
5 What are the 'four particular questions' which 'demand our attention' (p. 61)? How can they be answered?

2:1–23
2. Jesus' childhood (pp. 65–74)

1 What contrasts do you notice between Herod and the Magi? What can we learn from them in terms of examples to seek to follow and to avoid (pp. 65, 67)?
2 What 'essential quality in God' (p. 67) does this passage underline?
3 What 'characteristic danger for clergy and scholars' (p. 67) do we find here? How does this apply to you?
4 How can we explain the appearance of the star and the significance attached to it (pp. 68–69)?
5 What is 'highly symbolic' (p. 71) about the escape to Egypt? What would you say to someone who suggested that Matthew made up this bit of the story so that it fitted better with the Old Testament passages he wanted to quote?

'If we are determined to get our own way at all costs, we will go to any lengths to eliminate all trace of Jesus and his claims on our lives' (p. 72).

---

6 How does Matthew use the Old Testament to back up what he is saying (pp. 72–74)?
7 What 'clear message for the readers of his day' (p. 74) does Matthew have here? How is this relevant to us?
8 What encouragement can we draw from this passage about facing opposition to Christian faith (p. 74)?

3:1 – 4:25
3. The beginning of Jesus' ministry (pp. 75–87)

1 In what ways is John the Baptist 'an example to preachers' (p. 76)?
2 What can we learn from the way John sees his ministry (p. 76)?
3 What is significant about the theme of desert in this story (p. 77)? Where is there a 'desert' in your life?
4 In what ways was John's baptism different from other forms of baptism around at the time (pp. 77–78)?
5 What background information from the Old Testament and elsewhere illuminates what John says about the Holy Spirit (pp. 78–79)?
6 What problems are there in the fact that Jesus was baptized, received the Spirit and heard a voice from heaven? How may such problems be resolved (pp. 80–82)?
7 How would you answer someone who felt that being tempted is an indication 'that God's blessing has evaporated' (p. 82)?

'Temptation builds spiritual muscle' (p. 82).

---

8 In what ways were the temptations of Jesus 'uniquely appropriate to God's Son' (p. 83)? What then can we learn from them and how Jesus dealt with them (pp. 83–84)?
9 What was it about Jesus' background that Jews from places such as Jerusalem would have looked down on (pp. 84–85)?
10 What is it about fishermen that Michael Green suggests makes them 'particularly suitable' (p. 86) for joining Jesus in his work of fishing for people?
11 What 'three sides to the gospel Jesus proclaimed' (p. 86) do we find here? How do these relate to your situation?

5:1 – 7:29
4. The first discourse: the manifesto of the kingdom (pp. 88–112)

1 What is significant about where the Sermon on the Mount comes in Matthew's Gospel (p. 88)?
2 How is the parallel between Jesus and Moses underlined here (p. 89)?

3 What do you make of 'Jesus' prescription for the happy life' (p. 91)? Which of the Beatitudes do you find particularly challenging? Why?

4 What are the images of salt and light intended to communicate about life as a follower of Jesus (pp. 91–92)?

5 What is the main difference between the attitude of the Pharisees to God's law and that put forward by Jesus? In what ways does he sharpen the law's demands? Why (pp. 92–98)?

'Love is the mark which, above all else, should distinguish those who know themselves to have been found by a loving God' (p. 97).

---

6 Why does Jesus say what he does about the 'three main areas of traditional religious devotion' (p. 98)? How does this apply to you?

7 How can we account for the differences in the Lord's Prayer as set out by Matthew when compared with Luke (p. 99)?

8 In what ways does Jesus' pattern for prayer challenge your own way of going about prayer?

9 'Disciples are marked out clearly by their attitude to money' (p. 103). As you think about this, what does this say about you?

10 Why is worry 'a sin that is strictly forbidden' (p. 104)? What impact does this have on you?

11 What is particularly significant about what Jesus says in 7:12 (p. 107)?

12 How would you respond to someone who said that the Sermon on the Mount is 'a collection of ethical maxims such as might have been devised by any cultivated humanist' (pp. 107–108)?

'. . . at the end of the Sermon we are not permitted merely to admire the teaching; we are challenged to bow to the preacher' (p. 109).

---

13 Why is it unwise to try and defend Christianity and say that 'it is better than anything else' (pp. 109–110)? What would be a better strategy?

14 What is the purpose of this Sermon (pp. 111–112)? To what extent has it achieved its purpose with you?

B. Discipleship (8 – 10)

8:1 – 9:34
5. Who is this Jesus? (pp. 113–127)

1 What is particularly significant about the healing of the man with leprosy? What was so 'extraordinary' and 'eloquent' about it (pp. 114–115)?
2 In what way is the attitude of the pagan centurion 'a great example of the proper approach to Jesus' (p. 115)?
3 What are we to learn from the healing of Peter's mother-in-law (pp. 116–117)? How might this apply to you?
4 To what extent do you think the disciples of Jesus today should expect to imitate his healing ministry?
5 What does 8:18–22 tell us about following Jesus (p. 118)? How do these verses fit in with what has gone before and what follows?
6 What 'lesson would not be lost on Matthew's hearers' in connection with the stilling of the storm (p. 120)?
7 What does the story of the Gadarene demoniacs underline about Jesus (pp. 120–121)? In addition, what 'fascinating details' (p. 121) are there here? What is their significance?
8 What lies behind Matthew's accentuation of certain details in the story of the healing of the paralytic (p. 122)?
9 What is 'amazing' about the story of the calling of Matthew (p. 123)?
10 'There is no room for the Pharisee spirit in the kingdom' (p. 124). What does Michael Green mean by this? What modern manifestations of Pharisaism are you aware of?

'. . . faith is the hand that grasps the astonishing new thing presented in Jesus' (p. 126).

---

11 What points do the three stories in 9:18–34 'stress . . . in common' (p. 126)? What is particularly encouraging about these incidents?

9:36 – 10:42
6. The second discourse:
the mission of the kingdom (pp. 128–136)

1 Why does this section need 'to be read at two levels' (p. 128)? How will this help?
2 What 'important points need to be noticed' (p. 129) at the level of the historical mission of the Twelve?
3 What 'enduring principles' (p. 130) concerning mission are highlighted here?
4 'One of the main reasons for burnout in Christian ministry is ...' (p. 130). What does Michael Green identify here? How secure are you against this possibility?
5 What 'strategy in mission' (p. 132) does your church have? Why is this so important?
6 'All the time, mission centres round Jesus' (p. 133) What does this mean in practice?
7 What 'useful criteria for determining authentic Christian workers' (p. 133) does this passage suggest?
8 What is it that Michael Green suggests is 'neglected in the churches at large' (pp. 134–135)? How about your church?

'Until our lives have been filled with the Spirit of God, we shall not be likely to engage enthusiastically in evangelism and mission ... We need empowering if we are to achieve anything for God' (p. 135).

---

9 According to Michael Green, what is the most effective way for a church to grow (p. 135)? To what extent are you contributing to the growth of your church in this way?

C. Response (11 – 13)

11:1–30
7. Jesus' claim, and its ground (pp. 137–143)

1 What is the particular significance of chapter 13? How does Matthew work up to it (p. 137)?
2 How can Jesus say that *he who is least in the kingdom ... is greater than* John (verse 11)? What does he mean (p. 138)?

3 In what ways does Jesus seek to help John to understand who he, Jesus, really is (p. 140)? How does this help us?

'The word of God in the ancient Scriptures and the works of God displayed in the miracles of Jesus do indeed point him out as the King who has come to bring in the kingdom' (p. 140).

4 What is so 'amazing' (p. 140) and 'astounding' (p. 141) about 11:25–28? Why does this make Christianity 'at once so widely attractive and so widely hated' (p. 142)? What experience have you had of this?

5 Why does Jesus offer a particular invitation to 'the weary and the heavily burdened' (p. 142)?

6 What significance is there in the picture of the yoke (p. 143)?

12:1–50
8. Human response to Jesus: for and against (pp. 144–151)

1 How are we to account for the fact that 'so many people reject the most wonderful person who has ever walked this earth' (p. 144)? Do you find this astonishing?

2 What is surprising about the Pharisees' rejection of Jesus? Why then did they turn against him (pp. 144–145)?

3 What characteristics of Pharisaism do we find here (pp. 145–150)? Do you see any hints of these things in your own life?

4 How does Jesus respond to the Pharisees (p. 148)? In what ways is this instructive for us?

5 What does this passage have to teach us about demonization (pp. 149–150)?

'To discredit the possibility of the demonic is as foolish as to go overboard on it' (p. 150).

6 What 'very painful' aspect of Jesus' life is highlighted in verses 46–50 (p. 150)? What happened in the end?

7 To what extent are you depending on 'religious practices and religious pedigree' (p. 151)? Why aren't these enough? What do we need instead?

13:1–58
9. The third discourse:
the parables of the kingdom (pp. 152–162)

1 What are parables? Why did Jesus use them so much (pp. 152–153)?

2 In what way do these parables provide 'a fitting end to the first half of the Gospel' (p. 155)?

3 What is particularly challenging about the parable of the soils (pp. 155–156)? How does it apply to you?

4 Which question is the parable of the weeds in the wheat intended to address? What answer does it give (pp. 156–157)?

5 'Significance cannot be measured in terms of numbers' (p. 158). On what is this statement based? In what ways does this challenge and encourage you?

6 Why would Jesus' hearers have been surprised to hear him using yeast as an image of the kingdom? Why is it so appropriate (pp. 158–159)?

'God is like that. He takes distasteful characters and transforms them, and then transforms society through them' (p. 159).

---

7 What is the 'clear' message of the parables of the treasure and the pearl (p. 160)? Do you see the kingdom as being as valuable as this?

8 What are the practical implications for now of the parable of the net (pp. 160–161)?

9 What is significant about the way this chapter ends? What 'powerful parallelism' (pp. 161–162) is there here?

10 What must we be careful not to miss in what Jesus says about a prophet having no honour in his home area (p. 162)?

PART 2: TO JERUSALEM (MATTHEW 14 – 28)

D. Shadows (14 – 18)

14:1 – 17:27
10. Shadows of the future (pp. 165–189)

1 What observations about the structure of the second half of Matthew's Gospel help us to understand the author's intentions (p. 165)?
2 What would have been the significance of the death of John the Baptist for Matthew's original readers (pp. 165–166)? And for us?
3 'By feeding the multitude in this desert place, Jesus is making a statement and a claim' (p. 167) What is Michael Green referring to here?
4 What is 'fascinating' (p. 168) about the story of the walking on the water? How does it develop what we already know from the earlier story of the stilling of the storm? What encouragement can we draw from this?
5 In 15:1–20, what is it 'that separates the Pharisees from Jesus' (p. 170)? What practical steps can you take to avoid the attitudes of the Pharisees in this area?
6 What are the 'two characteristics' (pp. 170–171) God is looking for in his worshippers? Does he find them in you?
7 What significance is there in the move Jesus makes to Gentile territory in 15:21 (pp. 171–172)?
8 What 'subtle points' (p. 173) can you identify in this story of the Gentile woman?
9 What is the 'wonderful thing' (p. 174) about the feeding of the four thousand? Why is this so significant?

'Lack of trust often springs from forgetfulness of past blessing' (p. 174).

---

10 What was so damaging about the teaching of the Pharisees and Sadducees (pp. 175–176)? Can you think of any modern equivalents?
11 What is 'remarkable' (p. 177) about Simon Peter's recognition of Jesus' identity?

12 Why have 16:18–19 'attracted such acrimony among interpreters' of Matthew's Gospel (p. 179)? What do you think about this issue?

13 How does an understanding of what was going on in first-century Judaism help us to understand what Jesus means in 16:19 (pp. 180–181)?

'There is no plateau of spirituality to which we can ascend and be for ever thereafter raised above the weaknesses that assail others' (p. 181).

---

14 What were people in Jesus' time expecting of the Messiah? Where were they accurate? What illusions does Jesus have to shatter (pp. 182–183)?

15 What is so significant about the fact that these events take place in Caesarea Philippi (p. 183)?

16 What was the point of the transfiguration? What significance is there in Moses and Elijah appearing with Jesus (pp. 184–186)?

17 In what ways is the story of the epileptic boy both 'embarrassing' and 'encouraging' (p. 187)?

18 How would the story of the temple tax have been a help to Matthew's first readers? What does it say to us today (pp. 188–189)?

18:1–35
11. The fourth discourse: relationships in the kingdom (pp. 190–200)

1 What is the 'first and foremost characteristic' Jesus wants to see in his disciples (p. 190)? Why is this so important?

2 'The way we behave to children is one of the indicators of the way we behave to Jesus' (p. 191) What impact does this statement have on you?

3 Who are the *little ones* in your church? Do they receive the welcome Jesus wants them to have?

4 In the light of verses 8–9, is there any action you need to take? What exactly should you do?

5 What truths about pastoral care are underlined in 18:10–14 (pp. 193–194)? How do they apply to you?

6 What light does Jesus shed on how mistakes by fellow-believers should be handled (pp. 194–195)?

7　What does Jesus mean by telling his disciples to treat an excluded leader or member as *a pagan or a tax collector* (17; p. 196)?

8　Why does Jesus go on to talk about binding, loosing and prayer in this context (pp. 196–197)?

9　Why is forgiveness such an important ingredient of church life (pp. 197–198)? How might a bit more of it help in your situation?

'As Christians we are called to openness with those we feel have wronged us, and to frank forgiveness when apology is sincerely made' (p. 198).

10　What is the fundamental problem which the parable in verses 23–35 is designed to counter (pp. 198–199)?

11　Looking back over this chapter, to what extent do you share Jesus' priorities for the life of the church?

E. Judgment (19 – 25)

19:1 – 20:34
12. Judgments on issues (pp. 201–217)

1　What teaching does Jesus give here on marriage and divorce? What is revolutionary about what he says (pp. 201–205)?

2　What is 'staggering' (p. 205) about Jesus' attitude to children?

3　What do we learn from Jesus' encounter with the rich young man in 19:16–22 (pp. 206–209)?

4　Why are the disciples *greatly astonished* in 19:25 (p. 209)? In what way does their thinking need to change? And yours?

'Nobody can earn his way or pay her way into the kingdom. With humanity it is impossible. Not difficult: impossible. "But with God all things are possible . . ."' *(pp. 209–210).*

5　In what ways is the story in 20:1–16 'very Jewish' (p. 210)? What is surprising about it (pp. 211–212)?

6　'Many Christians who have worked hard for God over a long period will have a lowly place in the kingdom because their motives were not purged of the ideas of merit and reward' (p. 213). What do you make of this?

7 How do you measure greatness? How does Jesus measure it (pp. 213–216)? How might you go about closing the gap between your view and his?

8 What do the blind men in 20:29–34 have to teach us? How does their story relate to what has just gone before (pp. 216–217)?

21:1–27
13. Judgment on Israel (pp. 218–225)

1 In what ways does Matthew's account of the triumphal entry into Jerusalem reflect his theme of judgment (pp. 218–221)?

2 What implication for the church is brought out by the events of verses 1–13? How do you think Jesus would behave if he came to your church?

3 What challenge do verses 14–17 present to church leaders today (pp. 221–222)?

4 Why do people get so upset about what Jesus does in verses 18–22? Why does Jesus act as he does? What lessons does it have for us today (pp. 222–223)?

'God is no more bound to Christian churches with a long pedigree than he was to Israel with an even longer one' (p. 223).

---

5 What 'wise expedient' (p. 224) is there in verse 23 for Christians who are attacked for their faith?

21:28 – 22:46
14. Parables and controversies on judgment (pp. 226–238)

1 What is the parable of the two sons designed to convey (pp. 226–230)? What details here are 'worth noticing' (p. 226)?

2 What is so 'controversial' about the parable of the wicked tenants? What does it reveal about how Jesus saw himself (pp. 227–230)?

3 What would the Christian leaders among Matthew's first readers have taken 'to heart' from this (p. 230)? How about us?

4 In what way does Jesus 'go further' with the parable of the wedding feast (p. 230)?

> *'There is room neither for embarrassment nor for pride in the feast of the kingdom. Both attitudes ruin the enjoyment'* (p. 231).

5 Why does the wedding guest who comes improperly dressed receive such a harsh punishment? What truth is Jesus seeking to get across (pp. 231–232)?

6 How important to you is 'controversy for the truth' (p. 232)? Why do you think it is 'widely neglected' by today's Christian leaders (p. 233)?

7 What is so revolutionary in Jesus' reply to the question about paying taxes to Caesar (pp. 233–234)?

8 What is the background to the controversy about marriage at the resurrection? On what does Jesus base his belief in life after death (pp. 234–236)?

9 Why is Jesus' summary of the law 'exceedingly powerful and disturbing' (p. 236)?

> *'The criterion of whether love for God is real is whether or not it is reflected in our relationships with others'* (p. 237).

10 What is going on in 22:41–46? What is Jesus doing here (pp. 237–238)?

23:1–39
15. The fifth discourse:
(1) judgment on dead religion (pp. 239–248)

1 What three things 'ought to be borne in mind' (p. 239) as we approach this section?

2 How would you answer someone who accused Matthew of being anti-Semitic (pp. 240–241)?

> *'One of the weaknesses of the modern church is that we major on minor matters and leave pressing issues unaddressed'* (p. 241).

3 What are the 'five characteristics for which the Pharisees were rebuked' (p. 241)? How do these apply to you?

4 Verses 13–32 contain seven 'woes' on Pharisaism (pp. 242–245). What is the focus of each one? How do you think they would have struck Matthew's first readers? What significance do they have for us today?

5 What are the 'two main grounds' (p. 245) on which Jesus bases his criticism of the Pharisees? What steps can we take to guard against them ourselves?

6 How is Jesus' love for his nation revealed in verses 33–39 (pp. 246–248)? What implications did this have for Matthew's first readers? And for us?

24:1 – 25:46
16. The fifth discourse:
(2) the end of Jerusalem and of history
(pp. 249–265)

1 What links are there between what happens here and the events of the previous chapter (p. 249)?

2 What is this chapter 'primarily' about (p. 250)? How does the future fall of Jerusalem fit into this (pp. 251–253)?

3 What encouragements are Christians to draw from what Jesus says here about his return (pp. 253–254)?

4 In what way does the teaching of Jesus about the presence of 'signs' before the end seem to be ambiguous? What does he mean (pp. 254–255)?

5 What do you make of 24:30–31 (pp. 255–256)? Why is interpretation of these verses difficult? What conclusion do you come to?

6 Why is it foolish to try and work out the date of Christ's return? What should we be doing instead (pp. 256–257)?

7 What is the relationship between the return of the Jews to Palestine in 1948 and the second coming of Christ? Why do people get this wrong (p. 258)?

'The world is headed not for ultimate chaos and disaster but for the return of the King and his coronation' (p. 258).

---

8 What exactly does Jesus mean by telling his followers to *keep watch* (24:42) for his return (p. 259)? What does this mean for you?

9 What lesson does the parable of the disorderly servants have for us (pp. 259–260)?

10 What is the background to the parable of the ten virgins? In what ways is the parable surprising (pp. 260–261)? Are you wise or foolish? How do you know?

11 In what way does the parable of the talents have a particular message for the Pharisees (pp. 261–262)?

12 What 'fascinating parallel between spiritual and natural laws' (p. 262) does this parable highlight?

13 Why has the picture of the sheep and the goats been 'endlessly discussed' (p. 262)? What stands out from what Jesus says here (pp. 263–264)? Are you a sheep or a goat? How do you know?

'The more we learn to discern Christ challenging us through the poor, the more prepared we shall be to face him on the day of judgment' (p. 264).

F. Finale (26 – 28)

26:1–16
17. A study in contrasts (pp. 266–270)

1 What is the significance of the fact that this, the last section of Matthew's Gospel, ends with the account of Jesus' resurrection rather than with a block of teaching (p. 266)?

2 What do we need to notice in particular from verses 1–2 (p. 267)?

3 What do we know about Caiaphas and Judas? What motivated them to do what they did (pp. 267–268)? What lessons are there for us here?

4 What 'amazing probability' (p. 268) emerges from piecing together verses 6–13 with the parallel accounts in Mark and John?

'. . . we must never forget that no offering lavished on Jesus is wasted' (p. 269).

26:17–56
18. Jesus' last evening (pp. 271–280)

1 In what ways was the Passover meal 'the perfect feast to anticipate what Jesus had come to do' (p. 272)?
2 What is the question 'every disciple needs to ask' (p. 273)? Why? How do you answer it?
3 Why would what Jesus said about his body and blood have provoked 'astonishment and indeed horror' (p. 273)? What did he mean?
4 What differences are there between the old and the new covenants (pp. 275–276)? In what ways is this relevant for you?
5 In what way does holy communion 'witness to the "already" and the "not yet" of the kingdom' (p. 276)?
6 What do Jesus' experiences in Gethsemane teach us about prayer (pp. 278–279)?

'The prayer of Jesus in Gethsemane shows that we can be close to God, live a holy life, and pray with faith, earnestness and expectancy, and yet not get what we ask for' (p. 279).

26:57 – 27:31
19. The trials of Jesus (pp. 281–294)

1 What was illegal in the way Jesus' trials were conducted (p. 281)?
2 In what way is Caiaphas the judge 'himself judged' (p. 284) by these events?
3 What 'undertones' (p. 285) are there in the account of Peter's threefold denial of Jesus? What lessons are there for us here?

'The fact that the New Testament records such failures in its heroes is a remarkable testimony to its veracity and reliability' (p. 286).

---

4 What do the references to Jeremiah and Zechariah serve to underline about the events of the passion (pp. 288–289)?

5 In what ways is the royalty of Jesus stressed by Matthew's account (p. 290)?
6 What is ironic about the involvement of Barabbas in the story (pp. 290–291)?
7 How does knowing something of Pilate's background shed light on what he does here (p. 292)?
8 In the light of 27:25, how can Matthew be defended against the charge of anti-Semitism (pp. 293–294)?

27:32–66
20. The cross and the tomb (pp. 295–310)

1 In what ways does Matthew's account of the crucifixion continue to underline the royalty and innocence of Jesus (pp. 295–298)?
2 How would the example of the suffering Jesus have been a help to Matthew's first readers? And to us (pp. 297–298)?

'We worship a suffering God: that is the best answer to the problem of undeserved suffering' (p. 297).

---

3 How does Matthew highlight the fact that Jesus took our place by dying for us (pp. 298–301)?
4 'Christ the Victor is the key to the future' (p. 302) How does Matthew bring this out?
5 What is Matthew intending to convey in verses 51–54 (pp. 302–304)?
6 Why does Matthew give 'such prominence to the destruction and resurrection of the "temple" of Jesus' (p. 305)?
7 What does Matthew choose to emphasize in his description of the burial of Jesus? Why (pp. 306–310)?

28:1–20
21. The end of the beginning (pp. 311–323)

1 Can you identify the six strands of evidence with which Matthew enables us to argue for the truth of the resurrection of Jesus (pp. 312–316)?
2 How does Matthew counter the alternative Jewish explanation for what had happened (pp. 316–318)?

3 What are the five implications of the resurrection of Jesus which are highlighted by Matthew's account (p. 319)?

'It should be impossible for believers to refrain from mission'
(p. 319).

---

4 How does the Great Commission in verses 16–20 fit into the pattern of the rest of Matthew's Gospel (p. 320)?
5 What lessons for evangelism are there for us here (pp. 320–323)?